Bible
Speaks
today

the message of

OBADIAH, NAHUM AND ZEPHANIAH

Series editors:
Alec Motyer (OT)
John Stott (NT)
Derek Tidball (Bible Themes)

the message of

OBADIAH, NAHUM AND ZEPHANIAH

The kindness and severity of God

Revised edition

Gordon Bridger

ivp

INTER-VARSITY PRESS
Studio 101, The Record Hall, 16–16A Baldwins Gardens, London, EC1N 7RJ, UK
Email: ivp@ivpbooks.com
Website: www.ivpbooks.com

First published 2010
This edition published 2024

British Library Cataloguing-in-Publication Data
A catalogue record for this book is available from the British Library.

ISBN: 978–1–78974–436–1
eBook ISBN: 978–1–78359–633–1

Typeset in Great Britain by CRB Associates, Potterhanworth, Lincolnshire
Printed and bound in Great Britain by Ashford Colour Press, Gosport, Hampshire

Produced on paper from sustainable sources.

Inter-Varsity Press publishes Christian books that are true to the Bible and that communicate the gospel, develop discipleship and strengthen the church for its mission in the world.

IVP originated within the Inter-Varsity Fellowship, now the Universities and Colleges Christian Fellowship, a student movement connecting Christian Unions in universities and colleges throughout Great Britain, and a member movement of the International Fellowship of Evangelical Students. Website: www.uccf.org.uk. That historic association is maintained, and all senior IVP staff and committee members subscribe to the UCCF Basis of Faith.

To Elizabeth, my wife and partner in ministry
Rachel and Alasdair Paine
Sarah and Peter Sainsbury
Mary and David Hall
and their families

'I have no greater joy than to hear that
my children are walking in the truth' (3 John 4)

Contents

General preface ix
Author's preface xi
Chief abbreviations xiii
Select bibliography xiv

Introduction to Obadiah, Nahum and Zephaniah 1

The message of Obadiah
Introducing Obadiah 19
1. The sovereignty of God: who is really in charge? (1, 15, 21) 29
2. The judgments of God: who will answer for what? (2–15) 36
3. The triumph of God: what hope is there? (15–21) 52

The message of Nahum
Introducing Nahum 79
4. Divine judgment: theologically explained (1:2–15) 89
5. Divine judgment: historically illustrated (2:1 – 3:19) 136

The message of Zephaniah
Introducing Zephaniah 175
6. God's message of judgment (1:2 – 2:3) 186
7. Judgment and hope for the nations (2:4 – 3:8) 247
8. Hope and restoration for God's people (3:9–20) 285

GENERAL PREFACE

The Bible Speaks Today describes three series of expositions, based on the books of the Old and New Testaments, and on Bible themes that run through the whole of Scripture. Each series is characterized by a threefold ideal:

- to expound the biblical text with accuracy
- to relate it to contemporary life, and
- to be readable.

These books are, therefore, not 'commentaries', for the commentary seeks rather to elucidate the text than to apply it, and tends to be a work rather of reference than of literature. Nor, on the other hand, do they contain the kinds of 'sermons' that attempt to be contemporary and readable without taking Scripture seriously enough. The contributors to The Bible Speaks Today series are all united in their convictions that God still speaks through what he has spoken, and that nothing is more necessary for the life, health and growth of Christians than that they should hear what the Spirit is saying to them through his ancient – yet ever modern – Word.

ALEC MOTYER
JOHN STOTT
DEREK TIDBALL
Series editors

Author's preface

I first began to try to explain the Bible to others when I was a teenager at boarding school. My mother would sometimes encourage me to include in my letter home a written note on a passage of the Bible that I might have found helpful – a tactful way to get me to read the Bible at all! But it worked, and I began to find how exciting it was to wrestle with the meaning of the text, and to try to understand and apply what God was saying to me in a particular Bible passage.

This all came back to me when Dr Alec Motyer asked me to consider writing an exposition of three Old Testament books, Obadiah, Nahum and Zephaniah. I realized with a shock that after thirty years of parochial ministry I had never preached on any of them! However, in the same way that I had found my earlier efforts at school both exciting and exacting, I found these three little-known books both challenging and rewarding. I can only offer these expositions, however, as the work of a humble Bible student, and not as an Old Testament expert. But my prayer is that they may excite the reader and encourage the preacher to open up these Scriptures and teach them as part of 'the whole will of God'.

It will be obvious that I have leaned heavily on the expertise of others. The bibliography will give some indication of the main sources of inspiration. I was helped by reading a sermon on the book of Nahum by Prebendary Richard Bewes. He preached this as part of a series on Nahum at All Souls, Langham Place, London, in August 1988. I am also grateful to the vicar of Cromer, Revd Dr David Court, for encouraging me to preach on the book of Obadiah; and others have given me the opportunity to expound Obadiah, Nahum and Zephaniah on different occasions and in different places.

However, my greatest human resource has been the series editor, Alec Motyer. Alec has been to me a friend as well as a mentor. His expertise and penetrating comments, offered with disarming discernment and wit, have been both encouraging and illuminating. Obviously I take full responsibility for the final product; but Alec has helped me to dig deeper, and to find in these three prophets godly and courageous men who brought God's Word, inspired by the Holy Spirit, to situations not far removed from those which the church today is facing in many different parts of the world.

The first Old Testament BST commentary that I ever read was Alec Motyer's on the message of Amos. It inspired me to preach on that book! My hope and prayer is that these expositions will inspire you, the reader, not only to apply the teaching of these prophets to yourself, but also to inspire you to teach and preach this message to others.

There are, of course, other people who have contributed in different ways to the final product of this commentary. Some years ago, Margaret Smith had been my secretary when I was Rector of Holy Trinity, Norwich. She kindly agreed to make up for my inadequate computer skills by preparing the final manuscript for the publisher. Her help was invaluable, and, as always, unstinting. Philip Duce, in the IVP office, has as always given much practical help graciously and patiently, together with Colin Duriez, who has given of his expertise in the last lap of preparing the manuscript for the printer. I would also like to thank Wendy Bell, the librarian of Oak Hill Theological College, London, for her help in supplying books and articles when requested, with typical kindness and efficiency. Members of my own family as well as members of the church family in Cromer have also helped and encouraged me in different ways.

In particular, Elizabeth, my wife, has given me unswerving support, even though the whole project has taken longer than expected and has sometimes taken me away from necessary chores, and support for her. She has also made a number of helpful suggestions that have undoubtedly improved the final product. It is to Elizabeth, therefore, and to all our family that I dedicate this book, with the prayer that we all may continue to 'walk in the truth'.

GORDON BRIDGER

Chief abbreviations

BST	Bible Speaks Today
ESV	English Standard Version
IBD	*Illustrated Bible Dictionary* (IVP, 1980)
KJV	Authorized (King James) Version (1611)
NBC	*New Bible Commentary*, ed. D. Guthrie, J. A. Motyer, A. M. Stibbs, D. J. Wiseman (IVP, 1970)
NBC (21)	*New Bible Commentary: 21st-Century Edition*, ed. D. A. Carson, R. T. France, J. A. Motyer, G. J. Wenham (IVP, 1994)
NBD	*New Bible Dictionary*, ed. I. H. Marshall, A. R. Millard, J. I. Packer, D. J. Wiseman (IVP, 1996)
NICOT	New International Commentary on the Old Testament
NIV	New International Version (2011)
NKJV	New King James Version
NRSV	New Revised Standard Version (1995)
NT	New Testament
OT	Old Testament
RSV	Revised Standard Version (1971)
TOTC	Tyndale Old Testament Commentary
WBC	Word Biblical Commentary

Select bibliography

This list includes works referred to in the notes and recommended further reading.

Allen, L., *The Books of Joel, Obadiah, Jonah and Micah* (Eerdmans, 1976).
Baker, D. W., *Nahum, Habakkuk and Zephaniah*, TOTC (IVP, 1988).
Baker, D. W., T. D. Alexander and B. Waltke, *Obadiah, Jonah, Micah*, TOTC (IVP, 1988).
Bebbington, D., *Patterns in History* (IVP, 1979).
Boice, J. M., *The Minor Prophets*, 2 vols. (Zondervan, 1983, 1986).
Brown, L., *Shining Like Stars* (IVP, 2006).
Brown, R., *The Message of Deuteronomy*, BST (IVP, 1993).
Brueggemann, W., *Theology of the Old Testament* (Fortress Press, 1997).
Calvin, J., *Joel, Amos, Obadiah, Jonah, Micah, Nahum*, Commentaries, vol. 14 (Baker Book House, repr. 1996).
Chapman, C., *Whose Promised Land?* (Lion, 1983).
Cole, R. A., *Exodus*, TOTC (Tyndale Press, 1973).
Craigie, P. C., *The Books of Joel, Obadiah, Jonah and Micah* (St Andrew's Press, 1984).
Davis, D. R., *2 Kings* (Christian Focus, 2005).
——, *2 Samuel: Looking on the Heart* (Christian Focus, 2004).
Eaton, J. H., *Obadiah, Nahum, Habakkuk and Zephaniah* (SCM Press, 1961).
Gaebelein, F. E. (gen. ed.), *Obadiah, Nahum, Zephaniah*, Expositor's Bible Commentary, vol. 7 (Zondervan, 1985).
Grudem, W., *Systematic Theology* (IVP, 1994).
Harrison, R. K., *Introduction to the Old Testament* (IVP, n.d.; Eerdmans, 1969).
House, P. R., *The Unity of the Twelve* (Almond Press, 1990).

Kaiser, W. C., *Hard Sayings of the Old Testament* (Hodder & Stoughton, 1991).

Kidner, D., *Genesis*, TOTC (Tyndale Press, 1967).

Knight, G. A. F., *A Biblical Approach to the Doctrine of the Trinity*, Scottish Journal of Theology Occasional Papers, no. 1 (Oliver & Boyd, 1953, 1957).

Lewis, C. S., *Miracles* (Collins Fontana, 1960).

Lewis, P., *The Message of the Living God*, BST (IVP, 2000).

Mackay, J. L., *Jonah, Micah, Nahum, Habakkuk, Zephaniah* (Christian Focus, 2005).

McComiskey, T. E. (ed.), *The Minor Prophets*, vol. 2: *Obadiah, Jonah, Micah, Nahum, and Habakkuk* (Baker Book House, 1993).

——, *The Minor Prophets*, vol. 3: *Zephaniah, Haggai, Zechariah and Malachi* (Baker Book House, 1998).

Morgan, G. C., *Voices of Twelve Hebrew Prophets* (Pickering & Inglis, n.d.).

Morris, L., *The Biblical Doctrine of Judgment* (Tyndale Press, 1960).

Motyer, J. A., *Isaiah*, TOTC (IVP, 1999).

——, *Look to the Rock* (IVP, 1996).

——, *The Message of Exodus*, BST (IVP, 2005).

Packer, J. I., *Knowing God* (Hodder & Stoughton, 1973).

——, *Laid-Back Religion?* (IVP, 1987).

Robertson, O. P., *The Books of Nahum, Habakkuk and Zephaniah*, NICOT (Eerdmans, 1990).

Sizer, S., *Christian Zionism* (IVP, 2004).

Smith, G. A., *The Books of the Twelve Prophets*, vol. 2 (Hodder & Stoughton, 1928).

Stott, J. R. W., *Issues Facing Christians Today* (Marshall, Morgan & Scott, 1984; repr. 1990 by Marshall Pickering).

Stuart, D., *Hosea–Jonah*, Word Biblical Commentary (Thomas Nelson, 1987).

Szeles, M. E., *'Wrath and Mercy': A Commentary on Habakkuk and Zephaniah* (Eerdmans, 1987).

Tasker, R. V. G., *The Biblical Doctrine of the Wrath of God* (Tyndale Press, 1951).

Tidball, D., *The Message of Leviticus*, BST (IVP, 2005).

Webber, D., *The Coming of the Warrior-King: Zephaniah Simply Explained* (Evangelical Press, 2004).

Wenham, J. W., *The Goodness of God* (IVP, 1974).

Wilcock, M., *Discovering Six Minor Prophets* (Crossway, 1997).
Woods, J., 'The West as Nineveh: How Does Nahum's Message of Judgement Apply to Today?', *Themelios* 31.1 (October 2005).
Wright, C. J. H., *The Mission of God* (IVP, 2006).

Introduction to Obadiah, Nahum and Zephaniah

Some years ago at a teaching conference in a local church, I tried to expound the teaching of the book of Zephaniah. At the end of the final session, a woman came up to me and said, somewhat shamefacedly, 'I've been a Christian for forty years, and I didn't even know that Zephaniah was in the Bible!' Another friend told me that he had recently read through the book of Zephaniah, as he did not want to meet the prophet in heaven without knowing what his prophecy was about.

Obadiah, Nahum and Zephaniah are probably the least well-thumbed books of the Bible. Indeed if my own experience is anything to go by, they are rarely preached in our churches, even by those of us who are committed to the exposition of 'the whole will of God' (Acts 20:27). Julie Woods, in an article in *Themelios*,[1] points out that the books of Nahum and Obadiah have 'no place in the three-year lectionary' and are rarely preached. She quotes the view of Achtemeier on Nahum as: 'we often wish Nahum were not in the canon'; in other words Achtemeier wished that Nahum was not part of holy Scripture.[2] So why should we study and preach from these books? Would it not be better to concentrate on preaching from the New Testament? Or from the better-known major prophets of the Old Testament? Or the brilliant stories from the historical books? Or the apt and pithy sayings of wisdom literature?

---

1 J. Woods, 'The West as Nineveh: How Does Nahum's Message of Judgement Apply to Today?', *Themelios* 31.1 (October 2005), pp. 7–37.

2 Quoted in Woods, 'The West as Nineveh', p. 7, from E. Achtemeier, *Nahum–Malachi*, Interpretation: A Bible Commentary for Teaching and Preaching (John Knox Press, 1986), p. 5.

My own conviction, as I have studied these 'minor prophets' afresh, is that they tackle major themes that are especially relevant in today's church and world. Here are some reasons to encourage us to study these three minor prophets, Obadiah, Nahum and Zephaniah.

1. They claim to bring a message from God

All the Old Testament prophets claim to bring a message from God. They have been called by God to proclaim *his* Word, not their own.

The idea that truth comes from God, and is revealed in Scripture, is rarely acknowledged in postmodern twenty-first-century Britain. I remember reading about a crucial debate in the House of Lords on the moral and legal implications of allowing research on stem cells derived from human embryos under fourteen days old. This was reported in the *Times* newspaper in January 2001. The Bishop of St Albans was the only speaker who was reported as arguing from biblical revelation – though there were others who took part in the debate who might have done so. According to the report, the bishop criticized the utilitarianism of many of the arguments, and added: 'there seems to be no room whatever for a philosophical stance which might embrace, for example, any concept of truth which has revelation as one of its constituent parts'.

These seventh-century BC prophets, Obadiah, Nahum and Zephaniah, however, were valiant for truth. They claimed to be speaking God's Word to their contemporaries.

Obadiah, for example, introduces his prophecy with the words: *This is what the Sovereign LORD says about Edom – We have heard a message from the LORD* (1). On two further occasions in this short book (the shortest in the Old Testament), he uses the phrase *declares the LORD* (4, 8); and he follows the phrase *There will be no survivors from Esau* with the words *The LORD has spoken* (18).

Nahum describes his oracle against Edom as *The book of the vision of Nahum*, the word for *vision* meaning a revelation from God (see pp. 23, 79–80). Yahweh speaks directly through Nahum's words, as illustrated in the statement *'I am against you,' declares the LORD Almighty* (3:5).

Zephaniah begins his writings with the phrase *The word of the LORD that came to Zephaniah* (1:1). He often records that word in direct speech: *'I will sweep away everything from the face of the earth,' declares the LORD* (1:2). He ends the prophecy with the words: *'I will give you honour and praise among all the peoples of the earth when I restore your fortunes before your very eyes,' says the* Lord (3:20).

Obadiah, Nahum and Zephaniah all claim to bring a message from God. But how can we be sure that these claims are true? For many people have made such claims before, and have proved to be false prophets.

Peter Masters, in his book *The Healing Epidemic*, tells the story of a childless couple who had been medically examined and told that they could not have any children of their own. This was a great sadness to them, but they managed to come to terms with the situation. Then, one day, a member of their church claimed to have a 'word of knowledge' from God for them. This asserted that 'within twelve months' they would have a child. After eighteen months the couple were still childless, their pastor had spent many hours counselling them, and their faith had been shattered.

When the evangelist David Watson was dying of cancer, he mentioned more than once in radio broadcasts that many 'prophets' from different parts of the world had claimed that God had said to them, 'This sickness is not unto death.' It is not uncommon for such claims to be made, and then found to be false. Indeed in my own experience recently, a fellow Christian prefaced a decision with 'The Lord told me to do this', which made it difficult to question that decision. Yet it is important that we do question such claims. 'Test them all' was the apostle's word to the Christians at Thessalonica (1 Thess. 5:21). We should do that in order to hold fast to the truth. No claim to speak from God can be lightly accepted.[3]

So why should we accept the claims of Obadiah, Nahum and Zephaniah, and indeed other biblical writers, that *the word of the Lord . . . came* to them (Zeph. 1:1), and that they were writing and speaking God's word? Had they any right to say, 'Thus says the Lord'?

The teaching of Jesus is crucial

The key to understanding a true doctrine of Scripture lies with the teaching of Jesus, because of his uniqueness and authority as a teacher. If he was no more than a man, then his teaching would carry no more weight than anyone else's. The evidence of the Gospels, however, points to someone who is both God and man. He is the One who 'was God . . . was

[3] Peter Masters' story is quoted in D. Pytches, *Does God Speak Today?* (Hodder & Stoughton, 1989), pp. 77–78.

with God in the beginning . . . became flesh and made his dwelling among us' (John 1:1, 2, 14). To listen to Jesus is to listen to God, just as to see him is to see God (John 14:9). As we read the Gospels we see the kind of person Jesus *is* – sinless and selfless – and we wonder, 'Who is sinless and selfless but God?' We also notice the kind of things that Jesus *said* – his claim to forgive sins, to give life, to settle our destinies. His use of the divine name, and his claims that he would be crucified and rise again on the third day, all point towards his deity rather than to delusions. His claims came about just as he said. We also notice the kind of things that he *did*: healing the sick, feeding the hungry, stilling a storm, walking on water, raising the dead, and rising from the grave himself after his death and burial. No wonder that even the sceptical Thomas was able to say to the risen Lord, as he stood before him: 'My Lord and my God!' (John 20:28). It is the resurrection of Jesus that declares him to be the Son of God (Rom. 1:4) and confirms the authority of his teaching. If he had spoken a falsehood he would not have been raised from the dead. 'It is finished' covers his teaching as well as his saving work.

So what does the Lord Jesus teach us about the authority of Scripture, and the relevance of prophets such as Obadiah, Nahum and Zephaniah?

One of the most telling sayings of Jesus about the Old Testament scriptures came in a discussion that Jesus had with some Pharisees about marriage and divorce. This is how Matthew describes it:

> Some Pharisees came to him [Jesus] to test him. They asked, 'Is it lawful for a man to divorce his wife for any and every reason?'
>
> 'Haven't you read,' he replied, 'that at the beginning the Creator "made them male and female," and said, "For this reason a man will leave his father and mother and be united to his wife, and the two will become one flesh"?'

Notice how Jesus quotes a narrative part of the book of Genesis and claims that God, the Creator, is the one who is speaking about marriage. In other words, Jesus is implying that 'what Scripture says, God says' (Matt. 19:3–5; Gen. 1:27).

The Gospels again show us Jesus' high view of Scripture when they describe his temptation in the wilderness. When the devil says to Jesus, 'If you are the Son of God, tell these stones to become bread,' he answers, 'Man shall not live on bread alone, but on every word that comes from the mouth of God' (Matt. 4:3–4). Here Jesus is quoting from the Old Testament scriptures (Deut. 8:3), endorsing the view that Scripture comes from the mouth of God.

The same humble and obedient attitude to Scripture is illustrated in the way that Jesus sought to fulfil Old Testament prophecies concerning his role as Messiah (e.g. Mark 8:31). He saw himself as the Suffering Servant (Isa. 53; Mark 10:45) and the Son of Man (Dan. 7:13–14; Mark 8:31; 13:26, etc.). He believed that the Scripture *must* be fulfilled. So in the light of Scripture he began to teach the disciples that 'the Son of Man must suffer many things and be rejected . . . and . . . he must be killed and after three days rise again' (Mark 8:31).

From early days, Jesus read, memorized and studied the Old Testament scriptures. He never undermined their divine authority. Sometimes he rebuked his listeners with a phrase such as 'Have you not read?' or, 'You are in error because you do not know the Scriptures' (Matt. 22:29). Jesus was prepared to say, 'Scripture cannot be set aside' (John 10:35).

From the point of view of our study of Obadiah, Nahum and Zephaniah, the words of Jesus in the Sermon on the Mount are particularly significant. Here he endorses the continuing importance of the Law and the Prophets by saying:

> Do not think that I have come to abolish the Law or the Prophets; I have not come to abolish them but to fulfil them. For truly I tell you, until heaven and earth disappear, not the smallest letter, not the least stroke of a pen, will by any means disappear from the Law until everything is accomplished. Therefore anyone who sets aside one of the least of these commands and teaches others accordingly will be called least in the kingdom of heaven, but whoever practises and teaches these commands will be called great in the kingdom of heaven.
> (Matt. 5:17–19)

Jesus' post-resurrection teaching endorses this same high view of the Old Testament scriptures. In his conversation with two disciples on the Emmaus road, Jesus gently rebuked them for not knowing the Scriptures well enough:

> 'How foolish you are, and how slow to believe *all* that the prophets have spoken! Did not the Messiah have to suffer these things and then enter

> his glory?' And beginning with Moses and *all* the Prophets, he explained to them what was said in *all* the Scriptures concerning himself.
> (Luke 24:25–27; emphasis mine)

It is clear from Luke's account (Luke 24) that Jesus expected the Old Testament scriptures to be of continuing relevance to the church in its ministry to God's people and in its mission to the world. When the risen Lord appeared to the disciples in the upper room in Jerusalem, he said to them all:

> 'This is what I told you while I was still with you: everything must be fulfilled that is written about me in the Law of Moses, the Prophets and the Psalms.'
>
> Then he opened their minds so they could understand the Scriptures. He told them, 'This is what is written: the Messiah will suffer and rise from the dead on the third day, and repentance for the forgiveness of sins will be preached in his name to all nations, beginning at Jerusalem. You are witnesses of these things.'
> (Luke 24:44–48)

We have surely seen enough in the teaching of Jesus to endorse the inspiration and authority of Obadiah, Nahum and Zephaniah and the other biblical writers. Indeed, we have noticed that for Jesus 'what Scripture says, God says'. Since it is also true that the apostles made the same claims for their teaching (1 Cor. 2:13; 1 Thess. 2:13; 2 Tim. 3:15–16; 2 Pet. 1:21; 2 Pet. 3:15–16), it is worth remembering that Jesus endorsed their authority as teachers in the church. According to John's Gospel, Jesus said to the Twelve: 'The Advocate, the Holy Spirit, whom the Father will send in my name, will teach you all things and will remind you of everything I have said to you' (John 14:26). A little later he said to the same group of disciples:

> I have much more to say to you, more than you can now bear. But when he, the Spirit of truth, comes, he will guide you into all the truth. He will not speak on his own; he will speak only what he hears, and he will tell you what is yet to come. He will glorify me because it is from me that he will receive what he will make known to you. All that belongs to the Father is mine. That is why I said the Spirit will receive from me what he will make known to you.
> (John 16:12–15)

Notice that these promises are not made to all disciples, but to those called to be apostles, the foundation of the church, with Christ being the chief cornerstone (Eph. 2:20).

It was one of those apostles, Peter, who years later wrote about the prophets of the Old Testament, urging the first-century Christians to 'pay attention to [the word of the prophets] as to a light shining in a dark place, until the day dawns and the morning star rises in your hearts'. He then adds these important words:

> Above all, you must understand that no prophecy of Scripture came about by the prophet's own interpretation of things. For prophecy never had its origin in the human will, but prophets, though human, spoke from God as they were carried along by the Holy Spirit.
> (2 Pet. 1:19–21)

Because of the unique authority of Jesus and his endorsement of the authority of the Old and New Testament scriptures, we should have no fears about trusting the claims of Obadiah, Nahum and Zephaniah that *the word of the Lord . . . came* to them (Zeph. 1:1) and that they proclaimed what God had spoken. We have further confirmation because of the way that prophets were tested. In Deuteronomy 13:1–3, the writer points out that a false prophet leads people away from the Lord God to idolatrous worship. 'If a prophet . . . says, "Let us follow other gods . . . and let us worship them," you must not listen to the words of that prophet or dreamer.'

On those grounds Obadiah, Nahum and Zephaniah cannot be false prophets, as our study of their writings will make clear. Similar tests were applied in Deuteronomy 18:21–22:

> You may say to yourselves, 'How can we know when a message has not been spoken by the Lord?' If what a prophet proclaims in the name of the Lord does not take place or come true, that is a message the Lord has not spoken. That prophet has spoken presumptuously . . .

The defeat of the Edomites (Obadiah), the destruction of Nineveh and the decline and fall of Assyria (Nahum), and the fall of Jerusalem, and judgment and restoration for Israel (Zephaniah), have all been fulfilled, or are being fulfilled, in the worldwide church of the Lord Jesus Christ.

This is surely reason enough for us to study these three minor prophets. They are 'minor' because of the length of their writings, not because their message is less important than that of the other prophets. God spoke through Obadiah, Nahum and Zephaniah, and Jesus endorsed their authority as being part of holy Scripture. God continues to speak to us through Scripture. These three books are part of those scriptures that are 'God-breathed' (see comment on Zeph. 1:1) and therefore 'useful for teaching, rebuking, correcting and training in righteousness, so that the servant of God may be thoroughly equipped for every good work' (2 Tim. 3:16–17).

However, Obadiah, Nahum and Zephaniah not only claim to bring a message from God to their contemporaries, and by God's Spirit to us, but also . . .

2. They teach us some major truths

a. The importance of focusing on God

There is no doubt that each of these three prophets lived in difficult and even dangerous times, as we shall discover. They were called by God to speak into those times with boldness and clarity, and in a way that would inspire faith and hope. We may well find ourselves in a similar situation, and we would do well to learn the lesson they teach us about the importance of focusing, not on ourselves and our problems, but first and foremost on the living God. For their message was always God-centred; and the God of Obadiah, Nahum and Zephaniah is the God revealed in the whole of Scripture.

In the twenty-first century many people, if they think about God at all, think of him in impersonal terms. That is why so many people today are drawn by New Age forms of religion, or by certain types of Eastern mysticism or 'spirituality'. C. S. Lewis used to suggest that people preferred to think about God as 'a subjective God of beauty, truth and goodness inside our own heads . . . a formless life force surging through us, a vast power which we can tap'.[4] For others, God is 'the ground of our being', a concept rather than a person. For an increasing minority God does not exist at all, and in the UK militant atheism is becoming more vocal.

[4] C. S. Lewis, *Miracles* (Collins Fontana, 1960), p. 98.

In the writings of the prophets, however, including Obadiah, Nahum and Zephaniah, God is not some 'formless life force'. He is a personal God. He speaks, he warns, he punishes, he promises, he searches Jerusalem with lamps, he takes vengeance on his foes, and he rejoices over his own people with singing! He is the Lord (Yahweh), the covenant God, who makes promises and keeps them. Whatever the situation, God is with us in person.

In Obadiah, Nahum and Zephaniah, God is also the *Sovereign Lord*. All the biblical writers have a strong sense of God's sovereignty over nature, over the nations and over his own people. So Obadiah begins his message by saying: *This is what the Sovereign LORD says about Edom*, and ends by saying *and the kingdom [or kingship] will be the LORD's*.

Likewise Nahum's prediction of the fall of Nineveh witnesses to the same truth. God is sovereign over all the nations. He will destroy Nineveh (1:14), and restore the splendour of Jacob (2:2). Zephaniah speaks of God's sovereignty over the whole universe (1:2–3) as well as Jerusalem and Judah (1:4–5). He calls upon God's people to *Be silent before the Sovereign LORD, for the day of the LORD is near* (1:7). Zephaniah recognizes God's sovereignty over Philistia, Moab, Ammon, Egypt and Assyria. God is sovereign over all; and by focusing on the *Sovereign LORD* these prophets brought a message of hope rather than despair. We too must trust the Lord to work his purposes out for us.

Consistent with the rest of Scripture, Obadiah, Nahum and Zephaniah not only preach about a personal, sovereign Lord, but also turn our thoughts to a God who is righteous. The biblical doctrine of the righteousness of God, rightly understood, includes the thought of God's wrath against sin as well as his righteous activity in saving those who put their trust in him. See how this is worked out in relation to the cross of Christ in Romans 3:21–26. However, the doctrine of God's wrath is not often preached from the pulpits of our churches in the twenty-first century. God is a God of infinite love and goodness. It is not his wish that any should perish (2 Pet. 3:9). But we are reminded by these three minor prophets that God is absolutely just and righteous, and that he deals with sin and evil with perfect justice. So Obadiah speaks of God's anger against the evil deeds of Edom by saying: *the Sovereign LORD says . . . 'See, I will make you small among the nations; you will be utterly despised . . . you will be destroyed for ever'* (1, 2, 10). Nahum proclaims the same truth in setting out reasons for the destruction of Nineveh: *The LORD is a jealous and avenging God; the* L*ORD takes vengeance and is filled with wrath* (1:2). Likewise Zephaniah brings a word from God which says: *I will sweep away everything from the face of the earth . . . I will stretch out my hand against Judah . . . That day will be a day of wrath . . . Woe to the city of oppressors, rebellious and defiled! . . . The* L*ORD . . . is righteous* (1:2–4, 15; 3:1–5).

The concept of God's righteousness and wrath, and in particular Nahum's description of God as a jealous God, is not easily understood, or easy to preach, in our tolerant Western culture. These anthropomorphic terms need to be carefully explained.[5] At this stage it is perhaps enough to let the words of Walter C. Kaiser point us in the right direction:

> The anthropopathic descriptions of God (which describe God's emotions in human terms) help us to understand that God is not just an abstract idea, but a living and active person. He does have emotions similar to our human emotions of jealousy, vengeance, anger, patience and goodness – with the exception that none of these is tainted with sin.[6]

The jealousy of God is also a reminder to us of the goodness and mercy of the covenant Lord (Yahweh) who commits himself to his people with steadfast love (Heb., *ḥesed*). Obadiah believes in a God who will judge the wicked, but will also, in his love, deliver those who put their trust in him. *On Mount Zion will be deliverance; it will be holy, and Jacob will possess his inheritance* (17). Nahum has many strong things to say about judgment. But there is no doubt in his mind that God is a loving God. *The* L*ORD is good, a refuge in times of trouble. He cares for those who trust in him* (1:7). Zephaniah too has a marvellous description of God's love for his people: *The* L*ORD your God is with you, the Mighty Warrior who saves. He will take great delight in you; in his love he will no longer rebuke you, but will rejoice over you with singing* (3:17).

Each of these prophets, then, proclaimed a God-centred message to their contemporaries, and through the Holy Spirit to us. The God they proclaimed is personal, sovereign, righteous and loving. He is the God of Abraham, Isaac and Jacob. He is the faithful God of the covenant (Yahweh). He is the triune God. For the prophets point to Jesus, and in Jesus we see the living God (John 14:9). Also, we see in the cross of Christ the same

[5] See pp. 93–94, 224–225.

[6] W. C. Kaiser, *Hard Sayings of the Old Testament* (Hodder & Stoughton, 1991).

personal, sovereign, righteous, loving Lord working out his purposes for the church and the world (Acts 2:22–24). Our contemporaries too need to be presented with this revelation of the triune God. We need to learn from Obadiah, Nahum and Zephaniah about the 'kindness and sternness of God' (Rom. 11:22) as part of the 'whole will of God' (Acts 20:27).

In their writing, preaching and teaching, Obadiah, Nahum and Zephaniah focus on the living God. They look at their problems from his perspective. They look to him first. We need to learn that lesson. We are tempted to be subjective and problem-oriented in our preaching and personal discipleship. Many of us need the correction and direction that these God-centred prophets bring home to us.

Another major truth that can be found in the writings of Obadiah, Nahum and Zephaniah is the doctrine of sin and judgment.

b. The importance of facing up to sin and judgment

We live in an age of 'cover-up', where wrong deeds are made still worse by clumsy attempts to lie and cheat and cover them up so that we cannot be blamed. If President Nixon and Watergate is the best-known example internationally, there are many other examples, and we are all prone to the temptation. The prophets are skilled at exposing cover-ups. Think of the prophet Nathan and David, and the Bathsheba 'affair' (2 Sam. 11 – 12). Obadiah, Nahum and Zephaniah are no less skilled than Nathan, and we will often find that their teaching convicts us and exposes our sinfulness.

In his book *The Unity of the Twelve*, Paul House argues for a unity in the twelve minor prophets, and a development of the themes that the 'Twelve' focus on. So, for example, Obadiah stands alongside Hosea, Joel, Amos, Jonah and Micah as emphasizing 'covenant and cosmic sin'. Nahum and Zephaniah together stress covenant and cosmic 'punishment' and 'judgment', and Haggai, Zechariah and Malachi emphasize covenant and cosmic 'restoration'. This is not the place to examine House's argument in detail. But his general comment may give us some further clues about the way to preach these three books. House writes: 'Within the "Twelve" the great themes of prophecy emerge. Sin, punishment and future salvation are portrayed throughout the books, but are also set forth clearly in distinct sections of the Twelve.'[7]

[7] P. R. House, *The Unity of the Twelve* (Almond Press, 1990), p. 69.

House is surely right that sin, punishment and future salvation occur in each of our three books. But it is also true that Obadiah lays stress on the seriousness of the sin of Edom against God's covenant people; that Nahum sets out a reasoned case for God's judgment on the nations (especially Assyria); and that Zephaniah writes about the sins of Judah, as well as neighbouring pagan nations, and the inevitable judgment on *the day of the Lord* that this brings, while emphasizing in the end (Zeph. 3) the hope of salvation and restoration for all God's people throughout the world.[8]

Each of the prophets is fearless in pointing out sin and its inevitable consequences. Nahum in particular majors on the doctrine of judgment. But Obadiah and Zephaniah do not shrink from declaring God's judgment on sin. Sometimes the message is conditional. The people can be spared judgment if they repent (e.g. in Zeph. 2:1–3). Sometimes the prophet declares a day of judgment that is certainly coming, and that points forward to a final day of judgment for the whole world (Obad. 15–16; Nah. 3:18; Zeph. 1:3, 14–18; 3:8).

The message about sin and judgment was also an essential part of the preaching of Jesus and the apostles.[9] Today, in the twenty-first century, we are often very hesitant about proclaiming a doctrine of judgment and accountability to God. In the latter half of the last century the late Bishop John Robinson wrote:

> We live in this twentieth century in a world without judgment; a world where at the last frontier you simply go out and nothing happens. It's like coming to the customs and finding there are none after all. And the suspicion that this is in fact the case spreads fast; for it is what we should all like to believe.[10]

I suppose the situation is much the same today. We need the teaching of Obadiah, Nahum and Zephaniah to help us to face up to sin in our own lives, and in the church and in the nation, and to strengthen our nerve to preach and teach both sin and judgment in a loving and biblical way.

As well as the importance of focusing on God, and facing up to sin and judgment, Obadiah, Nahum and Zephaniah teach us the centrality of repentance and faith.

---

8 House agrees that Zephaniah links up with Haggai, Zechariah and Malachi in emphasizing restoration.

9 See Matt. 7:24–28; 25; Mark 13; Luke 21; John 5:19–27; Acts 17:30–31.

10 J. A. T. Robinson, *On Being the Church in the World* (Penguin, 1968), p. 165.

c. The importance of responding in repentance and faith

The prophets of the Old Testament are chosen by God to call people back to himself. For God is a covenant God, the God of Abraham, Isaac and Jacob. It is of his grace that he makes a covenant or 'agreement' with us. But his blessings are conditional on our obedience. God promises to bless those who obey his Word, and to punish those who are disobedient (Deut. 30:11–20). A vital part of this prophetic message, therefore, was a call for people to repent of their sins, and to cast themselves upon the mercy and goodness of the Lord for his pardon and forgiveness.

In the books of Obadiah and Nahum the call for repentance is muted. The certainty of judgment is made clear. The explicit call for repentance is missing. In the case of Nahum it has been rightly pointed out by many commentators that the book of Jonah (one of the twelve minor prophets) has majored on God's call to Nineveh to repent, and to trust in God's message proclaimed by Jonah. Nineveh had had its chance to repent, had responded positively, and then, some hundred years later, had hardened its heart. The message of repentance was already there in the story of Jonah. However, it is also true that the warning of God's certain judgment on the people of Nineveh in the prophecy of Nahum was in itself a call for them to examine themselves again and to repent. For Nahum clearly believed that *the LORD is good, a refuge in times of trouble. He cares for those who trust in him* (Nah. 1:7); and he also believed there was *good news* and *peace* (1:15) for those who fulfilled their *vows* and obeyed God's Word. Likewise, Obadiah's words of warning are an implicit call to repent and to look to *Mount Zion*, and all it represented, for salvation (Obad. 17). In Zephaniah, however, the call to repent and believe is made explicitly:

Gather together, gather yourselves together,
you shameful nation,
before the decree takes effect
and that day passes like windblown chaff,
before the LORD's fierce anger
comes upon you,
before the day of the LORD's wrath
comes upon you.
Seek the LORD, all you humble of the land,
you who do what he commands.

Seek righteousness, seek humility;
perhaps you will be sheltered
on the day of the LORD's anger.[11]

Jesus too called for repentance and faith during his earthly ministry (Mark 1:15). The apostles did the same (Acts 2:38; 17:30–31). The minor prophets expected a similar response. Those who follow in their steps will preach for a verdict. Do we hear that enough from the pulpits of our churches?

So far, then, we have seen that Obadiah, Nahum and Zephaniah all teach major biblical truths. They underline the importance of focusing on God, facing up to sin and judgment, and calling for the response of repentance and faith in God. There is one more major area of truth that is taught by all three prophets: the hope of salvation and restoration.

d. The importance of the hope of salvation and restoration

The teaching of Obadiah, Nahum and Zephaniah includes a great deal about sin and judgment. But all three prophets also offer us hope, and point us to God's future salvation and restoration. Zephaniah in particular majors on this future hope.

Interpreting biblical prophecy is like extending a telescope bit by bit until we can see a distant scene more clearly and in sharper focus. Obadiah writes about *Mount Zion* as a place of *deliverance*, and refers to *Israelite exiles* possessing *the land as far as Zarephath* (17–20). There is a partial fulfilment of these promises in the return of some of the exiles to Jerusalem and Judah. But extend the 'telescope' further, and we see, in the light of New Testament teaching, how the promise about 'the land', promised to Israel, is further fulfilled in the spiritual inheritance given to believers, Jew and Gentile; and if we extend the telescope still further, we see the ultimate fulfilment is to be found in heaven itself.[12]

Obadiah, Nahum and Zephaniah may not have as developed an eschatology, or a teaching about the last things, as we find in the major prophets Isaiah and Ezekiel. But they do teach us about a future hope that includes full and final salvation and restoration.[13] In today's world, which is so full

---

11 See commentary on Zeph. 2:1–3.

12 See pp. 65–75 for fuller explanation.

13 See pp. 65–75; 126–135; 282–310.

of pessimism and despair, the future hope of salvation, the hope of glory, is a truth to be treasured, lived by and passed on to others.

I hope we have said enough to encourage us 'to read, mark, learn, and inwardly digest'[14] the major truths brought to us by these three minor prophets. We have argued that it is important for us to read them and preach them because they claim (rightly) to bring a message from God, and because they teach us some major spiritual truths. There is a further reason to mention briefly.

3. They relate to the real world

The prophets of the Old Testament did not live in an ivory tower. They were in touch with the social and political issues of the day, as well as the spiritual and moral ones. So their preaching built a bridge from the Word of God to the world in which their contemporaries lived.

The biblical order of Obadiah, Nahum and Zephaniah is not the most likely chronological order (see individual expositions for more details). Chronologically, Zephaniah probably comes first. He preached during the reign of Josiah, king of Judah (640–609 BC), before or after the discovery of the Book of the Law.[15] Josiah was a reforming king, and Zephaniah clearly supported what he was doing. But there was still a great deal going on in Judah that deserved God's judgment; so Zephaniah warns God's people of the impending destruction of Jerusalem. The prophet understood the sleaze among the political leaders, and the unfaithfulness and 'spiritual adultery' of many of the priests; he was not afraid of applying God's word directly to them. He also had a message of judgment for the surrounding nations, including the superpower, Assyria. Assyria was still a force to be reckoned with, though it was beginning to decline during Zephaniah's ministry. The problems the prophet faced are not unlike those we face in church and state today. Encouragingly, his message is not without hope.

Nahum (c. 630–612 BC) brings a message of judgment upon Nineveh, the capital of Assyria. This would encourage God's people, for they had suffered much, as others had, at the hands of this cruel superpower, and needed the comfort of divine judgment; it would also be a warning for all

14 From the Collect for the Second Sunday in Advent, Book of Common Prayer (1662).

15 See exposition of the book of Zephaniah, p. 180, and 2 Kgs 22 – 23.

about the dangers of pride, both national and personal. Nahum's description of the decline and fall of Nineveh has many lessons to teach us today. The suffering, the crimes against humanity, the war crimes and the various displays of evil are still to be found in many parts of the world today. What is God's view of all this? Nahum helps us to face up to the reality of divine judgment, as well as reminding us that *The LORD is good, a refuge in times of trouble* (Nah. 1:7).

The fall of Assyria (and Nineveh) eventually led to the rise of Egypt. Josiah unwisely tried to stand up to them at Megiddo, but was defeated and assassinated in 609 BC. His son Jehoahaz was later defeated by Necho, the Egyptian leader, and was then succeeded by his brother Jehoiakin (609–597 BC). It was during his reign that Jeremiah experienced such bad times (Jer. 7:1 – 8:12) and Obadiah probably exercised his ministry. Obadiah's book was probably written around the time of the destruction of Jerusalem by the Babylonians in 586. His message to God's people deals with the problem of the Edomites who, in spite of their close kinship to Israel, had for years been a thorn in the side of Judah. In 586 they took sides with the Babylonians against God's people in Jerusalem. God's attitude to those who persecute 'his own' is made clear. Today we are living at a time of unprecedented persecution of the people of God. Obadiah addresses a very similar situation, and helps us to see such suffering from God's perspective.

We have seen that Obadiah, Nahum and Zephaniah all claim to bring a message from God, all teach some major spiritual truths, and all relate to the real world of their day. With the help of God, the Holy Spirit, we too can find in their teaching 'everything we need for a godly life' (2 Pet. 1:3). May that be our experience as we study, teach and preach these inspired scriptures.

The message of Obadiah

Introducing Obadiah

A friend of mine admits to a nightmare scenario about the book of Obadiah. He imagines a situation in which he is asked to read publicly from Obadiah at very short notice. He then finds to his horror that the table of contents at the front of his Bible has been torn out, and he has no idea where Obadiah can be found! Most of us would feel the same sense of panic in that situation.

Obadiah is the shortest book in the Old Testament. For many people it is a little-known book, written by an unknown prophet about a minor nation – Edom. So why should we bother to study it? There are two main answers to that question: first, because Obadiah brings a message from God which is part of holy Scripture; second, because holy Scripture inspired by the Holy Spirit is always relevant to our needs today.

However, before we consider those two propositions more carefully, we need to say something about the prophet himself and the times and dates of his ministry. So . . .

1. Who was Obadiah?

The book of Obadiah is so obscure that we don't know for certain that Obadiah is the actual name of the writer. The name 'Obadiah' literally means 'One who serves the Lord'. So it is possible that Obadiah is the anonymous title of a prophet who wanted to remain unknown, and who wanted to emphasize the message rather than the messenger. He was simply someone who served the Lord; and it was God's message that was important, not the prophet who proclaimed it. Certainly, God chooses those who are humble to proclaim his word. When God revealed to the prophet Jeremiah that he had chosen him – 'Before I formed you in the womb I knew you, before you were born I set you apart; I appointed you as a prophet to the nations' – Jeremiah's immediate response was the humble statement: 'Alas, Sovereign LORD . . . I do not know how to speak; I am too young' (Jer. 1:4–6; see also Exod. 3; 4; Isa. 6). So, the prophet might have sought anonymity as a humble servant of the Lord. Humility is certainly essential for those proclaiming God's word (1 Cor. 1:26–31; 1 Pet. 5:5–6).

However, it is also true that Obadiah was a common enough name in Israel and Judah.[1] So a prophet of that name may well have prophesied in Jerusalem, or even among the exiles. We can't learn much about him from such a short prophecy; but Eaton[2] suggests that he might possibly have belonged to a group of prophets, suggested by the phrase, *We have heard a message from the Lord* (1), and Obadiah's emphasis on the restoration of Zion and its temple (17, 21) suggests that they located themselves in the temple.

However, we've already begun to make assumptions about the time of Obadiah's ministry, without making a case for it.

2. When did Obadiah prophesy?

a. Some possible early dates

Some scholars place Obadiah's prophecy as early as the ninth century BC, in the reign of King Ahab, following a Jewish tradition found in the Talmud. Others suggest that the background to Obadiah's ministry might be the various attacks on Judah by the Edomites and others in the reign of King Jehoram (852–841 BC; see 2 Chr. 21:16–17). Jehoram, the eldest son of Jehoshaphat, succeeded his father in 852 BC. He established his position in Judah by putting to death his brothers and other princes of Israel. He reigned in Jerusalem for only eight years, married a daughter of Ahab, and 'did evil in the eyes of the LORD' (2 Chr. 21:6–20).

However, it was during Jehoram's short reign that the Edomites rebelled against Judah and set up their own rival king. Jehoram attacked the Edomites with his army, and at one stage of the battle found himself surrounded by the Edomites. He managed to escape on that occasion, but the Chronicler noted, 'To this day Edom has been in rebellion

---

[1] 1 Kgs 18:3–16; 1 Chr. 3:21; 7:3; 8:38; 9:44; 12:9; 27:19; 2 Chr. 34:12; Neh. 10:5; Ezra 8:9.

[2] J. H. Eaton, *Obadiah, Nahum, Habakkuk and Zephaniah* (SCM Press, 1961), p. 35.

against Judah' (2 Chr. 21:10). Could this be the background to Obadiah's ministry?

It's also possible that Obadiah ministered at the time when the Edomites attacked Judah in the reign of King Ahaz (735–715 BC; see 2 Chr. 28:17). The Chronicler comments:

> At that time King Ahaz sent to the kings of Assyria for help. The Edomites had again come and attacked Judah and carried away prisoners, while the Philistines had raided towns in the foothills and in the Negev of Judah . . . The LORD had humbled Judah because of Ahaz king of Israel, for he had promoted wickedness in Judah and had been most unfaithful to the LORD.
> (2 Chr. 28:16–19)

There is no doubt that the Edomites were a constant thorn in the side of God's people in Judah, and Obadiah would have been aware of that. The prophets lived in the real world, where there is constant conflict and threat. But although it is possible that Obadiah lived and worked in these earlier situations, it seems much more likely that he ministered at a later date.

b. A probable later date

The most likely background for Obadiah's ministry was the attack on Jerusalem and its destruction in 586 BC. This was carried out by the Babylonians and their allies, with the Edomites playing a major part. This certainly fits Obadiah's description of the fall of Jerusalem in his prophecy, and his dismay at the role played by the Edomites, who were the kinsfolk of the Judean people. This is how Obadiah described the Edomite involvement: *On the day you stood aloof while strangers carried off [our] wealth and foreigners entered [our] gates and cast lots for Jerusalem, you were like one of them* (11). A little later he says:

> *You should not march through the gates of my people*
> *in the day of their disaster . . .*
> *nor seize their wealth*
> *in the day of their disaster.*
> *You should not wait at the crossroads*
> *to cut down their fugitives,*

nor hand over their survivors
in the day of their trouble.
(13–14)

Those words of Obadiah are so vivid and immediate that some believe that Obadiah prophesied soon after the fall of Jerusalem in 586 BC, while those events were still fresh in his mind. The Psalm of the Exiles (Ps. 137), which began with the words 'By the rivers of Babylon we sat and wept when we remembered Zion', goes on to say: 'Remember, LORD, what the Edomites did on the day Jerusalem fell. "Tear it down," they cried, "tear it down to its foundations!"' (Ps. 137:1, 7).

We don't know whether Obadiah remained in Jerusalem or sat with the exiles in Babylon. But we do know that he shared the grief of those who mourned for Jerusalem and longed to see God's name and reputation honoured and vindicated; and it is clear that the part that the Edomites played was deeply embedded in the collective memory of God's people, and in the heart of Obadiah.[3]

Obadiah's prophecy foretells the future wiping out of the Edomites as a nation (8–10). So it is highly likely that Obadiah focused on such a message only after a calamitous event such as the destruction of Jerusalem in 586 BC, and the heavy involvement of the Edomites in siding with the enemies of Judah. The fact that the book of Obadiah comes before Nahum and Zephaniah in the Bible may be no more than a reflection of those traditions that speculated on an earlier, but less probable, date for Obadiah's ministry.

We are now in a better position to answer the question as to why we should study this rather obscure little book, written by a relatively unknown prophet about a minor nation and neighbour of God's people in Judah and Jerusalem. One answer to that question is that his message is inspired by God.

3. Obadiah's message is inspired by God

We live in a world today where many people, including some individual Christians, claim to have a hotline to God, and a message which is

[3] See note on Ps. 137, pp. 57–58.

authoritative. This is true of some major religions and many religious cults (see 'Introduction to Obadiah, Nahum and Zephaniah').

Obadiah also claims that his message comes from God. *The vision of Obadiah* (1a), which he refers to at the start of his prophecy, indicates 'a revelation communicated in those moments of special insight characteristic of prophecy . . . God's own disclosure of his forthcoming action'.[4] Motyer says that all thirty-five occurrences of the word for *vision* (*ḥāzôn*) in Scripture refer to 'truth disclosed by God; not necessarily a visual experience (e.g. Dan. 8:2), but by supernatural revelation'.[5]

This is precisely how Obadiah describes his *vision*. He goes on to say, *This is what the Sovereign LORD says about Edom – We have heard a message from the LORD* (1b). So we cannot be certain who Obadiah was, or precisely when he prophesied; but we can be sure that the living God gave Obadiah a message, a *vision* to lift the hearts of God's people; and that message was given to him as a revelation from God.[6] That message may have been given in part through the inspired writing and preaching of the prophet Jeremiah, who may well have been a contemporary of Obadiah. So we read in Jeremiah 49:14–16 almost the same words as we find in Obadiah verses 1 and 2. Obadiah appears to be quoting directly from Jeremiah.[7] So whether quoting other scriptures (Jer. 49:14–16), or receiving a direct revelation from God, Obadiah was able to bring a vision of God's way of dealing with the Edomites; and he claimed that this message was from God himself.

All the biblical writers claimed that their message came from God.[8] At the time of Jesus' ministry on earth, Obadiah was part of the Scriptures that Jesus endorsed. For example, when the risen Lord Jesus, 'beginning with Moses and all the Prophets . . . explained to them' (that is, to the two disciples on the Emmaus road in Luke 24) 'what was said in all the Scriptures concerning himself', Obadiah was part of those Scriptures described by Jesus as 'the Law of Moses, the Prophets and the Psalms' (Luke 24:27, 44). This was the traditional way to describe the threefold division of the Hebrew Bible. Psalms, the first book in division 3, was used as the title for the whole of the third part of the canon, which of course

[4] Eaton, *Obadiah, Nahum, Habakkuk and Zephaniah*, p. 33.

[5] J. A. Motyer, *The Prophecy of Isaiah* (IVP, 1993), p. 41.

[6] See 'Introduction to Obadiah, Nahum and Zephaniah', pp. 2–3.

[7] Jeremiah could, of course, be quoting from Obadiah if the latter was a pre-exilic prophet.

[8] See 'Introduction to Obadiah, Nahum and Zephaniah', pp. 2–8.

includes the book of Obadiah. The apostle Paul also wrote about the authority and inspiration of these scriptures when he reminded his colleague Timothy, a church leader in Ephesus, that all Scripture (and this would have included Obadiah) 'is God breathed' (2 Tim. 3:16). The apostle Peter taught the same truth when he wrote:

> Above all, you must understand that no prophecy of Scripture came about by the prophet's own interpretation of things. For prophecy never had its origin in the human will, but prophets, though human, spoke from God as they were carried along by the Holy Spirit.
> (2 Pet. 1:20–21)

So Obadiah may be the shortest book in the Old Testament, and written by a minor prophet.[9] But it is part of God's inspired Word (2 Tim. 3:15–16). It is, therefore, according to the apostle Paul, 'useful for teaching, rebuking, correcting and training in righteousness, so that the servant of God may be thoroughly equipped for every good work' (2 Tim. 3:16–17).

When Paul met the leaders of the church in Ephesus he told them: 'I have not hesitated to proclaim to you the whole will of God' (Acts 20:27). When he wrote to Timothy he warned him about those who neglected certain scriptural truths and whose teaching 'spread like gangrene' (2 Tim. 2:17). The effect of false teaching was gangrenous. Teaching the 'whole will of God', or 'sound doctrine',[10] resulted in healthy Christians.

The teaching of the book of Obadiah is part of God's inspired revelation to his people in every age. It's part of the total, wholesome biblical message. It's written for our profit and for our learning. We do ourselves harm if we neglect its teaching. But some may still wonder how a message about the Edomites can have any relevance to Christians in the twenty-first century!

So far, we have argued that the book of Obadiah is a message from God that is part of holy Scripture. Therefore, far from dismissing it or ignoring it, we should be eager to study it as part of the whole will of God. We must now consider another proposition.

---

[9] Obadiah is called a 'minor prophet' only because his prophecy is brief, and not because his message is unimportant. God's word through Obadiah is as important as any other message from the biblical prophets.

[10] 2 Tim. 4:3; 'sound' means 'hygienic' or 'healthy'.

4. Obadiah's message is relevant today

There are many conflicts between nations and different groups of people in the twenty-first century that have created great tensions, fear and suffering: for example, the present conflict between Israel and the Palestinians; or between North and South Korea; or between Sunni and Shi'ite Muslims in Iraq; or between Muslims and Christians in Nigeria; or between communists and Christians in China; or between liberals and conservatives in the worldwide Anglican Church. In some of these conflicts Christians are facing attacks upon themselves and their churches; and some of these people have been driven from their homes, and have become refugees in another country. Such people desperately need a vision from God, a message that will bring them some hope and comfort in their suffering.

The prophet Obadiah was almost certainly addressing a similar kind of situation. God's people in his day also needed a fresh *vision* from God, a message that would encourage them in the midst of their troubles (12–14), and through the dangers and disruption that they faced.

We too may find ourselves in a similar position. We may not be refugees or prisoners of war, but we could be facing conflict and pressure in our lives through the experience of redundancy, or divorce, or physical or mental suffering, or bereavement, or loneliness, poverty or homelessness, or simply facing unkindness from family, friends or neighbours.

There is a further factor in the hostility that God's people suffered in Obadiah's day that is common to the situations we are called upon to face. The tensions between Judah and Edom were continuing problems which seemed to be incapable of any lasting solution – just as many of our international, national, ecclesiastical and personal problems seem incapable of resolution for us today.

The fact is that the ill feeling between Edom and Judah went back a long way – as far back as ancient ancestors. For Edom and Judah traced their roots back to Jacob and Esau, the children of Isaac and Rebekah, and the grandchildren of Abraham and Sarah. Jacob and Esau were twins, Esau being the older. However, God had said, before the birth of the twins, that 'the elder' would 'serve the younger' (Gen. 25:23). Indeed, we read in the book of Genesis that after Rebekah became pregnant

> the babies jostled each other within her, and she said, 'Why is this happening to me?' So she went to enquire of the LORD.

The LORD said to her:

'Two nations are in your womb,
  and two peoples from within you will be separated;
one people will be stronger than the other,
  and the elder will serve the younger.'
(Gen. 25:22–23)

The writer goes on to tell us that when the time came for Rebekah to give birth

> there were twin boys in her womb. The first to come out was red, and his whole body was like a hairy garment; so they named him Esau. After this his brother came out, with his hand grasping Esau's heel; so he was named Jacob.
> (Gen. 25:24–26)

A more obvious reason for the growing hostility between the two brothers was the deceitful way in which Rebekah gave a 'helping hand' to further God's plans for Jacob. We are told that Rebekah said to Jacob:

> Look, I overheard your father say to your brother Esau, 'Bring some game and prepare me some tasty food to eat, so that I may give you my blessing in the presence of the LORD before I die.' Now, my son, listen carefully and do what I tell you: go out to the flock and bring me two choice young goats, so that I can prepare some tasty food for your father, just the way he likes it. Then take it to your father to eat, so that he may give you his blessing before he dies.
> (Gen. 27:6–10)

At first Jacob demurred. Then he agreed, and participated in the plot to deceive his father and to gain his father's blessing. He had already taken his father's birthright – Esau sold it 'for a single meal' (Heb. 12:16). So the twins drifted apart, with Esau aggrieved at his treatment at the hands of Jacob.

As they drifted apart, their families grew, and later became two neighbouring nations. Esau had been called 'Edom' (Gen. 36:19) and Jacob became known as 'Israel' (Gen. 32:22–32). So these names were adopted by the nations of which these two persons were the ancestors. Sadly, the animosity, which had begun with Jacob and Esau, continued through the years between these two nations, and in particular with the southern kingdom of Israel, namely Judah.[11]

The prophet Amos summed up the animosity between Edom and Judah when he explained the reason for God's judgment on Edom:

> This is what the LORD says:
>
> 'For three sins of Edom,
> even for four, I will not relent.
> Because he pursued his brother with a sword
> and slaughtered the women of the land,
> because his anger raged continually
> and his fury flamed unchecked . . .'
>
> (Amos 1:11)

To sum up, we are not told much about Obadiah. We cannot be sure that 'Obadiah' is his name, though for the purposes of this exposition we shall refer to him as that. We cannot be certain when he brought his message about Edom to the people of Judah, though it is most likely that it was shortly after the fall of Jerusalem in 586 BC. However, we can be sure that God gave him a *vision* to lift the hearts of God's people as they wrestled with continual problems that seemed to have no solution.

The destruction of Jerusalem, which involved the Edomites, would have been devastating for those who survived it. The loss of their homes, their property and possessions would have been bad enough; but that would have been compounded with fears about the future. Would they become refugees or prisoners? Would they be allowed to remain in Judah? And under what conditions? What would become of them if they were taken into exile? Furthermore, the fall of Jerusalem, and the dismantling of the monarchy, appeared to undermine the promises of Yahweh with respect to

---

[11] Here are some of the incidents recorded in Scripture which illustrate the continuing tensions and frustrations between these two nations: (1) Edomites prevented Israelites from passing through their land (Num. 20:14–21); (2) King Saul attacked Edom (1 Sam. 14:47), and King David defeated Edom (2 Sam. 8:13–14); (3) King Solomon occupied Edom against the will of her people (1 Kgs 9:26–28; 11:14–22); (4) in the ninth century BC Edom raided Judah, when Jehoshaphat was king (2 Chr. 20:1–2); (5) Edom rebelled against Jehoram (2 Kgs 8:20–22; 2 Chr. 21:8–10); (6) King Amaziah of Judah recaptured Edom (2 Kgs 14:7; 2 Chr. 25:11–12); (7) Edom raided Judah when Ahaz was king, and broke free from Judah's control (2 Chr. 28:17); and (8) Edom became a vassal of Assyria and later came under Babylonian rule (Obad. 11–14).

the dynasty of King David. Had not Yahweh made the following promise to David and his son Solomon?

> When your days are over and you rest with your ancestors, I will raise up your offspring to succeed you, your own flesh and blood, and I will establish his kingdom. He is the one who will build a house for my Name, and I will establish the throne of his kingdom *for ever.*
> (2 Sam. 7:12–13; emphasis mine)

There are many in today's world who face similar traumatic situations. There are war zones where refugees move from camp to camp without proper food, water or security. They are vulnerable to rape and other forms of aggression, including murder. Many have lost hope in the goodness and greatness of God. Sometimes Christians find themselves asking 'Where is God in all this?'

Obadiah addresses a similar situation, and his *vision* is badly needed today. We must ask what it was about Obadiah's message that had the potential to lift the hearts of his hearers, and equally our hearts today, whether it be in Jerusalem, Gaza, Nairobi, Mumbai, New York, London, Kyiv, or anywhere else in today's world. As we read through this short book we shall find that Obadiah teaches us three great truths to encourage us:

- The sovereignty of God (1, 15, 21)
- The judgments of God (2–15)
- The triumph of God (15–21)

Obadiah 1, 15, 21

1. The sovereignty of God: who is really in charge?

Years ago, when I was at boarding school, I vividly remember an evening when there was bedlam in the boys' dormitory, until an irate master came on the scene and demanded, 'Who is in charge here?' Because of the utter chaos in the dormitory it was only too obvious that nobody was in charge!

Sometimes it looks as if no-one is in charge when we read our daily newspapers, or watch the news on TV. Who's in charge in Zimbabwe, the Democratic Republic of Congo, Iraq, Afghanistan, Iran, North Korea and China? Also, we might well ask where God is in those areas of the world where the persecution of Christians goes on without any sign of relief. It may well be that some will wonder whether God is in charge in a personal situation where for a time disaster and tragedy come thick and fast – rather in the way that suffering and affliction came to Job in the Bible story (Job 1 – 2).

As we have already indicated, if Obadiah is writing at the time of the fall of Jerusalem in 586 BC, the people of God were likely to be asking the same kind of questions. Where is God in all this? Who is really in charge?

The answer that Obadiah gives, particularly in three key verses in his prophecy (1, 15, 21), is that in spite of appearances, God is sovereign and very much in charge.

No doubt Obadiah was pleased to bring a message to the people of God that demonstrated that God was addressing the Edomite problem. Israel and Judah had suffered for years from Edomite attacks, and there seemed to be no answer to this continuing problem. But now Obadiah has a message from God to encourage God's people: *This is what the Sovereign* *LORD says about Edom* (1). It's a message *about Edom*, and God's judgment on the Edomites, which teaches us that God rules over the world.

1. God is sovereign over the nations (1)

Before Obadiah spells out his main message about Edom, he seems to refer to another message from the Lord. *We have heard a message from the LORD: an envoy was sent to the nations to say, 'Rise, let us go against her for battle'* (1b). The reference to going against *her* seems to refer to Edom. That appears to fit the context best (1), while elsewhere Edom is sometimes referred to in the feminine form.[1]

Others, however, suggest that *her* refers to Jerusalem. The reference to an *envoy* may be a pictorial way of saying that it is Yahweh who brings a message about an assault on Jerusalem, and its destruction, which Obadiah later describes (11–14). In fact, both interpretations point to the truth that Yahweh is in control of the nations. He is in charge of history. He is 'the Mover in History' (Motyer). Or, as the prophet Amos put it: 'When disaster comes to a city, has not the LORD caused it?' (Amos 3:6b). It's possible, as P. C. Craigie suggests, that 'at the same time that Obadiah was receiving a message concerning Edom itself (2–15), he hears that the nations round about have been called to take action as well'.[2] This is the same message that Jeremiah proclaimed (Jer. 49:7–16); it is possible that Jeremiah quotes from Obadiah or vice versa, or that they both quote from another source. Whatever is the human source of this message about an *envoy . . . to the nations*, the lesson that Obadiah affirms is that the *Sovereign LORD* is involved in the stirring up of the nations against Edom. 'Yahweh is sovereign in the history of the entire world, and freely exercises his will therein' (Baker).[3] Or as Calvin put it: 'Wars are not stirred up at random, but by the secret influence of God.'[4]

The vision of Obadiah, then, focuses on *the Sovereign LORD* and what he has to say to us. When we face problems in our lives, we often focus on the problems rather than on the Lord himself – even when we are on our

---

1 See Lam. 4:21; see also Mal. 1:3–4, where Edom is sometimes feminine and sometimes masculine.

2 P. C. Craigie, *The Books of Joel, Obadiah, Jonah and Micah* (St Andrew's Press, 1984), pp. 200–201.

3 D. W. Baker, T. D. Alexander and B. Waltke, *Obadiah, Jonah, Micah*, TOTC (IVP, 1988), p. 31.

4 J. Calvin, *Joel, Amos, Obadiah, Jonah, Micah, Nahum*, Commentaries, vol. 14 (Baker Book House, repr. 1996), p. 422.

knees praying about them! Obadiah begins and ends his message with an emphasis on the sovereign rule of the covenant Lord (Yahweh). His final statement that *the kingdom will be the* L*ORD's* (21) probably means that 'the Lord will rule over all', for the Hebrew word that Obadiah uses (*mělûkâ*) means literally 'kingship'.

Obadiah's understanding of God's sovereignty is consistent with the teaching of the other biblical prophets, and indeed the Bible as a whole. In Scripture generally, the sovereign Lord exercises divine government and control over the universe at large (see Ps. 103:19; Dan. 4:35; Eph. 1:11); the physical world (Ps. 104:14; 135:6; Matt. 6:30); animal creation (Ps. 104:21, 28; Matt. 6:26); and the affairs of nations (Job 12:23; Ps. 22:28; 66:7; Acts 17:26) and individuals (Ps. 75:6; Matt. 10:30; Luke 1:52; Rom. 8:28; Jas 1:5).[5]

In his brief message Obadiah shows his confidence in the sovereign Lord to work out his purposes for God's people in spite of, indeed through, the evil and warlike actions of many of the nations. For Obadiah and the other biblical prophets, Yahweh is not a local deity confined to one place. He is sovereign over Israel and Judah, and is working out his judging and saving purposes for them; and he is sovereign over all the nations too (15). In his sovereignty he may use wicked nations, Israel's enemies, to fulfil his purposes (1; cf. Hab. 1). He will require all the nations to stand before him on the last day and give account of their behaviour (8, 15; see Matt. 24; Mark 13; Luke 21) and, according to Obadiah, the sovereign Lord will finally be acknowledged as the supreme ruler over all (21; cf. Phil. 2:9–11). As Baker has expressed it: 'Yahweh is sovereign in the history of the entire world, and freely exercises his will therein.'[6]

We do well to listen to Obadiah's teaching, and to trust in God's sovereignty in the many situations we face in the world today. For, as Peter Lewis has written:

> The testimony of the Scriptures is that there is nowhere in the world where God's writ does not run, there is no event where he is locked out, no process of thought and act where he is helpless. God is not at work in some things in history but in all of history; in all its events, processes, agents and actors. He is at work sinlessly but none the less sovereignly;

---

[5] W. Grudem, *Systematic Theology* (IVP, 1994), ch. 16.

[6] Baker, Alexander and Waltke, *Obadiah, Jonah and Micah*, p. 31.

> in advance and set-back, war and peace, in the rise and fall of Empires, in the powerful and the powerless, in all things both good and bad. The decisive thing however is that it is God acting always in his own character; the One who is holy and just, wise and good, but whose justice can be terrible and whose goodness has long been abused in our world and whose wisdom is beyond our partial assessments.[7]

There is another truth that can be deduced from Obadiah's teaching about the sovereignty of God.

2. God gives us the dignity of choice (15)

If God exercises his sovereign control over all events in the way we have described, in what sense are we free? If God is in charge of world events, what choices do people have? In his book *Systematic Theology*, Grudem answers those questions in the following way:

> Scripture nowhere says we are 'free' in the sense of being outside of God's control, or of being able to make decisions that are not caused by anything . . . nor does it say we are 'free' in the sense of being able to do right on our own apart from God's power. But we are nonetheless 'free' in the greatest sense that any creature of God could be free . . . we make willing choices, choices that have real effects. We are aware of no restraints on our will from God when we make decisions. We must insist that we have the power of *willing* choice; otherwise we will fall into the error of fatalism or determinism, and thus conclude that our choices do not matter, or that we cannot really make willing choices. On the other hand the kind of freedom that is demanded by those who deny God's providential control of all things, a freedom to be outside of God's sustaining and controlling activity, would be impossible if Jesus Christ is indeed 'continually carrying along things by his word of power' (Heb. 1:3). If this is true, then to be outside of that providential control would simply be not to exist! An absolute 'freedom', totally free of God's control, is simply not possible in a world providentially sustained and directed by God himself.[8]

---

[7] P. Lewis, *The Message of the Living God*, BST (IVP, 2000), p. 303.

[8] Grudem, *Systematic Theology*, p. 331.

Obadiah teaches both the sovereignty of God and the responsibility of humankind. The Edomites were given the dignity of choice. They were free to choose judgment (15) or salvation (21). A certain TV personality, who was notorious for his cruel brand of humour and his four broken marriages, was asked in an interview if he would have changed anything in his life if he could. He replied that he would like to have been a better man, not treating people merely as pawns, but that it wasn't his fault that he had behaved in the way that he had. 'You play', he said, 'with the cards you've got.' Obadiah had a very different message. The sovereignty of God does not rule out the responsibility of human beings. God gives us the dignity of choice. Obadiah teaches us that *The day of the Lord is near for all nations* (15). On that day we shall all have to give an account of ourselves to God.

There is a further truth we can deduce from Obadiah's teaching on the sovereignty of God.

3. God brings good out of evil (21)

Another question raised by Obadiah's teaching is the relationship between God's providential care and government of his world and the evil actions of people. Often God's sovereign actions in history are mysterious and unfathomable to our finite sinful minds. But sometimes we are given a glimpse of the ways in which our sovereign Lord is working out his purposes for his people. In Lindsay Brown's heartwarming description of the work of the International Fellowship of Evangelical Students (IFES) in many universities throughout the world, he gives us a number of such glimpses. For instance, he writes:

> Another example of our Sovereign Lord turning bad into good was in the aftermath of the Gulf War in the early nineties. This war, which issued from Iraq's attempt to seize and annex Kuwait, brought immense suffering in Iraq. Many fled the country to travel across the border to friendly Jordan. The trauma of those days led to the awakening of Mission awareness in the Jordanian Church, and the growth of Jordanian student ministry. Many Iraqis who crossed into Jordan were welcomed into the homes of Christians living in the Jordanian capital, and were stunned at the hospitality and kindness shown to them by Christians. When I visited Jordan in 2003, a local church leader told me so many

> Iraqis had become Christians that there were now more Iraqi Christians in Amman than Jordanian Christians.[9]

Brown goes on to tell us that the witness of some of these Christians also greatly impressed some members of the Jordanian government.

There are many such examples of God's sovereignty at work in the twentieth and twenty-first centuries. Biblical history is also full of such stories. The story of Joseph's rise to prominence in Egypt, in spite of the jealous and cruel behaviour of his brothers, the malice of Potiphar's wife, and the miscarriage of justice which led to years of imprisonment is a classic example (see Gen. 39 – 50). For God was on the throne, working his purposes out for Joseph and his family, and eventually for the nation of Israel, and ultimately for the salvation of the world (see Gen. 50:20; cf. Acts 2:23–24; Acts 7).

Obadiah teaches us to trust in that same sovereign Lord. The Lord (Yahweh) is the covenant God who promised to bless Abraham and his family and to make them a blessing to all the nations of the world. He also promised them *a land* (19–21) and a spiritual inheritance (see Gen. 12; 15; 17). Obadiah understood this, and believed that if God has spoken he will keep his word and fulfil his sovereign purposes for his people; *the kingdom will be the LORD's* (21).

In a world where there are so many conflicts, and suffering is rife, we need to put our trust in the sovereignty of God and to be encouraged by this truth. Obadiah teaches us that God is sovereign over the nations. But God is also sovereign over our personal lives. When the apostle Paul wrote to suffering Christians in Rome, he reminded them of God's sovereign purpose for them, and their need to trust God to work out his purposes for their lives. Paul, like Obadiah, has no doubts about the sovereignty of God. He writes confidently:

> And we know that in all things God works for the good of those who love him, who have been called according to his purpose. For those God foreknew he also predestined to be conformed to the image of his Son . . .
> (Rom. 8:28–29)

[9] L. Brown, *Shining Like Stars* (IVP, 2006), p. 47.

As a consequence of his trust in God's sovereignty, he was able to go on to say: 'What, then, shall we say in response to these things? If God is for us, who can be against us?' (Rom. 8:31).

I was talking on the phone to a friend of ours recently, who happened to be both a committed Christian and a lawyer. I was mentioning a concern I had about a certain situation in the neighbourhood and began to exaggerate the possible effect this might have on our property. 'Oh come on,' she said, 'we believe in the sovereignty of God, don't we?' Having given me excellent legal advice, she added, 'I'll pray for you!' That was exactly what I needed to hear. God's sovereignty does not rule out wise counsel and believing prayer, but to trust in the sovereign Lord, as Obadiah clearly did, and I was exhorted to do, certainly takes away anxiety. Needless to say, prayer was answered in God's way!

The beginning (1), the middle (15) and the end of Obadiah (21) focus on the sovereignty of God. God is in charge. We should be encouraged by this truth. But Obadiah also encourages us to remember the judgments of God. It is to that part of his teaching that we must now turn.

Obadiah 2–15

2. The judgments of God: who will answer for what?

It is difficult in today's world, even among Christians, to find those who take the doctrine of God's judgments seriously. Yet perhaps we ought not to be surprised by that. According to the story of Adam's temptation, disobedience and fall in the book of Genesis (Gen. 3:1–24), the first doctrine to be denied is judgment. The serpent, Satan, first casts doubt on God's word: 'Did God really say, "You must not eat from any tree in the garden?"' (Gen. 3:1). Satan then flatly contradicts God's word of judgment: 'You will not certainly die' (Gen. 3:4). Derek Kidner comments:

> It is the Serpent's word against God's, and the first doctrine to be denied is judgment. If modern denials of it are very differently motivated, they are equally at odds with revelation: Jesus fully reaffirmed the doctrine (e.g. Matt. 7:13–27).[1]

Obadiah and the other biblical prophets also teach positively about God's justice and his acts of judgment. So Obadiah teaches us not only that we should be encouraged by the sovereignty of God, but also that we should be encouraged by the judgments of God.

In the book on which the film *Schindler's List* is based, the author, Thomas Keneally, reflects on the dark possibility that there will be no judgment or accountability for those who perpetrated the horrors of the Jewish Holocaust during the Second World War. He describes a mother

---

[1] D. Kidner, *Genesis*, TOTC (IVP, 1967), p. 68.

and son brutally murdered by Nazis guards in full view of a three-year-old girl dressed in red. Keneally imagines Schindler thinking along these lines: 'They [the guards] permitted witnesses, such witnesses as the red toddler, because they believed that all the witnesses would perish too.'[2]

The fact is that the guards did what they liked because they thought they would never have to give account of their lives. They thought they could do what they liked, and that no-one would accuse them; that there was no God to judge them. We may well ask, 'Do we want to live in a world like that?'[3]

Obadiah and the biblical writers assure us that the world is not like that. God is just and acts with perfect justice. As we have already noticed, God has promised to judge the Edomites. *We have heard a message from the LORD: an envoy was sent to the nations to say, 'Rise, let us go against her for battle'* (1). God will judge those who are his enemies and his people's.

No doubt the people of Judah, whether at home or in exile, were delighted to hear Obadiah bring a message of judgment upon their unpleasant and difficult neighbours, the Edomites. But Obadiah is addressing Judah as well as Edom. If God could deal so firmly with the Edomites, what might he do with Judah, in the light of all the privileges she had received?

We too should read these verses in a similar way. We should recognize that the sins of Edom are sometimes our sins too. As the apostle Paul wrote to Christians in Corinth centuries later, after he had pointed out some of the failures of God's people under Moses: 'These things happened to them as examples and were written down as warnings for us, on whom the culmination of the ages has come. So, if you think you are standing firm, be careful that you don't fall' (1 Cor. 10:11–12).

So what does Obadiah teach us about God's judgments in this passage to encourage us? I want to suggest three main lessons.

- God's judgment means humbling the proud
- God's judgment means destroying the wicked
- God's judgment means facing the truth

---

2 T. Keneally, *Schindler's List* (Hodder & Stoughton Sceptre, 1994), p. 143.

3 See further the use of this story in R. Tice and B. Cooper, *Christianity Explored* (Good Book Co., 2009), p. 74.

1. God's judgment means humbling the proud (2–4)

God's judgment of the Edomites illustrates the saying that 'pride comes before a fall'. At the heart of their national failure lay their sinful pride. For example, they prided themselves on the natural resources of their land. George Adam Smith points out that Edom had 'a complacent form of satisfaction in a remarkable isolation and self-sufficiency, in large stores of wealth, and in a reputation for worldly wisdom . . . that felt no need of the divine'.[4] The land occupied by the Edomites (formerly the land of Seir; Gen. 32:3; 36:20–21, 30; Num. 24:18) stretched from the southern tip of the Dead Sea to the Gulf of Aqabah which leads into the Red Sea. This strip of land was about 100 miles long and was part of a rugged, mountainous area with peaks rising to 3,500 feet.[5] Edom, therefore, was difficult to attack and reasonably easy to defend. It seems clear that the people of Edom found it easier to trust in the security of their mountains than in the sovereignty of the Lord. They were deceived by their apparent impregnability. As God reminded them through Obadiah: *The pride of your heart has deceived you, you who live in the clefts of the rocks and make your home on the heights, you who say to yourself, 'Who can bring me down to the ground?'* (3).

Perhaps God's people in Judah and Jerusalem had been in danger of thinking that Jerusalem was secure and impregnable, whether or not they followed the Lord. Christians too can put their trust in a secure environment or in material prosperity or armaments (a 'new generation of nuclear weapons') rather than in the living sovereign Lord. God's message to Edom was clear: *'Though you soar like the eagle and make your nest among the stars, from there I will bring you down,' declares the Lord* (4).

In addition to the natural features of the country, which gave the Edomites a sense of security, they also prided themselves on their intellectual ability. Edom boasted of some shrewd and clever men; but human wisdom doesn't save us any more than rich natural resources. God's message was clear: *'In that day,' declares the Lord, 'will I not destroy the wise men of Edom, those of understanding in the mountains of Esau?'* (8).

History gives us many examples of God's judgments in humbling the proud, and of 'pride coming before a fall'. Many nations have had their day

[4] G. A. Smith, *The Books of the Twelve Prophets*, vol. 2 (Hodder & Stoughton, 1928), p. 178.

[5] See J. A. Thompson, 'Edom, Edomites', in NBD, pp. 290–292.

of success (as did the Edomites) and then have become arrogant and been humbled. In biblical history it happened to the Assyrians, the Babylonians, the Persians, the Greeks and the Roman empire. In modern times, in the twentieth century, it happened to Hitler's Nazi Germany, Mussolini's Fascist Italy, Stalin's Communist Soviet Union and Pol Pot's Cambodia, to name but a few. It will be interesting to see how long the proud atheistic leaders of North Korea will survive before their nation disintegrates; and what will happen to the UK, the USA and Japan? The credit crunch and economic recession in 2008 was frequently put down to the hubris of bankers, politicians and creditors. Pride comes before a fall – and God, our sovereign Lord, 'has brought down rulers from their thrones' (Luke 1:52).

As we have already indicated, Obadiah's message is also a warning to God's people. For those who know the Lord can also be deceived by pride. In the book of Deuteronomy Moses warns the Israelites of the dangers of a proud heart. God was about to lead them into the Promised Land:

> a land with brooks, streams, and deep springs gushing out into the valleys and hills; a land with wheat and barley, vines and fig-trees, pomegranates, olive oil and honey; a land where bread will not be scarce and you will lack nothing; a land where the rocks are iron and you can dig copper out of the hills.
> (Deut. 8:7–9)

God would provide for his people wonderfully, but Moses knew how easily the people could become proud and complacent. So he warns them:

> When you have eaten and are satisfied, praise the Lord your God for the good land he has given you. Be careful that you do not forget the Lord your God, failing to observe his commands . . . Otherwise, when you eat and are satisfied, when you build fine houses and settle down, and when your herds and flocks grow large and your silver and gold increase and all you have is multiplied, *then your heart will become proud* and you will forget the Lord your God, who brought you out of Egypt, out of the land of slavery.
> (Deut. 8:10–14; emphasis mine)

Then Moses gives Israel a similar warning to the one that Obadiah gave to Edom, and by implication to Judah: 'If you ever forget the Lord your God and follow other gods and worship and bow down to them, I testify against you today that you will surely be destroyed' (Deut. 8:19).

Pride comes before a fall for pagan nations and the people of God. God's judgments mean humbling the proud. But such judgments are for individual believers as well as the nation or the people of God. In Jonathan Aitken's moving autobiography *Pride and Perjury*, he tells his personal story of his fall from being a cabinet minister in John Major's Conservative government (he was Chief Secretary to the Treasury in 1994) to becoming a convicted perjurer, sentenced to eighteen months' imprisonment in 1999. Describing the reasons for his fall, he writes:

> Pride was the root cause of all my evils. Without pride there would have been no libel action; no attempt to defend the Ritz bill payment with a lie; no will to win the battle in court on an end-justifies-the-means basis. There would have been no deceit of friends, family and colleagues; no Sword of Truth speech; no involvement of my wife and daughter in the front line of the war with the *Guardian*. If I had been blessed with a small helping of humility instead of possessed by a surfeit of pride, the entire tragedy would have been avoided. The ancient Greeks who prophesied that hubris would always be followed by nemesis were right. So was C.S. Lewis in the twentieth century when he described pride as 'the complete anti-God state of mind'. My pride had been such a powerful, blinding, demonic state of mind that it could only be cured by the severest of lessons.
>
> Today I am grateful for the lessons I have learned.[6]

Jonathan Aitken's example is high profile and dramatic, as you will know if you have read his story. For most of us, pride affects our private lives in more low-profile situations. But, as Obadiah reminds us, pride can creep up on us and deceive us (3). It can lead us to what C. S. Lewis calls an 'anti-God state of mind'. To the proud, self-sufficient, apparently secure Edomites, God says: *'The pride of your heart has deceived you . . . you who say to yourself, "Who can bring me down to the ground?"'* (3). We can be equally arrogant, even if we are Christian workers or ministers. As we become more competent and professional as leaders, for example, we can begin to trust in our own wisdom and strength, and regard ourselves as above the temptations that face other people – whether these temptations be in the area of

[6] See J. Aitken, *Pride and Perjury* (HarperCollins, 2000), p. 358.

sexual morality or financial probity. *'Who can bring me down to the ground?'* we boast, just as the Edomites did with their false sense of security.

God's judgments humble the proud. God says to the proud Edomites:

'See, I will make you small among the nations;
you will be utterly despised . . .
Though you soar like the eagle
and make your nest among the stars,
from there I will bring you down,'
declares the Lord.
(2, 4)

God will humble the proud. We should be encouraged by that. Mary, the mother of Jesus, expressed this poetically in the song we call 'The Magnificat', shortly before Jesus was born.

My soul glorifies the Lord
and my spirit rejoices in God my Saviour . . .
He has performed mighty deeds with his arm;
he has scattered those who are proud in their inmost thoughts.
He has brought down rulers from their thrones
but has lifted up the humble.
(Luke 1:46–47, 51–52)

It was not only the Edomites who needed to know that because of their pride the Lord would humble them, make them small among the nations (2) and bring them down to earth (4). If there is this 'anti-God' kind of pride in the nation, in the church, or in our personal lives, God may well humble us and *bring [us] down* (4). We need to recognize that pride comes before a fall and that God humbles the proud. That is both a warning for the proud and an encouragement to the humble.

2. God's judgment means destroying the wicked (5–9)

Obadiah has courage. He does not hold back from warning the Edomites (and God's people in Judah) that judgment means destruction. There's nothing sentimental about his message.

a. God will destroy his enemies completely (5–9)

The prophet imagines a situation where some thieves break into a house during the night (5a). This could be a disaster, but probably not a complete disaster. They would steal as much as they wanted, but they would almost certainly leave some things untouched. God's judgment, however, would be more complete than that. Nothing that was evil would be left. *Oh, what a disaster awaits you*, says Obadiah (5).

Again, Obadiah imagines grape pickers leaving some grapes on the vine, and not stripping the vine of every grape. But God's judgment would deal with his enemies completely. The apostle Paul underlined that truth centuries later when he spoke of the final day of judgment for all nations, when

> the Lord Jesus is revealed from heaven in blazing fire with his powerful angels. He will punish those who do not know God and do not obey the gospel of our Lord Jesus. They will be punished with everlasting destruction and shut out from the presence of the Lord and from the glory of his might . . .
> (2 Thess. 1:7–9)

God will destroy his enemies completely.

But Obadiah also makes it clear that in judging wickedness, God will not tolerate false gods.

b. God will remove false gods completely (6–9)

The Bible teaches us that 'righteousness exalts a nation' (Prov. 14:34). It is equally true that wickedness corrupts a nation, and 'sin condemns any people' (Prov. 14:34b). According to Obadiah, Edom's sin included her dependence on the false gods of materialism (6), worldly wisdom (8) and military strength (9). God promised to remove these false gods completely.

i. The false god of material wealth (6)

As well as the mountain ranges which gave Edom military security, Edom also had access to a great deal of material wealth. George Adam Smith has written that 'on this rich fortress land the Edomites enjoyed a civilization far above that of the tribes who swarmed upon the surrounding deserts'. This encouraged a self-sufficiency bolstered by the various trade routes that passed through Edom:

> The masters of Mount Se'ir held the harbours of Ahaba, into which the gold ships came from Ophir. They intercepted the Arabian caravans and cut the roads to Gaza and Damascus. Petra, in the very heart of Edom, was in later times the capital of the Nabatean kingdom, whose commerce rivalled that of Phoenicia . . . the early Edomites were also traders, middle men between Arabia and the Phoenicians; and they filled their caravans with the wealth both of East and West . . .[7]

However, material wealth cannot of itself save a nation from disaster or from the judgment of God. We know from the experience of a country such as Zimbabwe in the twenty-first century that a nation full of natural resources, and with a strong economy in past years, can still become disastrously weak economically.[8] God's message to Edom, through Obadiah, was a warning about the vulnerability of material wealth. God's judgment upon Edom would lead to economic disaster – *how Esau will be ransacked, his hidden treasures pillaged!* Riches are no substitute for the living God; and God can take them away in a moment.

Jesus often warns us about the dangers of wealth. In his parable about the rich fool (Luke 12:13–21) he describes a man whose aim in life was to make more and more money:

> He said, 'This is what I'll do. I will tear down my barns and build bigger ones, and there I will store my surplus grain. And I'll say to myself, "You have plenty of grain laid up for many years. Take life easy; eat, drink and be merry."'
>
> But God said to him, 'You fool! This very night your life will be demanded from you. Then who will get what you have prepared for yourself?'
>
> (18–20)

Jesus added this comment: 'This is how it will be with whoever stores up things for themselves but is not rich towards God' (21).

The Edomites undoubtedly trusted in uncertain riches. We can easily do the same, and become like the man in the parable. Money can become our idol, our substitute for God.

---

[7] Smith, *The Books of the Twelve Prophets*, vol. 2, p. 180.

[8] In January 2009 the inflation rate in Zimbabwe stood at 231 million per cent. This made the currency worthless, and stopped almost all economic activity in that country. Furthermore, world recession brought home widely the same lessons to more developed countries.

But we cannot take our money or our stocks and shares with us when we die. When we face God as our judge, our money will not save us. God will take it away.

> Our life is but an empty show,
> Naked we come and naked go,
> Both for the humble and the proud,
> There are no pockets in a shroud.
> (John Alexander Joyce)

ii. The false god of worldly wisdom (8)

A further mark of God's judgment on Edom was the destruction of *the wise men of Edom* (8). It seems that Edom had gained a reputation for a certain kind of worldly wisdom and shrewdness. Obadiah talks about *the wise men of Edom, those of understanding* (8); and Jeremiah clearly looked back to a time when such men existed there, when he brought this message from God: 'This is what the LORD Almighty says: "Is there no longer wisdom in Teman?[9] Has counsel perished from the prudent?"' (Jer. 49:7).

George Adam Smith implies that their human wisdom had always been of a worldly kind:

> The wise men of Edom . . . were notorious. It is the race that has given to history only the Herods . . . clever, scheming, ruthless statesmen, as able as they were false and bitter, as shrewd in policy as they were destitute of ideals. 'That fox' cried Christ, and crying stamped the race.[10]

The New Testament makes it clear that there are two kinds of wisdom. The apostle James put it like this:

> Who is wise and understanding among you? Let them show it by their good life, by deeds done in the humility that comes from wisdom. But if you harbour bitter envy and selfish ambition in your hearts, do not boast about it or deny the truth. Such 'wisdom' does not come from heaven but is earthly, unspiritual, demonic. For where you have envy and selfish ambition, there you find disorder and every evil practice.

---

[9] Teman, the grandson of Esau (Gen. 36:11), gave his name to a tribe living in the north of Edom. 'Teman' was also used to describe the whole of Edom (Hab. 3:3). The inhabitants of Teman were renowned for their wisdom (see R. K. Harrison, *Jeremiah and Lamentations*, TOTC [IVP, 1973], p. 180).

[10] Smith, *The Books of the Twelve Prophets*, vol. 2, p. 182.

> But the wisdom that comes from heaven is first of all pure; then peace-loving, considerate, submissive, full of mercy and good fruit, impartial and sincere. Peacemakers who sow in peace reap a harvest of righteousness. (Jas 3:13–18)

God's judgment fell on the false god of worldly wisdom, the wisdom that James called 'earthly, unspiritual, demonic'. Individually, and as a church and nation, we need to seek the wisdom that 'comes from heaven', if we are to avoid the just judgment of God. That heavenly wisdom comes from Christ himself. For, as the apostle Paul wrote:

> God chose the foolish things of the world to shame the wise . . . It is because of him that you are in Christ Jesus, who has become for us wisdom from God – that is, our righteousness, holiness and redemption. Therefore, as it is written: 'Let the one who boasts boast in the Lord.' (1 Cor. 1:27, 30–31)

Obadiah teaches us the truth that one day the 'worldly wisdom' of Edom will be destroyed. The New Testament teaches us that one day Christ and his wisdom will be all in all. What an encouragement that is for the people of God!

iii. The false god of military power (9)

The Edomites also depended on the false god of military power and military alliances. Edom had a relatively small population and, with its almost impregnable security from military attacks because of the mountainous terrain within its borders, it did not need a large army. But when attacking other nations, such as Judah, Edom sometimes relied upon superpowers such as Assyria and Babylon.

However, God's message to Edom was the promise that he would sweep away the military power and alliances on which Edom depended: *All your allies will force you to the border; your friends will deceive and overpower you; those who eat your bread will set a trap for you, but you will not detect it* (7). The reference to eating bread may well refer to making alliances with others (Jer. 49:10); but this would not be able to save them from God's judgments. Indeed, God's judgment on Edom would be so terrible that even the brave warriors from Teman[11] would be terrified.

[11] See n. 9 above.

God's message to the people of Edom, and at the same time to the people of Judah, was simply that reliance on the false gods of material wealth, worldly wisdom and military power would never save them from God's just judgment. That message is as relevant to nation states today as ever it was in Obadiah's time. Yet the UK government has spent billions of pounds on what the politicians call a 'new generation' of atomic weapons (a point made to me in a private letter from Alec Motyer). God's judgments lead to the humbling of the proud and the destruction of the wicked, together with the removing of false gods.

God's judgment also leads to facing up to the truth about ourselves as we consider the reasons why God acts in this way. It is that aspect of judgment that now demands our attention.

3. God's judgment means facing up to truth (10–14)

Obadiah wants to make clear to the people of God that the Lord's judgment of Edom was not arbitrary. There were sound reasons for God acting as he did, as there always are. He had been very patient with the Edomites, in spite of their persistent attacks on Judah. Furthermore, it's possible that Obadiah had been an eyewitness of the way in which the Edomites gleefully cashed in on the Babylonian attack on Jerusalem in 586 BC (10–15). So now, as an encouragement for Judah, and also a warning, he explains to God's people why God must judge Edom. We ourselves, as well as Edom and Judah, need to face up to the truth about his judgment.

Here are some of the reasons that Obadiah gives for God's judgment on Edom.

a. Attacking God's people deserves his judgment (10)

God has a special place in his heart for his chosen, redeemed people. It was beautifully expressed to Moses in these words:

> The LORD did not set his affection on you and choose you because you were more numerous than other peoples, for you were the fewest of all peoples. *But it was because the LORD loved you* and kept the oath he swore to your ancestors that he brought you out with a mighty hand and redeemed you from the land of slavery . . . he is the faithful God, keeping his covenant of love to a thousand generations of those who love him and keep his commandments. But

> those who hate him he will repay to their face by destruction;
> he will not be slow to repay to their face those who hate him.
>
> (Deut. 7:7–10; emphasis mine)

The sin of Edom was that she showed her hatred and rejection of God by the way she treated his people, even though God's people in Judah were kinsfolk, sharing a common ancestor in Abraham. *Because of the violence against your brother Jacob, you will be covered with shame; you will be destroyed for ever* (10). Using violence against anyone is a violation of God's law to love our neighbour as ourselves. To use violence against a brother or sister is even more shameful and reprehensible; and as Jesus taught us, 'all who draw the sword will die by the sword' (Matt. 26:52).

Obadiah's message is uncompromising. Violence against God's people deserves and may lead to eternal destruction: *you will be destroyed for ever* (10; see also 2 Thess. 1:9; Matt. 24:31–46). Yet this is a message that is largely ignored today, at a time when Christians are facing more persecution worldwide than ever before.

In a publication called *Barnabas Aid*[12] I read of the persecution of Iraqi, Ugandan, Indian, Pakistani, Bangladeshi, Malaysian, Albanian and North Korean Christians, to take but a sample of reported stories. In northern Uganda, for example, a sixteen-year-old girl was killed by her father for becoming a Christian. In India, a Christian pastor near Bangalore was beaten by a mob, had kerosene poured over him, his Bible set on fire and thrown at him, and then, stripped of all his clothes, he was paraded through the town by his persecutors with the placard, 'I am one who converts people.' God has protected him and preserved his life. He is determined to carry on his ministry, for he knows God is with him, loves him and is sovereign over all. He refuses, of course, to take vengeance into his own hands. He knows, however, that God is both just and loving, and that those who are violent against God's people will face his judgment, as Obadiah reminds us. Attacking God's people deserves God's judgment. We all need to face up to that truth.

b. Standing aloof deserves God's judgment (11)

It seems that some Edomites did not actively join in the attack on Jerusalem but they stood aloof (11) – we might say 'sat on the fence'. They

---

[12] *Barnabas Aid*, September/October 2007.

looked down on their brother and rejoiced *over the people of Judah in the day of their destruction* (12), while others did the damage. But even though these Edomites may not have joined actively in the attack on Jerusalem, they were still behaving as if they were *one of them*; that is, as if they were on the side of the enemies of God and his people.

Standing aloof from God and his people is little better than attacking his people. Jesus taught the importance of real commitment, rather than 'standing aloof', when he said: 'Whoever is not with me is against me, and whoever does not gather with me scatters' (Matt. 12:30). When we stand aloof rather than positively take sides with Christ and his church, we tend to do more harm than good. We scatter and disrupt the work of God, rather than gather and become fully involved with God's work and his purposes.

Some of the Edomites stood by, while the Babylonian soldiers carried off the wealth of Jerusalem and cast lots for what was left in the captured city. But there was no doubt they were not fighting on the Lord's side. Such an attitude, Obadiah teaches us, also deserves God's judgment. Christian people too sometimes need to ask: 'Am I truly involved in the work of the gospel, or do I stand aloof? Am I a fellow worker with God? [See 2 Cor. 6:1.] Or does my non-involvement mean that I am scattering and setting back the work of God in the world?'

c. Supporting the enemy deserves God's judgment (12–14)

If some of the Edomites *stood aloof* (11), others of them seemed to be much more involved in helping the enemy (11c). It's against this group that God brings eight specific charges:

1. You should not look down on your brother in the day of his misfortune;
2. you should not rejoice over the people of Judah;
3. you should not boast so much;
4. you should not march through the gates of my people;
5. you should not look down on them in their calamity;
6. you should not seize their wealth;
7. you should not wait at the crossroads to cut down their fugitives;
8. you should not hand over their survivors in the day of their trouble.

These eight charges bring home the seriousness of supporting the enemies of God. The repetition of *You should not* – eight times in the original text – or

Do not (ESV) presses home God's displeasure at Edom's behaviour.[13] Yet, as Eaton comments, 'it is too late . . . the pleadings are a sad irony, for the choice of evil has already been made . . . they mirror the offences already committed, showing up their pitiless or despicable character.'[14] Obadiah uses the imperative *You should not* or *Do not* as a father might say to his son after he has been bullying and annoying his brother all morning: 'You should not do that!' or 'Do not do that!' The deed has already been done, and it displeases the father.

This list of charges against the Edomites begins with a clear indication of the heart of Yahweh's objection to their actions and attitude. The sinfulness of their actions lay chiefly in the fact that they were looking down on their brother in the day of his misfortune (12a), and rejoicing over the people of Judah in the day of their destruction (12b). The Edomites were kinsfolk to the people of Judah; they were brothers and sisters. They all looked back to Jacob and Esau, and to Esau's grandfather, Abraham. They shared a common inheritance. So Yahweh is deeply grieved that the Edomites, of all people, should look down on their brothers, and that they rejoiced over their defeat and destruction.

It is indeed sad and grievous to God when those who share a spiritual inheritance, and have so much spiritually in common, nevertheless despise their fellow believers or rejoice over their defeat and failure. It happens sometimes when a Christian takes another Christian to court. The apostle Paul specifically challenges Christians at Corinth about this:

> Is it possible that there is nobody among you wise enough to judge a dispute between believers? But instead, one brother takes another to court – and this in front of unbelievers! . . . You . . . cheat and do wrong, and you do this to your brothers and sisters.
> (1 Cor. 6:5–6, 8)

Sometimes this attitude is to be found in a local church where, in the midst of a power struggle, strong-minded people can look down on the leaders of the church and, when misfortune comes, can rejoice over, indeed contribute to, the distress of those leaders.

---

13 Michael Wilcock, in his guide to Obadiah in *Discovering Six Minor Prophets* (Crossway, 1997), p. 56, points out that in Obad. 11–14 the prophet uses the phrase *the day* ten times in RSV, and eight times in NIV; he suggests that this has the effect of the tolling of a bell, similar to the eight 'Do nots' of vv. 12–14.

14 J. H. Eaton, *Obadiah, Nahum, Habakkuk and Zephaniah* (SCM Press, 1961), p. 42.

Jesus had strong words to say to his disciples about looking down on and despising other believers. In the Sermon on the Mount he said to those who were wanting to follow him:

> You have heard that it was said to the people long ago, 'You shall not murder, and anyone who murders will be subject to judgment.' But I tell you that anyone who is angry with his brother or sister will be subject to judgment . . . Anyone who says, 'You fool!' will be in danger of the fire of hell.
> (Matt. 5:21–22)

So, in Jesus' teaching, this attitude of despising other people is tantamount to murder. Through Obadiah, God is saying to the Edomites: 'You should not do this!'

God also charged the Edomites not to boast so much when the people of Judah were facing the day of their trouble (12c). Was this a case of boasting that they had helped the Babylonians to capture Jerusalem, glorying in their own military strength and their powerful allies? Scripture warns us to avoid boasting in anything or anyone other than the Lord himself. 'Let the one who boasts boast in the Lord' (Jer. 9:24; 1 Cor. 1:31).

The remaining five charges against the Edomites (13–14) describe what seems to be an eyewitness account of the occupation of Jerusalem by the Babylonian army and their allies, with a detailed description of the part that the Edomites played. The Edomites identified closely with the enemies of God's people. They marched with the Babylonians through the gates of Jerusalem on the day when disaster struck God's people. God said they should not do it! (13a). Yahweh charges them again with looking down on God's people *in their calamity in the day of their disaster* (13b). Here Yahweh seems to be pointing out the heartlessness and coldness of the Edomites, who appeared to be unmoved by human suffering and unaware of the dishonour that the destruction of Jerusalem might bring to the name and reputation of Yahweh. God said that they should not be like this! The Edomites also exploited the situation further by looting the city (13c), and added insult to injury by intercepting those who were trying to escape from the invading army and handing them over as prisoners to the Babylonians (14). It's a grisly story of disloyalty, hatred, deceit and downright cruelty towards the people of God, whose ancestors they shared and whose values they ought to have supported. They should not have done this!

The Edomites deserved God's immediate judgments upon them, because they had supported the Babylonians and their allies in their attack on the people of God in Jerusalem. So God condemned their behaviour. He gave them reasons to repent. For we all have to face up to the truth of God's Word, which tells us that those who attack God's people deserve his judgment.

There is, however, a further reason to take notice of God's Word. *For the day of the LORD is near upon all the nations* (15, RSV). The NIV unhelpfully omits the initial word *For* or 'because', which is in the original text, and which clearly indicates a further reason for the Edomites to change their ways. All nations, and all people, are accountable to God. On that *day of the LORD* at the end of the age, we shall all stand before the throne of God. We shall have to give account of our lives. Obadiah now goes on to teach us (15–21) that God will act in justice and mercy on that *day*. God will triumph over his enemies, and deliver his people. It's a further message of encouragement for the people of God, and a warning to the Edomites. It is to that message that we must now turn.

Obadiah 15–21

3. The triumph of God: what hope is there?

We live in a day when despair and hopelessness are much more likely to dominate people's lives than hope. For some people this is because they can no longer believe in God – or at least in a personal God who cares about each of us and has a purpose for our lives. Stephen Hawking, one of the most brilliant thinkers of the twenty-first century, expressed his doubts about a personal God when he wrote about life on planet Earth in these terms:

> A medium-sized planet, orbiting round an average star in the outer suburbs of an ordinary spiral galaxy, which is itself only one of about a million million galaxies in the observable universe. Yet the strong anthropic principle would claim *that the whole vast construction exists simply for our sake. This is very hard to believe.*[1]

Obadiah, however, and all the biblical writers, believed in the sovereign Lord (1) who personally spoke to them (1, 4, 8, 18) and revealed his purposes for them and for the future of the world. So far, we have noticed that God has spoken of his sovereignty over Edom and his judgment of her wickedness. Now he reminds his people that he is sovereign over *all nations* (15), and that history is moving towards the climax of his final triumph – that *day of the Lord . . . for all nations* (15) when *the kingdom will be the Lord's* (21). In writing about the *day of the Lord* (15) Obadiah teaches us in these final verses two important truths: God will triumph over his enemies on that day (15–16); and he will deliver his people on that day (17–21).

---

[1] S. A. Hawking, *A Brief History of Time* (Bantam Press, 1988, 1995), p. 120 (emphasis mine).

1. God will triumph over his enemies on that day (15–16)

So far, Obadiah has spoken of the certainty of God's judgment of Edom, Judah's near neighbour and close kinsman. Now he speaks of the *day of the Lord* as a day of judgment for all nations, including Judah. Obadiah no doubt expected *that day* in his own lifetime, as every godly believer would have done. For just as every next king could be the royal Messiah, and every next prophet could be the prophet like Moses (Deut. 18:18), so every next looming disaster could be the *day of the Lord*. Obadiah is right to say *The day of the Lord is near* (15), always imminent, and we should be always ready for it. Sometimes biblical scholars can say critically (and somewhat patronizingly perhaps) that 'of course Paul expected Jesus to return during his own lifetime'. Should not our response be to say, 'Yes, of course he did – and he was right to do so. Don't you expect Jesus to return in our lifetime? His coming is always imminent.'

Jesus spoke a great deal about this final day (see Matt. 7:21–23; 12:36–37; 13:40–43; 25:41–46; John 5:22–30). For example, in his famous parable of the sheep and the goats he said:

> When the Son of Man comes in his glory, and all the angels with him, he will sit on his glorious throne. All the nations will be gathered before him, and he will separate the people one from another as a shepherd separates the sheep from the goats. He will put the sheep on his right and the goats on his left.
>
> Then the King will say to those on his right, 'Come, you who are blessed by my Father; take your inheritance, the kingdom prepared for you since the creation of the world. For I was hungry and you gave me something to eat . . . whatever you did for one of the least of these brothers and sisters of mine, you did for me.'
>
> Then he will say to those on his left, 'Depart from me, you who are cursed, into the eternal fire prepared for the devil and his angels. For I was hungry and you gave me nothing to eat . . . Truly I tell you, whatever you did not do for one of the least of these, you did not do for me.'
>
> Then they will go away to eternal punishment, but the righteous to eternal life.
>
> (from Matt. 25:31–46)

Jesus taught, as Obadiah did, that on that final day of the Lord, God would triumph over all his enemies, and that he would act with perfect and appropriate justice. As Obadiah put it: *As you have done, it will be done to you; your deeds will return upon your own head* (15).

Both Obadiah and Jesus also taught that in God's final triumph over all his unrepentant enemies, those who rebelled against God were in danger of eternal loss. This is behind the teaching of the next verse (16). Perhaps the Edomites are in Obadiah's mind when he describes a scene on the top of Mount Zion, which he calls here, *my holy hill.* Is he picturing the Edomites drinking in celebration of the victory of the Babylonians over Jerusalem (see also vv. 10–14), and so desecrating God's holy hill? Obadiah reminds the Edomites of another kind of drinking, the drinking of the cup of God's wrath. That is what all the nations can expect to experience if they continue to be enemies of God and his people. They will continually drink of God's wrath, and *be as if they had never been* (16c); that is, they will suffer eternal loss (see Isa. 51:17; Jer. 25; Nah. 1:2–6; Hab. 2:15–16; Mark 14:36).

The picture of the nations drinking the cup of God's wrath and becoming *as if they had never been* (16) is a hard saying for those who believe in the love and mercy of God. Yet there is a gut instinct in all of us that insists that sin and injustice deserve to be punished, and that in a moral universe justice must be done and be seen to be done. That kind of justice is expressed in the words, *As you have done, it will be done to you; your deeds will return upon your own head* (15); that is a principle that is based on the *lex talionis* (Exod. 21:23–25; Lev. 24:19–20; Deut. 19:21).

Lex talionis literally means 'law of the tooth'. It is described in the book of Exodus, in the context of a law court, in these words: 'if there is serious injury, you are to take life for life, eye for eye, tooth for tooth, hand for hand, foot for foot, burn for burn, wound for wound, bruise for bruise' (Exod. 21:23–25). Here the law is insisting on '*objective* and *exact* determination of penalties . . . whereby the punishment matches the offence committed in both kind and degree'.[2] So Obadiah reminds us that the *day of the Lord is near for all nations*, and that on that day the Lord will act with perfect justice. *As you have done, it will be done to you; your deeds will return upon your own head* (15).

The purpose of the *lex talionis* was to prohibit personal vengeance and to define just and exact punishment in the law courts. It was given in the

[2] J. A. Motyer, *The Message of Exodus*, BST (IVP, 2005), p. 240 (italics in original).

Old Testament as the basic principle of jurisprudence. 'Not a rule for personal life, but for the Judge on the Bench.'[3] In Leviticus, in the context of the law courts, we read:

> Anyone who takes the life of a human being is to be put to death. Anyone who takes the life of someone's animal must make restitution – life for life. Anyone who injures their neighbour is to be injured in the same manner: fracture for fracture, eye for eye, tooth for tooth. The one who has inflicted the injury must suffer the same injury.
> (Lev. 24:17–20)

In his exposition of this passage Derek Tidball writes:

> This law fulfilled a number of purposes. It emphasised . . . the sacredness of life. No one could take a life without surrendering his own, although due allowance was made for the difference between premeditated murder and manslaughter . . . the law was also designed to set a limit on the punishments meted out, to check the unleashing of vengeance and to forestall the igniting of spirals of retaliation. If an eye was lost no one had the right to take a life in return, or to blow up a house and render a family homeless. The punishment had to be equal to the crime, not more, not less. The punishment also had to be administered on behalf of the community and the offended parties by the courts and magistrates. This was not a charter for taking the law into one's own hands.[4]

For, as John Wenham points out: 'It remains fundamental to the welfare of any society that the evildoer should be punished with scrupulous fairness, and that the well-doer should be acquitted.'[5]

This principle of exact and retributive justice was in no way undermined in the teaching of Jesus in the Sermon on the Mount. Jesus taught:

> You have heard that it was said, 'Eye for eye, and tooth for tooth.' But I tell you, do not resist an evil person. If anyone slaps you on the right cheek, turn to them the other cheek also.
> (Matt. 5:38–39)

---

[3] A phrase used by Alec Motyer in a letter to me (March 2008).

[4] D. Tidball, *The Message of Leviticus*, BST (IVP, 2005), pp. 289–290.

[5] J. W. Wenham, *The Goodness of God* (IVP, 1974), p. 93.

In these words Jesus is not contradicting the principle of *lex talionis* as found in the book of Leviticus, or undermining the principle of retributive justice through the courts. He is simply pointing out that the words of Leviticus should not be used as an excuse to take personal vengeance or retaliation on another person, which some were ready to do. On a personal level the disciples of Jesus were to turn the other cheek. Jesus teaches us to love our enemies and to pray for our persecutors. Yet, in the law courts, justice should be done and be seen to be done; and on the final day of judgment justice will be carried out in a perfectly just and proportionate way. As the Lord says in Obadiah's prophecy: *The day of the LORD is near for all nations. As you have done, it will be done to you; your deeds will return upon your own head* (15).

Before we leave the *lex talionis* we should reflect on whether, in the British context, the punishment fits the crime as much as it ought to in English law. Many dismiss the teaching of the Old Testament, and the teaching of Jesus on the *lex talionis*, as outdated and irrelevant in a modern society. For example, in debates on the death penalty in the UK parliament, there is always someone who warns the House with some such phrase as 'we must not return to the savagery of "an eye for an eye and a tooth for a tooth"'. Hanging for sheep stealing, or deportation for stealing sixpence, may once have been part of English law. But it was not a proper use of the *lex talionis*, which is best understood as descriptive, rather than prescriptive. As William Kaiser has written: 'While some have thought that the text condoned excessive retribution, it actually curbed all retribution and any personal retaliation among Israel's citizens.'[6] Raymond Brown points out that 'in eighteenth century England two hundred offences were punishable by death; that was because the law of *Lex Talionis* had been forgotten or ignored'.[7]

So Obadiah teaches us that the *lex talionis* is fundamental to God's justice (15). It ought, therefore, to be fundamental to the exercise of justice in our law courts. Indeed, according to Deuteronomy 19:20, a proper application of exact justice serves to purify a community from evil and is good for society. For Christians the cross of Christ is the place where the law was perfectly satisfied, when Jesus became our perfect substitute, dying as 'the just for the unjust' to bring us to God. Obadiah looks beyond the

---

[6] W. C. Kaiser, *Hard Sayings of the Old Testament* (Hodder & Stoughton, 1991), p. 14.

[7] R. Brown, *The Message of Deuteronomy*, BST (IVP, 1993), p. 195.

cross to *the day of the LORD . . . for all nations* (15). On that day God will continue to act with exact justice: *As you have done, it will be done to you; your deeds will return upon your own head* (15). But the cross of Jesus tells us that if our sins have already been laid upon our Saviour and perfect substitute, we shall be saved from the wrath to come by our Lord Jesus Christ (see 1 Thess. 1:10).

There is, moreover, a further truth, suggested by the next phrase in Obadiah's prophecy: *But on Mount Zion will be deliverance* (17a). God is not only just; he is also loving. He is the God of salvation as well as judgment. His people should be encouraged by the teaching that God will triumph over his enemies on that day. They should also rejoice in the truth that God will deliver his people on that day.

2. God will deliver his people on that day (17–21)

Obadiah insists that the *day of the LORD* (15) is not only a day of judgment for all nations, but also a day of deliverance for God's faithful people. If Obadiah is prophesying soon after the fall of Jerusalem in 586 BC,[8] when many of God's people would already be in captivity, then there would be despair and discouragement among them. The psalmist brilliantly captures that mood and their reaction to the Babylonian and Edomite destruction of Jerusalem:

By the rivers of Babylon we sat and wept
  when we remembered Zion.
There on the poplars
  we hung our harps,
for there our captors asked us for songs,
  our tormentors demanded songs of joy;
  they said, 'Sing us one of the songs of Zion!'

How can we sing the songs of the LORD
  while in a foreign land?
If I forget you, Jerusalem,
  may my right hand forget its skill.
May my tongue cling to the roof of my mouth
  if I do not remember you,

[8] See note on pp. 20–22.

if I do not consider Jerusalem
  my highest joy.

Remember, LORD, what the Edomites did
  on the day Jerusalem fell.
'Tear it down,' they cried,
  'tear it down to its foundations!'
Daughter Babylon, doomed to destruction,
  happy is the one who repays you
  according to what you have done to us.
Happy is the one who seizes your infants
  and dashes them against the rocks.
(Ps. 137:1–9)

Psalm 137:8–9 are difficult verses. However, there are a number of things that need to be weighed up in order to understand them in their context.

1. The psalmist reflects the mood of those who have suffered terrible things at the hands of the Edomites and the Babylonians. These verses come to us with 'the shocking immediacy of a scream, to startle us into feeling something of that desperation which produced them'.[9]

2. The psalmist is not taking the law into his own hands, or gloating over the killing of innocent babies. *Happy is the one* should be translated as: 'How right is the one'. Alec Motyer points out that the Hebrew word *'āšar* means 'to be straight', which in this context means 'to do the right thing'.[10]

So the psalmist must surely be saying that God will act with perfect justice, 'doing the right thing' in judging the Babylonians and the Edomites in terms of God's moral principle set out in Obadiah verse 15. As Motyer comments, Psalm 137:9

> records the savagery of Babylonian 'justice' (cf. 2 Kgs. 8:12; Isa. 13:16), and as they did, so it will be done to them. Does the Psalmist say he wants it to be so? No, only that it will be so. That is the sort of world we live in under God.[11]

---

[9] D. Kidner, introduction to his *Psalms 1 – 72*, TOTC (IVP, 1973), p. 28.

[10] See J. A. Motyer on Ps. 137 in 'Psalms', NBC (21), pp. 577–578; see also Ps. 106:3; Prov. 14:21.

[11] Motyer, in 'Psalms', NBC (21), pp. 577–578.

So we should leave vengeance to the Lord (Rom. 12:19), and acknowledge that the judge of all the world does right (Gen. 18:25).

3. The teaching of Jesus helps us to hold on to the truth about God's judgments, while encouraging us personally to love and pray for our enemies (Matt. 5:44); to forgive those who sin against us (Matt. 6:14); and to repay evil with good (Matt. 5:38–42). It is Jesus who teaches us how much God values children when he says: 'Let the little children come to me, and do not hinder them, for the kingdom of God belongs to such as these' (Luke 18:16).

Obadiah may well have been preaching to people in the midst of great despair. He has encouraged them by speaking of God's sovereignty and his judgment of their enemies. Now he comes to the climax of his message. It's a message that assures them of God's deliverance and ultimate triumph, and that focuses on four promises: a new Jerusalem (17, 21a); a decisive victory (18); a future inheritance (19–20); and a divine kingdom (21b).

a. The promise of a new Jerusalem (17, 21a)

Obadiah had no doubt that Jerusalem had a future. Generations earlier, Moses had foreseen such a place as a sanctuary for God's people and a place where God would dwell in a special way:

> In your unfailing love you will lead
> the people you have redeemed.
> In your strength you will guide them
> to your holy dwelling . . .
> You will bring them in and plant them
> on the mountain of your inheritance –
> the place, LORD, you made for your dwelling,
> the sanctuary, LORD, your hands established.
>
> The LORD reigns
> for ever and ever.
> (Exod. 15:13, 17–18)

It was in King David's day that Jerusalem was captured and made the capital of Israel. Then the first temple was built in the reign of Solomon, David's son. The prophets, however, were continually pointing out the ways in which God's people were breaking the covenant that he had made with them. They warned of coming judgment, which came about in the north through the Assyrians (722 BC), and to Judah and Jerusalem in the south through the Babylonians (586 BC). Obadiah, however, brings a message of hope and the promise of a new Jerusalem to those who remained in Judah and to those already in exile.

On Mount Zion will be deliverance; it will be holy (17a). When Obadiah speaks of *Mount Zion* he is surely referring to the temple and all that it stands for. Jerusalem will once again be a place of *deliverance* and salvation. It will be a place of security and safety for true believers. It will be a *holy* place, set apart for God and for God's people exclusively (here described as *Jacob*). Obadiah seems to imply that all God's enemies, symbolized here as *Esau* (18), will be excluded from the holy city.

All this is an ideal picture of a new Jerusalem that God will bring about, for Yahweh, the covenant Lord, *has spoken* (18c).

But how were these promises about a new and restored Jerusalem fulfilled? And what message do they have for us?

i. The promises were partially fulfilled in the return of some exiles

Obadiah's prophecy was partially fulfilled when some exiles returned to Jerusalem under Zerubbabel (see Ezra 1; 2) and when Nehemiah directed the building of the city walls (c. 537 BC). In Ezra (Ezra 3:6, 11–13) we read of the rebuilding of the temple (c. 515 BC) during the time of Ezra and Haggai (see Ezra 1:3; 3:3, 8–10; Hag. 1). Ezra and Nehemiah also describe the rebuilding and restoring of a spiritual community, with a call to holiness of life.

It is clear, however, that the restoration of Jerusalem and the rebuilding of the temple, as well as the spiritual reforms that were carried out, never completely fulfilled the picture of a city that was *holy* and exclusive to God's holy people. When Malachi, for example, preached after the rebuilding of the temple, he pointed out a great deal that was wrong with the worship there and in the lives of the people (see Mal. 1:6–14). So we need to look to the New Testament for a further fulfilment of these promises from God in Obadiah.

ii. The promises were further fulfilled in the coming of Jesus

Jerusalem and the temple had not become *holy* and exclusive to God's people at the time of Jesus' earthly ministry. The people of Israel knew, of course, that God's presence with them was not confined to the temple (see

1 Kgs 8:27; Ps. 51:16–17; Isa. 66:1); and this truth is made even more explicit in the teaching of Jesus and his apostles. Jesus, for example, spoke of the destruction of the temple as God's judgment on a nation that did not recognize God's moment when it came (see Luke 19:41–44). Again, according to Luke's Gospel, Jesus wept and prayed over Jerusalem, and then 'he entered the temple courts [and] began to drive out those who were selling. "It is written," he said to them, "'My house will be a house of prayer'; but you have made it 'a den of robbers'"' (Luke 19:45–46). According to Bishop Tom Wright this was 'a prophetic sign, which commentators now take as signifying the coming destruction of the Temple itself and the end of all that it stood for in contemporary theology and politics'.[12]

So, if the temple was to be destroyed again (and it was in AD 70), where was the fulfilment of Obadiah's prophecy of a new Jerusalem (and, for that matter, the prophecies of Ezek. 34 – 47 and Dan. 9)? Where was *Mount Zion* which was *holy*, from which *deliverance* would come? The New Testament teaches us that Jerusalem and the temple, symbolized by *Mount Zion*, were to be found in Jesus, the Messiah (John 2:18–22), and in the community of believers, who were the temple of the Holy Spirit (see Eph. 2:19–22; 1 Pet. 2:11–12). Jesus had spoken enigmatically, and said, 'Destroy this temple, and I will raise it again in three days' (John 2:19). When the Jews replied, 'It has taken forty-six years to build this temple, and you are going to raise it in three days?' John commented: 'But the temple he had spoken of was his body. After he was raised from the dead, his disciples recalled what he had said. Then they believed the Scripture and the words that Jesus had spoken' (John 2:20–22). So Jesus spoke as if his coming to earth and dwelling among us, and his death and resurrection, made the temple redundant; and surely his one sufficient sacrifice on the cross made animal sacrifices unnecessary too. John Calvin believed that 'God deserted his Temple, because it was only founded for a time, and was but a shadow' of things to come.[13]

Another important scripture is to be found in the letter to the Hebrews. The writer tells those Christian believers who were tempted to return to Judaism:

---

12 See Matt. 21:12–13; Mark 11:15–17; Luke 19:45–46; John 2:13–22; for a fuller discussion see also N. T. Wright, *Jesus and the Victory of God* (SPCK, 1996), pp. 405–428.

13 J. Calvin, *Daniel 7 – 12, Hosea*, Commentaries, vol. 13 (Baker Book House, repr. 1996), p. 390. See also C. J. H. Wright, *The Mission of God* (IVP, 2006), p. 509.

> But you have come to Mount Zion, to the city of the living God, the heavenly Jerusalem. You have come to thousands upon thousands of angels in joyful assembly, to the church of the firstborn, whose names are written in heaven. You have come to God, the Judge of all, to the spirits of the righteous made perfect, to Jesus the mediator of a new covenant, and to the sprinkled blood that speaks a better word than the blood of Abel. (Heb. 12:22–24)

Mount Zion might be considered as 'the ultimate goal of God's people when they left Egypt' (Peterson). But the writer to the Hebrews reminds these Christians that they have come already to the heavenly Jerusalem, the city of the living God, if their names are written in heaven, and if they have been cleansed and forgiven by Jesus, the 'mediator of a new covenant' whose 'sprinkled blood . . . speaks a better word than the blood of Abel' (Abel's blood called out for vengeance; Jesus' blood promised forgiveness and acceptance). So the writer assures believing Christians that they belong to the heavenly Jerusalem, now, and one day they will enjoy the full rights of citizenship.[14]

This further fulfilment in Christ was no doubt hidden from Obadiah's eyes. But God showed him that deliverance would come from Jerusalem, and that the holy God would once again dwell among his people. Some commentators believe that the prophets glimpsed this further fulfilment rather as a person might glimpse several mountain peaks, some further away than others, indistinct now but becoming clearer in time. Indeed, the teaching of the New Testament leads us to look still further on to the final fulfilment of these great promises about the new Jerusalem and the temple as we find them in the prophecy of Obadiah. So not only are these promises partially fulfilled in the return of the exiles and further fulfilled in the coming of Jesus, but . . .

iii. The promises will ultimately be fulfilled in heaven itself

In the final analysis the Christian hope lies beyond the last day. It goes beyond any idea of Jerusalem remaining in the hands of the Israelis – let alone the worrying interpretation that the temple itself will be rebuilt before the return of Christ, and sacrifices re-enacted.[15]

---

[14] See David Peterson's comments in NBC (21), p. 1351.

[15] Some Christians, especially 'Christian Zionists', believe that a new temple will be built in Jerusalem before Christ returns, and some believe that animal sacrifices will be offered once more. This seems to me to be wholly incompatible with the way the New Testament treats the Old Testament prophecies about

So, the apostle Paul links Jerusalem with heaven when he writes to Christians in Galatia and refers to 'the Jerusalem that is above' (Gal. 4:26). The writer to the Hebrews tells them that God 'has prepared a city for them' in heaven (Heb. 11:16). And the apostle John, in the book of Revelation, links the new Jerusalem specifically with heaven, when he writes:

> Then I saw 'a new heaven and a new earth,' for the first heaven and the first earth had passed away, and there was no longer any sea. I saw the Holy City, the new Jerusalem, coming down out of heaven from God, prepared as a bride beautifully dressed for her husband. And I heard a loud voice from the throne saying, 'Look! God's dwelling-place is now among the people, and he will dwell with them. They will be his people, and God himself will be with them and be their God. "He will wipe every tear from their eyes. There will be no more death" or mourning or crying or pain, for the old order of things has passed away.'
> (Rev. 21:1–4)

It is this final picture of Mount Zion and all that it stands for that is the ultimate inheritance of the people of God (17c). Obadiah offers this future hope to encourage and motivate God's people at a time of hopelessness and despair. The prophet assures them that God will certainly bring to an end the time of disciplining judgment for his people. God promises to restore Jerusalem and all it stood for; and in doing so God looks beyond the partial restoration and deliverance brought about in the days of Ezra and Nehemiah to the days of Jesus and his followers, and ultimately to the new Jerusalem in the new heaven and earth, where righteousness will reign (2 Pet. 3:13).

In one of his writings, Jim Packer urges Christians to take more seriously this future hope of a new Jerusalem. He says:

> We have recast Christianity into a mould that stresses happiness above holiness, blessings here above blessings hereafter; health and wealth as God's best gifts, and death, especially early death, not as thankworthy deliverance from the miseries of a sinful world, but as the supreme

---

Jerusalem and the temple; and it also undermines the glorious gospel truth about 'the finished work of Christ' on the cross. (For a full discussion of these various interpretations, see Stephen Sizer, *Christian Zionism* [IVP, 2004]; and Colin Chapman, *Whose Promised Land?* [Lion, 1983]. For a Christian dispensationalist viewpoint, see Hal Lindsey, *Planet Earth* [Marshall Pickering, 1970, 1987, 1988].)

> disaster . . . Is our Christianity out of shape? Yes it is, and the basic reason is that we have lost the New Testament's two world perspective that views the next life as more important than this one and understands life here as essentially preparation and training for the life hereafter![16]

Obadiah, I believe, also has this two-world perspective and points us in the same direction. He also encourages God's people with the promise of a decisive victory.

b. The promise of a decisive victory (18)

There's a room in a Whitehall basement where Winston Churchill used to meet his war cabinet during the Second World War. On the wall there was a notice, which was placed so that all his colleagues could see it clearly. It was a statement attributed to Queen Victoria, and it read as follows: 'Please understand that there is no depression in this house. We are not interested in the possibilities of defeat: they do not exist.'

There's something of that spirit in the message that Obadiah brings to God's dispirited people. Obadiah indicates that the people of God, or at least a remnant of them (described here as *Jacob . . . and Joseph*), will in some way be caught up in God's victory over Edom (*Esau* stands for Edom; and Edom seems to symbolize the enemies of God in totality). The victory will be complete. There are no possibilities of defeat. The Lord has spoken, says Obadiah, and his promises never fail. God says: *Esau will be stubble, and they will set him on fire and destroy him. There will be no survivors from Esau* (18b).

On the surface it seems as if Obadiah envisages a military battle in which the fire and the flame of Israel overcome her enemies. It is more likely, however, that Obadiah is writing metaphorically. Fire and flame often symbolize the presence of a holy God (e.g. Exod.13:21; Lev. 6:12; Jer. 23:29; Matt. 25:41; Heb. 12:29; Rev. 20:14). So it is possible that Obadiah brings a message from God describing a spiritual victory over all the forces of evil in the world, symbolized by this total victory over Edom. For, as we have already noticed (17), deliverance will be from *Mount Zion . . . it will be holy.* In the light of the New Testament, perhaps there is a picture here of the flame of God's holiness, expressed in the lives of God's faithful remnant, overcoming the forces opposed to God. Whatever exact meaning

16 J. I. Packer, *Laid-Back Religion?* (IVP, 1987), pp. 62–63.

lies in these words, they describe a decisive victory over evil, and the ultimate triumph of God. There are no possibilities of defeat.

The apostle Paul captures something of the same spirit when writing to the Christians in Corinth. In spite of the difficulties and pressures of gospel ministry, about which he is open and honest (see 2 Cor. 2:1–6), he can still write:

> But thanks be to God, who always leads us as captives in Christ's triumphal procession and uses us to spread the aroma of the knowledge of him everywhere. For we are to God the pleasing aroma of Christ among those who are being saved and those who are perishing. To the one we are an aroma that brings death; to the other, an aroma that brings life.
> (2 Cor. 2:14–16)

For Christians the decisive victory, which makes holy living possible, is the death of Christ on the cross, followed by his resurrection and exaltation. There Christ defeated Satan. 'Having disarmed the powers and authorities, he made a public spectacle of them, triumphing over them by the cross' (Col. 2:15). It is as Christians claim that victory on the cross, and live lives of sacrificial discipleship and courageous testimony, that they share in Christ's victory. As the apostle John writes about Christians in the first century AD: 'They triumphed over him [Satan] by the blood of the Lamb and by the word of their testimony; they did not love their lives so much as to shrink from death' (Rev. 12:11).

Obadiah has no doubt that God will win a decisive victory over his enemies, symbolized here by Edom. He describes a situation in which God's people share in that victory. There are no possibilities of defeat, because the Lord has spoken. As Christians, we sometimes share in the sense of despair and discouragement that Obadiah's listeners probably felt. But we need to hear God's word through Obadiah. God promised to defeat the enemies of his people. Christ has already won a decisive victory at Calvary. The final victory is assured.

c. The promise of a future inheritance (19–21)

When Obadiah asserted that *Jacob will possess his inheritance* (17b), he meant more than the restoration of Jerusalem and its temple. The future inheritance of Israel is linked with God's covenant with Abraham, which included the promise: 'The whole land of Canaan, where you now reside as a foreigner, I will give as an everlasting possession to you and your descendants after you; and I will be their God' (Gen. 17:8). So God promises Israel a land and a relationship with himself.

For God's people in exile this was a precious promise. In Obadiah's day much of the land that God had promised them had been taken over by their enemies, including the Edomites. Obadiah now assures God's people that the Lord will be faithful to his covenant, and will give them the future inheritance that he had promised. It is that gracious work on behalf of his people that Obadiah now describes: *People from the Negev will occupy the mountains of Esau, and people from the foothills will possess the land of the Philistines. They will occupy the fields of Ephraim and Samaria, and Benjamin will possess Gilead* (19).

There is more than one way of interpreting verse 19. But the Negev is the wilderness south of Beersheba, and God is promising through Obadiah that some of the exiles will eventually move into Edomite territory (*the mountains of Esau*).

The *Philistines* (19b) had never been fully driven out of the Promised Land; but here God promises a future where God's people, *the people from the foothills* (the *Shephelah*, NRSV), will possess the land of the Philistines (at last!), and occupy Ephraim, Samaria and Gilead.[17] If Obadiah was preaching soon after the destruction of Jerusalem in 586 BC, when many of God's people were already in exile, and much of the Promised Land was occupied by the enemies of Israel, this message must have seemed astonishing, even unbelievable. But Obadiah is clear: *The LORD has spoken* (18). God is a God of surprises, and the God of the impossible. He is a faithful covenant God who keeps his promises. It is also possible that the reference to the occupation of Edom is intended to be symbolic rather than merely literal. As we have already noted, 'Esau/Edom' stood for Israel's inveterate foe, and on occasions illustrates symbolically the final overthrow of the world for its hostility towards the Lord and his people (see Isa. 34; Ezek. 35; Amos 9). Could Obadiah be pointing to the same 'end-time' reality here? Certainly in the promise of the land there is a hint of a deeper and more spiritual fulfilment. This is suggested in two ways in Obadiah's prophecy and its New Testament fulfilment.

[17] It may be that in this last section we have prose and not poetry, in which case this is perhaps a reminder that the promise of the repossession of the land was at least in part both factual and historical. Those who argue that a change to prose indicates a different writer from Obadiah have no other evidence to support that view.

First, God promises to unite his people spiritually; second, he promises to bless his people spiritually.

i. God promises to unite his people spiritually (19–20)

The overall picture in verse 19 promises the re-creation of a united people throughout the Promised Land. The prophets had never come to terms with the divided kingdom, as the story of Elijah's twelve-stone altar built in Israel illustrates (1 Kgs 18:16–46). Obadiah's message points forward to the time when God's people would be united. The next verse (20) paints the same picture: *This company of Israelite exiles who are in Canaan will possess the land as far as Zarephath; the exiles from Jerusalem who are in Sepharad will possess the towns of the Negev.* In other words, the Israelite exiles from the north, taken captive by Assyria in 722 BC (see 2 Kgs 17:6; 18:11), and the exiles from Jerusalem currently in Sepharad, will return to their homes, so that the entire nation of Israel from far south to far north will be restored, and the land occupied will surpass the territory held during the monarchy.

These promises were only partially fulfilled territorially when Israel gained control of the foothills (Shephelah), Ephraim, Samaria and Gilead under the Maccabees in the second century BC (see 1 Macc. 10:84–89). But surely Obadiah was pointing forward to a deeper, spiritual fulfilment of these promises? The promise is that the people of God will settle among their enemies, the Edomites and the Philistines. This is symbolic of a supernatural activity of God which will bring people together in spite of a great deal of ancestral prejudice and hostility. That hostility was not unlike that which affects the making of peace between Israelis and Palestinians today. The New Testament declares that such unity can be achieved, and has been, through the death, resurrection and exaltation of the Lord Jesus Christ. In New Testament times the hostility and prejudice that existed between Jew and Gentile is well known. Yet the apostle Paul can write to the Christians at Ephesus:

> But now in Christ Jesus you [Gentiles] who once were far away have been brought near by the blood of Christ. For he himself is our peace, who has made the two groups one and has destroyed the barrier, the dividing wall of hostility, by setting aside in his flesh the law with its commands and regulations. His purpose was to create in himself one new humanity out of the two, thus making peace, and in one body to reconcile both of them

> to God through the cross, by which he put to death their hostility . . . For through him we both have access to the Father by one Spirit.
> (Eph. 2:13–16, 18)

Obadiah reminds us that it is God's purpose to unite his people. It still is; and, as the apostle Paul teaches us, it has been made possible through the death of Christ. Jew and Gentile became one in Christ. As Paul wrote to the Christians in Galatia: 'There is neither Jew nor Gentile, neither slave nor free, nor is there male and female, for you are all one in Christ Jesus. If you belong to Christ, then you are Abraham's seed, and heirs according to the promise' (Gal. 3:28–29).

If, then, spiritual unity is part of God's plan for his people, we need to ask ourselves whether we live out that unity in our relationships at home and in the local church. There are clearly some churches where that unity is both moving and compelling. The Anglican church in Baghdad, Iraq, is one such church. The former vicar, Canon Andrew White, has spoken movingly of a unity of different races and backgrounds that has been a powerful witness to the wider community. The tragedy is that in our far more comfortable churches, love, care and acceptance of one another too often is missing. Instead there can be backbiting, a spirit of criticism, and that ugly kind of jealousy and pride that is the mark of most power struggles. The apostle Paul recognized those dangers in the same letter to the Ephesians that I have already quoted. He wrote:

> As a prisoner for the Lord, then, I urge you to live a life worthy of the calling you have received. Be completely humble and gentle; be patient, bearing with one another in love. Make every effort to keep the unity of the Spirit through the bond of peace. There is one body and one Spirit . . .
> (Eph. 4:1–4)

The prayer of the Lord Jesus should be enough to move us to be at peace with one another:

> I pray . . . for those who will believe in me through their [the apostles'] message, that all of them may be one, Father, just as you are in me, and I am in you . . . so that they may be brought to complete unity. Then the world will know that you sent me . . .
> (John 17:20–21, 23)

God's promise to unite his people spiritually also points us to the truth that God promises to bless his people spiritually. Obadiah's message about the repossession of the Promised Land, and the promise of a future inheritance, must have lifted the hearts of the exiles and renewed their confidence in the Lord.

ii. God promises to bless his people spiritually (20–21)

Jeremiah, who was probably a contemporary of Obadiah, had prophesied that the exile would last for some seventy years:

> This is what the LORD says: 'When seventy years are completed for Babylon, I will come to you and fulfil my good promise to bring you back to this place . . . Then you will call on me and come and pray to me, and I will listen to you. You will seek me and find me when you seek me with all your heart. I will be found by you,' declares the LORD, 'and will bring you back from captivity. I will gather you from all the nations and places where I have banished you,' declares the LORD, 'and will bring you back to the place from which I carried you into exile.'
> (Jer. 29:10, 12–14)[18]

Once again, we know that God kept his word and began to fulfil Obadiah's prophecies about the land as well as the predictions of other prophets (such as Isaiah, Ezekiel and Zechariah). In 539 BC King Cyrus of Persia captured Babylon, passing an edict to allow the exiles from Israel and Judah to return to Jerusalem (see 2 Chr. 36:22–23; Ezra 1:1–3; 2; cf. 1 Chr. 9:2). Their return was peaceful, which counters the idea that Obadiah is advocating a military conquest (see 17–21). The prophet Zechariah (who prophesied c. 520–518 BC) describes the return of the exiles in very similar ways to Obadiah. He writes about the return of the exiles from the north and the south, and says:

> I will strengthen Judah
>   and save the tribes of Joseph.
> I will restore them
>   because I have compassion on them . . .

[18] See also Jer. 16:14–15. For a discussion of other prophecies about 'the land', see Chapman, *Whose Promised Land?* pp. 100–130.

I will bring them to Gilead and Lebanon,
and there will not be room enough for them.
(Zech. 10:6, 10)

Clearly these promises in Obadiah and Zechariah were at least partially fulfilled in the subsequent history of Israel, following the return of the exiles. But God's promise to Abraham about the land was only one part of the future inheritance that God had promised his people (see Gen. 17:3–8); and the New Testament casts new light on the significance of 'the land'.

It is true that some modern Israelis hold on to the belief that God's promises about the Promised Land still have validity. Christian Zionists also believe that God's promises about the land in Obadiah, Isaiah, Jeremiah, Ezekiel and Zechariah will be fulfilled literally, and that the Six-Day War in 1967 and the unifying of Jerusalem under Israeli rule was a fulfilment of biblical promises.

However, there is another way, and I believe a more scriptural one, to interpret these prophecies in Obadiah and the other prophets: that is to understand them in the light of the teaching of Jesus and his apostles. We have already seen how Jesus understood the significance of the temple, and foretold its destruction rather than its further rebuilding. How did Jesus interpret the promises to Abraham? 'God said to him, ". . . The whole land of Canaan, where you now reside as a foreigner, I will give as an everlasting possession to you and your descendants after you; and I will be their God"' (Gen. 17:3, 8).

According to the Gospels, Jesus said very little about the promise of 'the land'. In the Sermon on the Mount he says: 'Blessed are the meek, for they will inherit the earth' (Matt. 5:5). Colin Chapman points out that the Greek word translated earth (*gē*) can also mean 'land'; and the Hebrew equivalent word (*'ereṣ*) is the word used for 'land' throughout the Old Testament. So Jesus is saying the meek will inherit the land. But what does Jesus mean by that? In the context, he is not talking about the kingdom of heaven as a piece of land but as the sphere of his reign over his disciples; and he is not limiting this future inheritance to the physical descendants of Abraham, but making the promises to all believers, Jews and Gentiles, who are poor in spirit, who mourn because of their sins, hunger and thirst for righteousness, show mercy, are pure in heart and meek before others, and are persecuted for righteousness's sake.

It is likely that the disciples still believed in the repossession of the Promised Land when they asked the risen Lord Jesus: 'Lord, are you at this time going to restore the kingdom to Israel?' (Acts 1:6).[19] Jesus said:

> It is not for you to know the times or dates the Father has set by his own authority. But you will receive power when the Holy Spirit comes on you; and you will be my witnesses in Jerusalem, and in all Judea and Samaria, and to the ends of the earth.
> (Acts 1:7–8)

Surely Jesus was not only trying to correct the disciples' idea about the *timing* of these events; he was also trying to correct the *idea* that was implied in the question (Acts 1:8). He wanted them to put on one side the idea of the kingdom which they had inherited from their Jewish background, and to accept a completely new idea of the kingdom of God: a kingdom which is spiritual and therefore has nothing to do with any territorial kingdom; a kingdom which is international and has no connection with any national kingdom. As the Lord Jesus said to Pilate: 'My kingdom is not of this world . . . my kingdom is from another place' (John 18:36; see also Acts 15:13–18; Amos 9:11–12).

In other words, Jesus is saying that his kingdom does not arise from this world, nor is it an earthly entity for which his servants could fight a war.

Certainly the apostle Paul emphasized the spiritual fulfilment of God's covenant promises to Abraham. All believers in Christ are Abraham's seed. As he explained to the Galatian Christians:

> You are all children of God through faith, for all of you who were baptised into Christ have clothed yourselves with Christ. There is neither Jew nor Gentile, neither slave nor free, nor is there male and female, for you are all one in Christ Jesus. If you belong to Christ, then you are Abraham's seed, and heirs according to the promise.
> (Gal. 3:26–29)

The apostle Peter also writes of a spiritual inheritance, even though a first-century Jew would naturally associate the word 'inheritance' with 'the land' (see Ps. 78:52, 54–55). Peter, however, contrasts the spiritual

[19] Chapman, *Whose Promised Land?* pp. 124–153.

fulfilment of the Old Testament prophecies about the land with the physical inheritance which ultimately fades and perishes. He writes:

> Praise be to the God and Father of our Lord Jesus Christ! In his great mercy he has given us new birth into a living hope through the resurrection of Jesus Christ from the dead, and into an inheritance that can never perish, spoil or fade. This inheritance is kept in heaven for you, who through faith are shielded by God's power until the coming of the salvation that is ready to be revealed in the last time.
> (1 Pet. 1:3–5)

Another example of this future spiritual inheritance is to be found in the letter to the Hebrews. The writer takes up the theme of the land in chapter 4, and describes it as God's 'rest'. This rest is clearly a spiritual one, which is to be entered into by faith:

> Therefore, since the promise of entering his rest still stands, let us be careful that none of you be found to have fallen short of it. For we also have had the good news preached to us, just as they did; but the message they heard was of no value to them, because they did not share the faith of those who obeyed. Now we who have believed enter that rest . . .
> (Heb. 4:1–3)

A little later the same writer describes Abraham seeking not only the physical Promised Land but also 'a better country – a heavenly one' (see Heb. 11:9–10, 16).

Finally, John, in the book of Revelation, describes the vision that God gave him of 'a new heaven and a new earth', where he saw

> the river of the water of life, as clear as crystal, flowing from the throne of God and of the Lamb down the middle of the great street of the city. On each side of the river stood the tree of life, bearing twelve crops of fruit, yielding its fruit every month. And the leaves of the tree are for the healing of the nations.
> (Rev. 22:1–2)

Surely Scripture teaches us that the promise of the repossessed land in Obadiah, and elsewhere, is fulfilled in the spiritual inheritance we have in

Christ and in the full salvation believers will enjoy in the new heaven and the new earth, where righteousness will reign.

This leads us on to Obadiah's final paragraph, which in many ways sums up all that has gone before. For in delivering his people, God promises not only a new Jerusalem, a decisive victory and a future inheritance, but also a divine kingdom.

d. The promise of a divine kingdom (21)

The phrase *Deliverers will go up on Mount Zion* literally means 'Those causing salvation will be on [Heb., *bĕ*] Mount Zion'. Here's a promise then that *Deliverers* or saviours will return to Jerusalem *to govern the mountains of Esau*. The mountains of Esau represent Edom. Edom, as we have already indicated, stands for all those who, like Edom, oppose God and his *kingdom* (literally, 'kingship') and his rule in the world.

Was Obadiah, then, foreseeing a restoration of the lineage of Davidic kings, a line that had been cruelly severed in 586 BC?[20] Would these kings become the *Deliverers* or saviours for whom Israel longed? Or would this promise only be fulfilled through the one who came as the Son of David and the Son of God (Rom. 1:3–6)? As is so often the case with biblical prophecy, the deepest interpretation of these words probably has a spiritual and eschatological meaning, especially in the light of Obadiah's final words: *And the kingdom [kingship] will be the LORD's* (21c).

Douglas Stuart helpfully explains this understanding of the text:

> The Christian . . . will see in Obadiah's prophecy, not merely a description of certain political realities and hopes for the sixth century BC in Palestine, but also the more general reality and hope of God's intervention on behalf of his people to rescue them from helplessness in the face of mortal danger, and to guarantee them a bright future of reward for their faithfulness. (See 1 Pet. 4:12–14.) The success of earthly powers arraigned against God's purposes can only be temporary, and the ultimate victory of God's people is assured.[21]

We should also notice that the word translated *govern* (21) is the standard verb 'to judge' (Heb., *šāpat*) in the basic sense of pronouncing a royal or

---

20 See D. W. Baker, in D. W. Baker, T. D. Alexander and B. Waltke, *Obadiah, Jonah, Micah*, TOTC (IVP, 1988), p. 43.

21 D. Stuart, *Hosea–Jonah*, WBC (Thomas Nelson, 1987), p. 22.

judicial decision, and 'putting things to right'. That is what the *Deliverer* or saviour will come to do, even in the mountains of Esau, where evil, wickedness and rebellion reigns. Even there God, the King, will triumph. No wonder the psalmist rejoiced at the prospect of God's judgment, and called upon the whole creation to celebrate:

> Let the mountains sing together for joy;
> let them sing before the LORD,
>   for he comes to judge the earth.
> He will judge the world in righteousness
>   and the peoples with equity.
> (Ps. 98:8–9)

Obadiah, then, has no doubt about the ultimate triumph of God – *the kingdom will be the LORD's*. And, of course, it already is the Lord's. As one commentator put it:

> The world has never escaped from the grasp and the grip of the government of God. There are so many things that we cannot understand today; but the one absolute certainty is that all these things are under the government of God. The fact remains, then, that the Kingdom shall be his, because in this sense it is already his.[22]

In the book of Revelation John describes the final triumph of God when he tells us that the seventh angel, at the end of the age, sounded his trumpet, 'and there were loud voices in heaven, which said: "The kingdom of the world has become the kingdom of our Lord and of his Messiah, and he will reign for ever and ever"' (Rev. 11:15).

While walking in Norfolk, my wife, Elizabeth, and I met a pastor and his wife who years earlier had worked with us in a local church. We began to talk about Christian friends we knew. Some had been through difficult times and appeared to have given up on their faith in God. Others had persevered and continued with the Lord. Elizabeth commented, 'Satan never gives up attacking Christians.' 'That's true,' said the pastor, 'but Jesus doesn't give up on us either!' Then he added with a smile: 'The Lamb is on the throne!'

[22] G. C. Morgan, *Voices of Twelve Hebrew Prophets* (Pickering & Inglis, n.d.), p. 74.

There's something of that confidence in God throughout this little book of Obadiah. The enemies of God (typified by Edom) never gave up their attacks on his people. But Obadiah reminds believers of the sovereignty of God, his judgments and his triumph. Whatever our circumstances may be, we can be encouraged and strengthened by these truths. The Lamb, who is our saviour and deliverer, is indeed on the throne. And the kingdom will be the Lord's!

The message of Nahum

Introducing Nahum

It may seem strange to have a *book* (1) in holy Scripture that focuses so much on an enemy of Israel: Assyria, and her capital city Nineveh.[1] Nahum tells us that his *book* is *A prophecy concerning Nineveh* (1). The Hebrew word for 'prophecy' (*maśśā'*) can sometimes mean 'burden'.[2] Certainly no word better expresses Nahum's prophecy, for it is indeed a weighty, even burdensome, message of judgment which Nahum declares with great boldness and clarity.

It must be said, however, that not all commentators on Nahum appreciate his clarity and bluntness. The Old Testament specialist Elizabeth Achtemeier is quoted as saying: 'All Scripture is inspired by God . . . but maybe with the exception of Nahum, we think.'[3] Furthermore, those of us who have no doubts about the place of Nahum in holy Scripture would probably have to admit that we have rarely, if ever, preached from the book of Nahum.

So why should we take the book of Nahum seriously and count it important to expound its teaching?

1. Why take the book of Nahum seriously?

a. The book of Nahum is a message from the living God

The *prophecy* or 'burden' concerning Nineveh is part of a *book* which is described as *the vision of Nahum the Elkoshite* (1). The word for *vision*

---

[1] It has a modern ring, however, as Assyria is in the region of modern Iraq, and the site of Nineveh is close to the modern city of Mosul.

[2] E.g. in Exod. 23:5 where it refers to a donkey's load; or Jer. 23:33 where it can be translated as 'the burden of the Lord'.

[3] Quoted in J. Woods, 'The West as Nineveh: How Does Nahum's Message of Judgement Apply to Today?', *Themelios* 31.1 (October 2005), p. 7.

means 'something communicated to the prophet by the revelation of God' (Eaton).[4] Some commentators point out that Nahum expresses that vision in superb poetry, and poetry was a natural mode of expression for all the great Hebrew prophets. But in Nahum, God's word is also found in direct speech claiming to be from God himself: *This is what the LORD says . . .* (see 1:12; 2:13; 3:5).

Nahum's claim has to be tested, of course, in the same way as that of the other prophets.[5] It seems clear that Nahum is predicting the fall of Nineveh and the collapse of the superpower Assyria, at a time when it must have seemed highly unlikely. If Nahum's predictions had not been fulfilled, then he could rightly be described as a false prophet (Deut. 18:22). In fact, Nineveh was destroyed exactly as Nahum predicted, and Assyria disappeared as a world power and was never a threat to Israel again (Nah. 1:8, 12–15; 2 – 3). The fulfilment of Nahum's predictions confirm the prophet's claim that his message was a revelation from God.

There are, however, some who object to the main thrust of Nahum's *vision.* They cannot believe that the loving God and Father of the Lord Jesus Christ can rightly be described as *a jealous and avenging God . . . [who] takes vengeance and is filled with wrath* (1:2). Some years ago that point was made very forcibly to me by a member of the church congregation which I served. A woman, who had only just become a Christian after years of atheism, came to me to complain about the preaching in our church. We had been preaching a series of sermons from the Old Testament, and she had felt uncomfortable with them. Taking out her Bible from the bag she was carrying, she opened it at the page that separated the Old Testament from the New. She then produced a pair of scissors, cut the Old Testament section from the New Testament and spoke dramatically along these lines: 'The Old Testament tells me about a God of wrath. The New Testament teaches me about a God of love.' She then handed me the New Testament and exclaimed, 'Preach that!'

After my initial rather startled reaction, I told my friend that I would continue to preach from the Old Testament as well as the New, and that both Testaments reveal the one true God who is a God of wrath as well as a God of love; a God who is both stern and kind (Rom. 11:22).

---

4 J. H. Eaton, *Obadiah, Nahum, Habakkuk, Zephaniah* (SCM Press, 1961), p. 52.

5. See note on Obad. 1:1 (pp. 30–32), Zeph. 1:1 (pp. 182–185) and 'Introduction to Obadiah, Nahum and Zephaniah' (pp. 2–8).

In this respect Nahum is no different from the other prophets. The prophet has much to say about the wrath of God and his judgments, as we shall see as we study his book; but he also speaks about the Lord's mercy and grace: *The LORD is slow to anger . . . the LORD is good, a refuge in times of trouble. He cares for those who trust in him* . . . (1:3, 7). The other prophets write in much the same way. Isaiah, for example, wrote, 'The LORD takes his place in court; he rises to judge the people' (Isa. 3:13), but he also writes, 'The LORD will have compassion on Jacob' (14:1); and who can forget the following words of love and mercy spoken to a rebellious people?

> Seek the LORD while he may be found;
> call on him while he is near.
> Let the wicked forsake their ways . . .
> Let them turn to the LORD, and he will have mercy on them,
> and to our God, for he will freely pardon.
> (Isa. 55:6–7)

We find the same balanced truths about the triune God in the teaching, character and life of Jesus. For example, we see the kindness and sternness of the Lord when Jesus weeps over Jerusalem while he warns his people of judgment to come (Luke 19:37–44). We see his anger at the hypocrisy of the Pharisees, and his compassion as he heals a man with a withered arm on the sabbath (Mark 3:5–6).

So, in Nahum's vision we find a message from the living God, the God and Father of our Lord Jesus Christ. It's a message of special interest because it sets out so clearly and rationally the character of God and the theological foundation for the doctrine of judgment. That foundation is laid down in the first chapter, where we learn that the Lord is a God who is angry (1:1–6) as well as a God who is good (1:7–15). Nahum then builds on that foundation by illustrating the principles of God's providence in relation to judgment and salvation in the contemporary story of the downfall of the superpower Assyria, and the destruction of her capital city Nineveh.

It is my contention, therefore, that the book of Nahum should have an honoured place in holy Scripture and not be sidelined. Nahum sets out to explain and illustrate a fundamental biblical doctrine, namely, the doctrine of judgment. It's a further reminder to us of the words of the apostle Paul to his young friend and fellow worker Timothy, that '*all Scripture* [my italics] is God-breathed' (and that includes the book of Nahum!). Paul goes on to point out the implication of that statement. All Scripture, therefore, 'is useful for teaching, rebuking, correcting and training in righteousness, so that the servant of God may be thoroughly equipped for every good work' (2 Tim. 3:16–17).

Those of us who are called to teach and preach in the local church, whether we teach adults or children, have a solemn responsibility to teach appropriately or aptly the 'whole will of God' (Acts 20:27). When the apostle Paul spoke to the leaders of the church in Ephesus, he reminded them of his own commitment to this kind of faithful teaching and preaching. He told them:

> You know that I have not hesitated to preach anything that would be helpful to you but have taught you publicly and from house to house. I have declared to both Jews and Greeks that they must turn to God in repentance and have faith in our Lord Jesus . . . Therefore, I declare to you today that I am innocent of the blood of any of you. For I have not hesitated to proclaim to you the whole will of God.
> (Acts 20:20–21, 26–27)

The apostle's reference to being 'innocent of the blood of any of you' is surely a reference to the book of Ezekiel (Ezek. 3:17–19), where the prophet speaks of his responsibility to warn God's people of coming judgment, unless they repented of their sins.[6]

So, if we believe that 'all Scripture is God-breathed' and that it is able to make us 'wise for salvation through faith in Christ Jesus' (2 Tim. 3:15), we must include in our message the doctrine of judgment. It is clearly set out in the book of Nahum. We must have the courage, as he did, to teach it with boldness. We must also have the compassion to teach it with tears.

The book of Nahum, then, is a message from the living God. He is the Lord, who, as the whole Bible tells us, is a God of wrath as well as a God of love, a God who judges as well as saves. However, before we look more closely at those two complementary aspects of his nature, we need to be clear that we should also study this book.

---

[6] God's words in Ezekiel were: 'When I say to a wicked person, "You will surely die," and you do not warn them or speak out to dissuade them from their evil ways in order to save their life, that wicked person will die for their sin, and I will hold you accountable for their blood' (Ezek. 3:18).

b. The book of Nahum is a message about the real world

A prophecy concerning Nineveh (1:1) may seem to be an irrelevant subject for a twenty-first-century Christian to consider. After all, what possible value can there be in pondering the destruction of a city in the seventh century BC, which happened to be the capital of a pagan nation, Assyria, that no longer exists![7]

Nineveh, however, was the capital of an aggressive superpower that was a constant threat and danger to God's people. The Assyrians were enemies of God. In Nahum's time they had already overrun the north of Israel, and taken many of God's people into exile. They were also a threat and menace to God's people in the south, in Judah. Aggressive superpowers, and the persecution of God's people, are part of today's world. It is one reason why the book of Nahum continues to have relevance in the twenty-first century. For the *prophecy concerning Nineveh* (1:1) brings both the promise of God's judgment and a message of hope and encouragement for God's people. It deals with issues that modern Christians have to face up to, and circumstances that are not unlike those that Christians face today.

In the real world of today, for example, we frequently hear of the widespread persecution of Christians. Angola is one twentieth-century example of this pattern. According to an article in the magazine *Barnabas Aid*:

> Angola was afflicted by four decades of continuous warfare, which only came to an end in 2002 AD. For fifteen years Angolans fought for independence from their Portuguese colonial masters. When this was achieved in 1975 the Marxist-leaning MPLA Party gained control of the Government, and was opposed by the Nationalist UNITA movement in a civil war that lasted for 27 years.

Only now is there relative peace and freedom. The article goes on to point out that during the period of MPLA rule:

> Christians suffered much persecution especially from 1975–85. The first President of newly independent Angola vowed to eradicate Christianity in his country within twenty years. Evangelicals were a particular target, with thousands abducted or killed. Scores of church ministers were also killed and many church buildings closed, seized or deliberately

[7] The remains of Nineveh lie just outside the city of Mosul (see n. 1).

> destroyed. On some occasions troops massacred whole congregations. The Marxist Government also imposed legal restrictions on Christians, forbidding open-air meetings, home meetings, or preaching anywhere outside of a church building. No new church buildings were allowed. The Security Police monitored pastors and all church activities . . . the MPLA's anti-Christian policies only began to lessen when they found that they needed the help of churches to try to meet the desperate physical needs of huge numbers of displaced people facing near starvation.

The article ends with a message of hope and confidence in the sovereign Lord: 'However, far from being destroyed by persecution, the church grew . . .'[8]

The story of Angola is only one of many stories about the persecution and suffering of Christians today. In a report in a Christian magazine in 2008,[9] mention was made of direct action against Christians in Bangladesh, China, the Congo, Egypt, India, Indonesia, Iran, Kazakhstan and Lebanon. In 2023, over 120 Christians were killed when violence broke out in Manipur, India. Thousands of buildings and homes belonging to Christians, together with hundreds of churches, were destroyed, and around 50,000 believers displaced.[10]

The book of Nahum addresses a situation that is not far removed from that which is described above. If, as seems likely, Nahum was writing at the time when Manasseh was king of Judah, then he would have experienced the suffering brought about by a king who is described as encouraging his people to do 'more evil than the nations the Lord had destroyed before the Israelites'. Faithful believers in Yahweh would have had a difficult time. Manasseh, wrote the narrator of 2 Kings, 'has done more evil than the Amorites who preceded him and has led Judah into sin with his idols' (2 Kgs 21:9, 11).

It is also clear from the book of Nahum, as we have already noted, that Assyria was still a superpower and a force to be reckoned with, and the people of God in Israel and Judah had to put up with the atrocities of the Assyrians for many years. Mackay says that

---

[8] *Barnabas Aid*, May/June 2008, p. 12.

[9] 'The World in Brief', *Evangelicals Now*, February 2009, p. 11. Sources given were 'Compass Direct'; 'Religion Today'; and 'Forum 18 News'.

[10] 'Update: Tensions in Manipur Intensify and Spread across India', *Open Doors*, 14 August 2023: <www.opendoorsuk.org/news/latest-news/manipur-violence> (accessed 17 September 2023).

> in terms of atrocities perpetrated, the Assyrian Empire has to be ranked with the concentration camps of Nazi Germany, the Cambodia of the Khmer Rouge and Pol Pot and the Uganda of Idi Amin . . . Assyria is but one instance of what happens when lust for power is combined with callous indifference to human suffering.[11]

In Nahum's time, when Ashurbanipal (669–626 BC) was ruler in Assyria, the empire was vast. It stretched from the Persian Gulf in the east, where so much of the Iran–Iraq War in the twentieth century was fought, through a slice of what is now Iran, all of Iraq, Syria, Israel and the Palestinian territories, and even into Africa, where the Assyrians attacked Egypt in 633 BC, destroying the capital city of Thebes (see Nah. 3:8–10).

We should remember that it is today's world that has invented the title of 'superpower'. Yet every generation has had its superpowers. There have always been nations that have sought world domination and, like Assyria, they have claimed the right to invade and occupy other nations with imperialistic pride. In my own lifetime the invasion of Poland and other European nations by Nazi Germany, the rolling in of Russian tanks across the borders of Hungary and Czechoslovakia (and more recently Ukraine), and even the American, British and Coalition forces invading Iraq, all echo the imperialistic intentions of Assyria and Nineveh in the seventh century BC. There is nothing new under the sun. Nahum's book has a message to superpowers as well as to the church and individuals. It's a message of judgment and hope; a message about the real world.

The book of Nahum, then, must be taken seriously because it is a message from the living God, which is about the real world in Nahum's day and ours. But before we look at the way in which God providentially deals with us in his world, and the theological basis for it, we need to answer two further questions. What do we know about Nahum? When did he write this book?

2. What do we know about Nahum?

We know very little about the prophet Nahum. He is not mentioned elsewhere in the Bible; and all we are told in this book is that he is called *Nahum the Elkoshite* (1). *Nahum* means 'comfort' or 'comforter'; and

[11] J. L. Mackay, *Jonah, Micah, Nahum, Habakkuk, Zephaniah* (Christian Focus, 2005), p. 191.

although his message brought no comfort to the Assyrians, he did bring a message of comfort to God's people. However, we do not know whether the meaning of his name was intended to have any significance.

An *Elkoshite* is presumably someone who came from Elkosh. But here again we do not know for certain where Elkosh was situated. Some link it to Qosh, which is about 30 miles north of modern Mosul.[12] There is also another tradition (noted by Jerome in the fourth century AD) that places Nahum's home in the north of Israel, in a village in Galilee, possibly in the area of Capernaum. Certainly the references to Bashan, Carmel and Lebanon suggest a knowledge of the northern kingdom (see Nah. 1:4); Robertson suggests that Nahum represents 'the surviving remnant of the north'.[13] Eaton, however, believes that Nahum ministered in the south. He suggests that Nahum was a professional prophet attached to the great royal sanctuary of pre-exilic Jerusalem, on the grounds that the book reflects 'themes and forms of the cultic tradition'.[14]

We cannot be certain of Nahum's background or where he ministered God's word, whether north or south. We do know that he claimed to be a prophet, speaking and writing God's word to his people at a difficult time in the history of Judah (see Nah. 1:1, 12–14; 2:13; 3:5). We do know that he had great courage to write about the defeat and destruction of a superpower such as Assyria; and great faith to be able to assure God's people, when Assyria was still at the height of her ability to conquer, subdue and damage her enemies, that *The LORD is good, a refuge in times of trouble* (1:7).

But can we be certain about the time of the trouble he refers to? We must now try to answer the question . . .

3. When did Nahum write this book?

We can be fairly clear about the approximate time of Nahum's ministry. In his prophecy he predicts the fall of Nineveh, the capital of Assyria. We know from other sources that Nineveh fell in 612 BC to the combined armies of the Medes and Babylonians. We also know that Nahum refers to the fall of Thebes, in Egypt, as something that had already taken place

12 D. W. Baker, *Nahum, Habakkuk and Zephaniah*, TOTC (IVP, 1988), p. 19.

13 O. P. Robertson, *The Books of Nahum, Habakkuk and Zephaniah*, NICOT (Eerdmans, 1990), p. 56.

14 Eaton, *Obadiah, Nahum, Habakkuk, Zephaniah*, p. 53.

(3:8–10); and we know the date for that event was 664 BC. So it is likely that Nahum ministered at some time between 664 and 612 BC. O. Palmer Robertson argues that Nahum began his public ministry in the latter days of King Manasseh, in Judah,[15] and continued during the early days of King Josiah (628–609 BC). Ashurbanipal of Assyria was still reigning in 627 BC, so, as Nahum makes clear, the Assyrians were still a power to be reckoned with.

It was at such a time of threat and danger from the enemies of Yahweh that God raised up Nahum the prophet to bring his message of judgment upon Assyria, and warning, hope and encouragement for God's people. We don't know for certain whether Nahum spoke from the midst of the occupied northern kingdom, or in Judah and Jerusalem in the threatened south. But we do know that his message was bold and clear; and both a burden and a *vision* or revelation from God (1).

In many parts of the world today God's people are facing persecution and opposition in many forms. Even in the UK, opposition to the Christian gospel has become increasingly aggressive. The popular Oxford scientist Richard Dawkins, for example, is not only an advocate for atheism, but also regards faith in God as an evil to be rooted out. Dawkins has written:

> It is fashionable to wax apocalyptic about the threat to humanity posed by the AIDS virus, 'mad cow' disease and many others; but I think that a case can be made that *faith* is one of the world's great evils, comparable to the smallpox virus but harder to eradicate. Faith, being belief that isn't based on evidence, is the principal vice of any religion.[16]

Another sign of such opposition in the UK can be seen in the way that religious 'equality' laws have been used against Christians. For example, according to a report drawn up by the Christian Institute in 2009, equality laws led to

> councils in Bideford and Worcester being urged to end over a hundred years of tradition by cancelling morning prayer meetings. In June 2005, Torbay Council removed a wooden cross from the wall of a Crematorium

---

15 Manasseh reigned c. 687–642 BC.

16 Quoted from an article in *The Humanist*, January/February 1997, entitled 'Is Science a Religion?' For a response to that quotation and other writings by Richard Dawkins, see John C. Lennox, *God's Undertaker: Has Science Buried God?* (Lion Hudson, 2007).

> Chapel and renamed the building a 'Ceremony Hall' . . . In some councils 'Christmas Lights' have been replaced by 'Festive Decorations', and some councils have even tried to rename Christmas with non-Christmas titles such as 'Winterval'. It has been reported that one hostel for homeless people run by Christians was told that it risked losing a substantial amount of public funding because it was 'too Christian'. The local council ordered it to stop giving thanks to God before meals, and said that Bibles should be removed from tables in case non-Christians coming to the shelter felt offended. Laws were introduced in the U.K. in 2007 that gave faith-based adoption agencies the stark choice of withdrawing from adoption services or abandoning their religious ethos.[17]

And so we could go on.

There are endless current examples of this kind; and they may appear as pinpricks compared to the persecution and pressure put upon the faithful people of God during Nahum's ministry. But the book of Nahum reminds us that God is looking for those who, like Nahum, will bring God's word to encourage God's people, and will sound a warning of judgment to those who are the enemies of God and his people. It is to that message, and its theological explanation, that we must now turn.

[17] Quoted from *Legal Defence Fund . . . A Briefing*, a publication of the Christian Institute, October 2009, p. 3. See also *Marginalising Christians*, Christian Institute, December 2009, pp. 1–71.

Nahum 1:2–15

4. Divine judgment: theologically explained

When we find ourselves facing danger and opposition, especially those attacks that focus on the people of God – physical, emotional and intellectual, as well as spiritual – we do well to look to God. There is a brilliant example of this in the story of the early church (Acts 4:1–31). After the apostles Peter and John had been arrested and then released, they were commanded 'not to speak or teach at all in the name of Jesus' (Acts 4:18). Luke goes on to tell us:

> On their release, Peter and John went back to their own people and reported all that the chief priests and elders had said to them. When they heard this, they raised their voices together in prayer to God. 'Sovereign Lord,' they said, 'you made the heaven and the earth and the sea, and everything in them. You spoke by the Holy Spirit through the mouth of your servant, our father David . . . They did what your power and will had decided beforehand should happen.'
> (Acts 4:23–25, 28)

So, with their thoughts centred on the sovereign Lord, they were moved to pray in that difficult situation a prayer of immense faith and courage: 'Now, Lord, consider their threats and enable your servants to speak your word with great boldness. Stretch out your hand to heal and perform signs and wonders through the name of your holy servant Jesus' (4:29–31). Soon Luke was reporting that, 'With great power the apostles continued to testify to the resurrection of the Lord Jesus. And God's grace was . . . powerfully at work in them all' (4:33).

The prophet Nahum tackled the threats to the people of God in his day in a similar way. He turned their attention to God; he focused on the sovereign Lord; he reminded them of the character of God; he told them what God is like. We do well to follow his example if we are facing difficulties or opposition in our church, in our place of work, in our home situation, or in our personal discipleship. If we focus on God, we see the problems and challenges of everyday life with a new perspective.

The story has been told of the difficulties that Hudson Taylor, the founder of the China Inland Mission,[1] encountered in the early part of the twentieth century. He believed that the work in China needed a thousand new missionaries to be found in the space of five years for the work to be established. He took the matter to the Lord in prayer and shared his concerns with Christian friends. The task seemed to be impossible to some of his friends. So they asked him how he could imagine that so many people could be found in so short a time. His answer was simple and convincing:

> When I look at the map of mainland China I cannot see *how* I could ask for less. And when I look at the promises of God in the Bible, I do not see *why* I should ask for less![2]

It was Hudson Taylor who used to interpret the phrase 'Have faith in God!' as, 'Hold to the faithfulness of God!' He had understood the importance of facing every challenging situation by focusing on the nature and character of God, just as the apostles had, and Nahum before them.

Nahum is often criticized for writing about God in a harsh and unsympathetic way. In fact he writes in a way that is consistent with the rest of God's revelation in Scripture. He writes about the goodness and the 'severity' of God (cf. Rom. 11:22, KJV). He writes theologically. He begins with that aspect of God's character that many people find hard to accept. He begins his *prophecy* (1) with a description of the severity of God (1:1–6).

1. The severity of God: the Lord is angry (1:2–6)

When I was a boy some of the best and most respected teachers at my school were those who not only taught well but also disciplined us.

---

[1] Now the Overseas Missionary Fellowship.

[2] I read this story in an article by Revd Richard Gorrie in *Crusade* magazine, March 1958.

Sometimes they were angry with us, especially if we failed to pay attention, behaved badly or acted rebelliously. If we had thought about it at the time, we would have realized that their anger meant that they cared enough about us to correct us and sometimes to punish us. Sometimes they got it wrong; but usually their anger was justified and their punishments fair, even if unwelcome. On the whole we respected most those teachers who were both kind and severe.

As Nahum begins to expound his *vision* from God, he starts with a revelation of God's severity and anger before he goes on to describe God's goodness and kindness. In the UK we live in a culture that in theory glorifies tolerance. The idea, therefore, that God might be intolerant of our sins, and be angry enough to punish us, is a concept that offends and is rejected by many. But Nahum will not let us get away with such a superficial view of God. He describes the Lord, who is to be feared and respected, as *a jealous and avenging God* (2). He warns us that *the LORD takes vengeance and is filled with wrath*, and *The LORD takes vengeance on his foes and vents his wrath against his enemies* (2). Furthermore, although he is *slow to anger* (a mark of his goodness and kindness), Nahum insists that he *will not leave the guilty unpunished* (3). Finally (3–6), he describes the awesome power of God in pouring out his wrath *like fire*, leaving us with the challenging questions: *Who can withstand his indignation? Who can endure his fierce anger?*

It is time, therefore, to look more closely at Nahum's teaching about the severity of God, as he sets out a number of propositions in these verses.

a. The severity of God is consistent with his faithfulness (1:2–6)

In emphasizing the severity and wrath of God (2), Nahum is keen to remind God's people that it is the faithful covenant God, *the LORD* (Yahweh), who *takes vengeance ... and vents his wrath against his enemies* (2).

The Hebrew nouns 'El' and 'Elohim' are most frequently used as the general word to describe God. (They were used to describe false gods too.) But we should notice that here (2–3) Nahum calls God four times in two verses by his covenant name, *the LORD* or 'Yahweh'.[3]

[3] The Hebrew word behind the name 'Yahweh' originally had no vowels, so that the name was spelt with the capitals YHWH and was considered too sacred to speak. So 'Adonay' (meaning 'my Lord') was substituted in reading and speaking, and the vowels of 'Adonay' were combined with the consonants to give 'Jehovah' or 'Yahweh'. See IBD, p. 571, for further discussion.

Strictly speaking, Yahweh is the only 'name' of God. When Abraham and Isaac built an altar to God, we read that Abraham 'called on the name of the LORD [Yahweh]' (Gen. 12:8; 13:4; 26:25). Even before the days of Abraham, we read that at the time that Seth had a son called Enosh, people began 'to call on the name of the LORD [Yahweh]' (Gen. 4:26). So the name Yahweh, the Lord, was there from the beginning of history.

The name 'Yahweh' was full of significance for the people of God. Were his people in Nahum's day afraid of further threats and action from the Assyrian superpower, or persecution from Manasseh's secret police? Did they feel vulnerable and weak, questioning, 'Where is our God now?' Then Nahum reminds them (and us) that the faithful covenant Lord (Yahweh) *takes vengeance on his foes and vents his wrath against his enemies* (1:2). Yahweh is faithful and keeps his promise to take *vengeance on his foes*, and to deliver those who put their trust in him (1:7).

We should notice that there is a link between the divine name 'Yahweh' and the Hebrew verb 'to be' (see Exod. 3:14). When Moses asks the Lord how he should answer the question 'What is his [God's] name?' God said: 'I AM WHO I AM [YHWH]'. Motyer comments that this points to 'the active presence of God . . . as a living force, vital and personal . . . in no situation is he the ornamental extra; in every situation he is the key active ingredient'.[4]

From the very beginning of his book, Nahum turns the eyes of God's people to the ever-present, faithful covenant God who is on their side, keeps his promises and *takes vengeance on his foes* (1:2).

The name 'YHWH' can also mean 'I will be what I will be'. That suggests a God 'for all seasons, all eventualities, all tasks and all needs' (Motyer). The Lord (Yahweh) is the all-sufficient God, the God of all grace. While Nahum writes bluntly of a God who *takes vengeance and is filled with wrath* (1:2), he wants God's people to know that the Lord's covenant faithfulness undergirds all he does; that he is angry with the deeds of the impenitent, but gracious and loving to those who put their trust in him.

There is a personal application for all this. Some years ago I heard a story from the life of one of the leading church ministers of his generation. His name was Prebendary Webb Peploe, who, when he was still a young man, lost one of his much-loved children while the family was on holiday. Returning from the funeral, the stricken father knelt in his study, pleading

---

[4] J. A. Motyer, *The Message of Exodus*, BST (IVP, 2005), p. 69.

with the Lord to make his grace sufficient in his hour of sorrow. He experienced no comfort, however, and his tears continued to flow. Then through his tears he suddenly saw a text card on the shelf with one word printed in capitals: 'My grace IS sufficient for you.' Webb Peploe prayed again, 'Lord, forgive me. I have been asking you to make your grace sufficient for me, and all the time you have been saying to me: "My grace IS sufficient." I thank you for sufficient grace and I appropriate it now.'[5]

Nahum wants us to know that when we turn to the faithful covenant Lord, whatever our problems or circumstances may be, the Lord's grace is sufficient and always available. As the Lord said to Moses: 'This is my name for ever, the name you shall call me from generation to generation' (Exod. 3:15c).[6] Alan Cole asks: 'What does "Yahweh" mean?' He goes on: 'It ultimately meant to them [the people of God in Moses' time] what the name Jesus has come to mean to Christians, a "shorthand" for all God's dealings of grace.'[7] As John wrote in his Gospel: 'Out of his fullness we have all received grace in place of grace already given' (John 1:16).

Scripture constantly reminds us that God is a faithful God. He keeps his promises; he takes vengeance on his foes, and graciously provides for his own. The faithfulness of God is consistent with his severity.

b. The severity of God is explained by his jealousy (1:2)

Now jealousy is not an attractive characteristic in a human being. It is a word that is usually used to describe a vice, not a virtue. However, when the Bible describes the Lord (Yahweh) as jealous, which it frequently does, there cannot be any sense of sinful jealousy. For 'God is light; in him is no darkness at all' (1 John 1:5). Yet one of the first truths taught to the Israelites about Yahweh was that he is 'a jealous God'. For example, the second commandment was introduced with the phrase: 'I, the Lord your God, am a jealous God' (Exod. 20:5). A little later Yahweh says to Moses: 'Do not

---

[5] The story is told in O. Sanders, *Problems of Christian Discipleship* (Overseas Missionary Fellowship, 1970), pp. 23–24.

[6] It is often pointed out that when God made himself known to Moses at the burning bush, revealing himself as 'Yahweh', he told Moses that he had appeared to Abraham, Isaac and Jacob as 'God Almighty' (*El Shaddai*). He added: 'but by my name the Lord [Yahweh] I did not make myself known to them' (Exod. 6:3). There is an apparent contradiction here. Some Old Testament specialists take the view that the name Yahweh was revealed for the first time to Moses, and that the earlier mention of the name was added by a later hand. Motyer's view, which I find persuasive, argues that the words spoken to Moses (Exod. 6:3) were 'not the disclosure of a new name as such, but the revelation of the meaning or "story" of a name known from earliest times (e.g. Gen. 4:26), and throughout the period of the Patriarchs'. For further discussion see Motyer, *The Message of Exodus*, pp. 67–74, 103–106; and IBD, p. 571.

[7] R. A. Cole, *Exodus*, TOTC (Tyndale Press, 1973), comment on Exod. 3:15.

worship any other god, for the LORD, whose name is Jealous, is a jealous God' (Exod. 34:14).[8]

So how should we understand the 'jealousy' of God? Perhaps a modern analogy can help us. Many of us live today in a Western culture where unfaithfulness to marriage vows is more acceptable than it was to previous generations. Nevertheless, it is still recognized that there is a proper jealousy that will be felt when a husband or a wife has an 'affair', and one is unfaithful to the other. It is right for the injured party to feel jealous in such a situation. Indeed the lack of jealousy in these circumstances would suggest the absence of true love and commitment to the unfaithful partner.

The 'jealousy of the Lord' is of that righteous kind. Packer helpfully explains:

> The Old Testament regards God's covenant as his marriage with Israel, carrying with it a demand for unqualified love and loyalty. The worship of idols and all compromising relations with non-Israelite idolaters constituted disobedience and unfaithfulness, which God saw as spiritual adultery, provoking him to jealousy.[9]

So Nahum reminds God's people that the *wrath* and *vengeance* of God is an expression of his jealous love. That jealous love leads him to judge his enemies wherever they may be (Nah. 1:2). It leads him to judge his own disobedient people (Zeph. 3:8). It also leads him to restore his people after a time of disciplining captivity (Zech. 1:14; 8:2).

What should all this mean for us? It certainly should encourage us to know that the Lord is so committed to us that he is jealous for our complete love and loyalty to himself. Furthermore, as Christians, we know that he has committed himself to us in a costly covenant of grace, which was sealed by his blood, when he laid down his life for us on the cross (Matt. 26:28; Mark 14:24; Luke 22:20; 1 Cor. 11:25). Such love encourages us to give our all to him. As the apostle Paul wrote: 'Therefore, I urge you . . . in view of God's mercy, to offer your bodies as a living sacrifice, holy and pleasing to God' (Rom. 12:1). Or, as Packer put it, 'The jealousy of God requires us to be zealous for God.'[10]

---

8 See also Num. 25:11; Deut. 4:24; 5:9; 6:15; Josh. 24:19; 1 Kgs 14:22; and many other places. See also a discussion of 'the jealous God' in J. I. Packer, *Knowing God* (Hodder & Stoughton, 1973), pp. 186–195.

9 Packer, *Knowing God*, p. 190.

10 Ibid., p. 192.

The truth about the jealousy of God should also challenge us to think about his plan for the world and our part in it. Let me quote Packer once more:

> Covenant love is the heart of God's plan for the world. And it is in the light of God's overall plan for his world that his jealousy must, in the last analysis, be understood. For God's ultimate objective, as the Bible declares it, is threefold . . . to vindicate his rule and righteousness by showing his sovereignty in judgment upon sin; to ransom and redeem his chosen people; and to be loved and praised by them for his glorious acts of love and self-vindication. God seeks what we should seek – his glory in and through men – and it is for the securing of this end, ultimately, that he is jealous.[11]

If the Lord is jealous for such a goal, we should be zealous in playing our part in it, or face the consequences of God's judgment on a complacent church (see Rev. 3:15–19). For God's severity is explained by his jealousy. His severity is an expression of his jealous and steadfast love.

c. The severity of God is expressed by his wrath (1:2–3)

While it is reasonable to understand the jealousy of God to be an expression of his covenant love, it is for many people much harder to understand how a God of love can also be described as *an avenging God* who *takes vengeance and is filled with wrath* (2). To be *filled with wrath* could literally be translated as: 'to be master of wrath'.[12] 'Master' here is not unlike calling someone 'a past master' at something; that is, referring to someone who has thoroughly 'mastered' an art.[13] The Lord really knows what he is doing when he takes vengeance on his enemies. It is an example of the severity of God, but it is consistent with the revelation of God's character throughout Scripture.

Nahum has no hesitation in writing about the severity and wrath of the Lord (Yahweh).[14] Yet the modern attitude, even among professing Christians, is to avoid speaking or preaching about the subject. Packer's words, written in 1972, are still true today. He wrote:

---

[11] Ibid., p. 191.

[12] J. L. Mackay, *Jonah, Micah, Nahum, Habakkuk, Zephaniah* (Christian Focus, 2005), p. 195.

[13] Suggested to me in private correspondence with Alec Motyer.

[14] Notice vv. 2, 3 and 6 in the first six verses.

> Those who still believe in the wrath of God (not all do) say little about it . . . To an age which has unashamedly sold itself to the gods of greed, pride, sex and selfishness, the church mumbles on about God's kindness but says virtually nothing about his judgment . . . the fact is that the subject of divine wrath has become taboo in modern society, and Christians by and large have accepted the taboo and conditioned themselves never to raise the matter.[15]

It is important to notice that there is nothing vindictive or capricious about the wrath of God. God's wrath is the reaction of his holiness to sin and evil in the world. Nahum teaches us that he *takes vengeance on his foes and vents his wrath against his enemies* (2c). Nahum is clearly insisting that God's enemies, and the enemies of his people, will not be allowed to get away with their wickedness and rebellion. God will not look away and let his enemies off the hook. *The* Lord *. . . vents his wrath against his enemies* (2d).[16]

We all recognize that there is such a thing as 'righteous indignation'; and although we may never achieve that kind of anger perfectly as humans, the biblical writers teach us that the Lord always acts in a way that is consistent with his perfect righteousness and love. As Abraham put it, 'Will not the Judge of all the earth do right?' (Gen. 18:25). Packer asks the question: 'Would a God who did not react adversely to evil in the world be morally perfect?' He goes on: 'Surely not. But it is precisely this adverse reaction to evil which is a necessary part of moral perfection, that the Bible has in view when it speaks of God's wrath.'[17]

It is certainly true that some Christians still feel that the doctrine of the wrath of God is inconsistent with the love of God. They cannot accept his severity as well as his kindness. Nahum is asking us to be humble enough to put our own limited understanding before the light of his own inspired *vision* (1) from the Lord. Nahum sets out for us a theological

---

15 Packer, *Knowing God*, p. 164.

16 The Hebrew word translated *vents* (NIV) literally means 'to guard' or 'to keep'. (The 1984 edition of NIV is perhaps closer to the Hebrew with the translation '*maintains* his wrath' [emphasis mine].) Nahum may be saying that the Lord 'keeps' his wrath for the appropriate time (see D. W. Baker, *Nahum, Habakkuk and Zephaniah*, TOTC [IVP, 1988], p. 26). Baker also points out that the structure in v. 2 focuses on the severity of God:

A. God is jealous;
  B. Yahweh is an avenger.
  B. Yahweh is an avenger;
A. God is wrathful.

17 Packer, *Knowing God*, p. 167.

description of the all-sufficient Lord, who is jealous for his people's love and loyalty, and for his own reputation, and according to his righteous nature promises to take action against his enemies and against evil. As Michael Wilcock points out: 'The Lord's power to destroy is an encouragement when we are aware of the evil around us, and a warning when we remember the evil within us.'[18]

d. The severity of God is modified by his patience (1:3a)

Nahum continues to lay a theological foundation for his teaching about divine judgment and vengeance or retribution. The Lord who takes action against *his enemies* (2), and promises that he *will not leave the guilty unpunished* (3b), is also described by Nahum as *slow to anger* (3a). God in his justice must punish those who rebel against him and his moral laws; and Scripture makes it clear that 'all have sinned and fall short of the glory of God' (Rom. 3:23), and that 'the wrath of God is being revealed from heaven against all the godlessness and wickedness of people' (Rom. 1:18). But Nahum reminds us that God is also *slow to anger.*

Nahum must have known the story of Jonah's mission to Nineveh some 100 years earlier, when he brought a message of judgment to that pagan city. The citizens of Nineveh deserved God's judgment, and Jonah hoped they would receive it (see Jon. 4). But the message of Jonah is about a patient God, who is *slow to anger,* even with the citizens of a pagan and idolatrous city. The narrator of the book of Jonah tells us: 'Then the word of the Lord came to Jonah a second time. "Go to the great city of Nineveh and proclaim to it the message I give you"' (Jon. 3:1–2). Jonah obeyed and preached a message of judgment: 'Forty more days and Nineveh will be overthrown' (Jon. 3:4). However, the preaching of God's word to Nineveh had a remarkable effect. We're told, 'The Ninevites believed God. A fast was proclaimed, and all of them, from the greatest to the least, put on sackcloth' (Jon. 3:5). The king himself made a proclamation: 'Let everyone call urgently on God. Let them give up their evil ways and their violence. Who knows? God may yet relent and with compassion turn from his fierce anger so that we will not perish' (Jon. 3:8–9). So God, with infinite patience and grace, spared the citizens of Nineveh from immediate judgment and punishment. 'When God saw what they did and how they turned from their evil ways, he relented and did not bring on them the destruction he had threatened' (Jon 3:10).

[18] M. Wilcock, *Discovering Six Minor Prophets* (Crossway, 1997), p. 107.

How patient God is! He will judge; he will punish wickedness; he will not leave the guilty unpunished. But he is also full of compassion, patient, merciful and forgiving. When the Lord (Yahweh) gave the Ten Commandments to Moses he revealed himself as 'the Lord, the compassionate and gracious God, slow to anger, abounding in love and faithfulness, maintaining love to thousands, and forgiving wickedness, rebellion and sin' (Exod. 34:6–7a). Yahweh was all that, even though he goes on to say that 'he does not leave the guilty unpunished' (Exod. 34:7b). Likewise in New Testament times, when some Christians were wondering whether God would ever judge and punish the wicked, especially their own persecutors, the apostle Peter could write:

> Do not forget this one thing, dear friends: with the Lord a day is like a thousand years, and a thousand years are like a day. The Lord is not slow in keeping his promise, as some understand slowness. Instead he is patient with you, not wanting anyone to perish, but everyone to come to repentance.
> (2 Pet. 3:8–9)

Divine judgment must be understood in the light of the patience and compassion of the Lord, as well as in the light of his severity and justice. The hymn writer John Newton (1725–1807) understood that well in his famous hymn 'Amazing Grace'. Newton had lived for many years as a notorious sinner and slave trader. He even found himself living in degradation as a slave for a time. He knew he deserved nothing but the judgment of God on his sinful life. But the Lord rescued him from the slavery of sin and 'the wrath to come', and Newton experienced God's amazing grace and patience. He wrote:

> Amazing grace! How sweet the sound
> That saved a wretch like me!
> I once was lost, but now am found,
> Was blind, but now I see.
>
> 'Twas grace that taught my heart to fear,
> And grace my fears relieved;
> How precious did that grace appear
> The hour I first believed.

Many of us would have written John Newton off, with the kind of comment that says: 'You've made your own bed – now lie on it!' I suppose we might well have done the same with some superpower like Assyria. Would we have given up the Soviet Union to destruction long before the collapse of communism, if it had been in our hands? The Lord who is *slow to anger* was patient enough to wait for the sudden collapse of communism, symbolized by the pulling down of the Berlin Wall, followed by the emergence of some 'green shoots' of evangelism in the churches and universities of the former Soviet Union.[19] How glad we should be that vengeance is in the Lord's hands and not in ours! The Lord is patient and compassionate. Would we have been glad to see Hitler assassinated earlier? Or Robert Mugabe destroyed years ago? No doubt we would. But the Lord is *slow to anger*. He's very patient with us. He does not want anyone to perish, but everyone to come to repentance (see 2 Pet. 3:8–9).

A further example of the Lord's patience is to be found in Jesus' teaching. Jesus taught his disciples to learn from the disasters and accidents that occur in everyday life, and to use them as motivation to repent of their sins before it was too late. So when news came to Jesus about certain atrocities committed against some Galileans, whose blood 'Pilate had mixed with their sacrifices' (Luke 13:1), Jesus made two observations. First, Jesus made it clear that these Galileans were not worse sinners than anyone else because they had suffered in this way. Second, he urged the people to examine themselves for, he told them, 'unless you repent, you too will all perish' (Luke 13:3). Again, when eighteen people were tragically killed when a tower in Siloam collapsed and fell on them, Jesus again made it clear that those unfortunate people were no more guilty than anyone else; yet the lesson to be learned from such tragedies is that death can come to us at any time, and after death, the judgment. So, we need to repent before it is too late (see Luke 13:1–5). The patient God warns us and delays final judgment.

In this way, Nahum teaches us that the avenging God is also the patient and merciful Lord. The fullest expression of the justice and the mercy of the Lord is to be seen at Calvary, where 'Christ also suffered once for sins, the righteous for the unrighteous, to bring you to God' (1 Pet. 3:18). On the cross Jesus drank from the cup of God's wrath (Matt. 26:39–42; Isa. 51:17) so that penitent sinners might drink from the cup of salvation

[19] See L. Brown, *Shining Like Stars* (IVP, 2006).

(Ps. 116:13). Nahum tells us that *the LORD will not leave the guilty unpunished.* The gospel tells us that although we all deserve to be punished, Christ the sinless one took the punishment in our place. As the apostle Paul wrote to the Christians in Corinth: 'God made him who had no sin to be sin for us, so that in him we might become the righteousness of God' (2 Cor. 5:21).

So Nahum teaches us that the Lord is *slow to anger* and patient with us. But, with perfect balance, he continues to remind us of the severity of the Lord. For the Lord who is *jealous* and patient is also *great in power* and *will not leave the guilty unpunished* (3).

e. The severity of God is controlled by his sovereignty (1:3–6)

We have already noted that when the early Christians faced opposition, they turned in prayer to the sovereign Creator, saying: 'Sovereign Lord . . . you made the heavens and the earth and the sea, and everything in them' (Acts 4:24). Once they remembered God's power as creator of all things, they saw the strength of their enemies in a different light. They were able to pray for boldness to speak God's word, whatever the opposition.

In a similar way, Nahum now makes plain to his contemporaries that the patient Lord is also the powerful Lord, sovereign in nature and history, and just in all his ways.

i. The Sovereign Lord is powerful in nature (3c–6)

Some time ago Elizabeth, my wife, and I took three of our grandchildren to the local zoo. We were walking in the open air when suddenly we found ourselves in the midst of an awesome storm. Black clouds had quickly gathered. Thunder rolled. Forked lightning pierced the sky. Heavy raindrops fell upon us. One of our granddaughters, who was four at the time, was understandably frightened until we took shelter in an underground cave where badger setts could be observed and we could keep dry. Relaxing for a moment, the four-year-old stretched out her arms and exclaimed somewhat dramatically, 'I'm too young to die!'

It's not only four-year-olds who are moved, even frightened, by a storm. Nahum paints a picture of the awesomeness of God in nature to humble us, and to give us a proper sense of 'fear' or reverence for our creator God:

The LORD is . . . great in power;
[he] will not leave the guilty unpunished.

His way is in the whirlwind and the storm,
and clouds are the dust of his feet . . .
The mountains quake before him
and the hills melt away.
The earth trembles at his presence,
the world and all who live in it.
(1:3, 5)

Nahum's description of the forces of nature active in the whirlwind, the storm and the earthquake is governed by his conviction that the Lord is in control of all that he has made. The biblical doctrine of God as creator begins with the assertion that 'In the beginning God created the heavens and the earth' (Gen. 1:1). As Motyer expresses it: 'All alike . . . the ground we tread, the earth we probe, the life we enjoy, the air we breathe, the food we eat . . . owe their being to the mind and hand of God.'[20] Scripture also teaches us that the Lord our creator holds all things together. As the apostle Paul said to the Athenians on Mars Hill: 'For in him we live and move and have our being' (Acts 17:28).[21] Nahum and the other biblical prophets believed that God was active in nature. The prophet Amos, for example, wrote:

He who made the Pleiades and Orion,
who turns midnight into dawn
and darkens day into night,
who calls for the waters of the sea
and pours them out over the face of the land –
the Lord is his name.
With a blinding flash he destroys the stronghold
and brings the fortified city to ruin.
(Amos 5:8–9)

In other words, everything is under the control of our powerful creator; and he is active in his creation. We say 'it rains' or 'the grass is growing'. The psalmist says, 'He waters the mountains . . . He makes grass grow for the cattle' (Ps. 104:13–14).

---

20 J. A. Motyer, *Look to the Rock* (IVP, 1996), p. 158.

21 See also Paul's words about Christ: 'For in him all things were created . . . He is before all things, and in him all things hold together' (Col. 1:16–17).

There is much to encourage us in all this; but Nahum's message also humbles us. The *whirlwind and the storm* (3c) are signs of the Lord's powerful activity in the world he has created. Michael Butterworth points out that

> the people of Nahum's day built their houses out of sun-dried mud bricks, with a roof made of wooden beams and twigs, covered with a layer of clay and whitewash. In a storm they would be aware of their smallness in the face of nature's power.[22]

Nahum is surely describing these awesome events in nature to emphasize the fact that although the Lord is mercifully *slow to anger*, we should not presume on his kindness and patience. He is an awesome and holy God who will not leave the guilty unpunished (3b). Yet even as the prophet emphasizes in these verses (2–6) the wrath and anger of the Lord, he is also reminding God's people that the Lord is with them, even in the midst of judgment. *His way is in the whirlwind and the storm.* 'He is quite at home there, that's where he walks about' (Butterworth). He is the sovereign Creator. He is in control.

There is much here to ponder in the light of storm, flood and earthquake disasters in our own times. Certainly God's awesome power in nature brings home to us our own weakness and dependence on him. The floods in New Orleans, the storms in Florida and the earthquake in Marrakesh are but three examples in the early twenty-first century of such disasters. They remind us of our weakness in the face of nature.

Nahum teaches us that his *way is in the whirlwind and the storm* (3c). The Lord is in control. He is with us in the storm. When Jesus was in the boat with his disciples and a sudden storm sprang up, and they were terrified, he stilled the storm with a brief word of command: 'Quiet! Be still! [lit. 'be muzzled']' (Mark 4:39). No wonder they asked one another, 'Who is this? Even the wind and the waves obey him!' Only God can control the weather (see Mark 4:35–41).

But how should we understand natural disasters that cause a great loss of life if the Lord's *way is in the whirlwind and the storm* (3c)?

First, we should note again the words of Jesus commenting on the disaster that overcame eighteen people killed by the tower that collapsed at

---

22 M. H. Butterworth, in NBC (21), p. 836.

Siloam (Luke 13:1–5). Jesus asked: 'Those eighteen who died when the tower in Siloam fell on them – do you think they were more guilty than all the others living in Jerusalem? I tell you, no!' We shall be careful, then, not to apportion particular blame on the citizens of New Orleans, Florida, Marrakesh, or for that matter, of Hull, Northampton or Cockermouth in the UK, because they suffered natural disasters.

We know from Scripture that sometimes in the past God has judged a particular place for a specific reason – for example, Sodom and Gomorrah (Gen. 18). But even then we must remember Jesus' words about the greater sin of those in Bethsaida and Capernaum who heard the words of Jesus and saw his works, and still rejected him. As Jesus said to them: 'It will be more bearable for Sodom on the day of judgment than for you', that is, the town that rejects Jesus (Matt. 11:24). On the day of judgment God will take into account the opportunities we have had to hear the gospel. So we must be careful not to pronounce final judgment on others; rather, we must be sure to examine ourselves.

Second, we should take notice of Jesus' words of warning that come to us whenever we hear of a disaster with a tragic loss of life. 'Unless you repent, you too will all perish' (Luke 13:5).

Disasters remind us that life is short; that death may come to us at any time; that this life is not all there is; and that we should be ready to meet God, to repent of our sins and to put our trust in the Lord. 'People are destined to die once, and after that to face judgment' (Heb. 9:27). Natural disasters remind us of all these things. The plagues at the time of the exodus were warnings to Pharaoh and his people, and a call for him to repent and to no longer harden his heart against the word of God (Exod. 7 – 11). The book of Revelation takes up the theme when the seven trumpets were sounded to call people to repent in readiness for the day of judgment. Some of those trumpet calls were linked with natural and ecological disasters (Rev. 8; 9).[23]

The Lord's way is *in the whirlwind and the storm* to warn us of judgment and the necessity for repentance. The words of C. S. Lewis still resonate with Christians: 'God whispers to us in our pleasures, speaks in our conscience, but shouts in our pains: it is his megaphone to rouse a deaf world.'[24]

---

[23] For a more detailed look at the questions raised by natural disasters, see J. W. Wenham, *The Goodness of God* (IVP, 1974).

[24] C. S. Lewis, *The Problem of Pain* (Geoffrey Bles: Centenary Press, 1940), p. 81.

The awesome power of the Lord is also depicted in the next phrase: *clouds are the dust of his feet.* While the armies of superpowers, such as Assyria, stir up the dust as they march towards the nations they seek to invade, Nahum teaches us that Yahweh is so powerful that *clouds are the dust of his feet* (3c). Furthermore, with a word, the Lord is able to do the seemingly impossible. *He rebukes the sea and dries it up; he makes all the rivers run dry* (4).[25] The stories of the exodus (Exod. 13 – 15) and the crossing of the River Jordan into the Promised Land (Josh. 3) are almost certainly in Nahum's mind. It was with 'an outstretched arm' (a symbol of great power) that the Lord delivered his people and destroyed his enemies. Nahum goes on to speak of Bashan, Carmel and Lebanon (4b). Bashan and Carmel were noted for their richly luxuriant pastures and woodlands, and the cedars of Lebanon were famous for their great strength and durability; yet the power of God was such that Nahum had no doubt that with a word *Bashan and Carmel wither and the blossoms of Lebanon fade* (4b). Mackay comments: 'If the glory of nature shrivels up before the Lord, how much more the pride of man?'[26]

The climax of this passage (1:2–6) comes in the next verse: *The mountains quake before him and the hills melt away. The earth trembles at his presence, the world and all who live in it* (5). Calvin comments:

> The world cannot for a moment stand, except as it is sustained by the favour and goodness of God: for we see what would immediately be as soon as God manifests the signals of his judgment. Since the very solidity of mountains would be as snow or wax, what would become of miserable men, who are like a shadow or an apparition? They would vanish away as soon as God manifested his wrath against them . . .[27]

So Nahum presses upon us the severe truth that even those things that seem to be most enduring – hills, the earth, the rocks – and the whole world and those who live in it (5), will ultimately be shattered and destroyed at the presence of the Lord. *His wrath is poured out like fire; the*

---

[25] *He makes all the rivers run dry* may be a warning to cities such as Nineveh, whose waters were a key part of their defence strategy, that they would be no match for the powerful Creator, Yahweh, and would not be able to defend themselves from his just judgment.

[26] Mackay, *Jonah, Micah, Nahum, Habakkuk, Zephaniah*, p. 197.

[27] J. Calvin, *Joel, Amos, Obadiah, Jonah, Micah, Nahum*, Commentaries, vol. 14 (Baker Book House, repr. 1996), p. 427.

rocks are shattered before him (6). Fire is sometimes used as a symbol of God's holiness and purifying judgment (Exod. 3:2; 19:18). Here the main emphasis is on the *wrath* of God (6b) 'spreading like fire' (Calvin) upon 'all the godlessness and wickedness of people' (Rom. 1:18). This wrath is God's holy reaction to sin in the lives of God's people as well as in the lives of those who know about God only from nature and not from Scripture. For, as the apostle Paul tells us:

> what may be known about God is plain to them . . . For since the creation of the world God's invisible qualities – his eternal power and divine nature – have been clearly seen, being understood from what has been made, so that people are without excuse.
> (Rom. 1:19–20)

No wonder Nahum ends this passage (1:1–6) with two rhetorical questions that clearly expect a negative response: *Who can withstand his indignation? Who can endure his fierce anger?* That anger is emphasized by the fact that Nahum uses four different words in the Hebrew text (6) to describe the anger of the Lord. Nahum wants us to be in no doubt that the Lord hates sin, that he is not a God to be trifled with, and that we all deserve his just judgment. None of us in our own strength can stand before him. Nature, with all its awesome power, reminds us how weak and puny we are before our sovereign Creator. So what should our response be?

King David gives us a fine example of his response to God's anger. In one of the psalms attributed to him, he writes:

> I cried to my God for help.
> From his temple he heard my voice;
>   my cry came before him, into his ears.
>
> The earth trembled and quaked,
>   and the foundations of the mountains shook;
>   they trembled because he was angry.
> Smoke rose from his nostrils;
>   consuming fire came from his mouth,
>   burning coals blazed out of it.
> (Ps. 18:6–8)

Natural and national disasters, as well as personal crises, should be occasions for seeking the Lord's help through prayer. They are a wake-up call to repentance. They are anticipations of a final day of judgment when, as the apostle Peter wrote:

> The heavens will disappear with a roar; the elements will be destroyed by fire, and the earth and everything done in it will be laid bare . . . That day will bring about the destruction of the heavens by fire, and the elements will melt in the heat. But in keeping with his promise we are looking forward to a new heaven and a new earth, where righteousness dwells. (2 Pet. 3:10–13)

So Nahum has brought home to us the power of the Lord in the world that he has made and sustains. He has emphasized the severity and anger of the Lord in order to humble us. However, before we go on to examine how Nahum balances the truth of God's severity with his kindness and goodness (1:7–15), we need to note briefly what he says here about the sovereign Lord in history.

ii. The sovereign Lord is powerful in history (4)

We have already noticed that Nahum is almost certainly referring to two historical events in the history of Israel, when he writes that the Lord *rebukes the sea and dries it up* (1:4). At the time of the exodus, as the Israelites made their escape from Egypt, they appeared to be trapped between the pursuing Egyptian army and the banks of the Red Sea. The narrator tells us:

> Then the LORD said to Moses, '. . . Tell the Israelites to move on. Raise your staff and stretch out your hand over the sea to divide the water so that the Israelites can go through the sea on dry ground . . . The Egyptians will know that I am the LORD . . .' Then Moses stretched out his hand over the sea, and all that night the LORD drove the sea back with a strong east wind and turned it into dry land. The waters were divided, and the Israelites went through the sea on dry ground, with a wall of water on their right and on their left . . . And when the Israelites saw the mighty hand of the LORD displayed against the Egyptians, the people feared the LORD and put their trust in him and in Moses his servant. (Exod. 14:15–16, 18, 21–22, 31)

The book of Exodus also tells us that the Lord not only delivered his people but judged the Egyptians: 'That day the LORD saved Israel from the hands of the Egyptians, and Israel saw the Egyptians lying dead on the shore. And . . . the Israelites saw the mighty hand of the LORD displayed against the Egyptians' (Exod. 14:30–31).

So when Nahum writes about the Lord who *rebukes the sea and dries it up* (4) he reminds us all about a God who acts in history both to deliver his people and to judge his enemies. He could also be referring to the crossing of the River Jordan by the Israelites when they entered the Promised Land under Joshua's leadership. We read in the book of Joshua that

> as soon as the priests who carried the ark reached the Jordan and their feet touched the water's edge, the water from upstream stopped flowing. It piled up in a heap a great distance away . . . while the water flowing down to the Sea of the Arabah (that is, the Dead Sea) was completely cut off. So the people crossed over opposite Jericho.
> (Josh. 3:15–16)

In describing God's power in nature and in history, Nahum has helped us to understand our weakness and dependence on a holy and sovereign Creator and Redeemer. He has called us, by implication, to face up to the two rhetorical questions (6) with humility and prayer. For without his help we cannot *withstand his indignation* or *endure his fierce anger*. Nahum has also encouraged us to put our trust and hope in God. For the Lord who is powerful in history has acted in such a way as to deliver his people from bondage (the exodus) and frustration (crossing the Jordan after years in the wilderness). Christian believers can likewise look back to a still greater historical event, when 'Christ Jesus came into the world to save sinners'. On the cross he bore the judgment and wrath of God that all sinners deserve. By his death, resurrection and exaltation he sets us free from the bondage of sin and the frustration of life without his Spirit (1 Tim. 1:15; cf. Rom. 8).

As we look back over the first six verses of the book of Nahum, we notice that the prophet has focused our attention on the Lord himself. He has taught us that *The LORD is a jealous and avenging God*. He hates sin and will judge sinners, for he is a holy and just God. But his jealousy means that he is wholly committed to his people. Therefore we should be zealous in giving him our wholehearted commitment and loyalty. He has also taught us that the Lord is a patient and avenging God. He will *not leave the guilty unpunished* (3b), so that we can be sure that justice will be done and be seen to be done. But he is also patient and *slow to anger*. Then if I am wise I will not presume upon his kindness and patience; rather, I will turn from my sins and put my trust in the Lord before it is too late. Finally (in this section) Nahum teaches us that the Lord is powerful and active in both nature and history. The lesson here is to be willing to humble ourselves before the Lord, and to be confident about a future which is in the hands of our faithful sovereign Creator who 'works out everything in conformity with the purpose of his will' (Eph. 1:11).

So far, then, Nahum has emphasized the severity of God and his anger against sin. This is a necessary part of his theological explanation of divine judgment. But now he further balances that truth with an emphasis on the kindness and goodness of God (1:7–15). It is to that truth that we must now turn.

2. The kindness of God: the Lord is good (1:7–15)

The Bible speaks about the goodness of God in several different ways. There is the idea of God's perfect moral goodness in contrast to the badness or evil in humankind. When the rich young ruler in the Gospel story addressed Jesus with the words 'Good teacher', Jesus responded by saying, 'Why do you call me good? No one is good – except God alone' (Mark 10:17–18). So when Nahum says *The Lord is good* (7a), he may well have the perfect goodness of a holy God in mind, in contrast to the sinful nature and the evil deeds of humankind.

The statement that *The Lord is good* also points to the way in which God is actively good towards all people. The psalmist wrote: 'The Lord is good to all; he has compassion on all he has made' (Ps. 145:9). Jesus made the same point in the Sermon on the Mount when he said that the same God who calls his followers to love their enemies and pray for those who persecute them also 'causes his sun to rise on the evil and the good, and sends rain on the righteous and the unrighteous' (Matt. 5:45).

So how does God demonstrate his goodness to all people? Nahum has already taught us that the Lord is angry about sin, and punishes the wicked; he *takes vengeance on his foes and vents his wrath against his enemies* (2). But how does he act with positive goodness in the world which he has made and sustains, and over which he reigns as sovereign Lord? In these next few verses (1:7–15) Nahum gives us a number of examples of the Lord's goodness.

a. 'The Lord is good, a refuge in times of trouble' (7b)

There is no doubt that Nahum would have had in his mind a number of different *times of trouble* that he and his contemporaries would be facing.

i. The troubles associated with the fear of divine judgment

Stephen Travis rightly points out that

> judgment is itself a neutral word. Whilst it implies accountability, it does not presuppose any particular verdict. According to the New Testament the Last Judgment, like an earthly judgment, may issue for any particular individual in a verdict of acquittal or condemnation.[28]

So the fear of divine judgment lies in the possibility that when the day of judgment comes I will be condemned, not acquitted.

Now Nahum has written eloquently about the severity of God (1:1–6), and the majesty and wrath of an awesome God whose *wrath is poured out like fire* (6b). He has already asked the question *Who can withstand his indignation? Who can endure his fierce anger?* (6).

Clearly, none of us can stand acquitted before such a holy and awesome God unless we make the Lord our refuge. As sinners who deserve nothing but the just judgment of God, we need to run to the Lord and take shelter in his goodness and grace. If we make the Lord our refuge, we need no longer fear divine judgment and condemnation.

Christians know where today that shelter can be found. It is Calvary, where Jesus died, 'the righteous for the unrighteous, to bring you to God' (1 Pet. 3:18). A. M. Toplady shows us how we may make Jesus our refuge, and escape the condemnation of a holy God, in his famous hymn, 'Rock of Ages':

> Rock of Ages, cleft for me,
> Let me hide myself in Thee;
> Let the water and the blood
> From thy riven side which flowed,
> Be of sin the double cure,
> Cleanse me from its guilt and power.

---

[28] S. Travis, 'The Problem of Judgment', *Themelios* 11.2 (January 1986), pp. 52–57.

Not the labours of my hands
Can fulfil thy laws demands;
Could my zeal no respite know,
Could my tears for ever flow,
All for sin could not atone;
Thou must save and thou alone.

Nothing in my hand I bring,
Simply to thy cross I cling;
Naked come to thee for dress,
Helpless look to thee for grace;
Foul, I to the fountain fly;
Wash me, Saviour, or I die!

While I draw this fleeting breath,
When my eyelids close in death,
When I soar through tracts unknown,
See Thee on Thy Judgment Throne;
Rock of Ages, cleft for me,
Let me hide myself in Thee.
(A. M. Toplady, 1740–78)

The apostle Paul wrote to the Christians in Rome: 'There is now no condemnation for those who are in Christ Jesus' (Rom. 8:1). When we make the Lord our refuge, we need not fear divine judgment.

Nahum, no doubt, also had another contemporary situation in mind when he spoke about *times of trouble.*

ii. The troubles associated with facing danger

Even if we cannot be sure of the exact time and place of Nahum's ministry (see pp. 86–87), we can be certain that he and his contemporaries often faced danger. Nahum probably preached in the reign of King Manasseh (687–642 BC). We have already noticed that the writer of 2 Kings tells us that Manasseh led the people astray 'so that they did more evil than the nations the LORD had destroyed before the Israelites' (2 Kgs 21:9). It would have been a dangerous time for true believers in Yahweh. Assyria was also a constant threat to those who lived in Israel and Judah. However, in spite of all the dangers that Nahum and his contemporaries faced, the prophet trusted in the Lord's protection. He could say confidently, *The Lord is good, a refuge in times of trouble* (7a).

One of the most moving stories of the Second World War tells of a courageous Christian woman, Corrie ten Boom, who with her family risked her life to hide Jews from the Nazis in occupied Holland. She and her family were eventually betrayed, and she was sent with her sister to a number of concentration camps, including the notorious Ravensbrück camp. Although her sister died before the war was over, Corrie survived those troubling times. After the war, she told her story in the book *The Hiding Place*. Her testimony was not only that she hid Jews in her house in Holland, but also that she was able to take refuge in the Lord, and so was given the strength to face up to danger and endure much suffering. She proved the truth of Nahum's words, *The Lord is good, a refuge in times of trouble.*

A further example of the truth of these words is found in the book *Kikuyu Conflict*, written in 1953 at the time of the Mau Mau troubles in Kenya. The author, Canon Cecil Bewes, relates many stories about the courage of African Christians, who were often the target of Mau Mau attacks. One day, for example, a Kikuyu teacher found himself confronted by one of the Mau Mau pointing a pistol at his head. Instantly a verse from the Bible, which he had read at family prayers that very morning, came into his mind: 'The name of the Lord is a fortified tower; the righteous run to it and are safe' (Prov. 18:10). The teacher immediately called out, 'Jesus, Tower!' and the shot from the pistol went wide. Another shot, and again the cry, 'Jesus, Tower!' There were four shots punctuated by the name of Jesus – four times the attack failed!

Cecil Bewes went on to say:

> There are stories of heroism, but also stories of suffering and cruelty . . . shining through it all is the quiet friendly serenity of the Christian brethren; first on the scene when any disaster occurs; courageous in their own afflictions, yet gentle and compassionate over the sorrows of others. I joined in one of the fellowship meetings: 'We are not afraid', said one of the leaders, 'our lives are in God's hands; and if we die we can only go to be with him. It has made the Lord Jesus real to us.' Another jumped to his feet. 'When they drag you out of your hut at night to make you take the oath', he said, 'that is the time for you to prove whether

> Jesus Christ means everything to you, or whether he means nothing at all.'[29]

The Lord is good. He takes away the fear of judgment. He helps those who take refuge in him to face danger. And since it is clear that not all escape death when facing danger, he also helps those who face death itself.

iii. The troubles associated with facing death itself

The writer A. N. Wilson has related how after spending many years mocking Christians and the Christian church, he now finds himself to be a committed Christian and churchgoer. He tells us that one reason for his newly found faith has been the witness of 'ordinary Christians' who, in Nahum's words, have found that *The Lord is good, a refuge in time of trouble* (7).

Wilson wrote:

> My belief has come about in large measure because of the lives and example of people I have known . . . not the famous, not saints, but friends and relations who have lived and faced death, in the light of the resurrection story, or in the quiet acceptance that they have a future after they die.[30]

As a minister I have often found myself alongside those facing terminal illness, in 'the valley of the shadow of death'. Those who have found the Lord as their refuge have often spoken of the goodness of the Lord, not only in the past when they were fit and well, but even as they face imminent death. John Wesley has been quoted as saying, with reference to Christians, 'Our people die well.' That would be my testimony time and time again as I have visited the sick and dying. Nahum is right. *God is good.* Those who take refuge in him can say that even as they face death itself. For, as the apostle Paul wrote in the light of the death and resurrection of Jesus, 'I am convinced that neither death nor life . . . nor anything else in all creation, will be able to separate us from the love of God that is in Christ Jesus our Lord' (Rom. 8:38–39).

---

29 T. F. C. Bewes, *Kikuyu Conflict* (Highway Press, 1953), pp. 55–57.

30 Article by A. N. Wilson in the *Daily Mail*, 11 April 2009.

b. The Lord 'cares for those who trust in him' (7)

Nahum goes on to assure those who *trust in him* that the same Lord knows them. The Hebrew word (*yāda'*), translated *cares for*, literally means 'to know' in an intimate and personal way. In Genesis (4:1), for example, the word is used to describe sexual relations between Adam and Eve. Jeremiah uses the same word to describe God's commitment to him even before he was born, 'Before I formed you in the womb I knew [*yāda'*] you' (Jer. 1:5); and Amos spoke God's word to Israel, 'You only have I known [*yāda'*] of all the families of the earth' (Amos 3:2, ESV), indicating the uniquely intimate covenant relationship with God's people. The phrase *those who trust in him* may better be translated 'take refuge in him', or 'run for shelter' to him. So, God's goodness and care for his people arises out of his loving and intimate knowledge of them. He knows and cares for those who take refuge in him.

It's an astonishing truth that the sovereign Creator, who is described so awesomely in the opening words of Nahum's prophecy, is also the good Lord who knows personally and intimately those who take refuge in him. The words of Jesus affirm the same truth when he says, 'I am the good shepherd. The good shepherd lays down his life for the sheep . . . I know my sheep and my sheep know me – just as the Father knows me and I know the Father' (John 10:11, 14–15).

It was that personal relationship with God through Christ that sustained Terry Waite through his five harrowing years as a hostage in Beirut. Waite writes honestly about the ups and downs of his spiritual experience in captivity. There were times when he experienced the 'dark night of the soul' and had no sense of God's presence with him. Yet, looking back over those five years of suffering that he and his family had endured, he concluded his moving account with these words: 'There is still a long, long way to travel, and I shall press on. God has been good to me, and to those whom I love.'[31]

The Lord knows and cares for those who take refuge in him. We may not recognize his goodness in the midst of a crisis or in the trauma of suffering but, like Terry Waite, we can look back and see how good he has been. However difficult the circumstances of our lives, we can trust God's Word when it says: *The Lord is good . . . he knows those who take refuge in him* (7, my translation). The Lord has committed himself to us, even to

[31] T. Waite, *Taken on Trust* (Hodder & Stoughton, 1993; and Coronet edn, 1994), pp. 460–461.

dying for us on the cross. He knows us through and through (see Ps. 139). Why should we not trust him?

c. The Lord is good – he defeats those who oppose him (8–15)

Some commentators take this next section of Nahum's book as emphasizing God's severity in judging Nineveh. But since the name 'Nineveh' only appears in the first verse as a general title to the whole book, and then appears again in chapter 2 (8), it seems to me that these verses (7–15) may still come under the heading of *The Lord is good* (7a). It is good that *The Lord is . . . a refuge in times of trouble* (1:7b), and that *He cares for [knows] those who trust [take refuge] in him* (7c). But surely it is also good that the Lord defeats his enemies, and the enemies of his people; so may it not be that this section (8–15) deals in more general terms with the Lord's defeat of his enemies, even though Assyria and Nineveh are not far away from the thoughts of the prophet, and Nahum is reminding us that God is good whenever he does this?

The NIV adds the name of Nineveh (8, 11, 14), but the name does not appear in the Hebrew script for those verses. Judah is added in the same way in verse 12.

In his exposition of the story of the death of King David's son Absalom (2 Sam. 18:1 – 19:8), Dale Ralph Davis makes this same point.[32] He tells the story of the famous Scottish preacher Alexander Whyte who, when he was a boy, caught his arm in a threshing machine. Everyone thought that there was no hope of saving the arm. Davis went on:

> A neighbour who was wise in down-home treatment wouldn't allow them to take the lad for . . . surgery. The pain became severe, so Whyte's mother called for the neighbour to come again. She examined the arm and said: 'I like the pain. I like the pain.' She was correct. The arm healed. The pain was a component of the healing. The two went together.

Ralph Davis goes on to say:

> That is the way it is in our text. If the kingdom of God under God's chosen King is to be saved, then the enemy who assaults that Kingdom must be destroyed. God gives no secure salvation to his church unless he brings

[32] D. R. Davis, *2 Samuel: Looking on the Heart* (Christian Focus, 2004), p. 192.

> decisive judgment on her enemies. We must stop praying, 'Deliver us from evil', unless we yearn for its destruction (see 1 Jn. 3:8). Otherwise we are like a patient ready to undergo cancer surgery who pleads with his doctor to 'deal gently with my cancer' . . . the preserving of God's kingdom involves the perishing of its enemies.

So I believe that Nahum is teaching us three things here: that God is good in overwhelming his enemies (8); frustrating their plans (9–11); and destroying their culture (12, 14).

i. The Lord overwhelms his enemies (8a)

The picture of *an overwhelming flood* (8a) immediately draws our attention to the judgment of God in the story of the flood in the days of Noah (Gen. 6 – 9). Noah 'was a righteous man, blameless among the people of his time, and he walked faithfully with God' (Gen. 6:9). But the story goes on:

> God saw how corrupt the earth had become, for all the people on earth had corrupted their ways. So God said to Noah, 'I am going to put an end to all people, for the earth is filled with violence because of them. I am surely going to destroy both them and the earth.'
> (Gen. 6:12–13)

However, in God's goodness he spared Noah and his family: 'And Noah and his sons and his wife and his sons' wives entered the ark to escape the waters of the flood' (Gen. 7:7); and after the flood had subsided, God in his goodness made a promise to Noah and his family, and to all humankind: 'Never again will I destroy all living creatures, as I have done. As long as the earth endures, seed time and harvest, cold and heat, summer and winter, day and night will never cease' (Gen. 8:21–22).

The Lord is good. In the midst of judgment there is mercy. The Lord will overwhelm his enemies; but the Lord knows and cares for those who take refuge in him (Nah. 1:7–8).

Those who believe that Nahum is thinking only of Nineveh in this part of his prophecy (see 8, NIV) point out that it was a flood that contributed significantly to the capture of Nineveh: *The river gates are thrown open and the palace collapses* (2:6).[33] If, as I believe, *an overwhelming flood*

---

33 Isaiah describes the capture of Jerusalem by the Assyrians in similar terms in Isa. 8:6–8.

points back to God's judgment in the days of Noah, then the words of Jesus in the Gospels come to mind to challenge us. For in his goodness Jesus warned the people of his day, and all of us today, that the lessons of the flood may not have been learnt, and that many of us will be as unready for the final day of judgment as people in Noah's day were unready for the flood. Remember that Jesus said:

> Just as it was in the days of Noah, so also will it be in the days of the Son of Man. People were eating, drinking, marrying and being given in marriage up to the day Noah entered the ark. Then the flood came and destroyed them all . . . It will be just like this on the day the Son of Man is revealed.
> (Luke 17:26–27, 30)

God is good to warn us to be ready for that final day of judgment. He will make an end of all those who oppose him. But we can heed his warning, as Noah and his family did, and make God our refuge (1:7–8).

Nahum adds another picture of judgment in verse 8 alongside his flood warning: *he will make a complete end of [his] adversaries* (ESV)[34] and *darkness shall pursue his enemies* (KJV), or as most other translations have it, *he will pursue his foes into darkness* (see NIV, ESV, RSV et al.). Light and darkness are frequent themes in Scripture. In the Old Testament, light is a symbol of God's presence and blessing (Ps. 27:1; Isa. 9:2), in contrast to darkness which symbolizes God's judgment and displeasure. In the New Testament, Jesus teaches us that people love darkness rather than light because their deeds are evil (John 3:19). If Nahum is saying that 'darkness pursues God's enemies', he is simply pointing out the consequences of sin. Sin separates us from God, takes away the sense of his presence, makes us lost souls. Darkness overwhelms us. Darkness pursues us, until we turn to the Lord and are able to say: 'The LORD is my light and my salvation' (Ps. 27:1).

Most translators prefer the translation: *he will pursue his foes into the realm of darkness* (8c). This seems to refer to God himself pursuing his enemies to ensure that they do not get away with 'the works of darkness' (Rom. 13:12, KJV). God's goodness and justice demands that those who

---

[34] Some translate as: 'he will make an end of *her place*', which accounts for the inserting of 'Nineveh' at that point.

oppose God face up to judgment, and experience the darkness of that separation from God that they themselves have chosen. Some commentators support the view that Nahum is referring here to Nineveh. Eaton, however, sees a demonic figure behind Nineveh, and the goddess Ishtar, one of Nineveh's female deities. He explains this verse by saying: 'The prophet announces that God will sweep away her citadel and drive her allies to the darkness of the nether world where they belong.'[35]

Whatever way we understand these two pictures of God's judgment – flooding and darkness – Nahum is encouraging us to see the goodness of God in dealing with sin and evil. God will *make an end of . . . his foes* (8). He overcomes those who oppose him. Christians likewise rejoice that Jesus by his death and resurrection has overcome his enemies and decisively defeated them. In the words of the apostle Paul, Jesus, 'having disarmed the powers and authorities . . . made a public spectacle of them, triumphing over them by the cross' (Col. 2:15). We too can overcome Satan, and demonic powers, by claiming Christ's victory over our enemy. As the book of Revelation puts it, 'the accuser of our brothers and sisters [Satan] . . . has been hurled down. They triumphed over him by the blood of the Lamb and by the word of their testimony' (Rev. 12:10–11).

I remember a group of students coming to see me in Edinburgh because the flat that they had rented as student accommodation had a strange atmosphere of oppression and foreboding, which they did not understand but believed was satanic in some way. We prayed together in the name of the Lord Jesus. We claimed the victory of Christ at Calvary over all spiritual wickedness (Col. 2:15). We asked the Lord, on the basis of his victory over Satan on the cross, to banish any evil spirit that was present; and the Lord heard our prayers and gave lasting relief and peace to that group of Christian students. The Lord defeats the enemy. He is good to those who take refuge in him.

ii. The Lord frustrates the plans of his enemies (9–11)

Nahum now makes clear that the enemies of God plot against the Lord. So even if the prophet has in his mind the threat to Judah from the Assyrian superpower, the deepest sin of Assyria and its leaders is in the fact that they are plotting *against the Lord*. It is always important to recognize sin for what it really is. When King David sinned by taking Uriah's wife

[35] J. H. Eaton, *Obadiah, Nahum, Habakkuk, Zephaniah* (SCM Press, 1961), p. 60.

Bathsheba from him, and by sending Uriah to his certain death at the front line, David sinned against Uriah and Bathsheba. But he realized that his greatest sin was against the Lord himself:

For I know my transgressions,
and my sin is always before me.
Against you, you only, have I sinned
and done what is evil in your sight;
so you are right in your verdict
and justified when you judge.
(Ps. 51:3–4)

God is justified in judging those who plot against him (9). He carries out his judgment in part by frustrating the plans of his enemies. Whatever they plot against the Lord, he will bring to an end; *trouble will not come a second time* (9c). So when God in his sovereignty frustrates the plans of his enemies, there is no possibility that those plans will be resurrected. God's judgment is complete. There will be no second chance.

There is a hint (11) that behind every plot to attack Yahweh and his people lie the rulers in Assyria, including Sennacherib and Ashurbanipal. It is also possible that Nahum sees behind them and all God's enemies a spiritual enemy, identified by reference to 'Belial'. In the Old Testament 'Belial' is a general description of what is worthless. Hence it goes on to mean 'wickedness', or in verse 11 'a counsellor of worthlessness'. A little later (15c) Nahum seems to use Belial (NIV: 'the wicked') as a proper name. Certainly, the phrase *devises wicked plans* could be translated as 'advises Belial'. Later, Belial was a name identified with 'the spiritual forces of evil in the heavenly realms' (Eph. 6:12) and Satan (Rev. 12:10–12).

Clearly, Nahum's point is that whatever they plot, and whoever is behind it, God will frustrate their plans and defeat his enemies. In some respects, of course, they will defeat themselves, becoming *entangled among thorns* (10a), unable to escape without hurt from the consequences of their life and lifestyle.

They will be entangled among thorns may well be a reference back to the book of Genesis (3:18). There God declares that his judgment on Adam's disobedience includes God's curse on the earth so that the ground produces 'thorns and thistles for you'. In other words, those who plot against the Lord come under the curse of God, deserving his judgment.

There is also the thought that those under God's curse find themselves *entangled* and unable to free themselves from the consequences of their sin. It is possible to see this happening to those who become addicted to alcohol or drugs. But it also happens less spectacularly to those who, for example, find themselves in a wrong relationship, or those who become obsessed by money, or sex or ambition.

The reference to being *drunk from their wine* may refer to a drink culture that destroys their rationality and ability to think sensibly about themselves and their lives. It's a problem that is particularly relevant in the UK today. But being *drunk from their wine* may also be a metaphor for the effects of sin in general that befuddle the mind. Certainly the book of Revelation describes the 'woman . . . dressed in purple and scarlet', the symbol of an evil and immoral empire, as holding in her hand a golden cup 'filled with abominable things and the filth of her adulteries . . . the woman was drunk with the blood of God's holy people, the blood of those who bore testimony to Jesus' (Rev. 17:4–6). Immorality and the persecution of God's people deserve the judgment of God; and that is exactly what he promises through Nahum: *they will be consumed like dry stubble* (10c). It's not a pretty picture; but it is not inconsistent with the goodness of God who insists that those who plot evil against him will suffer loss. Their plotting against God and his people will be frustrated and defeated.

Surely it is a matter of immense encouragement that the Lord frustrates the plans of his enemies. King David once found himself in a tricky position where he was likely to lose both his crown and his life. Absalom, his rebellious son, was on the edge of carrying out a successful coup against his father, when he decided to seek the advice of his aides. Ahithophel, who had been disloyal to David, was his most experienced advisor. He gave Absalom good advice about attacking David and his supporters quickly. Astonishingly, Absalom then turned to a less trusted advisor, who suggested another plan which would involve delay; that advisor was Hushai, a spy in Absalom's camp. Absalom followed his advice, and was defeated and killed. Where was God in all this? The narrator tells us: 'The Lord had determined to frustrate the good advice of Ahithophel in order to bring disaster on Absalom' (2 Sam. 17:14).[36]

Sometimes we find ourselves in situations where the work of the kingdom suffers every kind of difficulty and opposition, and where

[36] For the whole story read 2 Sam. 16 – 17.

enemies of God seem to be all around. Nahum continually reminds us that the Lord is sovereign. He will bring to an end those who plot against the Lord. He will frustrate their plans. He uses individuals (such as Hushai) and nations (such as Assyria) to do this. It really is true that 'God works for the good of those who love him, who have been called according to his purpose' (Rom. 8:28). Sometimes, when others oppose us and the work of God, and even seek to do us harm, we can say with Joseph, 'You intended to harm me, but God intended it for good' (Gen. 50:20).[37]

iii. The Lord will destroy the culture of his enemies (12, 14)

At the end of the Second World War in 1945 it was not only that Berlin and other German cities were destroyed, and the Third Reich Nazi machine dismantled; but a whole atheistic and dehumanizing culture was also condemned. It was not totally destroyed, and a few very small minority groups continue to keep the Nazis' dream alive. But it can fairly be said that the Nazi culture has been largely destroyed.

Culture has been defined as 'an integrated system of beliefs, values, customs and institutions . . . which bind a society together, and give it a sense of identity, dignity, security and continuity'.[38] But it is clear that there comes a time in some cultures when evil has flourished to such a degree that it is too late for the culture to change or be transformed, and judgment and destruction are inevitable.

Nahum is convinced, as we shall see in the rest of the book, that Assyria and Nineveh have reached that point, although at the time they *have allies and are numerous* (12a). Yet the Lord says: *they will be destroyed and pass away*. Nahum emphasizes that *The Lord has given a command concerning you, [Nineveh]*[39] (14a) and that command will certainly lead to the destruction of their whole evil way of life.

If Nahum has Assyria in his mind as he writes, the words of judgment, *'You will have no descendants to bear your name'* (14b), will be especially

[37] Dale Ralph Davis, when commenting on the story from 2 Sam. 16 – 17, wrote: 'The plot against Yahweh's king has gone to pot. Why? Yahweh has ordained it. More often than not that is the manner of God's work. His sceptre is unseen, his sovereignty hidden behind the conversations and decisions and activities and crises of our lives. We see only grocery lines and diaper changes and school assignments; but through and over and behind it all Yahweh rules. He is not absent, but neither is he obvious' (Davis, *2 Samuel*, p. 175).

[38] Quoted from the Willowbank Report 1079:7 in Eddie Gibbs, *I Believe in Church Growth* (Hodder & Stoughton, 1981), p. 88.

[39] As 'you' (14a) is masculine singular, it is possible that Nahum has a king of Assyria in his mind, probably Ashurbanipal (669–627 BC). 'Nineveh' is in brackets because it does not appear in the Hebrew text; but if the king is referred to, he represents the capital city Nineveh, Nineveh represents Assyria, and Assyria represents all evil cultures that plot against the Lord and his people.

appropriate for the descendants of Ashurbanipal. According to inscriptions outside the biblical record, Ashurbanipal had recorded his wish that his son would honour and preserve his name. It was a matter of personal pride for the king.[40]

But God is our judge. He has the final word. He knows the true value of the legacy we will leave for future generations. To those who rule over a culture that is hostile to him, there are these stark words: *'You will have no descendants to bear your name.'*

O. P. Robertson gives an example of the evil nature of the Assyrian culture from the Annals of Ashurnasirpal.[41] That king left a record engraved in stone which included these boasts:

> I built a pillar over against his city gate, and I flayed all the chief men who had revolted, and I covered the pillar with their skins; some I walled up within the pillar, and some upon the pillar on stakes I impaled, and others I fixed to stakes round about the pillar; many within the borders of my own land I flayed, and I spread out their skins upon the walls; and I cut off the limbs of the high officers, of the high royal officers who had rebelled.[42]

Such atrocities are not, of course, limited to ancient times. The Holocaust during the Second World War, the labour camps in the Stalinist Soviet Union, the killing fields of Cambodia, and the suffering and cruelty of recent regimes in Africa, Asia and the Middle East all remind us that 'the heart is deceitful above all things' (Jer. 17:9), and that 'there is no one righteous, not even one' (Rom. 3:10). Furthermore, the UK, the USA and the Coalition forces during the recent conflicts in Iraq and Afghanistan were not immune from charges of inhumane treatment of prisoners and other atrocities in the theatre of war. It is surely of God's goodness that we are not destroyed as Assyria would be in time. But we need to be on our guard against our own nation and culture becoming more and more deserving of God's judgment. I heard a bishop in the Church of England say to a large company of Christian people recently that we may need to be more

---

40 D. D. Luckenbill, 'Ancient Records of Assyria and Babylonia', quoted in O. P. Robertson, *The Books of Nahum, Habakkuk and Zephaniah*, NICOT (Eerdmans, 1990), p. 79.

41 II, a9, c. 800 BC.

42 G. Roux, *Ancient Iraq* (Penguin, 1992), pp. 263–264, lines 89ff., quoted in Robertson, *The Books of Nahum, Habakkuk and Zephaniah*, p. 82.

*counter*cultural in the UK today because so much of our present culture has become secular, anti-Christian and worthless.

Christians today have a responsibility to seek to influence and even transform our culture in the light of the gospel and biblical truth. We can begin to do this as we pray for our leaders and our nation (2 Chr. 7:14; 1 Tim. 2:1–4). We can do it by preaching and teaching the Word of God (2 Tim. 3:10 – 4:5). We can do it as we live godly lives, being salt and light in the world, and refusing to allow the world to squeeze us into its mould (Matt. 5:13–15; Rom. 12:1–21). We can do it as we bear witness to Christian values in the public space (Acts 1:8; Acts 17), which in our day and age may well include writing letters to our local government MP or similar people, and seeking other opportunities to 'give the reason for the hope that [we] have' (1 Pet. 3:15–17).[43]

Certainly Nahum did his part in bringing the Word of God to bear on contemporary cultures. He was sure that God would judge a culture that turned people's eyes away from the living God to that which promised much but was in fact worthless. The Assyrians, for example, had many gods and liked to collect gods from other nations which they had overrun, and put them in their own temples in Assyria. In God's sight, however, these gods were no more than *images and idols*, made by human hands. So Yahweh pronounced: *I will destroy the images and idols that are in the temple of your gods* (14c). These idols promised much but gave nothing. They led to death, not life; to frustration, not salvation.[44]

Through Nahum, God says: *I will prepare your grave, for you are vile* (14d). This may mean that the Assyrian culture will be buried and destroyed, because it is worthless and evil. Or it could refer to the last king of the Assyrians who might well have been killed and buried by his enemies the Babylonians. Proud leaders are sensitive about the manner of their death. Was Ashurbanipal to suffer the final indignity of a grave prepared by God's decree but carried out by his victorious enemy? How

[43] For a helpful summary of different Christian views on the relationship between the gospel and culture, see Gibbs, *I Believe in Church Growth*, pp. 84–130.

[44] In J. B. Pritchard's *Ancient Near Eastern Texts Relating to the Old Testament* (Princeton University Press, 1969) there is, according to D. R. Davis, a moving and revealing 'prayer to every god'. Davis comments: 'The worshipper prays to all the gods and goddesses, the ones he knows and those he doesn't know. Some god or goddess has inflicted illness and suffering upon him. He does not know which god or goddess he has offended; he does not know what his offence has been. Indeed, he alleges, this miserable agnosticism plagues mankind as a whole . . . no one knows whether he is committing sin or doing good as he lives out his life. That is paganism . . . nebulous, hopeless, cruel; but Yahweh is kind; he declares our guilt to us' (Davis, *2 Samuel*, pp. 218–219).

are the mighty fallen! Yet God is good to warn us that he will destroy the cultures of those nations that plot against him and attack his people.

d. The Lord is good – he delivers the afflicted (12–13)

In his autobiographical account of life as the 'Vicar of Baghdad', in post-Saddam-Hussein Iraq, Andrew White gives a moving account of his perceived role in an incredibly dangerous city. He writes:

> However dreadful the tragedy, My Lord is there. Amidst the greatest havoc I have witnessed in post war Iraq, or in Gaza, or in Bethlehem during the siege, I have still seen [God's] glory . . . I have seen the heavens opened and glimpsed something of the majesty, might and love of God.
>
> When life is full of despair, it is only the glory of God that truly sustains. There have been times when everything has gone wrong, when friends and colleagues have been killed, and there has seemed to be no hope. It is at times like this that I ask God to show me his glory . . . so as I circulate among the powerful people in the Pentagon, Congress and Parliament, I ask to see God's glory, and in all these places I have seen it. It is when the power and glory come together that we witness change. That is why I say that my work is about the power and the glory . . . the power of those who run the world and the glory of God who runs the Universe. For too long people have tried to keep them separate; but God is at work in time and space, and they have to be brought together . . . Egypt, Assyria . . . that is Iraq . . . and Israel are all places where I work, and I have a profound sense that in the midst of all this conflict the Lord is here and his Spirit is with us. All my hope for this broken world rests in God. And it is a huge hope . . .[45]

This moving and lengthy quotation from Andrew White's book has a great deal of the spirit of Nahum about it. Nahum also worked in a dangerous place at a dangerous time. Powerful nations threatened the peace of Jerusalem and the security of God's people. Nahum, like White, pointed people to the glory and majesty of God, and sought to bring God and the people together.

So far, we have seen that Nahum has spoken about the severity of God (1:1–5) and his anger and judgment on sin and evil in the world. Then he

[45] A. White, *The Vicar of Baghdad* (Monarch, 2009), pp. 171–173.

went on to describe the goodness of God (6–15), caring for those who take refuge in him, and defeating their enemies and his. But we have omitted to comment on two verses (12–13) that tell of God's disciplining judgment and liberating salvation.

i. God disciplines the nations (12)

In spite of the fact that the NIV adds the name 'Judah' (12c), when Judah is not found in the Hebrew text, it is possible that Nahum is referring to God's disciplining judgment more generally, and not confining his meaning to Judah. The Assyrians, for example, had overrun many nations and afflicted them. So Yahweh may be saying to these nations: *Although I have afflicted you . . . I will afflict you no more. Now I will break their yoke from your neck and tear your shackles away* (12–13). Yahweh is Lord of all nations. He longs that all people will turn to him in repentance, faith and obedience. He afflicts the nations in order that he might deliver them and bring them to himself. The prophet Isaiah certainly shares that vision and hope as he looks into the future:

> In that day there will be a highway from Egypt to Assyria. The Assyrians will go to Egypt and the Egyptians to Assyria. The Egyptians and Assyrians will worship together. In that day Israel will be the third, along with Egypt and Assyria, a blessing on the earth. The LORD Almighty will bless them, saying, 'Blessed be Egypt my people, Assyria my handiwork, and Israel my inheritance.'
> (Isa. 19:23–25)

God's disciplining judgments – his 'megaphone to a deaf world' – applies to every nation. Did the UK not learn as a nation (if briefly) to turn to God in prayer during the bombing in London in the Second World War? Should we not have learned the same lesson following the terrorist attacks on New York and London in more recent times? To say, of course, that God might use such attacks as a megaphone to warn us to return to him does not mean that the instruments of such attacks are therefore without guilt. The apostle Peter made this clear when speaking about the crucifixion of Jesus: 'This man was handed over to you by God's deliberate plan and foreknowledge; and you, with the help of wicked men, put him to death by nailing him to the cross' (Acts 2:23). Scripture teaches us to hold to both truths: the sovereignty of God and the responsibility of humankind.

In Nahum's day many who lived in Israel in the north and Judah in the south would be aware of the afflictions and sufferings endured by God's people. The Assyrians and their allies had oppressed the land and dominated the people. They introduced foreign gods, and persecuted and mocked the people of God (2 Kgs 18). But none of this was outside the sovereign purpose of God. Nahum teaches us: *This is what the LORD says . . . I have afflicted you* (12).

Throughout biblical history the people of God have experienced the disciplining judgments of God. The psalmist saw the hand of God in such afflictions in his personal life when he wrote: 'Before I was afflicted I went astray, but now I obey your word' (Ps. 119:67). He went on to say: 'It was good for me to be afflicted so that I might learn your decrees' (119:71). The suffering persecuted church often bears witness to the goodness of the Lord in the midst of afflictions. The fast-growing church in China, for example, has suffered many, but Christians in that country testify to the way in which such afflictions have brought them to a deeper trust in the Word of God, and a deeper knowledge of God himself.

In the New Testament, Christians also bear witness to the goodness of God in his disciplining judgments. For, as the writer to the Hebrews puts it: 'No discipline seems pleasant at the time, but painful. Later on, however, it produces a harvest of righteousness and peace for those who have been trained by it' (Heb. 12:11). We should notice that we don't learn these lessons from afflictions automatically. We have to be 'trained' or exercised by them as we wrestle and pray and think through the lessons that the Lord wants to teach us in the midst of suffering (Rom. 5:1–5; 2 Cor. 1:3–11; Heb. 12:12–13; Jas 1:2–12).

But what does God's promise mean – *I will afflict you no more*? It may mean that the Assyrians, as instruments of God's disciplining judgment, will no longer afflict God's people. This came true according to God's promise. For God said: *they will be destroyed and pass away* (1:12). After the fall of Nineveh, Assyria was destroyed and never again afflicted God's people. Or this promise could be looking forward to the final day of judgment when God's people will be secure and free from all suffering. O. Palmer Robertson writes:

> Possibly the prophet views Nineveh as a typical representation of Israel's archenemy, and her destruction as symbolic of God's final act of judgment. Whoever might prove to be the archenemy of God's people in

> the future generations could be sure from Nineveh's experience that God would destroy them and deliver his people. God remains vitally concerned for his people in all their afflictions. When the right time comes for their deliverance, he shall break them free from all oppression.[46]

In the book of Revelation, John gives us a vision of heaven and the end of all afflictions. For those who belong to God, whose names are 'written in the Lamb's book of life' (Rev. 21:27), John wrote:

> 'He [God] will wipe away every tear from their eyes. There will be no more death or mourning or crying or pain, for the old order of things has passed away.' He who was seated on the throne said, 'I am making everything new!'
> (Rev. 21:4–5)

On that day God's promise, *I will afflict you no more*, will be finally fulfilled.

God is good. He may afflict his people, but it is for their good. Furthermore, he speaks not only of his disciplining judgments, but also of his liberating salvation (1:12–13).

ii. God sets people free (13)

Nahum is aware that some of God's people have already experienced the political oppression of a superpower in their own backyard, and the humiliation of being chained as a prisoner in a forced labour camp in a foreign country. The *yoke* (13), therefore, may be a metaphorical reference to political oppression. The *shackles* (13b) must refer to other forms of oppression and captivity. But Nahum would also have in mind the spiritual bondage that is a universal experience. At the time of the exodus the Hebrews were slaves and needed to be brought out of slavery and into freedom; but the deeper significance of that event was a spiritual one. The Passover teaches us that a lamb needed to be slain to redeem God's people and to save them from their sins; and the New Testament tells us that 'Christ, our Passover lamb, has been sacrificed [for us]' (1 Cor. 5:7) and that Jesus is 'the Lamb of God, who takes away the sin of the world' (John 1:29). So, when Nahum brings God's promise – *Now I will break their yoke from*

[46] Robertson, *The Books of Nahum, Habakkuk and Zephaniah*, p. 78.

your neck and tear your shackles away (13) – he is pointing beyond political oppression and slavery to freedom from sin, and fulfilment in Jesus.

It was Jesus who taught that 'everyone who sins is a slave to sin' (John 8:34); and the whole Bible makes it clear that 'all have sinned and fall short of the glory of God' (Rom. 3:23) and that 'there is no one righteous, not even one . . . All have turned away, they have together become worthless' (Rom. 3:10, 12; Ps. 53:3). Few modern writers have given a better description of the enslaving power of sin than William Somerset Maugham in his semi-autobiographical novel, *Of Human Bondage*. Philip, the central character in the story, is brought up in the Christian faith, but after a visit to Paris decides he no longer believes in God. As an atheist he concludes that he no longer needs to live by Christian moral standards, especially with reference to sexual morality. He throws away restraints and sets out to enjoy himself. A friend says to him, 'You seem to be a contented slave of your passions.' Philip replies, 'A slave because I can't help myself, but not a contented one.' Through the character of Philip, Maugham reflects:

> Philip was astonished at the weakness of his will. It seemed to him that he was swayed by every light emotion, as though he was a leaf in the wind. And when passion seized him he was powerless. He had no self control . . . He thought of what he was going to do and, when the time came to act, he was powerless in the grasp of instincts, emotions, he knew not what . . . his reason was someone looking on, observing the facts but powerless to interfere.[47]

The apostle Paul expressed the power and the bondage of sin even more strikingly. He writes as a Christian believer when he says: 'We know that the law is spiritual; but I am unspiritual, sold as a slave to sin. I do not understand what I do. For what I want to do I do not do, but what I hate I do' (Rom. 7:14–15).

Nahum brings good news to those who were experiencing different forms of bondage, including spiritual bondage. God will set them free: *I will break their yoke from your neck and tear your shackles away* (13). Jesus came to make that possible. He set out the aims of his mission in the synagogue of Nazareth, quoting from Isaiah, and applying the description to himself:

---

[47] W. S. Maugham, *Of Human Bondage* (Penguin, 1968), p. 384.

> The Spirit of the Lord is on me,
> because he has anointed me
> to proclaim good news to the poor.
> He has sent me to proclaim freedom for the prisoners
> and recovery of sight for the blind,
> to set the oppressed free,
> to proclaim the year of the Lord's favour.
> (Luke 4:18–19; Isa. 42:7)

It is clear that Jesus did not 'set free' prisoners of war. He 'set free' those in the bondage of sin and guilt (e.g. Luke 7:41–50), in Satan's bondage (Luke 8:26–39), in the grip of greed and dishonesty (Luke 19:1–10) and in bereavement (John 11:1–44). The word for 'set free' (*aphesis*) can be used in the more general sense of 'discharge'; but it can also mean 'forgive', and Jesus' mission was to make forgiveness possible (see Matt. 26:27–28; Mark 2:1–12). He came 'to give his life as a ransom for many' (Mark 10:45), paying the price for our sins by his sacrificial death on the cross (2 Cor. 5:21; Gal. 3:13; 1 Pet. 1:18–19; 2:24; 3:18). The freedom Jesus offers is primarily a spiritual freedom.

Today many people speak about freedom in terms of living in a democracy rather than under a dictator. There is of course nothing about that in the teaching of Jesus. That is not to say that he did not identify with that part of the prophecy from Isaiah which saw the Servant's ministry as showing compassion and concern for the poor, the captive, the blind and the oppressed. But his primary purpose was setting people free from the bondage of sin and all its terrible consequences.

Few have described that inner experience of being 'set free' better than the hymn writer Charles Wesley:

> Long my imprisoned spirit lay
> Fast bound in sin and nature's night;
> Thine eye diffused a quickening ray –
> I woke, the dungeon flamed with light;
> My chains fell off, my heart was free,
> I rose, went forth, and followed Thee.
> (Charles Wesley, 1707–88)

So, 'if the Son [Jesus] sets you free, you will be free indeed' (John 8:36).

e. Responding to what God does for his people (15)

Nahum now pauses (15) to call upon God's people to respond to what God in his severity and goodness has done and will do. This verse also links the theological explanation of chapter 1 with the historical illustration of judgment in chapters 2 and 3.

Nahum has taught us that God in his severity will take *vengeance on his foes* (1:2b). He goes on to state that in God's goodness, he will be *a refuge in times of trouble* and that he *cares for those who trust in him* (7); he will defeat those who oppose him (8–12). In this concluding verse (15) he emphasizes again the importance of *completely* destroying *the wicked.*[48]

In his goodness God also disciplines those he has *afflicted* (12b) and sets free those who are in bondage (13). Divine judgment is an expression of God's severity and goodness. In his severity God always hates sin. As the prophet Habakkuk said to God, 'Your eyes are too pure to look on evil; you cannot tolerate wrongdoing' (Hab. 1:13). But equally Nahum insists that God is always good and a refuge to those who put their trust in him (7).

What, therefore, should be our response to all that God has done or will do for his people? Yahweh now clearly addresses Judah (15b), and makes a threefold call to his people to respond by rejoicing in good news, celebrating in worship, and fulfilling their promises.

i. Look to the messenger – a call to rejoice in good news (15a)

Most of us know what a relief it is to hear good news after a period of suffering, oppression or failure, when our spirits are likely to be very low. In Judah the oppression of the Assyrians must have broken the spirit of many of God's people. But now, at last, Nahum can point to some good news: *Look, there on the mountains, the feet of one who brings good news, who proclaims peace!* (15a).

The *mountains* may be those around Jerusalem, making the promise of *peace* very close. Or they may be a metaphor for a very public proclamation of this good news; it would not be done in a corner, or in secret. The mention of the *feet* of the messenger suggests someone who has travelled some distance, perhaps from the scene of battle and a famous victory. The heart of the message was *peace*, the word used being *šālôm*, which means much more than 'a ceasing from hostilities' or 'the ending of a conflict'.

[48] The word for 'wicked' is *Belial*, a name that was associated later with the spiritual power of wickedness behind the 'flesh and blood' enemies that were attacking God's people (2 Cor. 10:3–5; Eph. 6:11). See p. 118.

Šālôm is a word that conveys 'wholeness'. It embraces 'peace with God', and wholeness in relation to him; it conveys harmony in our relationships with other people, and peace within ourselves, described by the apostle Paul as 'the peace of God, which transcends all understanding' (Phil. 4:7); and it includes harmony with the environment.

By lifting our eyes to the messenger who brings *good news* (15), God is calling his people to rejoice in this message of peace, and all its implications, and to celebrate what God has done and will do for his people.

Isaiah used very similar language when he prophesied the deliverance of Israel from the Babylonians (Isa. 52:4–7). He used the word 'beautiful' to describe the feet of the messenger, because it is a beautiful and privileged ministry to bring good news to those in captivity; and whether God's people are delivered from the Egyptians (Exod. 12 – 14), the Assyrians (Nah. 1:13–15) or the Babylonians (Isa. 52:5–6), they are called to rejoice in God's mighty saving power. So the prophet Isaiah wrote:

> This is what the Sovereign LORD says:
>
> 'At first my people went down to Egypt to live;
> lately, Assyria has oppressed them . . .
>
> And all day long
> my name is constantly blasphemed.
> Therefore my people will know my name . . .
>
> How beautiful on the mountains
> are the feet of those who bring good news,
> who proclaim peace,
> who bring good tidings,
> who proclaim salvation,
> who say to Zion,
> "Your God reigns!"'
> (Isa. 52:4–7)

These acts of God's redemption in history all point to Christ's mighty act of redemption in his life, death, resurrection and exaltation. So the apostle Paul quoted these words from Nahum and Isaiah to promote the work of evangelism for the whole world, for Gentiles as well as Jews. He reminds the

Christians in Rome that 'Everyone who calls on the name of the Lord will be saved'. He then goes on to say:

> How, then, can they call on the one they have not believed in? And how can they believe in the one of whom they have not heard? And how can they hear without someone preaching to them? And how can anyone preach unless they are sent? As it is written: 'How beautiful are the feet of those who bring good news!'
> (Rom. 10:14–15)

Nahum's words about *the feet of one who brings good news, who proclaims peace*, point forward to salvation and peace beyond the deliverance from the Assyrians or even the Babylonians, to salvation in Christ and peace with God, and all that follows in the life of the Spirit. That's an encouragement to Christians to share this good news with others. It's also a challenge to Christians to support in prayer, giving, and other practical help, those who are engaged as evangelists in our own country, as well as those who are sent as missionaries with the gospel of peace to other nations. For as the apostle Paul wrote some 2,000 years ago: 'How can they hear without someone preaching to them? . . . As it is written: "How beautiful are the feet of those who bring good news!"'

ii. 'Celebrate your festivals' – a call to celebrate in worship (15b)

Nahum has been shown by God that a messenger is coming to bring news of victory over Assyria, with a message of peace. God calls his people not only to rejoice in the good news, but also to celebrate by reinstating worship services in the temple. *Celebrate your festivals, Judah* (15b).

This call to worship may be a call to the people to meet together before the messenger arrives, and while their dangers and problems are still unresolved. Sometimes a believer will cease to worship with other believers when he or she is going through difficulties in life. For example, someone might say after a bereavement in his family, 'I can't go back to church. I have so many doubts and problems, I would be a hypocrite if I did go back.' Or someone else might simply feel down and depressed about the circumstances of her life; and so, just when she needs the help of God's grace most, she keeps away from meeting God's people and receiving his grace and strength as she worships him. Through the sacrifices, the worship of Israel made available the grace of God for the people of God. For that reason Nahum called for God's people to celebrate their festivals. Jesus also called his disciples to meet together and to break bread 'in remembrance' of his death (Matt. 26:26–29; Mark 14:22–25; Luke 22:14–20; cf. 1 Cor. 11:23–25). He taught them to love, encourage and support one another (John 15:1–17; 17:20–26; cf. Acts 2:42). The writer to the Hebrews also urged Christians facing persecution

> to consider how we may spur one another on towards love and good deeds, not giving up meeting together, as some are in the habit of doing, but encouraging one another – and all the more as you see the Day approaching.
> (Heb. 10:24–25)

So Nahum urges God's people in Judah to reinstate their festivals and, therefore, to purify their worship, and to celebrate and give thanks to God for all he has done and will do for his people. The circumstances of their lives may be grim and traumatic at the moment; but peace and victory are round the corner. Nahum seems to be saying, 'Celebrate your festivals *now*!'

We do not know for certain what festivals Nahum has in mind. O. Palmer Robertson makes the helpful suggestion that

> Israel's three annual festivals and their new covenant counterparts might be considered as the natural vehicles by which God's people might give expression to their continuing joy in salvation. *The Passover Meal*, which finds its NT counterpart in the celebration of the Lord's Supper . . . *The festival of Pentecost*, which corresponds to the new covenant reality of the outpouring of the Holy Spirit . . . The fruit of the Spirit in a person's daily experience provides continual cause for celebration. *The harvest festival of Booths* reminds of the abundance of provision that God makes for his people, even as they continue along their pilgrim pathway.[49]

Nahum reminds us that God calls us to celebrate his mighty acts in corporate worship. We encourage one another as we do so (Heb. 10:24–25). In the new covenant 'festivals', we look back in remembrance and thanks

[49] Robertson, *The Books of Nahum, Habakkuk and Zephaniah*, p. 85 (italics mine).

for all that God has done for us in Christ, especially by his death for us on the cross (1 Cor. 11:17–34); we look up in gratitude to God for his daily provision of our needs, physical, material and spiritual (Phil. 4:19); and we look forward to his final victory over sin and evil and all that opposes God, which is signified by the promise here of the complete defeat of the Assyrian empire. *No more will the wicked [Belial] invade you; they will be completely destroyed* (15c).

Worship together in temple and church, however, must be followed by 'worship' and obedience in everyday life (Rom. 12:1–3). So God asks for a further response.

iii. 'Fulfil your vows' – a call to keep our promises (15b)

A friend of mine, who has now gone to heaven, told me some years ago that during the Second World War, when he was a soldier, he had made a promise to God. My friend was not a Christian then, but he promised the God he was not sure existed that he would search for the truth about him if he survived the war. He told me, smiling, that he was proof of the truth of the old adage that 'there are no atheists in the trenches'. His life was spared. When he went up to Oxford University after the war he kept the promise he had made to God. He fulfilled his vow. He read the Bible, sought out the truth of the gospel and became a committed Christian. He spent the rest of his life serving Christ within his profession and in his local church.

In Nahum's day, people also made promises and took vows. In Moses' day the people had corporately pledged obedience to God's law (Deut. 29 – 30). These were still binding on Judah. Individuals also made vows to God, sometimes before a battle; sometimes, no doubt, during it. One disastrous vow before a battle was taken by Jephthah, at the time of the judges in Israel (see Judg. 11). The book of Judges tells us:

> And Jephthah made a vow to the LORD: 'If you give the Ammonites into my hands, whatever comes out of the door of my house to meet me when I return in triumph from the Ammonites will be the LORD's, and I will sacrifice it as a burnt offering.'
> (Judg. 11:30–31)

The tragedy of this story is that the first person he met was his much-loved only daughter. One of the lessons from this tragic story is that we should be very careful what promises we make to God. In the book of Deuteronomy we read:

> If you make a vow to the LORD your God, do not be slow to pay it, for the LORD your God will certainly demand it of you and you will be guilty of sin. But if you refrain from making a vow, you will not be guilty.
> (Deut. 23:21–22)

In other words, don't make promises to God that you cannot keep; and in the light of the foolishness of Jephthah's promise, and its tragic ending, we should add that we should be quick to repent if and when we find that we have promised something we should not have promised. Scripture teaches us to be careful and thoughtful about what we say. Sometimes in the Christian church we expect congregations to sing songs that make promises to God which we may find it impossible to keep. We need to remember the words, 'Whatever your lips utter you must be sure to do, because you made your vow freely to the LORD your God with your own mouth' (Deut. 23:23).[50] That should warn us about careless speech and impossible promises. That should also make us quick to repent.

Keeping our vows and promises to God is important. Indeed practical obedience of this kind demonstrates the reality of our worship. The psalmist sums this up perfectly:

> LORD, who may dwell in your sacred tent?
>   Who may live on your holy mountain?
>
> The one whose way of life is blameless,
>   who does what is righteous,
>   who speaks the truth from their heart,
> whose tongue utters no slander . . .
> *who keeps an oath even when it hurts . . .*
>
> Whoever does these things
>   will never be shaken.
> (Ps. 15:1–5; emphasis mine)

[50] For a helpful treatment of the difficult story of the vow of Jephthah, see M. Wilcox, *The Message of Judges*, BST (IVP, 1992), pp. 117–120.

But what happens to those who refuse to walk in God's way, and turn their back on him? The theological answer lies in the just judgment of a God who is both severe and good. Nahum now presents us with a historical illustration of how that divine judgment works out in practice – in the destruction of Nineveh (Nah. 2; 3).

Nahum 2:1 – 3:19

5. Divine judgment: historically illustrated

1. The destruction of Nineveh – describing the action (2:1–13)

In the first section of his book Nahum has given a theological explanation of God's judgment as he has described the severity and goodness of God, and his dealings with the nations in general terms (ch. 1). Now he focuses on a particular illustration of divine judgment – the destruction of Nineveh, the capital of the superpower Assyria in the seventh century BC (ch. 2).

Nahum begins this chapter with a call to the citizens of Nineveh to prepare for their attacker (2:1), and a promise of deliverance for God's people (2). He then describes the attack on Nineveh (3–5), the destruction of the city (6–10) and the rout of the Assyrian army (11–13).

Nahum tells the story of the fall of Nineveh in a poetic and vivid way; and the message is clear. The Lord is behind these events in history. He is sovereign over all nations. *The LORD has given a command concerning you* (1:14) certainly applies to Nineveh. So Nahum describes what the Lord will do, and what in his sovereignty he has decreed. The fall of Nineveh is a classic illustration of divine judgment and retribution, and of the sovereignty of God in history.

There are a number of lessons that we can learn from this next section (ch. 2).

a. God's purposes will be fulfilled, however puzzling his actions (1)

It is easy to forget that Nahum is writing before the fall of Nineveh (612 BC). In normal circumstances the citizens of Nineveh would expect to defend their city without too much difficulty. The command to *Guard the fortress, watch the road, brace yourselves, marshal all your strength!* (1) would have been sufficient to see off any threat from the enemy. However, this time it is different. Nahum warns the Assyrians, *An attacker advances against you . . .* (1). In the first instance this refers to the combined forces of Babylonians, Medes and Scythians, who were to sweep through Mesopotamia, and eventually attack and destroy Nineveh in 612 BC; but, second, the *attacker* is surely a reference to the sovereign Lord, as the warrior king, who is coming to judge Nineveh because of her wickedness. Certainly, Nahum makes clear that Yahweh is *against* the Assyrians, and that he uses other nations as his instruments of judgment (13). All of this reminds us that although God's message may be blunt and severe, his goodness may be seen in his patience in warning those who face the certainty of destruction unless they repent. I recently saw a television programme retelling the story of the sinking of the *Titanic*. One of the reasons for that tragic disaster was the failure to heed warnings about dangerous icebergs. The warnings had been given but not heeded. Nineveh was not without its warnings of coming destruction as well. In our personal lives, too, God often warns us about the consequences of wrong choices, and shows us how we may avoid disaster. The psalmist puts it like this:

> How can a young person stay on the path of purity?
>   By living according to your word.
> I seek you with all my heart;
>   do not let me stray from your commands.
> I have hidden your word in my heart
>   that I might not sin against you.
> (Ps. 119:9–11)

There is a way to escape from God's retribution; and that is to read and obey God's Word and to heed its warnings. We need preachers like Nahum, who will bring a message not only of encouragement, but also of warning. The apostle Paul was quite clear about that when he wrote to Timothy, 'Preach the word; be prepared in season and out of season; correct, rebuke and encourage – with great patience and careful instruction' (2 Tim. 4:2).

Nahum's description of the destruction of Nineveh as part of God's purpose, however, does raise some puzzling questions.

i. Has not God already chosen Assyria to be his servant and his instrument to discipline Israel?

The answer to this question is 'yes'. Yahweh is free to choose any nation to be his instrument to further his purposes. The prophet Isaiah, for example, tells us that Yahweh calls Assyria and Egypt, as well as Israel, 'my people . . . my handiwork . . . my inheritance' – indicating his relationship to all nations (Isa. 19:23–25). Again, the prophet Isaiah describes Assyria as 'the rod' of God's anger, God's instrument to discipline Israel (Isa. 10:5, 15). This leads to another question.

ii. If Assyria is God's instrument to fulfil his purposes, why does God promise to destroy Assyria?

The answer to this question is that Assyria clearly went beyond the mandate that God gave her. Isaiah explained what happened when he wrote: 'Woe to the Assyrian, the rod of my anger . . . I send him against a godless nation . . . But this is not what he intends . . . his purpose is to destroy, to put an end to many nations' (Isa. 10:5–7).

Isaiah clearly recognizes the tension between the will of Yahweh, using Assyria as a just punishment, and the will of Assyria, acting out her own imperialist ambitions. Isaiah points out both the sinfulness of Assyria's motivation, and execution of the sovereign purposes of God. So God says:

> I will punish the king of Assyria for the wilful pride of his heart and the haughty look in his eyes. For he says:
>
> 'By the strength of my hand I have done this,
>   and by my wisdom, because I have understanding.
> I removed the boundaries of nations,
>   I plundered their treasures;
>   like a mighty one I subdued their kings.' . . .
>
> Does the axe raise itself above the person who swings it,
>   or the saw boast against the one who uses it?
> (Isa. 10:12–13, 15)

The story of the nations is often puzzling for both ancient and modern believers. But Isaiah and Nahum, and indeed all the biblical writers, are clear that Yahweh is sovereign over all nations. In his sovereignty he used

Assyria to discipline Israel; but Assyria was also responsible for the way she carried out that task. Alec Motyer explains helpfully:

> There is only one Agent and he does all things well. Under him, history is the outworking of moral providences. The Assyrian holocaust was not 'let loose' on the world. It was sent, directed where it was merited [Isa. 10:6], kept within heaven's limits; and in the end Assyria was punished for its excesses [Isa. 10:12].[1]

There's a warning here to nations such as the UK and the USA, and their allies. We might like to think that toppling a cruel dictator, such as Saddam Hussein in Iraq, was a way of bringing God's judgment on an evil regime.[2] But even if that were true, the teaching of Isaiah and Nahum about the motives and actions of Assyria, and her accountability to God, makes it clear that the leaders of the Coalition nations are also accountable to him. To be fair to him, Tony Blair, the British prime minister who took the UK to war with Iraq, has acknowledged his accountability; and I imagine that George W. Bush, the American president, would have agreed with him. The fact is that each one of us is accountable to God. As the apostle Paul wrote: 'It is written: "'As surely as I live,' says the Lord, 'every knee will bow before me; every tongue will acknowledge God.'" So then, each of us will give an account of ourselves to God' (Rom. 14:11–12).

So Yahweh, in his sovereignty, humbles one nation and exalts another. He uses Assyria to discipline Israel, and judges Assyria because she exceeds the mandate God gave her and acted with arrogance and greed. This leads us to another question that might puzzle us.

iii. Does this make Yahweh, in his sovereign acts, harsh and unloving?

As we read on in Nahum's prophecy and reflect on his description of the attack on Nineveh, there is much that reminds us of the horrors of warfare, both ancient and modern. For example, there is the overrunning of the city by enemy troops and chariots (3–4); the flooding of the city and the subsequent panic (6–10); the imagery of the savage lion and his activities, recalling the brutality of the Babylonian and Scythian troops against citizens as well as soldiers (11–13). It's the Assyrians who are the victims

---

1 J. A. Motyer, *The Prophecy of Isaiah* (IVP, 1993), p. 113.

2 Many people, Christians included, believed it was wrong to invade Iraq, and that the lack of any real plan to stabilize the situation after the invasion was even more regrettable and reprehensible.

of war here. Yahweh was *against* them (13), for reasons we have touched on. But did he love them? Did he care about them?

Nahum has already answered that question in the opening words of his book. *The Lord is slow to anger* (1:3) . . . *The Lord is good, a refuge in times of trouble. He cares for those who trust in him* (1:7). Furthermore, Yahweh's love is not confined to Israel. 'The Lord Almighty will bless them, saying, "Blessed be Egypt my people, Assyria my handiwork, and Israel my inheritance"' (Isa. 19:25; 56:3, 6–7; Amos 9:7). Again in the book of Jonah, as we have already noted, we are given a further glimpse into the heart of Yahweh, and see how much God loves Nineveh, and how readily he forgave her when she repented after the preaching of Jonah (Jon. 3). Yahweh is *slow to anger.* He was loving and patient towards Nineveh, and the Assyrian people she represented. However, when Nineveh no longer repented of her sins, went beyond the mandate Yahweh gave her, acting arrogantly and brutally against her enemies, Yahweh could no longer bless her. God was *against* her; and Nineveh received the just reward of her sins and her war crimes. We must never presume on the kindness of God.

So Nahum is clear in his teaching, with the other prophets, that Yahweh is sovereign over all the nations, and that he is working his purposes out, not only through Israel, but also through pagan nations such as Assyria and Babylon. Nahum's confidence that an *attacker* (2:1) will advance against Nineveh, and destroy it, is based on the assertion that *This is what the Lord says* (1:12). Later, the prophet Habakkuk will raise the question as to why the attacker of the Assyrians (the Babylonians and their allies) will then go on to attack and capture Jerusalem, taking many of God's people into exile. 'Why are you silent while the wicked swallow up those more righteous than themselves?' the prophet asks Yahweh (Hab. 1:13b). Judah had sinned, but surely the sins of the Babylonians were greater, Habakkuk suggests. Nahum doesn't ask that question, but his attitude of unquestioning faith in the sovereignty of God, and his confidence that a holy and just God will judge Assyria, is a lesson for us as well as for Nahum's contemporaries. Sometimes we may wonder why the evil actions of certain leaders and nations continue to flourish without any sign of a change. For years it seemed to be like that in Hitler's Germany, Stalin's Russia and Mao's China. Yet, by the end of the twentieth century, change had taken place in all three nations.

Sometimes we have to trust in God's sovereignty, and wait for his timing, even when we are puzzled by his actions and unclear about his purposes in a particular situation. Nahum clearly believed that, but it has rarely been better expressed than in the words of the prophet Habakkuk, in the climax of his prophecy:

> I will wait patiently for the day of calamity
> to come on the nation invading us.
> Though the fig-tree does not bud
> and there are no grapes on the vines,
> though the olive crop fails
> and the fields produce no food,
> though there are no sheep in the sheepfold
> and no cattle in the stalls,
> yet I will rejoice in the LORD,
> I will be joyful in God my Saviour.
> (Hab. 3:16–18)

God's actions may be puzzling, the circumstances of our lives may be grim and traumatic, yet Nahum and Habakkuk remind us that, in the words of an old hymn, 'God is working his purpose out, as year succeeds to year'.[3]

Before we look in more detail at the way in which Nineveh was taken and destroyed, however, we must note another side to this message of judgment. For we have already learnt from Nahum that the severity of God must be balanced by his goodness. Here again Nahum links the sovereign Lord's righteous acts of judgment with his merciful acts of restoration for those who put their trust in him (Nah. 1:7–15; 2:1–2).

b. God's people will be restored, however much they have suffered (2:2)

In Lindsay Brown's moving story of the history of the International Fellowship of Evangelical Students[4] there are many stories of Christian students suffering for Christ in countries that have suffered years of occupation and fighting. Time and time again it was the future hope of glory that sustained them in their suffering. For example, a young student in Vietnam wrote in a letter:

---

3 A. C. Ainger, 1841–1919.

4 L. Brown, *Shining Like Stars* (IVP, 2006).

> This is probably my last communication with IFES. Pray for me and the students and the church in Vietnam, for wisdom to face the coming trial. Our Lord has risen, we are going to suffer, to die and be raised up with him in glory . . .[5]

The people of God in Nahum's day also experienced deprivation and suffering due to enemy occupation and fighting. Their towns had been destroyed, and their livelihood taken away from them, for their vines had been ruined (2b). But Nahum had a message of hope for them: *The LORD will restore the splendour of Jacob like the splendour of Israel, though destroyers have laid them waste and have ruined their vines* (2).

We cannot be certain of Nahum's meaning. Possibly *Jacob* refers to Judah, the southern kingdom, and *Israel* the united kingdom as it was in the days of King David and his son Solomon. So Nahum may be predicting that in the future 'the divided and scattered people of God would be found united once more'.[6] On the other hand, the titles *Jacob* and *Israel* do not always refer in the prophets to the divided nation. Elijah, for example, refused to recognize the division when he built his altar on Mount Carmel with twelve stones (1 Kgs 18:31). The reference to laying waste to the land and ruining the vines might suggest the restoration of land and the return of economic prosperity; but surely Nahum is looking for a much deeper spiritual restoration? If we go back to the story of Jacob in the book of Genesis, we find the clearest clue to the meaning of this verse. 'Jacob' stands for the man, warts and all; 'Israel' stands for the man God intends him to be, the man restored by God's grace. So, does Nahum mean that the Lord promises to take his people as they are – like Jacob, truly belonging to God, mixed up, flawed in obedience and commitment, and not above sharp practices – and make them into Israel, the people of God as he intended them to be? The fulfilment of such a promise can be seen in the church, the followers of Jesus, the family of God, the continuing seed of Abraham (Gal. 3:29), the Israel of God (Gal. 6:14–16).

So Nahum offers hope for God's people in the midst of their suffering. The Lord promises to take them as *Jacob* with all the limitations and weaknesses that his name reflects, and to make them into *Israel*, restoring them and changing them 'from glory to glory' (2 Cor. 3:18, KJV).[7]

---

[5] Brown, *Shining Like Stars*, p. 52.

[6] J. L. Mackay, *Jonah, Micah, Nahum, Habakkuk, Zephaniah* (Christian Focus, 2005), p. 209.

[7] I am grateful to Alec Motyer for suggesting this line of interpretation.

Christians will see the ultimate fulfilment of this promise of restoration in the glory that is to come when believers will see Jesus face to face. The apostle John saw it like this:

> Dear friends, now we are children of God, and what we will be has not yet been made known. But we know that when Christ appears, we shall be like him, for we shall see him as he is. All who have this hope in him purify themselves, just as he is pure.
> (1 John 3:2–3)

In this one verse (2:2) the Lord promises his people hope, restoration and glory. Such a promise should lift our spirits when we face conflict, suffering and a feeling of hopelessness at the circumstances of our lives. Indeed the very sufferings we are enduring can contribute to the renewing and restoring of our lives (Rom. 5:1–5; Heb. 12:4–13; Jas 1:2–12). Nahum wants us to know that God's people will be restored, however much they have suffered.

c. God's enemies will be destroyed, however great their resources (2:3–10)

The description of the attack of the Babylonians, Medes and Scythians on the city of Nineveh is so vivid in these verses (2:3–10) that some might think that Nahum was an eyewitness, and that he was writing after the fall of Nineveh. Nahum, however, claims that this is his *vision* from the Lord (1:1).

In striking language he describes an attack of foot soldiers and chariots on Nineveh. The 'red' *shields* (3) may refer to bloodstained shields used in previous battles; or red could be the colour of the Babylonian army. *The warriors are clad in scarlet* suggests the bright colour of their uniforms; the detail about the metal on their chariots flashing in the sunlight, and the *spears of juniper* (3b), suggests some first-hand knowledge of the invaders from previous encounters; and the description of the *chariots* storming through the streets of the city, looking like *flaming torches* and darting about *like lightning* (cf. tanks in modern warfare), is vivid and dramatic.

How then would Nineveh cope with the invaders, and what can we learn from this vivid description of warfare?

I think the main lesson we should learn is that in spite of Nineveh's reputation for solid security and fabulous riches, her people were incapable of saving themselves from the armies of the Babylonians, Medes and Scythians, who had become God's instruments of judgment and retribution. When Nahum writes *Nineveh summons her picked troops* (5), he could well be referring to the advance guards of these armies, who *stumble* (5a) in their haste to overrun the city, and who dash to the city wall to put up *the protective shield* (5b) that would help them to ward off the missiles of the Assyrian defenders. Or Nahum could be referring to the Assyrian soldiers, who in spite of their reputation and their protective shield, were stumbling in panic as they took up their defensive positions. Either way, the Assyrians and Nineveh are looking decidedly vulnerable. Only repentance before God can ward off the judgment of God. Military strength (and in our day, even nuclear capability) is not able to frustrate the purposes of the sovereign Lord.

The strategy of the invading forces seemed to be to flood part of the city by opening the sluices or the *river gates* (6a). The river defence system was meant to ensure the security of Nineveh. It turned out to be the weak spot that provided an entrance into the city for the invading armies, and led to the collapse of the *palace* (6b). That in turn would lead to the end of effective leadership in Nineveh (6).

Nahum tells us that it *is decreed* (7) that the city's population be exiled and the captives taken away. After all, the Assyrians were expert at taking that action against other nations, including Israel. No doubt the Babylonian leaders announced the decree, but Nahum knows that it was the sovereign Lord who is behind it all (1:14). The fact is that Nineveh was ripe for judgment and retribution as the next few verses illustrate (7–10). Nahum has already told us that military strength won't save Nineveh. He now goes on to tell us that idols and money won't save her either.

The city's *female slaves moan like doves and beat on their breasts* (7b). Were these *female slaves* temple prostitutes? Certainly there were young women who worked in the temples of Assyrian gods. They were not carrying out sexual favours for financial gain, like prostitutes in our modern culture, but they were wholly devoted to their god. In the book of Genesis, a person carrying out a similar task (Gen. 38:21) is called a 'holy woman' – that is, belonging to the distinct sphere and service of some god. So the *moaning* of these women in Nineveh was not because their hope of financial gain was gone, but because their 'god' had failed them. They had devoted the whole of their lives to a god who in the end could not deliver them. They had turned their back on the one true God who could save them and satisfy them, and, according to the apostle Paul, they had no excuse. 'For since the creation of the world God's invisible qualities – his eternal power and divine nature – have been clearly seen, being understood from what has been made, so that people are without excuse' (Rom. 1:20).

According to the Bible there is no excuse for idolatry. Yet today we become devoted to our own idols as surely as these Assyrian women did; and the consequent sorrow, disappointment and shame will be much the same. It is easy to point the finger at other people when we are looking for modern examples of idolatry. We see people making idols of their home or family or work or pleasure, and, being devoted to them at the expense of love for God and love for other people, they find that they are disillusioned and dissatisfied. When we worship the creature instead of the Creator, judgment follows (Rom. 1:18–25). If we sow to the flesh (that is, to our own selfish desires), we shall reap corruption (Gal. 6:7–10). But those of us who are involved in Christian ministry can also have our idols. I remember visiting a retired clergyman who had spent at least forty years in one parish, and then found on retirement that he had nothing to live for any more. As I listened to his story, it seemed as if he had devoted himself to the 'god' of 'religious activity' rather than to the living Lord. Once the 'religious activity' had been taken from him, his whole world collapsed; he felt deep depression. Like the Assyrian slaves, he *moaned* with a sense of deep disillusionment. I found myself thinking about the words of the apostle Paul: 'If you think you are standing firm, be careful that you don't fall' (1 Cor. 10:12). Idolatry was one reason for the destruction of Nineveh. The Assyrians thought their idols were sources of strength: they found them to be, as the female slaves discovered, a reason for overwhelming disappointment and ultimate destruction.[8]

For many people, money can easily become a 'god', and materialism is one of the most destructive idols of our age in the developed world. Nahum seems to be referring to the failure of money and other resources of wealth to deliver Nineveh when he picks up again the theme of water. *Nineveh is like a pool whose water is draining away* (8). Perhaps Nahum is using the image of a pool full of water to suggest the resources and riches that the Assyrians had plundered from nations they had defeated and exploited. But now, before the sovereign Lord, the pool was draining away. First, the

---

[8] NB: For further discussion of idolatry, see Ps. 115:2–8; Isa. 44:6–23.

people were trying to escape from the enemy on their doorstep; and however much the leaders in Nineveh tried to prevent the exodus by calling out 'Stop! Stop!', no-one turned back (8b). Then Nahum describes how the wealth that they had stolen from others was taken from them. It was described as *endless* (9b), but in fact it all disappeared (10).

Money cannot save us either; nor does it solve all our problems. Jesus warned his disciples about the dangers of putting our trust in riches. He said:

> Do not store up for yourselves treasures on earth, where moths and vermin destroy, and where thieves break in and steal. But store up for yourselves treasures in heaven, where moths and vermin do not destroy, and where thieves do not break in and steal. For where your treasure is, there your heart will be also.
> (Matt. 6:19–21)

In recent years the world has faced multiple economic crises, a credit crunch and a deep recession, with large banks closing down and financial traders in panic mode. Never have the words of the apostle Paul seemed so relevant:

> Command those who are rich in this present world not to be arrogant nor to put their hope in wealth, *which is so uncertain*, but to put their hope in God, who richly provides us with everything for our enjoyment.
> (1 Tim. 6:17; emphasis mine)

Assyria's people had long moved away from their state of repentance following the preaching of Jonah. They had become complacent and put their trust in idols and wealth seized from other nations. Through God's revelation to Nahum, the prophet sees the certain end to such complacency and arrogance. Nineveh must be *pillaged, plundered, stripped!* The people are terrified. *Hearts melt, knees give way, bodies tremble, every face grows pale* (10).

God is no respecter of reputations. He doesn't judge a superpower according to its wealth or military strength. God looks on the hearts of people, not on the outward appearance. So where he sees evil, God punishes it. There's a present activity of judgment where God gives people over to their sinful desires, with all the consequences that inevitably follow. The apostle Paul explained this in describing the corrupting behaviour of the Roman empire:

> Therefore God gave them over in the sinful desires of their hearts to sexual impurity for the degrading of their bodies with one another. They exchanged the truth about God for a lie, and worshipped and served created things rather than the Creator – who is for ever praised. Amen. (Rom. 1:24–25)

But there is also a future judgment when evil will finally be destroyed. The overthrow and destruction of Nineveh is a pointer to that final day of victory. On that day, according to John's vision in the book of Revelation, Jesus will come to claim final victory over all evil. This is how John describes it:

> I saw heaven standing open and there before me was a white horse, whose rider is called Faithful and True. With justice he judges and wages war. His eyes are like blazing fire, and on his head are many crowns. He has a name written on him that no one knows but he himself. He is dressed in a robe dipped in blood, and his name is the Word of God. The armies of heaven were following him, riding on white horses and dressed in fine linen, white and clean. Coming out of his mouth is a sharp sword with which to strike down the nations. 'He will rule them with an iron sceptre.' He treads the winepress of the fury of the wrath of God Almighty. On his robe and on his thigh he has this name written:
>
> KING OF KINGS AND LORD OF LORDS.
>
> (Rev. 19:11–16)

In the end, God's enemies will be destroyed, however great their resources. The destruction of Nineveh offers hope to all who see no end to the oppression of their foes and the power of evil. Jesus reigns. His victory is certain.

d. God's word will be vindicated, however confident human boasting (2:11–13)

In one of his commentaries, Dale Ralph Davis recounts the story of the destruction of the home of one of the great boasters of the Nazi regime, Hermann Goering. He wrote:

> On Hitler's birthday, April 20th 1945, Reichsmarschall Hermann Goering stood outside his castle and estate fifty miles west of Berlin. This was Karinhall – the repository of Goering's unquenchable appetite for opulence and luxury. Anyone with eyes could see that the Third Reich was being flushed down the historical drain. So Goering was getting out. Twenty four Luftwaffe trucks lined the road outside Karinhall; they were stuffed with the antiques, paintings and silver Goering hoped to salvage. The convoy was making a break for the south. Goering swept a last view over the wings and buttresses of his huge castle. An engineering officer indicated all was ready. Goering walked across the road, grabbed the handle of a detonator, and pushed the plunger. Karinhall exploded into a mass of rubble.

Davis commented: 'That is where all the pride, arrogance, swaggering and greed ends . . . at the plunger of a detonator.'[9]

Nahum has been describing a situation which is not unlike the end of the Nazi empire, with all its arrogance, cruelty and boasting. The imagery of the lions (11–12) aptly describes the cruelty of the Assyrians. Nineveh is likened to *the lions' den* (11), where the young lions were fed and felt secure. It's a picture that suggests the security and strength of the citizens of Nineveh, provided for by the powerful Assyrian army. However, that security and absence of *fear* (11b) was achieved by the cruellest of means. Just as a lion *killed enough for his cubs and strangled the prey for his mate, filling his lairs with the kill and his dens with the prey* (12), so the Assyrian armies savaged their foes, exploited their lands for loot, and made themselves rich at the expense of other more vulnerable nations.

The imagery of the *lion* was an appropriate one for the Assyrians. It was an image that was often found on stone reliefs commissioned by Assyrian kings. Palmer Robertson points out that the kings of Nineveh often described their actions in terms of lion behaviour. '"I am lion brave," claimed one ruler, Ashernaserpal. "Like a lion I raged," boasted King Sennacherib.'[10]

Certainly the kings of Assyria did not hesitate to boast of their cruelty and their war crimes in their description of Assyrian victories. Much the

---

[9] D. R. Davis, *2 Samuel: Looking on the Heart* (Christian Focus, 2004), p. 186; Davis quotes from C. Ryan, *The Last Battle* (Simon & Schuster, 1966), pp. 402–403.

[10] See footnote in O. P. Robertson, *The Books of Nahum, Habakkuk and Zephaniah*, NICOT (Eerdmans, 1990), p. 95.

same happened in Hitler's Third Reich when the Nazis kept meticulous records of the Holocaust and other war crimes. King Ashurbanipal, for example, boasts of horrendous bestiality in the treatment of prisoners:

> They suspended their corpses from poles, tore their skin off and affixed it to the city walls. I let dogs, swine, wolves, vultures, the birds of the heavens and the sweet water-fish devour their cut off limbs . . . the people who lived in the city, and had not come out, and had not acknowledged my rule, I slew . . . I chopped off their heads and cut off their lips.[11]

There is much more boasting along these same inhumane lines. The tragedy is that humankind is so infected by sin and wickedness that every generation repeats these kinds of inhumane actions in war and also in times of peace. It is good that organizations such as Amnesty International draw attention to war crimes and to the breaching of human rights; but it is only the gospel of Jesus Christ that has the power to change lives and to forgive sins.

Nineveh has been called 'the concentrated centre of evil in the ancient world'. But Nahum asks, looking ahead to the fall of Nineveh and the defeat of the Assyrian army, *Where now is the lions' den?* Where has all the strength and savage power of the Assyrians gone? Nahum is so sure that it will be gone that he writes as if it has already happened and the word of the Lord Almighty (or the Lord of Hosts) has brought it about. For it is the Lord of Hosts who declares:

> *I am against you . . .*
> *I will burn up your chariots in smoke,*
> *and the sword will devour your young lions.*
> *I will leave you no prey on the earth.*
> *The voices of your messengers*
> *will no longer be heard.*
> (13)

Nahum describes Yahweh as 'the Lord of Hosts' only twice in his prophecy (2:13; 3:5; NIV has *the LORD Almighty*). Yahweh's greatness is to

[11] Selections from the Annals of Ashurbanipal, as cited by W. A. Maiar, *The Book of Nahum: A Commentary* (Concordia, 1959), and quoted in Robertson, *The Books of Nahum, Habakkuk and Zephaniah*, p. 99.

be seen in contrast to the Assyrian gods who are made by human hands. But the translation 'Lord of Hosts'[12] suggests a further thought. This phrase can mean 'possessing every potentiality and power'. He is the Lord, who in his own nature is not in fact a bare 'one', but a multiplicity in unity. The 'Hosts' within the divine nature are in fact the persons of the Trinity: Father, Son and Holy Spirit. They are incognito in the Old Testament, but revealed in the New Testament. This makes the progression from the Old Testament to the New a sharpening of the focus, as the prologue to John's Gospel and other New Testament passages make clear (Matt. 28:19–20; John 1:14; 14:15–21).

So it is the triune God – Father, Son and Holy Spirit – who says to the evil superpower that Assyria had become, *I am against you* (13); and when God speaks, his word is effective. He promises Nineveh, *I will burn up your chariots in smoke, and the sword will devour your young lions. I will leave you no prey on the earth* (13b). And that is exactly what happened. God spoke, and it was done. God is faithful in keeping his promises of judgment and retribution as well as his promises of salvation. Furthermore, God says, *The voices of your messengers will no longer be heard* (13c). The Assyrians loved to mock their enemies. This has a modern ring about it, even in countries such as the UK and the USA – where there is a Christian presence, and where in the past the culture has been strongly Christian. The mocking of the church, and even on occasions the mocking of Jesus Christ in films and on television, has become a feature of our increasingly secular societies. So, is the promise that the *voices of your messenger will no longer be heard* (13c) a reference to the way in which Sennacherib's men mocked Jerusalem with their taunts in the days when Hezekiah was the king of Judah? The field commander of the Assyrian army sent a message to King Hezekiah and God's people which included these boastful and arrogant words:

> Do not listen to Hezekiah, for he is misleading you when he says, 'The Lord will deliver us.' Has the god of any nation ever delivered his land from the hand of the king of Assyria? . . . How then can the Lord deliver Jerusalem from my hand?
> (2 Kgs 18:32–33, 35)

[12] I am grateful to Alec Motyer for drawing my attention to this interpretation of 'The Lord of Hosts' as expounded by G. A. F. Knight, *A Biblical Approach to the Doctrine of the Trinity*, Scottish Journal of Theology Occasional Papers, no. 1 (Oliver & Boyd, 1953).

Hezekiah's response was to put his trust in Yahweh's word, for Isaiah had told him:

> This is what the LORD, the God of Israel, says: I have heard your prayer concerning Sennacherib king of Assyria. This is the word that the LORD has spoken against him . . .
>
> Because you rage against me
>   and because your insolence has reached my ears,
> I will put my hook in your nose
>   and my bit in your mouth,
> and I will make you return
>   by the way you came.
>
> (2 Kgs 19:20–21, 28)

It was the word of God that prevailed, as it always does. God's word will always be vindicated, in contrast to the arrogant words of human beings. Yahweh speaks through Nahum and says to Nineveh: *The voices of your messengers will no longer be heard* (13c). In the end it is God's word that triumphs; the mocking arrogance of those who oppose him and his people will finally be silenced. Remember Sennacherib. Remember Hitler and Goering. *Where now is the lions' den?*

So Nahum has helped us to learn some important lessons from his description of the fall of the superpower Assyria. We have noted that God's purposes will be fulfilled in history, however puzzling God's actions may sometimes be. We have learned that God's people can be restored, however much they have suffered, and that God's enemies will finally be destroyed, however great their strength and resources. Finally we have learned that God's word will be vindicated, however confident human boasting may be. Once more Nahum is bringing us a message of judgment on evil, and hope and restoration for those who put their trust in the Lord. But there is still more to learn about the reasons for such severe judgment. It is to that consideration we must now turn.

2. The judgment of Nineveh – understanding the reasons (3:1–11)

We have already seen that the message of Nahum is predominantly one of divine judgment. But he is no mere demagogue shouting denunciations in the public square. On the contrary he offers calm statements and reasoned arguments; and his book should be read in that spirit. He has already presented an argued case for judgment on the citizens of Nineveh. The Lord is *against* them (3:5) because, for example, they are animated by an 'anti-God' spirit (see 1:9). That is not to say that they desire an atheistic society; but they are against Yahweh, the God of Israel. They would be at home, I imagine, in the multicultural UK, which often feels ill at ease with the first commandment, 'You shall have no other gods before me' (Deut. 5:7). It is even more embarrassed by the words of Jesus, 'I am the way and the truth and the life. No one comes to the Father except through me' (John 14:6). The Assyrians rejected Yahweh and his exclusive claims, but were happy to worship as many other 'gods' as people wanted.

So the Assyrians were perfectly happy with religion (1:14); but not with a holy God, who makes demands, seeks personal devotion and offers salvation (1:15). Queen Victoria's prime minister, Lord Melbourne, is supposed to have said, 'Things have come to a pretty pass when religion is seeking to invade a man's private life.' But, as Nahum makes plain, that is part of the essence of biblical religion. It is also that part of religion which is most criticized and condemned by non-Christian and post-Christian societies. But for Nahum the Lord is *against* those whose religion does not lead to the worship of the true and only God, and to a life of obedience (2:13).

The Assyrians also believed in a strong economy, and a defence programme that would keep their citizens secure and prosperous. But the Lord was *against* them because they were motivated by imperialist intentions and greed, and acted with extreme cruelty. They had attacked the people of God, and taken away the freedom of some of them (1:13); and they had ruined their means of livelihood (2:2). They had stolen the treasures of other nations, and they had lived up to their national image (the lion), by treating their enemies in bestial and savage ways.

We cannot be certain, of course, whether the Assyrian kings exaggerated their claims to act cruelly so as to impress their enemies. But according to Julie Woods[13] the Assyrian reliefs show

> bodies impaled on sticks, tongues being cut out, people being led by lip rings, heads being carried and piled up, dismembered bodies with

[13] J. Woods, 'The West as Nineveh: How Does Nahum's Message of Judgement Apply to Today?', *Themelios* 31.1 (October 2005), p. 16.

scattered limbs and severed heads serving as ornamental decorations on walls and structures and totem poles made of human heads.

No wonder Nahum anticipates the reaction of most people to the destruction of Nineveh with these words: *All who hear the news about you clap their hands at your fall, for who has not felt your endless cruelty?* (3:19).

As Nahum comes towards the end of his *prophecy concerning Nineveh* (1:1), what more can he say about the sins of the city which so offend Yahweh? Why does Nineveh, and the whole Assyrian empire, deserve such severe judgment?

a. God is against aggressive behaviour (3:1–3)

Although the book of Nahum is about the attack of the Babylonians on Nineveh, so that the Assyrians are the victims in this description of war, the phrase *the city of blood* (3:1) refers to the bloodthirstiness of the Assyrians (*of blood* is literally 'of bloods', the plural in Hebrew signifying 'blood shed by violence'[14]). In the sovereign purpose of God the Assyrians were used to discipline Israel. But they had far exceeded the mandate God gave them, and had become aggressive and cruel in attacking not only Israel but other smaller nations as well. It is because of her aggression that Nineveh is called *the city of blood*. She had been so aggressive that Nahum describes her as *full of plunder, never without victims!* (3:1; see also 2:12). The picture Nahum paints is one of a nation eager and glad to be at war with neighbouring nations – 'trigger happy', as we might say. Nahum may well be describing in these next few verses what will happen when the Babylonians attack the people of Nineveh. But it will only happen to them because they have done the same to others. *The crack of whips, the clatter of wheels, galloping horses and jolting chariots! Charging cavalry, flashing swords and glittering spears!* (2–3). But war is not a game; there's a cost in human lives when one nation invades another. Nahum reports the cost of aggressive action against another nation as a kind of news headline: *Many casualties, piles of dead, bodies without number, people stumbling over the corpses . . .* (3). Every time we see a similar report flashing across our television screens after a terrorist bomb attack in Iraq, or a Russian missile barrage on a Ukrainian city, we need to remember the human cost of such warfare.

---

[14] Mackay, *Jonah, Micah, Nahum, Habakkuk, Zephaniah*, p. 220.

This is not the place to enter into a long discussion on pacifism. But Christians who are prepared to serve in the armed forces usually try to apply those tests that make the case for a 'just war'. In Dr John Stott's book *Issues Facing Christians Today*[15] he reduces the seven traditional conditions[16] for a 'just war' to three. His three are:

1. Its cause must be righteous. It must be defensive, not aggressive. Its objective must be to secure justice, to protect the innocent and to champion human rights. Stott continues, 'Just causes are not served by unjust motives. So there must be no hatred, no animosity, no thirst for revenge.'
2. Its means must be controlled. Stott argues that there must be no wanton or unnecessary violence. 'Action must be proportionate.'
3. Its outcome must be predictable. Stott writes, 'There must be a calculated prospect of victory and so of achieving the just cause for which the war was begun.'

In private correspondence Alec Motyer points out that

> the only truly just war ever attempted was in the Garden of Gethsemane when Peter drew the sword in defence of Jesus, only to be told 'Those who draw the sword will perish by the sword' – surely implying that in human hands 'just war' is impossible.

There is still a need, in my view, to consider how 'just' a cause is before embarking on any kind of action using force of arms. The use of force can be 'relatively just' and is sometimes the least of two evils.

It is difficult to apply these principles to the specially sanctioned wars commanded and directed by Yahweh. For one thing, no-one today can claim to enjoy Israel's privileged position as a 'holy nation', God's covenant people, a theocracy. But the Bible makes it clear that Assyria was God's instrument in disciplining Israel, and yet she clearly went beyond the mandate that God gave her. For that she was judged.

---

15 J. R. W. Stott, *Issues Facing Christians Today* (Marshall Pickering, 1990), p. 88.

16 The seven are: formal declaration; last resort; just cause; right intention; proportionate means; non-combatant immunity; and reasonable expectation.

In the light of God's revelation in his Word (including the book of Nahum), the Western nations, including the UK and the superpower America, do need to be warned against aggressive trigger-happy wars against other nations, especially when the desire for oil or other kinds of wealth can so easily become the chief motivation. Nineveh and the Assyrian superpower were judged because of their aggressive behaviour. On an international, national and even personal level we need to be warned that God is against such behaviour. We are all accountable to the Lord who is sovereign over all nations.

b. God is against deceitful behaviour (3:1)

Another characteristic of a nation that deserves the judgment of God is that of lying or deceitfulness. Nazi Germany, with its lying propaganda under the direction of the notorious Dr Goebbels, is a twentieth-century example of that. But Western nations today are sometimes guilty of untruthful propaganda or dishonest spin; and our Western culture is deeply engrained with deceit. This was well illustrated in an article in the *Times* newspaper by Mark Henderson.[17] Henderson wrote:

> The country is experiencing a white collar crime wave created by solid citizens who do not consider themselves to be dishonest, but think nothing of padding insurance claims, dodging tax with cash-in-hand payments, cheating each other in second-hand deals and stealing from their employers.
>
> Almost two-thirds of adults in England and Wales admit to indulging in minor fraud but rarely think their behaviour is criminal, a study at Keele University has revealed. They are also its victims; 73% have been cheated themselves, most commonly by supermarkets, holiday operators, restaurants and second-hand traders . . . the respectable dishonest now damage the economy almost five times more than burglars. In 2000 the cost of burglary was £2.7 billion as against £13.8 billion for fraud.
>
> A predatory dishonesty has become so deeply rooted in the psyche of middle class Britain that many otherwise honest people are quite happy even to cheat their peers . . .[18]

[17] Friday, 12 September 2003.

[18] The *Times* article is based on research carried out by Stephen Farrall and Susanne Kardstedt at Keele University and presented to the British Association for the Advancement of Science Festival on Thursday, 11 September 2003.

God hates deceitful behaviour, Nahum teaches us. Nineveh deserved the judgment of God because it was a *city of blood, full of lies* (3:1). London, New York, Paris and other great cities may also deserve God's judgment today; and all of us, as individuals, need to examine our own hearts, so that we speak and reflect truth, not lies.

However, the 'expenses scandal' among Members of Parliament in the UK and in Europe, in 2009, and 'Partygate' in 2021–22 involving the British prime minister and his staff, were further examples of the deceitfulness of the human heart. The erosion of trust in the whole political system in the UK is a consequence of the deceitful actions of many, though not all, of the Members of Parliament from all political parties. The churches in the UK have become so marginalized that their comments and example have made little impact and their opinions are rarely sought.

The apostle Paul wrote to the Christians in Ephesus to remind them, among other things, that truth, not lies, should characterize their lives in Christ:

> You were taught, with regard to your former way of life, to put off your old self, which is being corrupted by its deceitful desires; to be made new in the attitude of your minds; and to put on the new self, created to be like God in true righteousness and holiness.
>
> Therefore each of you must put off falsehood and speak truthfully to your neighbour, for we are all members of one body.
> (Eph. 4:22–25)

God's people must bear witness to the truth. It's easy to point the finger at others. We must examine ourselves. For God is against deceitful behaviour.

c. God is against shameful behaviour (3:4–7)

The aggression and deceitfulness of Nineveh arose out of sinful and selfish motives that led to still more unspeakable and shameful actions. God likens Nineveh to a prostitute selling her wares to anyone who can be enticed and brought under her influence. She lusted after the wealth of other nations. She used any method, however evil, to seduce and exploit people. This included witchcraft and the occult (4). Thousands of tablets have been uncovered in the Mesopotamian valley which show how much the Assyrians were in the grip of the occult. Hundreds of incantations have come to light. Astrology flourished. Amulets associated with moths, birds, pigs, scorpions, cows, rats, dogs, sheep, hens and even grasshoppers were worn by many to ward off evil spirits.

However, it was the end result of idolatry and the occult which was the most shameful aspect of Assyria's behaviour. She *enslaved nations by her prostitution and peoples by her witchcraft* (4b). Assyria's aim was to enslave and exploit other people for her own selfish gain; and she stooped very low to achieve this in a most inhumane way. Here is what one Assyrian king boasted:

> 3000 captives I burned with fire . . . their young men and maidens I burned in the fire . . . from some I cut off their hands and their fingers. From others I cut off their noses, their ears and their fingers; of many I put out their eyes . . .[19]

It was the inhumane and shameful actions of the Assyrians that brought this strong condemnation from the Lord: *I am against you* (5). And Yahweh doesn't mince his words to Nineveh. Has she, like some common prostitute, lifted her skirts to entice others to her? Then, says Yahweh, *I will lift your skirts over your face. I will show the nations your nakedness and the kingdoms your shame* (5). In other words, the Lord promises to show the nations what Nineveh is really like. Again, have the Assyrians shown contempt for their enemies, and pelted them with filth? Then, says the Lord, *I will pelt you with filth, I will treat you with contempt and make you a spectacle* (6).

God's judgment of us, though crudely expressed here, is like that. The punishment fits the crime – for God will act with perfect justice. God sees us as we really are. The light of his holiness exposes the darkness in our lives. As the writer to the Hebrews put it, 'Nothing in all creation is hidden from God's sight. Everything is uncovered and laid bare before the eyes of him to whom we must give account' (Heb. 4:13). Or, as Jesus taught, 'There is nothing hidden that will not be disclosed, and nothing concealed that will not be known or brought out into the open' (Luke 8:17).

Some years ago, my brother-in-law, Richard Bewes, was leading a boys' camp at which many of the boys attending had very little, if any, Christian background. As Richard passed by one of the tents during a Bible-study

---

[19] From a document describing the first twenty-eight years of Ashurneserpal II, 885–860 BC, quoted in J. M. Boice, *The Minor Prophets*, vol. 2: *Micah to Malachi* (Zondervan, 1983, 1986), p. 68.

session, he heard the leader point out from the passage the truth that 'God sees all we do'. 'If that's the case,' he said to the children, 'what should we do about sinning?' In a flash one boy blurted out, 'Do it behind 'is back!'

But that is one thing we can't do! God does see all we do; and the day of judgment, as for Nineveh here, will reveal all and show us as we really are. This clearly applies to individuals as well as to nations. So we would do well to have the same spiritual ambition as the apostle Paul, who longed to 'be found in him [Jesus], not having a righteousness of my own that comes from the law, but that which is through faith in Christ – the righteousness that comes from God on the basis of faith' (Phil. 3:9).

Nahum teaches us, however, that God is also against the shameful behaviour of nations. Julie Woods,[20] in her helpful article on the book of Nahum, points out:

> The fact that Nahum does not talk to an individual till the end of the book, but to a nation, may well indicate that God is concerned with nations . . . Atrocities committed in the name of a nation appear to bring judgment on the whole nation.

She goes on to argue that 'abuse of power and injustice does not always take the form of brutal murders and tortures'. She gives other examples of injustice:

> The wealthiest fifth of nations dispose of 84.7% of the world's GNP, its citizens account for 84.2% of world trade and possess 85.5% of savings in domestic accounts . . . In the 1960s there was general optimism that poverty could be eliminated with the correct agricultural programmes. But since 1960 the gap between the richest and the poorest fifth of nations has more than doubled.

She concludes, 'If we were to examine honestly what has led to this state of affairs, we would have to conclude that it can be summed up in two words – power and greed.'

So the powerful nations of today, as with Assyria in Nahum's day, need to see themselves as God sees them. We too are guilty of greed and lust for

---

[20] Woods, 'The West as Nineveh', p. 22.

power, as was Nineveh; and greed and power often lead to shameful behaviour. In the case of Nineveh God was ready to act in judgment. All would see it. So God says to Nineveh, *All who see you will flee from you and say, 'Nineveh is in ruins – who will mourn for her?'* (7). In the light of her shameful behaviour, God is only able to add the sad words, *Where can I find anyone to comfort you?* (7c).

It is true to say that God loves us with infinite patience, and that, as Nahum has already taught us, he is *slow to anger* (1:3). Nineveh had turned her back on Yahweh so completely, and had behaved so abominably, that no-one sought to support her. It seems too that God had given her up to her sinful lifestyle, as she no longer showed any signs of repentance. As the apostle Paul said of another corrupt society, Rome: 'God gave them over in the sinful desires of their hearts to sexual impurity . . . They exchanged the truth about God for a lie, and worshipped and served created things rather than the Creator' (Rom. 1:24–25). It's a solemn warning for us all.

d. God is against arrogant behaviour (3:8–11)

It was the prophet Isaiah who expressed most clearly the arrogance, complacency and self-sufficiency of the Assyrians when they were still a superpower. Isaiah prophesied:

> When the Lord has finished all his work against Mount Zion and Jerusalem, he will say, 'I will punish the king of Assyria for the wilful pride of his heart and the haughty look in his eyes. For he says:
>
> '"By the strength of my hand I have done this,
> and by my wisdom, because I have understanding.
> I removed the boundaries of nations,
> I plundered their treasures;
> like a mighty one I subdued their kings.
> As one reaches into a nest,
> so my hand reached for the wealth of the nations;
> as people gather abandoned eggs,
> so I gathered all the countries;
> not one flapped a wing,
> or opened its mouth to chirp."'
>
> (Isa. 10:12–14)

Zephaniah's comment on Nineveh was even more succinct: 'This is the city of revelry that lived in safety. She said to herself, "I am the one! And there is none besides me"' (Zeph. 2:15).

In this passage Nahum seeks to prick the balloon of Assyrian arrogance by reminding Nineveh of some lessons from history. In 663 BC the Assyrian army had ransacked the Egyptian city of Thebes. So Nahum asks the Assyrians in Nineveh, *Are you better than Thebes?* (8). In other words, has it not occurred to you that Thebes, with its strong position on the River Nile (in the south of Egypt), its natural water defences and its powerful allies (such as Cush, Put and Libya), is similar in strength to Nineveh itself, and yet was completely overrun by the Assyrians! *Are you better than Thebes, situated on the Nile, with water around her? The river was her defence, the waters her wall. Cush* [Ethiopia] *and Egypt were her boundless strength. Put* [Somalia] *and Libya were among her allies* (8–9).

Thebes was also regarded as a sacred city of Egypt, 'founded on primeval waters' (Eaton). But like Nineveh, which also trusted in other gods, Thebes, for all her apparent strength and security, was completely defeated by the Assyrians and overrun. Notice the way that Nahum describes that massive defeat: *Yet she was taken captive and went into exile. Her infants were dashed to pieces at every street corner. Lots were cast for her nobles, and all her great men were put in chains* (10). The resources and fame of Thebes, and her religion, were not able to spare her a bloody war and an overwhelming defeat. They did not prevent babies being killed, or leaders and distinguished citizens being sent into captivity (10). So Nahum asks, *Are you better than Thebes?* (8).

We too need to learn the lessons of history. Great nations rise and fall. That was true for Egypt, Assyria, Babylon, Persia, Greece and Rome. In the twentieth century we saw the rise and fall of Hitler's Third Reich, Stalin's Soviet Union and Mao's China. We have seen similar 'judgments' on Pol Pot's Cambodia, Amin's Uganda and Mugabe's Zimbabwe, to name but a few arrogant and cruel regimes. Mary, the mother of Jesus, reminds us that in history, God 'has performed mighty deeds with his arm; he has scattered those who are proud in their inmost thoughts. He has brought down rulers from their thrones but has lifted up the humble' (Luke 1:51–52).

So God is against arrogance and self-sufficiency, whether found in Nineveh or Thebes, Berlin or Moscow, Shanghai or Phnom Penh, Kampala or Harare, New York or London – or anywhere in God's world. Nineveh was no better than Thebes when it came to her behaviour in the sight of a holy God. So, in spite of her apparent invincibility, like Thebes she was soon to fall. *You too will become drunk; you will go into hiding and seek refuge from the enemy* (11). To *become drunk* may well refer to drinking the cup of God's wrath (Ps. 75:6–8). In the judgment that was soon to come, the proud, arrogant Assyrians would be hiding from their enemies and drinking from the cup of God's wrath.

Nahum's picture of the defeated Assyrians as panicking refugees (11b) was in fact an accurate one. After the Medes and Babylonians had assaulted and captured Nineveh in 612 BC, the city was destroyed by fire. A number of Assyrians went into hiding and escaped to Haran (250 miles west of Nineveh); but there was no lasting security there. They were defeated by the Babylonians in 610 BC and again in the battle of Carchemish in 605 BC. That battle 'eliminated the last vestiges of Assyrian presence in the Fertile Crescent'.[21] Both for Thebes and Nineveh, their leaders sought to *go into hiding and seek refuge from the enemy* (11). But they found no lasting security, nor could they escape the just judgment of God.

God is against aggressive, deceitful, shameful and arrogant behaviour – and all of that was to be found in Nineveh, among the Assyrians. But what about ourselves? Do we not act sometimes with the same kind of self-sufficiency, boasting of the money that we will make and the plans we will carry out? The apostle James warned the first-century Christians of similarly arrogant attitudes. Perhaps he had businesspeople in mind when he wrote:

> Now listen, you who say, 'Today or tomorrow we will go to this or that city, spend a year there, carry on business and make money.' Why, you do not even know what will happen tomorrow. What is your life? You are a mist that appears for a little while and then vanishes.
> (Jas 4:13–14)

We easily forget how short life is; how it disappears as suddenly as the morning mist. And we need to remember, as the writer to the Hebrews put it, that 'people are destined to die once, and after that to face judgment' (Heb. 9:27). God judges the proud and arrogant. 'He has brought down

---

[21] Robertson, *The Books of Nahum, Habakkuk and Zephaniah*, p. 119.

rulers from their thrones but has lifted up the humble' (Luke 1:52). The humble person will not boast or brag like the Assyrians; he should rather say: 'If it is the Lord's will, we will live and do this or that' (Jas 4:15).

There is no doubt that Nineveh and the Assyrians deserved the judgment and retribution of a holy God. Nahum now goes on to tell us about some of the signs of the decline and fall of Nineveh, and the inevitability of God's judgment and retribution.

3. The decline and fall of Nineveh – warning the nations (3:11–19)

The sinking of the *Titanic* on 15 April 1912 was a disaster that might have been avoided if early warnings about icebergs in her path had been acted on immediately. But hubris was not far from the minds of owners and crew. Disaster for such a magnificent liner seemed to them impossible. One of the passengers who survived, a Christian missionary, Sylvia Caldwell, quotes famously the words of a deckhand: 'Yes lady, God himself could not sink this ship!'[22]

The disaster that Nahum now spells out for Nineveh could also have been avoided if early warnings had been acted on. Some 100 years earlier Nineveh had repented in response to the preaching of Jonah and his warnings of judgment, and had avoided disaster; but later, Nineveh had gone her own disastrous way, and ignored God's warnings, so that Nahum's message spells out her doom: *Nothing can heal you; your wound is fatal* (19a). There's a warning here.

a. A warning about marks of decline (3:11–18)

As Nahum describes the decline and fall of Nineveh, we see that the marks of that decline are in themselves 'warnings' of God's judgment to come. So, with immense courage, Nahum calls upon the king of Assyria (18) and all people everywhere (19) to note certain marks of decline in Nineveh. There are a number of examples.

i. The self-indulgence of the citizens (11)

It is possible, as I have already suggested, that the phrase to *become drunk* (11) is a reference to the symbolic picture of drinking the cup of God's

[22] Quoted in R. Bewes, *Great Quotations of the 20th Century* (Christian Focus, 1999), p. 14.

wrath. The psalmist, for example, speaks of God's judgment in these terms:

No one from the east or the west
  or from the desert can exalt themselves.
It is God who judges:
  he brings one down, he exalts another.
In the hand of the LORD is a cup
  full of foaming wine mixed with spices;
he pours it out, and all the wicked of the earth
  drink it down to its very dregs.
(Ps. 75:6–8)

Certainly Nineveh is on the point of drinking the cup of God's wrath to 'its very dregs'. But there is another way to interpret these words. Drunkenness, and other forms of excessive self-indulgence, may well have become increasingly a feature of Assyrian society. As a result, she became less ready to face the enemy on the point of attacking her (11a). Soldiers as well as citizens may well have preferred to go into hiding (11b) than to stand up and defend the city against foreign invaders. Clearly the picture is of 'someone who has lost control of his faculties, and is unable to act with calm and deliberation'.[23] The picture of Saddam Hussein, hiding in a hole in the ground in Iraq at the time of his capture, conjures up the same kind of attitude.

Self-indulgence and lack of self-control is frequently a mark of a declining culture, whether it be with respect to alcohol, sex or money. Drunkenness is a major problem in the UK, for example, especially among young people; and a lack of self-discipline in sexual and financial matters is also a worrying feature of British culture. Liberty has become licence for many, and rights rather than responsibilities have come to the fore. The mention of drunkenness suggests that this kind of personal and moral decline might well have become a feature of Assyrian society.

If this is the thrust of Nahum's message here, he may well be implying that God's people should be careful not to travel on the same path of self-indulgence. Certainly the New Testament emphasizes the importance of self-discipline. So, in writing to Timothy about the qualities to look for in

[23] Mackay, *Jonah, Micah, Nahum, Habakkuk, Zephaniah*, p. 228.

Christian leaders, Paul says: 'Now the overseer is to be above reproach, faithful to his wife, temperate, self-controlled, respectable, hospitable, able to teach, not given to drunkenness, not violent but gentle, not quarrelsome, not a lover of money' (1 Tim. 3:2–3). In contrast to the self-control required of Christian leaders, he paints a very different picture of the culture of 'the last days', which is very much closer to the Assyrian culture. The apostle writes: 'People will be lovers of themselves, lovers of money, boastful, proud, abusive, disobedient to their parents, ungrateful, unholy, without love, unforgiving, slanderous, without self-control . . . lovers of pleasure rather than lovers of God' (2 Tim. 3:2–4).

When a nation shows increasing signs of its citizens losing self-control and becoming self-indulgent, it is a warning to all of us. It's a sign of a declining culture; and as the apostle Paul reminds the Christians in Rome in the first century AD, there is really no excuse to live without God in God's world. 'The wrath of God is being revealed from heaven against all the ungodliness and wickedness of people, who suppress the truth by their wickedness' (Rom. 1:18).

If self-indulgence was one mark of a declining nation, too much trust placed in military resources was another. So Nahum reminds the king of Assyria (18) of the inadequacy of the military.

ii. The inadequacy of the military (12–15)

Superpowers normally put a great deal of trust in military force and might. This was certainly true of Assyria, whose leaders had great confidence in their military strength for their security as well as for their imperialistic strategies and plans for expansion. In defence, Assyria's trust was in her many fortresses, which gave a false sense of security to her citizens. Nahum, however, points out that military might does not guarantee security and permanence. *Fortresses* (12), he tells us, will be picked off as easily as ripe figs are shaken off fig trees (12a). Soldiers under attack can become as weak and effeminate as unarmed women (13a, ESV). The gates of the city of Nineveh have become wide open to the enemy (13b), and the wooden bars of the gates, and indeed the whole city, is vulnerable to fire (13c, 15a). According to Babylonian and Greek records, Nineveh was in fact set on fire by the Babylonian and Scythian armies.

Nahum is so certain of the imminent siege and attack on Nineveh that he calls upon the citizens to prepare for the worst. *Draw water for the siege* (14a) – for much of the water supply would need to be drawn from outside the city walls. *Strengthen your defences! Work the clay, tread the mortar, repair the brickwork!* (14b). Is there irony here; a reference to the taunting of God's people by the Assyrians when they laid siege to Jerusalem (2 Kgs 18)? Certainly, to obey these words would require hard work and immense effort if Nineveh was to be saved. Nahum's message seems to be that however much effort is put into defending the city, it will all be in vain. *There* [where all the work is going on?] *the fire will consume you; the sword will cut you down – and it will devour you like a swarm of locusts* [or grasshoppers?] (15a).[24]

However powerful our defence systems, or our military, it is vain to put our trust in them, rather than in the living God. Indeed Nahum insists that even if the people of Nineveh worked hard to improve the defences of the city, God would still bring destruction upon them. In fact, even if the size of the army increased suddenly so that it multiplied *like grasshoppers . . . like locusts* (15b), it would still be unable to defeat the enemy. The words of the psalmist come to mind: 'Unless the LORD builds the house, the builders labour in vain. Unless the LORD watches over the city, the guards stand watch in vain' (Ps. 127:1).

Of course, it's not only pagan cities such as Nineveh who need to learn this lesson. Nahum would no doubt always have Judah and the people of God in mind when he brought God's word to Nineveh. God's people, then and now, need to remember that our own efforts will never be enough to overcome our enemies, especially Satan, our spiritual enemy. As Calvin wrote on these verses (14–15): 'Thy frugality, exertion and care not only will avail thee nothing, but will also turn out to thy ruin; for the Lord pronounces accursed the arrogance of men when they trust in their own resources.'[25] That is why the apostle Paul urges the Christians at Ephesus not to trust in themselves, but to 'be strong in the Lord and in his mighty power'. He goes on, 'Put on the full armour of God so that you can take your stand against the devil's schemes' (Eph. 6:10–11).

The inadequacy of the military, and a nation's reliance on military force rather than on the living God, was another mark of a declining empire. Now Nahum has the failure of another group in his sights: the traders and merchants.

---

[24] The Hebrew word can be translated 'locusts', if it refers to an early stage of the locust's development.

[25] J. Calvin, *Joel, Amos, Obadiah, Jonah, Micah, Nahum*, Commentaries, vol. 14 (Baker Book House, repr. 1996), p. 408.

iii. The greediness of the traders (3:16–17)

It is clear that Nineveh had become a centre for trade in the region. The number of merchants had increased year on year (16) until the city was full of them. Yet there is a certain irony in Nahum's words. For what was now beginning to happen with the merchants was a sign of the decline, not the growth, of the Assyrian economy. At first the number of merchants in Nineveh had increased greatly *till they [were] more numerous than the stars in the sky* (16b). But in Nahum's day, times were changing. The bubble was bursting. The 'boom' had brought much trade and great wealth to the city; but now 'the bust' had begun. For the very same merchants that flocked to Nineveh because of its prosperity were now moving away, stripping the city of its assets, and departing to unknown places (17c): *like locusts they strip the land and then fly away* (16c).

It's not only the traders who had been rocking the boat. The *guards* and *officials* (administrators) who once swarmed like locusts in every part of the life of the capital (bureaucracy gone mad?) had also left the city and its administration to its own devices. *Your guards are like locusts, your officials like swarms of locusts that settle in the walls on a cold day – but when the sun appears they fly away, and no one knows where* (17).

In the declining years of the once-powerful Assyrian empire many traders and civil servants clearly worked in Nineveh out of greed and self-interest. Once there were more riches to be found elsewhere, they deserted the city. It's exactly the kind of action that took place in the 'credit crunch' of 2008. Jesus taught his disciples about the dangers of greed and wealth. When he asked one rich young man to 'go, sell your possessions and give to the poor . . . Then come, follow me,' he went on to say to his disciples:

> Truly I tell you, it is hard for someone who is rich to enter the kingdom of heaven. Again I tell you, it is easier for a camel to go through the eye of a needle than for someone who is rich to enter the kingdom of God.
> (Matt. 19:21, 23–24)

Jesus never taught that it is impossible to be rich and to follow him. Several of his followers were, by the standards of the time, 'well off'. Some of the women who ministered to Jesus were probably wealthy (Matt. 27:55; Luke 10:38; 23:55–56), as were secret disciples such as Nicodemus and Joseph of Arimathea (John 19:38–42). But the love of money can become 'a root of all kinds of evil' (1 Tim. 6:10), and an idol that we worship. In the story of the rich young ruler (Matt. 19:16–30) we read that the young man was not able to count the cost and follow Jesus, and to sell his possessions and give the proceeds to the poor. Matthew comments that 'he went away sad, because he had great wealth' (Matt. 19:22). Jesus calls his followers to lay up 'treasure in heaven' (Matt. 19:21) rather than on earth. Making money must never become our driving ambition. We cannot serve God and money (Matt. 6:24).

Nahum would no doubt be mindful of similar lessons to be learned by God's people from the decline and fall of Nineveh. The traders had stripped the land of riches and then flown away to more congenial places. The civil servants had joined them (17). There is nothing new under the sun.

There's one further mark of a declining superpower that Nahum mentions.

iv. The idleness of the leaders (3:18)

Nahum now addresses the king of Assyria (Ashurbanipal?) for the first time in his prophecy. He was a cruel and corrupt king; and as head of state he was responsible for the leaders around him. We have seen in the twentieth and twenty-first centuries how easily a corrupt leadership can affect a whole nation. Nahum may simply be pointing out that the leaders in Nineveh had become idle and useless. 'Shepherd' (18) was a familiar term in Near Eastern countries to describe a leader. So, Nahum points out to the king: *your shepherds slumber; your nobles lie down to rest.*[26]

If it is their idleness that Nahum is focusing on, then it is clear that it led to a complete failure to care for the needs of the citizens of Nineveh. He accuses them of a complete dereliction of duty: *Your people are scattered on the mountains with no one to gather them* (18b).

No doubt Nahum also has in mind God's people as he speaks of idle leaders. Manasseh, the king of Judah, was certainly a corrupt king; Nahum may have been born in his reign. Josiah was a reforming king. But what of his successors? They were very different (2 Kgs 23:31 – 24:20). The failure of leadership was often on the minds of the prophets, especially after the fall of Jerusalem in 586 BC, during the exile. Ezekiel famously describes the leaders of Israel in these words:

---

[26] Some commentators point out that Nahum may be saying that these leaders are on the point of experiencing 'the sleep of death', as in the psalm which says: 'The valiant lie plundered, they sleep their last sleep' (Ps. 76:5).

> 'Woe to you shepherds of Israel who only take care of yourselves! Should not shepherds take care of the flock? . . . You have not strengthened the weak or healed those who are ill or bound up the injured. You have not brought back the strays or searched for the lost. You have ruled them harshly and brutally. So they were scattered because there was no shepherd . . . They were scattered over the whole earth, and no one searched or looked for them.
> (Ezek. 34:2–6; see 1–31)

It was Ezekiel who looked to the Lord to be the Good Shepherd:

> For this is what the Sovereign LORD says: I myself will search for my sheep and look after them . . . I will bring them out from the nations and gather them from the countries, and I will bring them into their own land.
> (Ezek. 34:11–13)

And it was Jesus who fulfilled these words when he said, 'I am the good shepherd; I know my sheep and my sheep know me . . . and I lay down my life for the sheep . . . there shall be one flock and one shepherd' (John 10:14–16).

Nahum does no more here than to remind the king of Assyria of the dangers of idle and corrupt leadership. It is for us to learn from the bad examples in Scripture, and then to look to the good shepherd, Jesus, who models perfectly what leadership should mean in the kingdom of God. Sometimes leadership in the church is idle and ineffective. Bad leadership was one of the marks of decline in the pagan Assyrian empire. It can have a similar corrosive effect in the church of Jesus Christ. We do well to follow the apostle Paul as he followed Christ. In speaking to the church leaders from Ephesus, he said:

> I declare to you today that I am innocent of the blood of any of you. For I have not hesitated to proclaim to you the whole will of God. Keep watch over yourselves and all the flock of which the Holy Spirit has made you overseers. Be shepherds of the church of God, which he bought with his own blood.
> (Acts 20:26–28; see 20:13–38)

Weak and idle leadership is so often the reason for the decline and fall of a nation, and for the deteriorating state of the church. That is why the apostle Paul urges Christians to pray for those in positions of leadership in the state. He wrote to Timothy: 'I urge, then, first of all, that petitions, prayers, intercession and thanksgiving be made for all people – for kings and all those in authority, that we may live peaceful and quiet lives in all godliness and holiness' (1 Tim. 2:1–2). Good leadership in government, even in a pagan nation like Rome, is more likely to lead to a favourable environment for evangelism. For the apostle follows the exhortation to pray for leaders with the words, 'This is good, and pleases God our Saviour, who wants all people to be saved and to come to a knowledge of the truth' (1 Tim. 2:3–4).

Jesus' prayer in John chapter 17 models the importance of praying for church leaders. Jesus not only trained the disciples, but also prayed for them specifically and as a priority: 'I am not praying for the world, but for those you have given me, for they are yours' (John 17:9). Nahum has taught us that weak leadership is a sign of decline in a nation; and we know that this is equally true in the church. Praying for leaders, then, should not be regarded as an optional extra, but rather a daily necessity. The teaching of the apostle Paul, and the example of Jesus, show us the way.

Here then are four marks of the decline and fall of the Assyrian superpower – warning signs to a nation that had once repented following the preaching of Jonah (Jon. 3) but had now turned its back on the living God. The self-indulgence of the citizens, the inadequacy of the military, the greediness of the traders and the idleness of the leaders all contributed to a declining nation which was under the judgment of God. Nahum now concludes his book by warning the king of Assyria (18) and other nations of the certainty of God's judgment and retribution for persistent sin.

b. A warning about certain judgment (3:19)

There is no doubt that the main focus of the book of Nahum is on the justice and judgment of God. God is just, and he must act in a way that is consistent with his character. Thank God we live in a moral universe where ultimately justice will be done and be seen to be done (Rom. 2:5–6)!

Chris Wright tells the story of an Indian man he met at a conference who had been converted to Christ through reading the Old Testament. He continues the story:

> He grew up in one of the many backward and oppressed groups in India, part of a community that is systematically exploited and treated with

> contempt, injustice and sometimes violence. The effect on his youth was to fill him with a burning desire to rise above that station in order to be able to turn the tables on those who oppressed him and his community. He threw himself into his education, and went to college, committed to revolutionary ideals and Marxism. His goal was to achieve the qualifications needed to gain some kind of power and thus the means to do something in the name of justice and revenge. He was contacted in his early days at college by some Christian students and given a Bible, which he decided to read out of casual interest, though he had no respect at first for Christians at all.
>
> It happened that the first thing he read in the Bible was the story of Naboth, Ahab and Jezebel in 1 Kings 21. He was astonished to find that it was all about greed for land, abuse of power, corruption of the courts, and violence against the poor – things that he himself was all too familiar with. But even more amazing was the fact that God took Naboth's side and not only accused Ahab and Jezebel of their wrongdoing, but also took vengeance upon them. Here was a God of real justice, a God who identified the real villains and took real action against them. 'I never knew such a God existed!' he exclaimed. He read on through the rest of Old Testament history and found his first impression confirmed. This God constantly took the side of the oppressed and took direct action against their enemies. Here was a God he could respect, a God he felt attracted to, even though he didn't know him yet, because such a God would understand his own thirst for justice.[27]

Nahum wants us to be clear that 'such a God exists'. When he writes, *Nothing can heal you; your wound is fatal* (19a), he may initially be addressing the king of Assyria with these words (18–19). Certainly, King Ashurbanipal died of his wounds before he could escape from Nineveh and the Babylonian invaders. But the king also personified the city of Nineveh and the whole Assyrian empire; and the message of Nahum is clear. God will judge Nineveh and the Assyrians. Judgment is certain. There will be no escape from it; justice will be done. *Nothing can heal you; your wound is fatal* (19a) is as appropriate a message for Nineveh and Assyria as it was for the king himself. Yahweh is a just and holy God. His wrath is an expression of that holiness and justice (1:2). Nineveh and the whole Assyrian empire

[27] Editorial in *Themelios*, 17.2 (January–February 1992), p. 3. This story is quoted in D. R. Davis's exposition of 1 Kgs, *The Wisdom and the Folly* (Christian Focus, 2002), p. 312.

had turned their back on God, and acted with unspeakable and *endless cruelty* (19c). They had gone beyond their mandate as an instrument in God's hand to discipline Israel. They deserved his just judgment.

Wright's Indian friend was overjoyed to find a God of justice. Nahum tells us: All *who hear the news* (19b) about the judgment and destruction of Nineveh *clap their hands at [her] fall, for who has not felt [her] endless cruelty?* (19). No doubt for some, this joy at the decline and fall of Nineveh was a piece of gloating over the destruction of a long-time enemy. But surely Nahum has taught us to see that we can properly rejoice at the justice of God, at his concern for the victims of oppressive regimes, and his deliverance of those victims from their enemies. We have learned from Nahum that God is kind as well as severe, merciful as well as just. He is *slow to anger* (1:3) and *cares for those who trust in him* (1:7). Before God pronounced final judgment on the people of Nineveh, he sent them Jonah to call them to repentance and show them a better way to live. For perhaps a hundred more years he continued to be patient with them. But, as Nahum teaches us, if we persist in rejecting God and his word, he gives us over to sin and judgment (Rom. 1:24–32). Justice will be done.

> Tho' the mills of God grind slowly
> Yet they grind exceeding small.[28]

There is a message here for all of us. We are all guilty before a just and holy God. But God is merciful to sinners. He sent his Son, Jesus Christ, to die, 'the just for the unjust', to bring us to God (1 Pet. 3:18, KJV). He calls the nations, and every individual within them, to repentance and faith (Mark 1:15; Acts 2:38–39).

Some people have pointed out that there is no call for repentance in the book of Nahum. Others have argued that the whole book is a call for repentance implicitly. Others have pointed to the unity of the twelve minor prophets, of which Nahum is one; many of them emphasize the importance of repentance. Nahum focuses on the certainty of God's judgment and retribution on those who refuse to repent.[29]

There are two books in the Old Testament that end with a rhetorical question: Jonah and Nahum. The book of Jonah ends with a question that

---

[28] From the poem 'Retribution' by F. Von Logau (1605–55), tr. H. W. Longfellow (1807–82).

[29] P. E. House, *The Unity of the Twelve* (Almond Press, 1990).

draws attention to God's mercy and compassion for the great city of Nineveh. Yahweh asks Jonah, 'Should I not have concern for the great city?' (Jon. 4:11). Jonah had gone to Nineveh to preach about God's judgment, having initially disobeyed God's call. The prophet had warned the Ninevites: 'Forty more days and Nineveh will be overthrown' (Jon. 3:4). Then the king and all the people repented and believed God's word. 'The Ninevites believed God. A fast was proclaimed, and all of them, from the greatest to the least, put on sackcloth' (Jon. 3:5).

Jonah was unhappy that God spared Israel's enemy. But God sought to teach him and all God's people to show the same compassion and mercy for their enemies that God showed. Hence the final question in the book of Jonah: 'Should I not have concern for the great city of Nineveh?' The book of Jonah helps us all to face up to our prejudices and to reflect the divine love, which is patient and kind, 'not wanting anyone to perish, but everyone to come to repentance' (2 Pet. 3:9).

The book of Nahum, however, has a different emphasis. The rhetorical question at the end (3:19) focuses on the need for justice and retribution on those who have persisted in acting with great brutality towards God's people and many others: *for who has not felt your endless cruelty?*

We need to grasp both truths about God, as Nahum has patiently taught us in his book. God is merciful, and forgives those who turn to him in penitence and faith. Equally God is just, and will judge sin and defeat evil. The clearest revelation of these two truths can be seen in the person of the Lord Jesus Christ, and in particular in his death on the cross. There God the Father, acting with perfect justice and perfect love, condemned our sin in the sinless Son of God, and so made it possible for us to be accepted and forgiven. 'Therefore, there is now no condemnation for those who are in Christ Jesus' (Rom. 8:1; 3:21–26; 2 Cor. 5:21; 1 Pet. 2:24; 3:18).

Nahum has given us a theological explanation of divine judgment based on the severity and goodness of God (ch. 1). He has also given us a historical illustration of divine judgment based on the decline and fall of Nineveh (chs. 2; 3). There is no doubt that God's judgment will fall on persistent sin and impenitent sinners. We can be grateful for Nahum's blunt and clear teaching about that. We can be grateful too that 'God so loved the world that he gave his one and only Son, that whoever believes in him shall not perish but have eternal life' (John 3:16).

The message of Zephaniah

Introducing Zephaniah

Most of us like to find out as much as we can about the author of a serious book. We like to know something about the person's background, the major influences of his or her early life, the experiences that have shaped the ideas that this gifted individual wants to share with us. Sometimes we are told a great deal about the writer, sometimes very little.

On the whole we are not told a great deal about the Old Testament writers. Zephaniah tells us that the *word of the Lord* (1:1) came to him, and we shall consider the significance of that claim a little later. But we are also given a few hints about his background and position in the society of his day (1). This is important, for God is sovereign. He knows all about us, and uses every experience and circumstance of the life of believers to prepare them and fit them to serve him, and to fulfil his purpose in the world. The apostle Paul wrote about this to the Christians in Rome in the first century AD: 'And we know that in all things God works for the good of those who love him, who have been called according to his purpose' (Rom. 8:28).

There is a danger that we might read too much into the opening words of the book of Zephaniah about his background. But there are things we can reasonably conjecture.

1. Zephaniah benefited from a godly home

The name *Zephaniah* (*ṣĕpanyâ*) includes the name of the Lord (*yâ* or *yah*) and literally means 'the Lord has hidden' or 'the Lord has caused to be hidden'. Why would his parents have given him this name if they were not believers in the Lord, Yahweh? It is possible, of course, that they had no reason other than they liked the name or they had a favourite Uncle Zephaniah whom they hoped would be a good model for their son to follow! Or there might be a deeper reason. If the name incorporates a perfect active tense, it could be 'a perfect of unchanging commitment': Yahweh 'hides' – he always does; he's like that. He's committed himself to it. So it's possible that Zephaniah's parents gave him his name as a reminder to themselves and to their son that Yahweh would look after him, hide him and protect him. Certainly that would fit the times during which Zephaniah was born (c. 696 BC), times of apostasy and persecution. For Zephaniah was probably born during the reign of Manasseh (687–642 BC), the father of Amon, king of Judah (1). Manasseh had turned to the Lord at the end of his life (see 2 Chr. 33:10–20), but before his 'conversion' he gave followers of Yahweh a torrid time (2 Kgs 21; 2 Chr. 33). The treatment of God's people was as brutal as the killing fields of Cambodia or the massacre of the Kurds in Iraq under Saddam Hussein in the twentieth century. The chronicler who wrote about Manasseh's cruelty concluded: 'Moreover, Manasseh also shed so much innocent blood that he filled Jerusalem from end to end – besides the sin that he caused Judah to commit, so that they did evil in the eyes of the LORD' (2 Kgs 21:16). Zephaniah, however, was protected by the Lord and prepared for prophetic ministry. It is likely that he benefited from a godly home.

In the New Testament the apostle Paul reminds his young fellow worker Timothy of the spiritual benefits of a godly home. He writes: 'I am reminded of your sincere faith, which first lived in your grandmother Lois and your mother Eunice and, I am persuaded, now lives in you also' (2 Tim. 1:5). In the same letter he urges Timothy to build on that early teaching: 'continue in what you have learned and have become convinced of' (2 Tim. 3:14). Christian parents and grandparents should be eager to endorse those words, and we should be thankful if God has given us that start in life, as he almost certainly did for Zephaniah.

But whether this be true of Zephaniah or not (for we must beware of reading too much between the lines), the truth of his name remains. The sovereign Lord has a plan for each of our lives. As the Servant of the Lord declares in Isaiah's prophecy: 'Before I was born the LORD called me; from my mother's womb he has spoken my name. He made my mouth like a sharpened sword, in the shadow of his hand he hid me' (Isa. 49:1–2).

2. Zephaniah came from a privileged background

We're told that Zephaniah's father is a man called *Cushi* (1). This is an Egyptian name, and some have suggested that he may have been of

Ethiopian origin and a slave or civil servant in the royal household. We can't be sure.

More significant perhaps is the mention of *Hezekiah* as the great-great-grandfather of Zephaniah. Is this King Hezekiah, the earlier reforming king of Judah (2 Chr. 29 – 32)? Again we can't be sure. But why does the ancestry stop once Hezekiah is mentioned? Could it be to relate Zephaniah to the royal house? This certainly fits in to what we find Zephaniah saying and knowing. The palace was the seat of government then and the centre of the civil service. A boy growing up in the extended royal family was in a good position to know what was going on in those circles, and as we study the message of Zephaniah we will find that he is well informed about the religious, civil and political issues of the day. His association with the palace enables him to be critical of the royals (1:8–9), the priesthood (1:4; 3:4), the judges and civil leaders (3:3), the merchant bankers and the complacent rich (1:11). He seems to be speaking from first-hand knowledge. Furthermore, when he began his public ministry, and the *word of the Lord . . . came* to him, King Josiah was carrying out his reforms in Judah (640–609 BC), and Zephaniah was clearly supporting them (Zeph. 1:4–13; 3:1–5).

It is encouraging for us to know that the sovereign Lord can use every experience of our lives to shape us into the kind of person he wants us to be. We see that spelled out very clearly, for example, in the life of Moses (Exod. 1 – 3) and Joseph (Gen. 37 – 50). These both spent part of their lives in privileged and royal circles. But it's equally true for those whose background was very different, such as Elijah and Amos and, for that matter, the disciples of Jesus. Indeed the apostle Paul was prepared to say to the Christians in first-century Corinth:

> Brothers and sisters, think of what you were when you were called. Not many of you were wise by human standards; not many were influential; not many were of noble birth. But God chose the foolish things of the world to shame the wise; God chose the weak things of the world to shame the strong. God chose the lowly things of this world and the despised things – and the things that are not – to nullify the things that are, so that no one may boast before him.
> (1 Cor. 1:26–29)

In Zephaniah's case, God seems to have used his privileged background, a godly home and his probable association with the palace as a way of preparing him for prophetic ministry in the reign of Josiah (1:1). Whatever our background, the same sovereign Lord is prepared to use the circumstances and experiences of our lives to prepare and equip us to serve him in our day.

There is a further matter that is suggested by the opening words of the book of Zephaniah.

3. Zephaniah lived and worked in challenging times

Zephaniah was almost certainly born during the reign of Manasseh, the son of Hezekiah. As we have already noted, Hezekiah may have been the great-great-grandfather of Zephaniah. He was also a great reforming king of Judah. He had introduced some important religious reforms and had stood up to the threats of a superpower, Assyria. He trusted in the Lord, and through prayer had seen the mighty Assyrian army turned away from the gates of Jerusalem (2 Kgs 18 – 20; 2 Chr. 32; Isa. 36 – 37).

King Manasseh, however, was a different proposition, and undid most of the work his father had done. He led Judah back to submit to Assyria, along with other neighbouring nations. He reintroduced pagan practices, defiled the temple, and encouraged idolatry, the occult and even child sacrifice (2 Kgs 21). He also persecuted genuine believers in Yahweh (Jer. 2:30). Zephaniah was born at that time.

There was a glimmer of light in the darkness, however, for the word of God was not completely stifled in those days. The writer of 2 Kings put it like this: 'The Lord said through his servants the prophets: "Manasseh king of Judah has committed these detestable sins . . . Therefore . . . I am going to bring . . . disaster on Jerusalem and Judah"' (2 Kgs 21:10–12). The prophets were still proclaiming God's word in the days of Manasseh.

It is worth reflecting that in the days of the old covenant as well as the new, God never ceases to keep his word alive. In the days of the evil King Ahab, for example, Elijah despaired because he thought he was the only faithful believer left in the land. But God reminded him that thousands had not bowed the knee to Baal (1 Kgs 19:18). So it was in the twentieth century, and so it is today. In earlier decades in the former Soviet Union and in China, for example, there were times of great darkness when the persecution of Christians raged. Yet in both those great continents the church is not only surviving but growing. Samuel Lamb, a Chinese pastor who spent twenty years in prison in China because of his Christian faith, wrote in 2003: 'Before the government confiscated our church, the church numbered 900 members. After confiscation the church had grown to 2000 members. More persecution, more growing!'[1] Today there are in China more Christians than there are members of their Communist Party.

In Cambodia, only about 2,000 of the church's 12,000 Christians survived the killing fields perpetrated by the Khmer Rouge in the late 1970s. Yet God still preserved a remnant of his people to keep the light of his truth shining, both in Cambodia itself and in refugee camps in neighbouring countries. By 2008, after ten years of relative freedom, the Evangelical Fellowship of Cambodia estimated that around 130,000 Christians were meeting in some 2,000 small congregations in Cambodia. Recent data confirms this progress. According to the World Christian Database, Cambodia's Christian population grew more than any country in South-East Asia from 2000 to 2015; by 2020, almost 3% of its population was Christian.[2]

Dark though the days of Manasseh were, God kept Zephaniah safe and kept his word alive. As he grew up, Zephaniah saw the situation change under God's sovereign hand. In 643 BC Manasseh was captured by Assurbanipal of Assyria, and then had a remarkable spiritual conversion (2 Chr. 33:10–17). Unfortunately this was too late to undo the damage he had caused; when his son Amon succeeded him, Judah was once again led astray. God is still in control, however. Amon was toppled by a 'people's revolution' (2 Kgs 21:23–24) and Josiah, a child of only eight years of age, was placed on the throne in 641 BC (2 Kgs 22:1; 2 Chr. 34:1). From early days Josiah began to seek the Lord, and at the age of twenty he initiated his religious, moral and spiritual reforms. At the same time, Assyria began to decline as a world power.

God was now to give Judah a fresh opportunity to return to him, through the reforming efforts of Josiah, backed by the preaching and teaching of Huldah the prophetess (2 Kgs 22:14–20), Zephaniah and, a little later, Jeremiah, Nahum and Obadiah.

God does not leave himself without witnesses in each generation, however dark it might become for true believers. But it is also true that each generation has to face up to its own responsibility to bear witness to the

---

[1] Quoted in an article by Andrew Boyd in *Prophecy Today*, September 2003, p. 17.

[2] James Thompson, 'Born Again and Again: Cambodian Evangelicals Celebrate 100 Years', *Christianity Today*, 25 January 2023: <www.christianitytoday.com/news/2023/january/cambodia-evangelicals-100-anniversary-protestant-missionary.html> (accessed 17 September 2023).

truth. A time of reform, even a revival of true religion, in Hezekiah's time, was soon engulfed by the forces of evil under Manasseh and Amon. It was up to Josiah, Zephaniah and other prophets such as Jeremiah to call on God's people to return to God and embrace reform. Every generation needs those who will have the courage to call people to repent and return to God.

Can we be even more precise about the time of Zephaniah's ministry? The answer to that question is tied up with a very significant event in the reign of Josiah. During the refurbishment of the temple in Jerusalem (622 BC), there was a most exciting discovery. This is how the Chronicler described it: 'While they were bringing out the money that had been taken into the temple of the LORD, Hilkiah the priest found the Book of the Law of the LORD that had been given through Moses' (2 Chr. 34:14). It is generally supposed that the scrolls that were discovered contained the words of the book of Deuteronomy. Furthermore, we know that King Josiah had begun his reforms before these scrolls were found; that Huldah the prophetess was called to interpret these scriptures (2 Kgs 22:14–20); that the terms of the covenant explained in those scriptures were renewed by the people; and that later Jeremiah was expounding those same words (Jer. 11:1–8).

So where exactly does Zephaniah's public ministry fit in?

Some have argued that the messages contained in the book of Zephaniah are most likely to have been delivered before the discovery of the Book of the Law, and the renewing of the covenant. Surely, it is said, Zephaniah could not have spoken about so many unreformed areas of Judah's life if the covenant had already been renewed nationally?

Others have argued that if the Book of the Law is indeed Deuteronomy, then the frequent quotations from that book in the preaching of Zephaniah suggest that he is supporting Josiah's reforms after the momentous discovery. The reference to *every remnant of Baal* (1:4) also suggests that some reforms had already taken place, but that a remnant remained which had to be dealt with. It's the same today. Reform in one part of the church goes on side by side with other parts unreformed and untouched. It is also the case that there can be blessing in one locality while neighbouring churches are withering and needing to be renewed by the Word of God. We may have an abundance of Bibles and many different versions today, together with ease of printing and distribution, yet in some churches the teaching of the Bible is so thin that a rediscovery of its message, relevance and power to change lives is as necessary as the rediscovery of the Law of

God in Josiah's time. It's his Word that the Spirit of God uses to bring about reform and renewal in the church. It always has been; it always will be (Neh. 8; Ezek. 37; 1 Thess. 2:13).

Before we move on to consider the message that Zephaniah delivered to his contemporaries, we do well to reflect on a further point from these opening words. Zephaniah mentions three names, all of which are referred to in the genealogy of Jesus (Matt. 1:10–11): Hezekiah, Amon and Josiah. We can understand how good reforming kings such as Hezekiah and Josiah are chosen by God to be part of that line that leads to Jesus, the Messiah. But it is harder to understand why Amon should be included. He only reigned for two years, and in that short time he was a disaster. We're told that

> he did evil in the eyes of the LORD, as his father Manasseh had done. He followed completely the ways of his father, worshipped the idols his father had worshipped, and bowing down to them. He forsook the LORD, the God of his ancestors, and did not walk in obedience to him.
> (2 Kgs 21:20–22)

Yet the biblical doctrine of the providence of God assures us that he was still on the throne and working his purposes out even while Amon reigned. We do well to remember that God is sovereign when tyrants such as Hitler, Stalin, Mao, Pol Pot – or Saddam Hussein and Robert Mugabe – appeared to be all-powerful as they persecuted Christians and crushed their people in the twentieth and twenty-first centuries. The psalmist put the Amons and the Hitlers in perspective when he wrote:

> Why do the nations conspire
> and the peoples plot in vain?
> The kings of the earth rise up
> and the rulers band together
> against the LORD and against his anointed . . .
> The One enthroned in heaven laughs;
> the Lord scoffs at them.
> (Ps. 2:1–2, 4)

The times we live in may be as challenging and difficult for us as for Zephaniah. But the biblical record of those crucial years of prophetic ministry reminds us again and again that God is sovereignly working his purposes out through individuals and nations. There is a profound truth in the words of an old Christian song that proclaimed:

God is still on the throne
And He will remember His own.
Tho' trials may press us
And burdens distress us,
He never will leave us alone.
God is still on the throne
And He will remember His own.
His promise is true,
He will not forget you,
God is still on the throne.[3]
(Mrs F. W. Suffield, 1884–1972)

We must soon turn to the message of Zephaniah, but before we do so, we need to examine the claim that is made in the opening words of the book: *The word of the* L*ORD* ... *came to Zephaniah* (1:1).

4. Zephaniah claimed that his message came from God

That is some claim! The Hebrew word for *came* (1) literally means 'to be'. So the force of the phrase is that the word of the Lord 'became a living, present reality to him'. Zephaniah claims that God spoke to him, and that his message to his contemporaries in Jerusalem and Judah was from the living God. The prophet doesn't tell us *how* God spoke to him. He may have heard a voice or seen a vision. He presumably found himself thinking God's thoughts. Perhaps God spoke to him as he reflected on existing scriptures, especially those rediscovered in the reign of Josiah (2 Chr. 34). There are certainly many echoes of Deuteronomy in the book of Zephaniah (e.g. 1:13 and Deut. 3:19–20; 28:30 and Deut. 26:19). However, we need to look elsewhere to understand more fully the nature of the authority and inspiration of Zephaniah and the Bible as a whole.

Zephaniah is not the only Old Testament prophet to claim divine authority for his teaching. Indeed they all claim to speak God's word to

[3] *CSSM Choruses*, book 2.

their contemporaries.[4] Take Jeremiah, a contemporary of Zephaniah, for example. This is how he describes the way God called him to speak God's word:

> The word of the LORD came to me, saying,
>
> 'Before I formed you in the womb I knew you,
> before you were born I set you apart;
> I appointed you as a prophet to the nations.'
>
> 'Alas, Sovereign LORD,' I said, 'I do not know how to speak; I am too young.'
>
> But the LORD said to me, 'Do not say, "I am too young." You must go to everyone I send you to and say whatever I command you . . . '
>
> Then the LORD reached out his hand and touched my mouth and said to me, 'I have put my words in your mouth. See, today I appoint you over nations and kingdoms to uproot and tear down, to destroy and overthrow, to build and to plant.'
> (Jer. 1:4–7, 9–10)

The New Testament writers made similar claims. The apostle Paul, for example, can write to the Christians at Thessalonica and say:

> we also thank God continually because, when you received the word of God, which you heard from us, you accepted it not as a human word, but as it actually is, the word of God, which is indeed at work in you who believe.
> (1 Thess. 2:13)

Again Paul claims verbal inspiration when he writes to the church at Corinth and says: 'This is what we speak, not in words taught us by human wisdom but in words taught by the Spirit, explaining spiritual realities with Spirit-taught words' (1 Cor. 2:13).

Furthermore, in an intriguing passage in the second letter of Peter, the apostle endorses this view of Paul's letters by putting them on a par with the other scriptures. Peter wrote:

---

[4] Exod. 4:14–16; 6:28 – 7:2; Isa. 1:10; 6:8; Jer. 1:9; Ezek. 2:7; 3:4; Hos. 1:1; Joel 1:1; Amos 1:3; Obad. 1:1; Nah. 1:1; Hab. 1:1–5; Hag. 1:1–10; Zech. 1:1.

> Bear in mind that our Lord's patience means salvation, just as our dear brother Paul also wrote you with the wisdom that God gave him. He writes the same way in all his letters, speaking in them of these matters. His letters contain some things that are hard to understand, which ignorant and unstable people distort, as they do the other Scriptures . . . (2 Pet. 3:15–16)

The apostle Paul summarizes his doctrine of Scripture (probably referring not only to the Old Testament scriptures but also to apostolic teaching; see 1 Cor. 2:13; 2 Pet. 5:15–16) by writing: 'All Scripture is God-breathed [*theopneustos*] and is useful for teaching, rebuking, correcting and training in righteousness' (2 Tim. 3:16). The Greek word *theopneustos* suggests that Scripture was 'breathed out' by God, not 'breathed in' by him. John Stott writes: '"Inspiration" is doubtless a convenient term to use; but "spiration" or even "expiration" would convey the meaning of the Greek adjective more accurately.' Stott goes on to say:

> There is no theory or explanation of inspiration here, for no reference is made to the human authors, who, moved by the Holy Spirit, spoke from God (2 Pet. 1:21). Nevertheless it is clear from many passages that inspiration, however the process operated, did not destroy the individuality or the active co-operation of the human authors. All that is stated here is the fact of inspiration, that all Scripture is God breathed. It originates in God's mind and was communicated from God's mouth by God's breath or Spirit. It is then rightly termed the 'Word of God', for God spoke it.[5]

Now that is exactly what is claimed for Zephaniah's message (1:1) when it is said that the *word of the LORD . . . came to Zephaniah*. It is the understood claim of every biblical writer.[6]

Because of the unique authority of Jesus, and his endorsement of the divine authority of the Old Testament scriptures and the teaching of the apostles,[7] we should have no fears about trusting the claim of Zephaniah that the *word of the LORD . . . came* to him. We have further confirmation

[5] J. R. W. Stott, *Guard the Gospel: The Message of 2 Timothy*, BST (IVP, 1973), pp. 101–102.

[6] For a brief examination of Jesus' teaching on the authority and inspiration of Scripture, supporting the claims of the prophets, see the main introduction, pp. 3–8.

[7] See 'Introduction to Obadiah, Nahum and Zephaniah', pp. 3–8.

because of the way that false prophets were tested. In Deuteronomy 13, the writer points out that a false prophet leads people away from the Lord God to idolatrous worship (Deut. 13:1–2). 'If a prophet . . . says, "Let us follow other gods . . . and let us worship them," you must not listen to the words of that prophet or dreamer.' On those grounds Zephaniah cannot be a false prophet, as our study of this book will make clear. Similar tests were applied in Deuteronomy 18:

> You may say to yourselves, 'How can we know when a message has not been spoken by the Lord?' If what a prophet proclaims in the name of the Lord does not take place or come true, that is a message the Lord has not spoken. That prophet has spoken presumptuously . . .
> (Deut. 18:21–22)

Zephaniah's words about the destruction of Jerusalem came spectacularly true in 586 BC as well as in AD 70. So, unlike some modern so-called prophets whose prophecies have not always come true, Zephaniah is vindicated as a true prophet by the events that followed his warnings.

As we turn now to the message of Zephaniah it is important for us to remember that according to Jesus and his apostles this is a word from God. Because this message is 'God-breathed', it is profitable 'for teaching, rebuking, correcting and training in righteousness, so that the servant of God may be thoroughly equipped for every good work' (2 Tim. 3:16). My prayer is that God might use the study of the message of Zephaniah to equip us for a life of Christian discipleship and service. The *word of the Lord . . . came to Zephaniah* (1:1). May it come to us too, through the inspired writings of the prophet.

Zephaniah 1:2 – 2:3

6. God's message of judgment

There are two major themes in the book of Zephaniah: judgment and hope. The theme of God's judgment is dealt with first (1:2 – 2:3). The prophet then writes about judgment and hope for all nations (2:4 – 3:8). Finally he sets out his teaching on hope, restoration and salvation (3:9–20).

The message of judgment does not sit comfortably in the postmodern, pluralistic, tolerant culture of the West in the twenty-first century. I suspect that it is not often preached from the pulpits of many of our churches. Many preach about the love of God, but not the wrath or judgment of God.

This abandonment of what the apostle Paul called the 'severity of God' goes back a long way (Rom. 11:22, KJV). The theologian Richard Niebuhr wrote about liberal Protestantism at the end of the nineteenth century in this vein: 'A God without wrath brought men without sin into a kingdom without judgment through the ministrations of a Christ without a cross.'[1]

That may be a description of extreme liberalism in the church. Yet this liberal influence has been felt in many theological colleges and seminaries throughout the Western world, and the consequences of watering down the biblical gospel have been catastrophic. Leon Morris, for example, quotes the words of McNeile Dixon with reference to this:

> The kind-hearted humanitarians of the 19th century decided to improve on Christianity. The thought of Hell offended their susceptibilities. They closed it, and to their surprise the gates of Heaven closed with

[1] H. R. Niebuhr, *The Kingdom of God in America* (Wesleyan University Press, 1988), p. 193.

> a melancholy bang. The malignant countenance of Satan disturbed them. They dispensed with him, and at the same time God took his departure.[2]

Dixon's point is that once you take away from the revelation of God's character in the Bible, the God you believe in becomes a god in your own image, and not the true God at all. Similarly, if the reality of evil, judgment and hell are dismissed, heaven becomes meaningless too.

I recently discussed with an Anglican minister a series of leaflets that he had written for his congregation, which challenged a number of important biblical doctrines. Sometimes he caricatured certain interpretations of those doctrines, but this is what he said about the doctrine of hell and judgment: '"Going to hell", the place of endless punishment, was widely thought to be the fate of the wicked and the unbaptized; and fear of hell was (and to some extent perhaps still is) an important agent of social change.' He then went on to say:

> Hell today has little hold over anyone, and tends to be mentioned only in jokes. Civilized adults don't make jokes about truly painful subjects; and because jokes about hell are not thought to be on the edge of acceptability, it shows that hell has, for almost everyone, lost its horrors . . .

He concluded:

> The traditional view of heaven and hell being our pay-off at the end of life, either reward or punishment as appropriate, rested on the idea of judgment, which in turn required a judge. The problem is that the sort of God involved, the God of theism, has come to seem less and less plausible to more and more people.[3]

It is probably right to say that fewer and fewer people in the Western world believe in a God of judgment and in the reality of heaven and hell. Yet Zephaniah challenges our culture and unbelief and gives us a balanced view of the character of God which reveals him as a just judge and a loving

---

[2] Quoted in L. Morris, *The Biblical Doctrine of Judgment* (Tyndale Press, 1960), p. 2.

[3] T. Windross (formerly vicar of St Peter's, Sheringham, England), 'Why Bother to Think about Heaven and Hell?'; one of a series of 'Why Bother?' leaflets.

saviour. The prophet brings us a message from God which says: *The whole world will be consumed by the fire of my jealous anger* (3:8). At the same time, he can write movingly about the love of God for his people when he says: *The* L*ORD your God . . . will take great delight in you; in his love he will no longer rebuke you, but will rejoice over you with singing* (3:17).

Zephaniah's balanced message of a God who is both just and loving needs to be heard in the twenty-first century AD as much as it was necessary in the seventh century BC. Notice that he focuses first on the fact that God's judgment is coming on the whole world.

1. God's judgment is coming on the whole world (1:2–3)

The fierceness of these words (2–3) must have caused both shock and surprise to those who heard them. It's not the way most of us would begin a sermon or start a book. There would probably be complaints to the church council, or letters to the bishop, if a preacher today focused so strongly on the theme of judgment. Yet Zephaniah, although he later writes most movingly about the love of God (in ch. 3), begins this book with an uncompromising message of judgment. Indeed the order is significant. First judgment, then love. For how can we understand the wonder of saving love if we do not first face the fact of judgment and the need to be saved?

It seems clear that Zephaniah's audience is primarily God's people in Judah and Jerusalem, although he applies God's message to the whole world. We can assume that first he preached this message to the people in Jerusalem, and that it was written down later. Clearly he speaks and writes as one speaking the very words of God (1; see also 1 Pet. 4:11).

In these opening words Zephaniah teaches us several things.

a. Judgment is from a personal God

Most of us find it more comfortable to think of judgment as an impersonal activity that is going on all the time in the world that God has created. The apostle Paul writes about this in his letter to the Christians in Galatia: 'Do not be deceived: God cannot be mocked. A man reaps what he sows. Whoever sows to please their flesh, from the flesh will reap destruction' (Gal. 6:7–8). Indeed it's true that inevitable consequences follow from self-centred living. We have choices. So if, for example, I choose to drink too much alcohol, the consequences of that choice may be to give me a 'drink problem', or to cause me to commit a drink-driving offence, or, ultimately, to turn me into an alcoholic. What we sow we reap; and many of us have discovered that our lives and careers have been destroyed by sowing to please our sinful nature.

We have also known for a long time that sexual promiscuity brings sexually transmitted diseases (Rom. 1:18–32). That is not to say that every individual who suffers with AIDS is guilty of promiscuity, for we all know of AIDS sufferers who, for example, have been infected because of a contaminated blood transfusion or babies infected by their mothers. However, the apostle Paul is not ruling God out of this apparent 'impersonal activity' of judgment. He teaches that 'the wrath of God' (Rom. 1:18) was being revealed when people 'received in themselves the due penalty for their error' (Rom. 1:27). The Bible teaches that the creation was ordered by the Creator, and its inbuilt procedures only operate by the direct action of his will. In other words, behind the 'impersonal activity' lies the personal activity of God.

It's that personal activity of God in judgment that Zephaniah emphasizes when he passes on God's message to his people: *'**I will** sweep away everything . . . **I will** sweep away both man and beast; **I will** sweep away the birds . . . [w]hen **I** destroy all mankind on the face of the earth,' **declares the Lord**'* (1:2–3; emphasis mine). So the consistent message of Zephaniah and the biblical writers is that God is personally involved in judgment, whether it be through the consequences of our sowing to please our 'flesh' (Gal. 6:7–8) or through the judgments of history (Isa. 10:5–16) or, as here, through the forces of nature (Amos 4:7), where God's wrath is involved through the inbuilt processes of sowing and reaping as well as through interventionist acts.

At first the idea that God is personally involved in judgment seems frightening. Indeed the biblical revelation of God as a person is a truth that many people shrink from as being far too challenging and demanding. C. S. Lewis made this point years ago in his book on miracles. He put it like this:

> An impersonal God – well and good. A subjective God of beauty, truth and goodness, inside our own heads – better still. A formless life-force surging through us, a vast power which we can tap – best of all. But God Himself, alive, pulling at the other end of the cord, perhaps approaching

> at an infinite speed, the hunter, king, husband – that is quite another matter . . . There comes a moment when people who have been dabbling in religion ('Man's search for God'!) suddenly draw back. Suppose we really found Him? We never meant it to come to *that*! Worse still, supposing He had found us?[4]

Yet we need not shrink from coming to know God as a person. Zephaniah teaches us that the God who *will sweep away everything from the face of the earth* (2) is not some impersonal power at the centre of the universe, threatening our lives. On the contrary God is a person, who is both just and loving, and who takes personal responsibility for seeing that justice is done and seen to be done, so that wickedness is punished and his character is vindicated.

In New Testament terms, of course, the God of Zephaniah is revealed in Jesus. It is Jesus who is described as 'the Word [who] was with God, and . . . was God . . . [and] became flesh and made his dwelling among us' (John 1:1, 14). To see Jesus is to see God (John 14:9). As we observe the life, teaching and atoning death of the Lord Jesus, we see clearly both the justice and the love of God. Jesus, for example, spoke many parables about a final day of judgment (e.g. Matt. 7:15–20; 24:42–51; see Luke 16), but he also showed his love and compassion by weeping over Jerusalem. He did this because he saw the inevitable judgment that would fall upon those who did not recognize the time of God's coming (Luke 13:34–35; 19:41–44). Again, on the way to the cross Jesus warned some women, whom he addressed as 'daughters of Jerusalem', to mourn for their sins and for the judgment that was coming (Luke 23:28–31). In his love he also prayed for his executioners with the words 'Father, forgive them, for they do not know what they are doing' (Luke 23:34).

Above all, the love and justice of God is revealed in the atoning death of Jesus. The apostle Paul wrote that on the cross, 'God was reconciling the world to himself in Christ' (2 Cor. 5:19). The apostle went on to explain that God reconciled himself to sinners by making Jesus 'who had no sin to be sin [or, a sin offering] for us, so that in him we might become the righteousness of God' (2 Cor. 5:21). We can only begin to understand this if we accept that God is both just and loving. Through the death of Jesus on the cross God showed his justice by judging our sin in the sinless body

[4] C. S. Lewis, *Miracles* (Geoffrey Bles, 1947), p. 114.

of Jesus. God showed his love by forgiving our sins and offering us the free gift of the righteousness of Jesus. When a person becomes a Christian there is a real exchange. By faith I lay my sins on Jesus. By grace God clothes me with Christ's righteousness. The apostle Paul sums it up with these words: 'God presented Christ as a sacrifice of atonement . . . he did it to demonstrate his rightousness at the present time, so as to be just and the one who justifies those who have faith in Jesus' (Rom. 3:25–26; see also Isa. 53:6; Mark 10:45; John 1:29; Gal. 3:13; 1 Pet. 2:24; 3:18).

So, when with Zephaniah we come to think of God as personally involved in the final judgment of the world, we should also think about Jesus, who reveals God to us as both just and loving. We need to remember that Jesus told his disciples: 'the Father . . . has entrusted all judgment to the Son, that all may honour the Son just as they honour the Father' (John 5:22–23).

In April 1989 there was a horrendous disaster at the Hillsborough football ground in Sheffield, in which many spectators were killed and injured. The story is told of a Christian doctor who, after he had finished the medical work he had been asked to do, was invited to have a word with some of the bereaved, many of whom had lost a son or a father. The doctor approached a man who was deeply distressed, and sought without words to draw alongside him to comfort him. After some time he thought it appropriate to offer to say a prayer for the man in his deep sorrow and distress. So he asked the man whether he might pray to God for him. The bereaved man reacted bitterly and said words to this effect: 'What does God know about losing a son?' It is precisely because 'he gave his one and only Son' that we know that God is loving as well as just (John 3:16).

There is one further point to make about the warning of judgment that Zephaniah introduces at the beginning of his prophecy. It is a sign of God's love that he does warn his people about forthcoming judgment. To be forewarned is to be forearmed. As I live by the sea in north Norfolk, I do not regard the warnings about rising sea levels caused by global warming and the possibility of flooding along the north Norfolk coastline as nothing more than doom and gloom, and a warning that can be safely ignored. On the contrary, I believe that those who give these warnings are people who have our best interests at heart. I am eager to hear what they have to say. I don't want to be ignorant about any possible future disaster. I want to respond responsibly to these warnings.

In the same way, God has my interests at heart when with great love and compassion he warns me about judgment to come. If we did not know about the wrath to come, we would not flee from it. It's an essential part of our humanity that we are to live in the light of foreseen consequences. Zephaniah helps us to do so.

This leads us to a second truth about judgment in this passage.

b. Judgment is fully deserved

When people face a personal tragedy in their lives, they will sometimes say: 'What have I done to deserve this?' or: 'Why has God done this to me?'

There are no easy answers to these questions. We know from the teaching of the Bible that suffering is not always the direct result of that particular sufferer's sin. So Job, for example, is described as a man who was 'blameless and upright' (Job 1:1). Yet he experienced disasters that came upon his property and upon his family, and he experienced suffering in his own body (Job 1:6–22; 2:1–10). Jesus taught the same truth. When his disciples saw a man who was blind from birth, they asked him: 'Who sinned, this man or his parents, that he was born blind?' Jesus' answer was clear: 'Neither this man nor his parents sinned . . . but this happened that the works of God might be displayed in him' (John 9:2–3). Likewise, when people asked Jesus about a massacre of Galileans and the collapse of a tower in Siloam that killed eighteen people, Jesus made it clear that these things did not happen to these particular people because they were more guilty of sin than anyone else in Galilee or Siloam. Jesus did say, however, 'But unless you repent, you too will all perish' (Luke 13:1–5). We are all sinners. We all deserve the judgment of God. Disasters of this kind help us to remember that life is short, and that we all have to stand before the judgment seat of Christ (2 Cor. 5:10). They remind us too not to take God's grace and protection for granted.

Zephaniah tells us that the judgment we deserve will be a sweeping clean of all evil and wickedness in the world: *I will sweep away everything from the face of the earth* (2). The Creator is also the Judge. He acts with perfect justice because humankind has rebelled against the Creator, worshipping idols rather than the true and living God.

Zephaniah's account here of God's final judgment seems to have in mind the story of Noah, and God's punishment of a generation that had turned its back on its Creator and thoroughly deserved that judgment. The language that describes God's action reverses the order of creation, sweeping away *both man and beast*, then *the birds in the sky and the fish in the sea* (3). Finally there is the statement: *'I destroy all mankind on the face of the earth,' declares the* LORD (3).

There is some dispute about the meaning of the Hebrew text behind the phrase *the idols that cause the wicked to stumble* (3). A better translation might be: *I will sweep away . . . the rubble with the wicked* (ESV) or *I will consume . . . the stumbling blocks along with the wicked* (NKJV). The word for 'stumbling block' is *mikšôl*, rather than the word in the Hebrew text, *makšēlâ*. But there is a link between the two words. If the word for 'stumbling block' is permitted, then God is saying through Zephaniah that he will finally destroy all those things that cause people to stumble and sin, especially idolatry. Robertson suggests that this would include the 'twisting of the good things of creation into a cause for sin'. This was done in Zephaniah's day through the making of idols and worshipping them. It is done no less certainly today by those who worship and bow down to the god of materialism and profit, or by those who exploit the environment and harm God's creation. The apostle Paul said that covetousness is idolatry (Eph. 5:5) – the root sin behind the materialism of today.

Zephaniah is very clear that human sin has affected the whole of creation: *man and beast . . . birds in the sky . . . and the fish in the sea* (3). Sin corrupts the environment (Gen. 3:16–19; Rom. 8:19–20) and affects the economic base of human existence (Lev. 18:25).

In 2006, for example, Sir Nicholas Stern, a former chief economist at the World Bank, presented a paper to the UK government which stated that 'the scientific evidence is now overwhelming' that climate change is under way and presents 'very serious risks'. Such changes, he argues, would 'transform the physical geography of the world', with many millions of people facing starvation, water shortage or homelessness. Commenting on this report in the *Times* newspaper on 3 October 2006, Lewis Smith wrote:

> The melting of glaciers would initially cause floods, but would then leave a sixth of the world's population facing water shortage. Sea rises would threaten cities, including London and New York, and a rise of 2°C. would put 15–40% of wild life at risk of extinction. Falling crop yields could leave hundreds of millions of people, especially in Africa, at risk of starvation; and, once temperatures have risen by 4°C. global food production is likely to be seriously affected. Scientists are clear that the

> higher the temperature rise the worse the impact on people and economies will be.

Stern argues that the stabilization of greenhouse gas levels in the atmosphere is possible and will not halt economic growth. But when Christian Aid's senior climate change analyst, Andrew Pendelton, commented on Stern's report, he said:

> Sir Nicholas' Report is of major international significance, and should leave no one in doubt about the need for immediate action on climate change. However, talk of economic change is all very well; but the real danger remains for poor people in the developing world, whose future depends on our willingness to act. If we follow the Report's conclusions, we may avert economic bankruptcy, but we are still teetering on the brink of moral bankruptcy. Stern's figures mean that the world's average temperature would almost certainly increase beyond the two-degree mark that scientists agree is safe. *This would condemn millions of poor people in the front line of climate change to death.*[5]

Human sin and selfishness inevitably leads to the pollution of the environment, and to God's judgment on the nations and the whole planet. Such judgment is deserved. For selfishness and idolatry is at the heart of the rebellion of humankind against God our Creator (Rom. 1:18–32).

c. Judgment will finally come

The idea that the climax of world history will be the destruction of the planet, as we know it, is a world view that is shared by some secular writers. Whether the end will come through a nuclear explosion, or a meteorite striking the earth, or a cosmic 'black hole' sucking up the planet, or in some other way, there is emerging a consensus that the world is more likely to end in a bang than a whimper. Sadly, while scientists are prepared to talk about the end in these ways, while offering little hope to humankind, Christian leaders are often silent about God's final day of judgment and the hope of salvation that is offered with it.

Zephaniah, however, wants us to know at the very beginning of his prophecy that God's judgment will finally come to the whole world. When

[5] Quoted in *Church of England Newspaper*, no. 5844, 3 November 2006.

he writes ***I will sweep away everything from the face of the earth***, he uses two Hebrew words (*'āsōp, 'āsēp*) to convey to his listeners that God's final judgment will be total and certain. These two words convey the idea of 'gathering up', 'sweeping away' or 'bringing to an end'. Together they indicate total annihilation. God will sweep clean all the wickedness and evil in the world when he comes to judge at the end of the age.

Jesus' parable of the wheat and the weeds speaks of the final judgment in a similar way (Matt. 13:24–30; 36–43). Wheat and weeds grow together until the harvest. Then the owner of the farm says, 'Let both grow together until the harvest. At that time I will tell the harvesters: first collect the weeds and tie them in bundles to be burned; then gather the wheat and bring it into my barn' (Matt: 13:30). In explaining the story, Jesus says: 'The Son of Man will send out his angels, and they will weed out of his kingdom everything that causes sin and all who do evil' (Matt. 13:41; see 13:36–42). There will be a gathering up and a weeding out on the last day. Zephaniah's message is no different at this point from the teaching of Jesus.

The rest of the New Testament teaches the same truths. Indeed, the apostle Peter explains to his readers why God was delaying this final act of judgment. He writes:

> With the Lord a day is like a thousand years, and a thousand years are like a day. The Lord is not slow in keeping his promise, as some understand slowness. Instead he is patient with you, not wanting anyone to perish, but everyone to come to repentance.

Peter goes on to describe the day in words that are similar to Zephaniah's description: 'But the day of the Lord will come like a thief. The heavens will disappear with a roar; the elements will be destroyed by fire, and the earth and everything in it will be laid bare' (2 Pet. 3:8–10).

What message does this teaching send to the people of God? Peter is clear that it challenges us to a life of godliness and holiness:

> Since everything will be destroyed in this way, what kind of people ought you to be? You ought to live holy and godly lives as you look forward to the day of God and speed its coming. That day will bring about the destruction of the heavens by fire, and the elements will melt in the heat. But in keeping with his promise we are looking forward to a new heaven and a new earth, where righteousness dwells. So then, dear friends, since

> you are looking forward to this, make every effort to be found spotless, blameless and at peace with him.
> (2 Pet. 3:11–14)

Zephaniah also makes his teaching about final judgment a wake-up call to the people of God in Jerusalem and Judah. We shall consider his teaching more fully later. But we do well to notice how soon he calls on the people to be *silent before the Sovereign Lord* (7); to *wail* and mourn because of coming destruction (11); and to *gather together* to seek *the Lord* and to seek *righteousness* and *humility* (2:1–3).

We do well to ask ourselves, in the light of final judgment, what kind of people we ought to be. A final day should concentrate the mind, as in a less important matter a final examination does. One day we shall all stand before the judgment seat of Christ (2 Cor. 5:10). We are accountable to God. How ready shall we be?

There is a further point to draw out of Zephaniah's teaching here. The prophet is not describing some chance cosmic disaster. He has taught us that the sovereign Lord is personally in charge, and the end comes only in accordance with his will and word, and in his time. *'I will sweep away everything from the face of the earth'* – God is in charge! The sovereign Creator, the faithful and loving covenant Lord, will have the last word (Rom. 8:20–21). The whole world stands under his judgment. 'Will not the Judge of all the earth do right?' (Gen. 18:25).

2. Judgment begins at home (1:4–6)

The idea that God would stretch out his hand against Judah and Jerusalem (4) would have been far from the thoughts of God's people. It was one thing to acknowledge a final day of judgment for the whole world. It was quite another matter to face up to the message that judgment would come to them. After all, they were the children of Abraham, and the Lord had said to Abraham:

> I will make you very fruitful; I will make nations of you, and kings will come from you. I will establish my covenant as an everlasting covenant between me and you and your descendants after you for the generations to come, to be your God and the God of your descendants after you. The whole land of Canaan, where you now reside as a foreigner, I will give as

an everlasting possession to you and your descendants after you; and
I will be their God.
(Gen. 17:6–8)

God kept his promises. He chose Judah and made the descendants of Judah a royal family (Gen. 29:32–35; 49:8–10; Ps. 78:68–69). They settled in the Promised Land, having been delivered from slavery in Egypt when God 'stretch[ed] out [his] hand' to save them (Exod. 7:5). Furthermore, those who lived in Judah and Jerusalem at the time of Zephaniah's ministry were able to enjoy the privileges of temple worship. They were able to come into the presence of God and to listen to teaching from the Word of God. They could receive by faith the means of grace, symbolized by the sacrifices offered in obedience to God. They were greatly privileged. Many of us share the same privileges today. Indeed, our privileges are greater because of the riches of our inheritance in Christ (Eph. 1:3–14; Col. 1:3 – 2:5).

Zephaniah reminds us, however, that with privilege comes responsibility. Furthermore, he brings us God's message that if we fail to act responsibly, we deserve judgment. The prophet Amos, a century before Zephaniah, had preached the same message. Through him, God had said to Israel: 'You only have I chosen of all the families of the earth'; and then went on to say, '*therefore* I will punish you for all your sins' (Amos 3:2; emphasis mine).

Those who profess to believe in God are accountable to him. The privilege of belonging, at least outwardly and nominally, to the people of God does not save us from God's judgment of our sinful behaviour. If we are Christians, justified by grace through faith in Jesus, we need not fear final judgment. As the apostle Paul wrote to the Christians in Rome, 'Therefore, there is now no condemnation for those who are in Christ Jesus' (Rom. 8:1). Jesus has borne the judgment we deserve and has 'suffered once for sins, the righteous for the unrighteous, to bring [us] to God' (1 Pet. 3:18). But that does not alter the fact that we are all accountable to God. As the apostle Paul put it, 'For we must all appear before the judgment seat of Christ, that each of us may receive what is due to us for the things done while in the body, whether good or bad' (2 Cor. 5:10).

So, if we profess to be Christians, but in fact live hypocritical ungodly lives, we should examine ourselves in the light of God's warning of judgment. It's with that situation in mind that the apostle Peter writes to first-century Christians and says that 'it is time for judgment to begin with

God's household' (1 Pet. 4:17). It is in this context that the apostle Paul wrote to the Christians at Corinth warning them about their selfish and self-indulgent behaviour at the Lord's Supper, and pointing out that

> everyone ought to examine themselves before they eat of the bread and drink from the cup. For those who eat and drink without discerning the body of Christ eat and drink judgment on themselves. That is why many among you are weak and ill, and a number of you have fallen asleep.
> (1 Cor. 11:28–30)

He goes on to say:

> But if we were more discerning with regard to ourselves, we would not come under such judgment. Nevertheless, when we are judged in this way by the Lord, we are being disciplined so that we will not be finally condemned with the world.
> (1 Cor. 11:31–32; see also Heb. 12)

Jesus also warned those who professed to be his followers, hearing but not obeying his word, of the danger of judgment. In the Sermon on the Mount he contrasts the wise man who heard and obeyed his word with the foolish man who heard the word but did nothing about it. The foolish man built his house on sand – there was no firm foundation to his life. So, when the storm came, 'that house . . . fell with a great crash' (Matt. 7:24–27). Those who heard the teaching of Jesus were greatly privileged. But because they did not obey the teaching, they faced the judgment of God. Judgment begins at home; judgment begins with me.

A few weeks after the striking of the Twin Towers in New York on that fateful day in September 2001, Anne Graham Lotz, the daughter of the evangelist Dr Billy Graham, was asked, 'How could God let something like September 11th happen?' Part of her reply was as follows:

> I believe that God is deeply saddened by this as we are; but for years we've been telling God to get out of our schools, to get out of our government and to get out of our lives. And being the gentleman that he is, I believe that he has calmly backed out. How can we expect God to give us his protection if we demand that he leaves us alone?[6]

[6] Part of an interview in the USA on TV's *The Early Show*, conducted by Jane Clays and circulated worldwide by email.

Christians in America were no doubt shocked that such a disaster could take place in a country where a large proportion of its citizens claim to be Christian and regularly attend church. We don't know all that God is saying to the Western world through such a horrendous disaster. But Anne Graham Lotz was surely right to face up to the questions and the implications for a professedly Christian country. Zephaniah's message was clearer still for Judah and Jerusalem and the people of God in his day. It was a message that came from God (1). In spite of all their privileges, God says, *I will stretch out my hand against Judah and against all who live in Jerusalem* (4).

Here, Zephaniah's teaching goes beyond the idea that judgment is no more than God removing his protective hand from us, giving permission for some disaster to intervene. When God says, through Zephaniah, *I will stretch out my hand against Judah and against all who live in Jerusalem*, he is going beyond 'God permitting' to 'God directing'. As the prophet Amos put it, 'When disaster comes to a city, has not the LORD caused it?' (Amos 3:6).

But why did God promise to *stretch out [his] hand against Judah and . . . Jerusalem*?

The answer to that question lies in the corrupt religion that was still being practised in Jerusalem and Judah in spite of the reforms of Josiah. In these verses (4–6) Zephaniah gives us some examples.

a. Some people worshipped Baal, not the Lord

The terms of God's covenant with his people were clear. God said, 'I am the LORD your God, who brought you out of Egypt, out of the land of slavery. You shall have no other gods before me' (Deut. 5:6–7). However, time and time again Israel broke this covenant in spite of the warnings of the prophets; and some worshipped Baal rather than the Lord (Yahweh).

In Zephaniah's day King Josiah had begun to remove the altars of Baal and to drive out the pagan and idolatrous priests and their evil practices. Zephaniah clearly supported these reforms. But it is also clear that there was a *remnant of Baal* (4) that still existed and *the idolatrous priests* were still encouraging corrupt worship.

God is against corrupt and false religion. He is a jealous God and asks for our exclusive loyalty. Notice the force of his words through the prophet Zephaniah: *I will stretch out my hand against Judah and . . . Jerusalem.*

I will destroy[7] *every remnant of Baal worship in this place,*[8] *the very names of the idolatrous priests* (4). God promises to remove the names of the idolatrous priests even from the memories of God's people. It has been suggested that the exile, when God carried out his disciplining judgment on his people, took away 'the addiction of Baal worship'. God's judgments have a purifying effect.

The Hebrew word Baal (*ba'al*) literally means 'master', 'lord', 'possessor' or even 'husband', and the term came to be used for Canaanite and Assyrian gods. Zephaniah was preaching during the time when Assyria was still a world power. But the mention here of *every remnant of Baal worship* and *the idolatrous priests* (the Chemarim) makes it more likely that there is a reference here to those Canaanite Baals that had been a constant temptation to Judah for generations and in particular during the days of Manasseh and Amon (2 Kgs 21:1–9). We know enough about Baalism of that time to suggest its relevance to the twenty-first century and to the church today. For example . . .

i. Baalism was a prosperity religion

Those who worshipped Baal in Zephaniah's day hoped that they would store up riches and prosperity for themselves. They believed that Baal could make the land more fertile and productive, and that if they pleased and stimulated Baal its plants, animals and people would be fruitful and multiply. So, many of the people worshipped the god of fertility and prosperity rather than the one true Creator God who could supply all their needs.

Today, we have our modern Baals associated with prosperity. 'Baal was another name for the gross national product; and wherever people see bank balances, prosperity or sound economy, productivity and mounting exports, as the essence of their security, Baal is still worshipped.'[9]

In the Gospels, Jesus frequently warns us about materialism and putting our trust in wealth. On one occasion he said, 'Be on your guard against all kinds of greed; life does not consist in an abundance of possessions.' He then went on to tell the story of the rich fool who, having made a great success of his farming, said to himself, '"You have plenty of grain laid up for many years. Take life easy; eat, drink and be merry." But God

[7] To 'destroy' is the same Hebrew word that is used of final judgment in v. 3c and literally means 'to hew down, to erase or to annihilate'.

[8] Probably referring to the temple and possibly Jerusalem too.

[9] J. A. Motyer, in T. E. McComiskey (ed.), *The Minor Prophets*, vol. 3: *Zephaniah, Haggai, Zechariah and Malachi* (Baker Book House, 1998), p. 912.

said to him: "You fool! This very night your life will be demanded from you. Then who will get what you have prepared for yourself?"' Then Jesus added, 'This is how it will be with whoever stores up things for themselves but is not rich towards God' (Luke 12:15–21).

The temptation to dabble in prosperity religion comes in other more subtle ways too for Christians in the twenty-first century. Few of us take seriously enough the challenge in the old slogan, 'Live simply that others may simply live.' Indeed some Christians are taught to believe in a 'prosperity gospel' that claims that Christians may become rich and prosperous if only they have enough faith to claim and believe the promises of God. An example of this was found in the teachings and practices of one well-known evangelist, whose workers put out an envelope on everyone's seat in the meeting hall with the words, 'The more you give, the richer the Lord will make you.' One young couple I know were so deceived and then disillusioned by this prosperity teaching which their local minister taught in their church that they no longer belong to any church. That is not to excuse their action, but it illustrates the harm to which the 'prosperity gospel' can lead.

Jesus teaches us in the Sermon on the Mount that we are not to be anxious about food, drink or the clothes we need to wear; rather, we are to seek first his kingdom and his righteousness. Then, as he puts it, 'all these things will be given to you as well' (Matt. 6:31–34). But clearly Jesus is not saying that if we put him first he will inevitably make us rich materially! Surely he is saying that if we put him first in our lives, he will meet our needs.

The apostle Paul in his second letter to the Corinthians may appear to support a prosperity gospel. He certainly teaches that generous giving brings generous spiritual blessings (2 Cor. 9:8, 10–11). He reminds us that as we give, God meets our every need and provides for every good work materially and spiritually. God does this in full measure. The apostle assures us: 'God is able to bless you abundantly, so that in all things at all times, *having all that you need*, you will abound in every good work' (2 Cor. 9:8; emphasis mine). But the phrase 'having all that you need' is a translation of the Greek word *autarkeia*, which in Greek thought described a person 'who has taught himself to be content with very little and never to want anything'.[10] So they are necessities, not luxuries, that God provides.

10 See W. Barclay, *The Letters to the Corinthians*, Daily Study Bible (St Andrew's Press, 1961), pp. 260–265.

Furthermore, Paul argues that as we share with others what God has entrusted to us, the resources of God's people are multiplied (2 Cor. 9:10) and a spiritual harvest follows. Many spiritual blessings flow from generous sacrificial giving (2 Cor. 9:8–14). But this is very far from the prosperity gospel teaching that 'the more you give (materially), the richer the Lord will make you'. In the providence of God that may sometimes be true; but God does not promise great material wealth to the generous giver, but rather great spiritual riches, and the supplying of material needs.

Baalism in Zephaniah's time was a prosperity religion; and there was a remnant in Judah and Jerusalem (4) who worshipped the god of prosperity and fertility rather than the one true God who could meet all their needs. We need to learn from their mistakes and guard ourselves from materialism and from the false emphases of the so-called prosperity gospel. God is against false and corrupt religion and the disobedience of those who practise it. He is also against those who teach people to be materialistic and those who espouse a false gospel. For Zephaniah the outcome was certain. Baalism would not triumph, any more than any false religion will. *I will destroy every remnant of Baal worship in this place, the very names of the idolatrous priests.* To 'destroy' includes the idea of 'erasing from the memory'. When God has completed his work of judgment, nothing will be left of false religion, and nothing will be remembered. False religion has no eternal significance.

ii. Baalism was a sexually corrupt religion

It's important to understand that Baal was not thought of as a 'person', but rather an impersonal force allegedly promoting fertility. As a force, Baal could not in any real sense be the object of prayer. Rather, the hope was that worshippers of Baal would make enough noise to attract Baal's attention (1 Kgs 18:26–29); or, to put it another way, worshippers of Baal set out to do on earth what they wished Baal would do from heaven, in the hope that Baal would catch on and imitate. Hence, human acts of fertility and sexual acts were performed where Baal could see and be stimulated to bring about the fertility of land, animals and people. So, when it is said that Baalism encouraged cult prostitution, it is not implying 'sex for money', which is encouraged in red-light districts in our culture; on the contrary, Baalism encouraged 'sex for devotion'. It was part of a corrupt religion.

Some religious cults today are equally misguided about the moral legitimacy of 'sex for devotion'. Some Mormon churches, for example, still practise polygamy. Sometimes, professing Christian churches cross the line when it comes to sexual morality. In the 1980s there were notorious cases of sexual immorality identified with a distorted theology taught at the large 'Nine O'Clock Service' in Sheffield. Equally misguided were those in the 1960s who advocated a sexual morality that stood for the principle that 'there is nothing prescribed except love'. A leading churchman actually argued that in certain circumstances an act of adultery could be an 'act of holy communion'. Those who argue for the alleged spiritual benefit derived from a physically expressed homosexual relationship are surely equally blind to the clear teaching of the Bible on sexual morality (see Gen. 2:24; Matt. 19:1–6; Rom. 1:18–32).

Zephaniah makes it clear that God is against Baalism and its corrupt sexual morality, even when it claims to be an act of religious devotion, for 'God is light; in him there is no darkness at all' (1 John 1:5). God is absolutely pure, and cannot tolerate wrongdoing (see Hab. 1:13). He has laid down in Scripture the proper place for sexual relations, which is within marriage and nowhere else. The classic statement about that is in Genesis 2:24, which is quoted by Jesus in his teaching on marriage and divorce:

> Haven't you read . . . that at the beginning the Creator 'made them male and female,' and said, 'For this reason a man will leave his father and mother and be united to his wife, and the two will become one flesh'? So they are no longer two, but one flesh. Therefore what God has joined together, let no one separate.
> (Matt. 19:4–6)

In God's mind (as revealed in Scripture and endorsed by Jesus) sexual immorality deserves the judgment of God. The gentle way in which Jesus dealt with the woman 'caught in adultery' is important for us to observe and to follow (John 8:1–11). But we must also notice that Jesus did say to her, 'Go now and leave your life of sin' (John 8:11). Our attitude must be the same.

Whenever religious people are misguided about sexual morality, as in Baalism, God is grieved. God says, *I will destroy every remnant of Baal worship in this place* (4). For Baalism was a sexually corrupt religion.

iii. Baalism was a frenzied religion

Zephaniah mentions *the idolatrous priests* (4c) who led people away from the Lord to worship Baal. We know that these priests (*kĕmārîm*) burned incense (2 Kgs 23:5). But the name is also linked to a word (*kāmar*) which means 'to be hot' or 'excited' (see also Gen. 43:30; 1 Kgs 3:26). Certainly the worship of Baal seemed to be linked to religious excitement, even frenzy, and the priests may well have been called 'the frenzied ones'.[11]

Paganism is a fast-growing movement in the West in the twenty-first century. Some pagan cults are characterized by frenzied dancing which may take place when they meet together for their various pagan ceremonies. Even in some Christian worship an overemphasis on excitement or unusual 'signs and wonders' can become unhelpful and an end in itself.

When the apostle Paul was faced with a church that gloried in many people speaking in tongues at the same time and without interpretation, he reminded them that the 'spirits of prophets are subject to the control of prophets. For God is not a God of disorder but of peace' (1 Cor. 14:32–33). In the same passage he writes that 'in the church I would rather speak five intelligible words to instruct others than ten thousand words in a tongue' (14:19).

Jesus himself contrasted frenzied pagan worship with Christian prayer in the Sermon on the Mount. He said: 'And when you pray, do not keep on babbling like pagans, for they think they will be heard because of their many words. Do not be like them, for your Father knows what you need before you ask him' (Matt. 6:7–8). Is there a danger that some of our evangelical churches become 'frenzied' in the number of activities they promote?

So, the frenzy associated with Baal worship also comes under the judgment of God, when he says: *I will destroy . . . every remnant of Baal worship, the very names of the idolatrous priests* (4c).

iv. Baalism was a cruel religion

There is some evidence that human sacrifice was sometimes associated with the worship of Baal. Robertson asserts, 'Under the corruptions of Baalism, the priesthood apparently offered the defenceless infant as a sacrifice. Instead of providing for the removal of sin, the priesthood instigated depravity of the worst sort.'[12]

---

11 1 Kgs 18:26. For further discussion, see Motyer, in McComiskey (ed.), *The Minor Prophets*, vol. 3, p. 912.

12 O. P. Robertson, *The Books of Nahum, Habakkuk and Zephaniah*, NICOT (Eerdmans, 1990), p. 263.

Before we yield to the temptation to take the moral high ground in today's world, we need to reflect on the fact that even in the UK recently there has been suspicion of child sacrifice; we need to acknowledge also the cruel way in which children are treated in many parts of the world; and we need to consider whether our society, with its mounting numbers of unborn children killed by abortions, does not equally deserve God's judgment in the twenty-first century.

So one major reason for the warnings of God's judgment on his chosen people in Judah and Jerusalem was the fact that some people were still worshipping Baal rather than him. God is against such corrupt and false religion. *I will stretch out my hand against Judah and against all who live in Jerusalem. I will destroy every remnant of Baal worship in this place* (4).

Zephaniah goes on to give another example of corrupt religion.

b. Some people worshipped the stars, not the Lord

'I will destroy ... those who bow down on the roofs to worship the starry host' (4–5). It has been well said that when people cease to believe in God and the Bible, they will believe in anything. Some years ago there was a television series on religion which was given the overall title of *Desperately Seeking Something.*[13] It focused on a number of bizarre examples of what was available for those who were seeking some kind of 'spiritual' experience. We were introduced to Druids, the Golden Dawn Occult Society, Taoist priests, the 'Barefoot Doctor', and a number of groups that were offering various kinds of New Age therapies. We were reminded at least that men and women are always desperately seeking something or someone who will satisfy their deepest needs and give some meaning and purpose to their lives.

It was no different in Zephaniah's day. It seems that as some people loosened their hold on the worship of the one true God who made the stars, some turned to the stars themselves to give meaning to their lives. It may be that some became followers of an Assyrian astrological cult that had introduced the worship of stars into Judah in the reigns of Manasseh and Amon (2 Kgs 21:3–5), or perhaps they were reverting to an early Canaanite belief in the stars. Either way, God had made it clear that such worship was idolatry and corrupt. He had said in his Word:

---

[13] On the UK television network Channel 4.

> When you look up to the sky and see the sun, the moon and the stars – all the heavenly array – do not be enticed into bowing down to them and worshipping things the LORD your God has apportioned to all the nations under heaven.
> (Deut. 4:19; see also 17:3; Jer. 44:25)

Zephaniah describes these idolaters as those who bow down on the housetops to worship the starry hosts (1:5). He may be suggesting private 'worship' at home, rather as people today read their horoscopes in the daily paper or listen to it privately on breakfast television. Or it could mean that worship 'was offered directly to the heavenly bodies without using idols'.[14] Whatever the exact significance, it was clear that some people were looking to the heavens for guidance rather than to Yahweh himself.

It is difficult to determine how far such superstitious practices have affected Christian people today. Certainly astrology has become a major industry in the West. The writer Sue Crawford has claimed:

> Most of us can't resist reading our own horoscope; and many of us (half of all women and a quarter of all men in the UK) look at the stars regularly. Astrologers now offer services to share dealers, blue-chip companies and even politicians . . .[15]

In the light of all this, it would be surprising if the church was not in some degree influenced by these superstitious practices. In Zephaniah's day those who worshipped the stars from the tops of their houses had lost their grip on the doctrine of creation. They failed to acknowledge how great God is. No-one wrote of God's greatness more powerfully than the prophet Isaiah, when he said:

> 'To whom will you compare me?
>   Or who is my equal?' says the Holy One.
> Lift your eyes and look to the heavens:
>   who created all these?
> He who brings out the starry host one by one
>   and calls forth each of them by name.

---

[14] Motyer, in McComiskey (ed.), *The Minor Prophets*, vol. 3, p. 913.
[15] From an article by Sue Crawford in *Woman and Home*, January 2001.

> Because of his great power and mighty strength,
> not one of them is missing.
> (Isa. 40:25–26)

Zephaniah tells us, however, that some people in Judah and Jerusalem turned from the Creator to his creation. People do the same today when they read their horoscopes and depend on them for guidance rather than on the Lord, the creator of the whole world; and it is becoming more and more obvious that those who write about our stars write about them as if they really do direct and determine our lives. Furthermore, the fact that the Bible warns us against astrology must mean that there is 'something there' to fear and to be taken seriously. Others ignore God as Creator by worshipping nature itself, or by adopting a rigid atheistic view of how the world came into being.

Worshipping the creation rather than the Creator is an act of rebellion and disobedience that deserves the judgment of God. The apostle Paul wrote to the Christians in Rome:

> The wrath of God is being revealed from heaven against all the godlessness and wickedness of people, who suppress the truth by their wickedness, since what may be known about God is plain to them, because God has made it plain to them. For since the creation of the world God's invisible qualities – his eternal power and divine nature – have been clearly seen, being understood from what has been made, *so that people are without excuse.*
> (Rom. 1:18–20; emphasis mine)

Those who *bow down on the roofs to worship the starry host* in Judah and Jerusalem are without excuse. God's promise to *destroy [them]* happened when Jerusalem was destroyed in 586 BC and many of them were taken into captivity. Those of us who depend on the stars rather than the Lord face the same bleak future.

Zephaniah now goes on to tell us another reason why God's hand was stretched out against Judah and Jerusalem.

c. Some people 'worshipped' Molek and the Lord

'I will destroy . . . those who bow down and swear by the LORD and who also swear by Molek' (4–5). Another feature of the corrupt religion that

was still present in Jerusalem and Judah was the syncretistic worship of some of the people. To *swear* or to take an oath was a religious action that was both an act of witness and a profession of faith. The original Hebrew means that these people swore 'to' Yahweh and swore 'by' Molek. To swear 'to' Yahweh was a witness to their loyalty to him in words. To swear 'by' Molek was to witness to their desire to live their lives by the principles and practices of this Ammonite god. ('They worshipped the LORD, but they also served their own gods in accordance with the customs of the nations from which they had been brought', 2 Kgs 17:33.)

It was King Solomon, years earlier, who had allowed the worship of Molek to come into Judah. We are told that as Solomon grew old his wives turned his heart after other gods, 'and [he] did not wholly follow the LORD, as David his father had done' (1 Kgs 11:6–7, ESV). Solomon's weakness led to syncretistic worship; and it was left to King Josiah to desecrate 'Topheth, which was in the Valley of Ben Hinnom, so no one could use it to sacrifice his son or daughter in the fire to Molek' (2 Kgs 23:10). Josiah also desecrated the high places that were east of Jerusalem, including the high places for Molek (2 Kgs 23:13).

In spite of Josiah's reforms, however, some still practised syncretistic worship. Syncretism involves the mixing of different religious systems, practices and loyalties. It's a feature of Western culture in the twenty-first century. We live in a pluralistic society; and for many people, pluralism means not only that we have many different religions in postmodern Britain, but also that each religion is equally valid. This is perfectly illustrated in New Age religion, which combines ideas and practices from different religions in a 'pick-and-mix' way.

No doubt those who encouraged such syncretistic practices believed they were acting in a more culturally relevant way than Zephaniah or Josiah. But God's Word had always been clear: 'You shall have no other gods before me' (Deut. 5:7). Elijah, centuries before Zephaniah, had challenged the Israelites to make up their minds to give God total and exclusive loyalty. He had summoned 450 prophets of Baal and 400 prophets of Asherah, and in front of them had addressed the people: 'How long will you waver between two opinions? If the LORD is God, follow him; but if Baal is God, follow him' (1 Kgs 18:21).

Jesus challenges us in the same way when he warns us that we cannot serve God and money: 'No one can serve two masters. Either you will hate the one and love the other, or you will be devoted to the one and despise the other. You cannot serve both God and Money' (Matt. 6:24).

The Bible speaks about God as a jealous God. He has a right to our exclusive loyalty. To compromise, to hedge our bets, to 'pick-and-mix' our religion or to engage in multifaith worship is to invite the judgment of God. Yet in our multifaith society in the UK today there is enormous pressure to say that 'all religions lead to God', or that the three monotheistic faiths of Islam, Judaism and Christianity all teach the same things and worship the same God. It is not politically correct to challenge this view, or to emphasize the exclusive claims of Jesus as 'the way and the truth and the life' (John 14:6).

There is an even more subtle form of syncretism. This takes all Christian sects and traditions equally seriously on the grounds that all have insights to contribute to the whole picture. That is obviously a humble and attractive position to adopt. But loyalty to the Lord Jesus Christ and to the Word of God will surely move us to acknowledge the deeper truth, as somebody has written, that 'the greatest non-Christian religion is unbiblical Christianity'. Our first loyalty must be to the Lord. Our loyalty to him involves loyalty to his Word. To acknowledge unbiblical 'Christianity' as well is to be guilty of that kind of syncretism which Zephaniah says God condemns, when he warns the people with the promise: *I will destroy . . . those who. . . swear by the Lord and who also swear by Molek* (4–5). God is against syncretism.

There was a further reason for God to stretch out his hand against Judah and Jerusalem.

d. Some people no longer followed the Lord

'I will stretch out my hand against . . . those who turn back from following the Lord and neither seek the Lord nor enquire of him' (4, 6). There were people in Judah and Jerusalem who at one time had appeared to be following the Lord, and then turned their back on him. They had been regular, no doubt, in attending temple services. They had listened to the Word of God as it was expounded by the prophets and the priests, and they had sought to live by that Word in their daily lives. The Hebrew words for to *seek* (*biqqeš*) and to *enquire* (*dāraš*) are synonyms. Together they speak of seeking and cultivating fellowship with the Lord. They point to the fact that the worship of God, whether private or public, should never be a casual affair. It involves focus and seriousness as well as joy, and

'a conscious and directed effort'.[16] Here, however, God is pointing out that some people are no longer doing this.

Zephaniah would also have been familiar with the story of Moses in the book of Deuteronomy, when he had warned the people against worshipping idols and had encouraged them 'to seek the place the LORD your God will choose from among all your tribes to put his Name there for his dwelling. To that place you must go' (see Deut. 12:4–7). Sadly, some people in Zephaniah's day no longer obeyed God's Word in this respect. They may have been devoted worshippers once, but now they no longer sought to have fellowship with him, nor did they seek his help or go to the place where they could be with other worshippers and call on the name of the Lord. God was not a living reality in their lives; and their backsliding and apostasy brought upon themselves the disapproval of the Lord (6).

There is a kind of logic about the order of the corrupt practices that Zephaniah has described. Idolatry (Baalism and the worship of the stars) led to syncretism. Abandonment of Yahweh as the one true God led to belief in many gods or none. This in turn led to individual backsliding and the apostasy of many people who had once been regular worshippers in the temple in Jerusalem.

The same process has been going on in most of the countries in Western Europe that once boasted a Christian culture. In the UK, for example, there has been a massive decline in the number of people attending church since the 1960s. Part of this is due to the materialism that is a dominant feature of our culture. Syncretism, which is seen to be 'politically correct' in a multifaith, multicultural Britain, has also played its part; and the theological liberalism that has discarded the supremacy and sufficiency of Scripture, and sometimes the Bible itself, must surely share some of the blame. Following all this, there are many people today who have turned back from following the Lord and *neither seek the LORD nor enquire of him* (6). This is true even for those who claim that they still believe in God (over 70% of the population in the UK). Many say that they believe, but they behave as though God does not exist. In practical terms they are atheists, and in reality they do not know God. Their religion is empty and powerless.

So God's words, through the prophet Zephaniah, should challenge us deeply. We too can be guilty of worshipping our Baals (money, prosperity, sex) rather than our living, loving Lord. We too can fail to acknowledge

---

16 Robertson, *The Books of Nahum, Habakkuk and Zephaniah*, p. 265.

God as Creator, and worship the stars or creation itself rather than the Creator. We can be unduly influenced by the pressures of a multifaith society so that we fall too easily into syncretistic worship. Or we can be like those who once worshipped the Lord regularly with his people, but now no longer go to church to seek his presence or his help.

God warns us here of the dangers of such behaviour, and the reality of judgment beginning with the family of God. But he also gives us hope. A little later in Zephaniah's prophecy, God pleads with his people to *gather together* to seek *the Lord*, to seek *righteousness*, to seek *humility* (2:1, 3). However, before Zephaniah delivers that message, he spells out in more detail the imminence of the day of judgment and introduces the important theme of *the day of the Lord*.

3. Time is running out! (1:7–13)

Today, in the twenty-first century, those who speak most urgently about coming disasters and 'time running out' for our planet tend to be the scientists and environmentalists who warn us about the dangers of global warming and the failure of most of us to do anything about it.

Zephaniah was no less urgent in warning God's people in Judah and Jerusalem about their need to face up to their own sinful actions which would inevitably lead to God's judgment upon them. Time was running out and, he warned them, *the day of the Lord is near* (7).

In the Bible, the phrase 'the Day of the Lord' suggests an important and decisive event. It has been described as 'a moment or period in which destiny is settled'.[17] Sometimes the phrase was used to describe a day when God delivered or blessed his people and judged their enemies. So Isaiah could write, 'For the Lord has a day of vengeance, a year of retribution, to uphold Zion's cause' (Isa. 34:8). The prophet Amos, however, wrote about the Day of the Lord in a significantly different way. He wrote, for example, 'Woe to you who long for the day of the Lord! Why do you long for the day of the Lord? That day will be darkness, not light' (Amos 5:18).

Zephaniah has already asserted that judgment begins with God's people. Now he warns that *the day of the Lord* may very well be a day of judgment, that time is running out, and that the Day of the Lord is both near and inescapable.

---

[17] See J. A. Motyer's comment on Zeph. 1:7 in McComiskey (ed.), *The Minor Prophets*, vol. 3, p. 917.

a. The Day of the Lord is near

The Hebrew prophets were constantly reminding God's people of his covenant and agreement with them, and warning them of the ways in which they could so easily bring God's judgment upon themselves. In the book of Deuteronomy (rediscovered during Zephaniah's lifetime) God had made it abundantly clear that to obey God led to the blessings of God upon the lives of his people. Equally, to disobey God invited his judgments (Deut. 27–28). So Moses set before the people these choices:

> If you fully obey the LORD your God and carefully follow all his commands that I give you today, the LORD your God will set you high above all the nations on earth. All these blessings will come upon you and accompany you if you obey the LORD your God. You will be blessed in the city and blessed in the country . . . You will be blessed when you come in and blessed when you go out.
> (Deut. 28:1–3, 6; see 28:1–14)

> However, if you do not obey the LORD your God and do not carefully follow all his commands and decrees I am giving you today, all these curses will come on you and overtake you: You will be cursed in the city and cursed in the country . . . You will be cursed when you come in and cursed when you go out. The LORD will send on you curses, confusion and rebuke in everything you put your hand to, until you are destroyed and come to sudden ruin because of the evil you have done in forsaking him . . . The LORD will cause you to be defeated before your enemies.
> (Deut. 28:15–16, 19–20, 25; see 28:15–68)

Time and time again the prophets warned God's people and called them back to him. But time and time again Israel ignored God's word and rebelled against him. Zephaniah has already told the people of Judah and Jerusalem that they deserve God's judgment. For they have chosen to break his covenant with them. Now he tells them that *the Day of the Lord*, a day of judgment, is near. Time is running out.

In the passage before us (7–13) Zephaniah uses a vivid illustration to bring home the imminence of this day of judgment, and the seriousness of the people's disobedience in breaking the covenant. He tells them: *Be silent before the Sovereign LORD, for the day of the LORD is near. The LORD has prepared a sacrifice; he has consecrated those he has invited. On the day of the Lord's sacrifice I will punish . . .* (7–8). Later I will come back to Zephaniah's call for silence. Suffice it to say at this point that Zephaniah is calling attention to the sovereignty of God and our need to acknowledge that truth and to listen to what God has to say to us. For the Day of the Lord is near. But what does Zephaniah mean when he speaks of the Lord preparing a sacrifice (7)? Robertson argues that the prophet is speaking here in strong covenantal terms. As we have already noted (2–3), Zephaniah understands God's universal judgment as a reversal of the order of creation. Now perhaps he pictures the sacrificial feast described in Genesis 15 as part of God's covenant with Abraham (Gen. 15:9–18). In that story Abraham sacrifices some animals by cutting them up and setting their parts opposite to one another in preparation for God's passing through. To break the covenant is to invite destruction, just as the birds of prey destroyed the animal carcasses. It's a vivid picture of the judgment of God upon those who break his covenant of grace (see also Isa. 34:8; Jer. 7:33; 16:4; 19:7; 34:18–20).

It's worth noting that the New Testament describes the final day of judgment with similar imagery. In the book of Revelation, John writes:

> And I saw an angel standing in the sun, who cried in a loud voice to all the birds flying in mid-air, 'Come, gather together for the great supper of God, so that you may eat the flesh of kings, generals, and the mighty, of horses and their riders, and the flesh of all people, free and slave, great and small.'
> (Rev. 19:17–18)

According to Zephaniah, then, Judah and Jerusalem are ready for God's imminent judgment, described in these sacrificial terms because they have broken God's covenant. But what does Zephaniah mean by the phrase *he has consecrated those he has invited*? (7b). It is possible that the invited guests are the heathen nations who would be there to observe God's judgment on Judah. However, it is more likely that they refer to the nations that God consecrated or 'set apart' to be instruments of that judgment. Certainly the biblical doctrine of God's sovereignty reveals a God who is Lord of all nations, and who in his loving purposes for the whole world uses even pagan nations to carry out his sovereign will.

The prophet Isaiah spells out this doctrine when, through him, God speaks of Assyria as 'the rod of my anger, in whose hand is the club of my wrath! I send him against a godless nation' (Isa. 10:5–6). Israel is the godless nation, but Assyria is the pagan nation that God uses to punish Israel! We must be clear that this does not mean that the Assyrians cannot help their actions or that they are not responsible for their wicked deeds in warfare against God's people. Motyer comments, 'The Assyrian holocaust was not let loose on the world; it was sent, directed where it was merited (v. 6), kept within heaven's limits; and in the end Assyria was punished for its excesses.'[18]

Motyer also points out that Isaiah uses the figure of the horse and its rider to illustrate the mystery of divine sovereignty and human responsibility:

> The Assyrians are the horse, the Lord is the Rider. To the horse belongs all the restless energy and huge strength of its nature; to the Rider belong all direction and skill of management . . . the Lord rides upon world history for the accomplishment of holy purposes.[19]

The prophet Habakkuk also wrestles with this mystery. God tells him that he is raising up the Babylonians, 'that ruthless and impetuous people', to execute judgment on Israel (Hab. 1:6, 12). The prophet is mystified: 'Why are you silent while the wicked swallow up those more righteous than themselves?' (Hab. 1:13). Habakkuk is willing to wait for his answer to come in God's 'appointed time' (Hab. 2:3); and as he reflects on past history when God delivered Israel from the bondage of Egypt (Exod. 1 – 3), he finds he is able to say: 'I will be joyful in God my Saviour. The Sovereign LORD is my strength; he makes my feet like the feet of a deer, he enables me to tread on the heights' (Hab. 3:18–19). God has never failed his people in the past; Habakkuk is sure he won't do so in the future.

Zephaniah doesn't explore the mystery of God's sovereignty and human responsibility. But he knows that the sovereign Lord *has prepared a sacrifice*, that he will judge Judah and Jerusalem, and that he will consecrate and call to that task those nations he has invited. He is Lord of the nations; he works all things after the counsel of his will.

This same truth about God's sovereignty can also give us hope as we reflect on many desperate situations in trouble spots in our world today.

---

18 J. A. Motyer, *The Prophecy of Isaiah* (IVP, 1993), p. 113.

19 See comment on Isa. 37:28–29 in Motyer, *The Prophecy of Isaiah*, p. 283.

What hope is there in the Middle East, for example, apart from the truth about God's sovereignty over all the nations of the world? Zephaniah's message that God is sovereign, and that he is both Judge and Deliverer, not only offered hope to Judah and Jerusalem, but offers hope to us as well.

There is a further point that has been made about the picture of judgment as *the day of the LORD's sacrifice* (8). Motyer writes:

> To speak of 'the day of the Lord' as a day of sacrifice places it within the long biblical tradition that where there is sin there must also be death . . . and this because Yahweh is the Holy One . . . Zephaniah takes the word of divine grace (the provision of a sacrifice for sin) and makes it the vehicle of the message of wrath; those who have long despised the sacrifice that God provides, become the sacrifice their sin merits.[20]

Although Zephaniah is convinced that the day of sacrifice has been prepared, the Day of the Lord is imminent and that time is running out, he is not teaching at this point that *the day of the LORD* is necessarily the day of final judgment, though that final day is never far from his mind (1:1–3, 18; 3:8). The judgments he writes about here were presumably fulfilled when the Babylonians destroyed Jerusalem and took many people into exile in 586 BC. Here he pleads with the people to take God seriously. *Be silent before the Sovereign LORD, for the day of the LORD is near* (1:7). The Hebrew word for *be silent* conveys a sense of awe in the presence of God, the Judge of all the world. The prophet Habakkuk captures that same sense of awe in the context of God's judgment of the nations when he writes: 'The LORD is in his holy temple; let all the earth be silent before him' (Hab. 2:20).

The apostle Paul also writes about the appropriateness of silence for those who have come to realize their sin and guilt before the moral law of God. 'Now we know that whatever the law says, it says to those who are under the law, so that every mouth may be silenced and the whole world held accountable to God' (Rom. 3:19).

In the West we live in a busy, noisy world which has lost that sense of awe before a holy God. The church may have contributed to that loss by failing to speak of the holiness and justice of God as much as the love of God. As Christians, we often fail to show in our lives a proper sense

20 For further discussion, see Motyer, in McComiskey (ed.), *The Minor Prophets*, vol. 3, p. 917.

of awe and wonder before almighty God. Perhaps we need to capture afresh the challenge in those words of Zephaniah: *Be silent before the Sovereign LORD, for the day of the LORD is near.* Christians live in 'the last days' – the time between the first and second comings of Jesus Christ. Jesus taught us to think about that day as *near*, and called us to be ready for his coming to judge and to save (Matt. 24 – 25; Mark 13; Luke 21). Zephaniah has more to tell us about that final *day of the LORD* (18). But before we consider that teaching further, we do well to notice how inescapable God's judgments are.

b. The Day of the Lord is inescapable

Zephaniah knew the situation well in Jerusalem. He does not hesitate to assure certain groups of people within the city that God would punish (8, 9) and search out (12) their wrongdoing and rebellion against him. Time was running out. There would be no escape. First, he warns the civil leaders: *I will punish the officials and the king's sons and all those clad in foreign clothes* (8).

The privilege of leadership carries with it a responsibility towards God and towards those who are led. This is often denied in our Western secular culture. How often we hear people defend what they do in private as of no relevance to their public office. God's word through Zephaniah is very different.

The Hebrew word for officials (*śarîm*) is a more general word for civil leaders, and would not be limited to 'the royals'. Sometimes, for example, it referred to military leaders. Josiah himself is presumably exempt from God's judgment as he was a godly man and a reforming king; but his sons, including Jehoahaz and Jehoiakim, later rebelled against God and led God's people astray (2 Kgs 23:31–36). They had broken God's covenant. They deserved God's judgment. There would be no escape for them.

It is possible that the reference to *all those clad in foreign clothes* (8) includes others as well as the civil leaders who flouted the religion of Yahweh by wearing clothes that identified with a pagan culture. Some believe that this included some of the priests in the temple. However, Baker argues convincingly that 'the flow of thought does not suggest priests in the garb of an alien religion . . . but the princely households frivolously dazzled by supposed foreign sophistication'.[21] It may seem

[21] D. W. Baker, *Nahum, Habakkuk and Zephaniah*, TOTC (IVP, 1988), p. 95.

harsh for God to disapprove so strongly about people not wearing Hebrew dress, but we need to remember that those who wore foreign clothes were not only identifying with a pagan culture but also 'eroding the distinction between the Lord's people and the world around, and exemplifying a failure of loyalty to him and a carefree attitude towards his Law'.[22]

As Christians too our lifestyle matters. We need to be sensitive, for example, about the clothes we wear, especially in a culture which is sex-obsessed. Another contemporary example could be the way that some people today wear amulets or lucky charms, even though they may be churchgoers and professing Christians. One person I know wears a necklace with a locket around her neck which carries a picture of an Eastern religious guru. She believes this will bring her luck. The Christian friend who has been sharing the gospel with her believes that this locket is a sign of her basic disloyalty to God and a hindrance to her genuine conversion.

Those who dressed unhelpfully in Zephaniah's day were identifying with the pagan culture and religion in such a way as to be disloyal to the one true God. Their clothes symbolized their basic attitude to God, and although God looks on the heart rather than the outward appearance, our clothes and our lifestyle often reflect our innermost thoughts and the true nature of our heart before God. As a boy I was brought up within an evangelical subculture that regarded smoking, drinking alcohol, dancing, and going to the theatre and cinema as part of a 'worldly' lifestyle that a 'keen' Christian would not adopt out of loyalty to God. Today that approach is regarded by most Christians as absurd and legalistic. However, Zephaniah teaches us that God does take note of our lifestyles. We are called to be 'holy', that is, distinct, different, separated from the world and dedicated to God. So if the clothes we wear, and the lifestyle we adopt, reflect an attitude of disloyalty to God, God is displeased.

Some time ago I read of a young Christian couple who were anxious to maintain a godly attitude while living in a world that largely ignores God. They had saved up enough money to get a mortgage and to buy their first ever property. It was not very large, but it was their own. Aware, however, of the dangers of a 'worldly' lifestyle, they wrote the following prayer which they often prayed: 'O God, who has given us so richly of this world's goods to enjoy, help us to live so lightly to them, so wholly to You, that were they all removed tomorrow, we should scarcely notice the difference.'

---

22 For further discussion, see Motyer, in McComiskey (ed.), *The Minor Prophets*, vol. 3, p. 919.

The civil leaders in Jerusalem in Zephaniah's day had no such attitude. They would rather wear sophisticated clothes that identified with a pagan culture than humbly identify with the people of God and the Word of God. Such disloyalty to God deserved the judgment of God; and such just judgment, God says, is inescapable. *On the day of the Lord's sacrifice I will punish the officials and the king's sons and all those clad in foreign clothes* (8).

Today our secular leaders often argue that their private lives and lifestyle should not be judged by the media or the public. Zephaniah reminds us that we are all accountable to God; we cannot escape his judgment.

Zephaniah now turns to a second group that has broken God's covenant and deserves God's inescapable judgment: the religious leaders (9). *On that day I will punish all who avoid stepping on the threshold, who fill the temple of their gods with violence and deceit* (9).[23]

The religious leaders are condemned first of all for 'leaping' *over the threshold* (NRSV). This almost certainly refers to a Philistine superstition (1 Sam. 5:5). The Philistine god Dagon stood at the threshold of the temple at Ashdod. It seems that the worshippers at this pagan temple would not walk on the threshold but instead jumped over it as a mark of respect or perhaps superstitious fear. Possibly some religious leaders and others were observing this ancient pagan superstition in the Jerusalem temple – *their master's house* (9b, NRSV) – so corrupting the worship of the Lord. We too need to be constantly on our guard against corrupting Christian worship with superstitious practices.

It may well be that some of the religious leaders were carrying out these rituals without realizing their origin or significance and without proper thought. God is looking for our thoughtful worship. Jesus set the standard. True worshippers will worship the Father in spirit and in truth, for they are the kind of worshippers the Father seeks; 'God is spirit, and his worshippers must worship in the Spirit and in truth' (John 4:23–24). The apostle Paul also called for thoughtful worship in his letter to the Christians in Rome: 'Therefore, I urge you, brothers and sisters, in view of God's mercy, to offer your bodies as a living sacrifice, holy and pleasing to God – this is your true [literally, 'logical' or 'reasonable'] and proper worship' (Rom. 12:1). When Paul wrote to the church in Corinth about worshipping

---

[23] See also v. 9, NRSV: *On that day I will punish all who leap over the threshold, who fill their master's house with violence and fraud.*

God, he said: 'I will pray with my spirit, but I will also pray with my understanding; I will sing with my spirit, but I will also sing with my understanding' (1 Cor. 14:15). Those who are called to lead worship in church need to take this responsibility seriously. Zephaniah does not hesitate to warn us about God's judgment on those who allowed unthinking superstition to corrupt the liturgy in the temple of the Lord.

These same religious leaders were also guilty of filling *their master's house* [the temple?] *with violence and fraud* (9b, NRSV). To do *violence* (Heb., *ḥāmās*) is often linked with social and political disruption. But sometimes the word is used with reference to doing violence to the truth under oath (e.g. Deut. 19:16). If this is the meaning here, then these religious leaders were guilty of distorting the true meaning of God's Word and so deceiving God's people.

Church leaders today are sometimes guilty of doing violence to the Scriptures so that their congregations are not fed with the pure Word of God but with the husks of human opinions. In a book entitled *Fragmented Faith*, Leslie Francis of the University of Wales produced some shocking statistics about the distorted faith of many Anglicans in the UK. These statistics were based on returns from 5,762 lay and 1,800 clergy readers of the *Church Times*. From these returns Francis deduced that 3% of the clergy (about 300) did not believe in God at all; 10% of the clergy did not believe in God as a personal Being. Two fifths of the clergy did not believe in the virgin birth or Jesus' miracles; nearly one quarter were unable to affirm the bodily resurrection of Jesus; one quarter did not believe in heaven; and a majority could not accept Jesus' teaching on hell.[24]

The apostle Paul sets a different standard for ministry. He wrote to the Christians in Corinth, 'We do not use deception, nor do we distort the word of God. On the contrary, by setting forth the truth plainly we commend ourselves to everyone's conscience in the sight of God' (2 Cor. 4:2). The apostle had the same sense of urgency as Zephaniah when he spoke of the importance of teaching the truth in the light of God's judgment and the final Day of the Lord. He wrote to young Timothy, a leader in the church at Ephesus:

> In the presence of God and of Christ Jesus, who will judge the living and the dead, and in view of his appearing and his kingdom, I give you this

[24] Quoted in an article by James Alder, entitled 'Bits and Peaces', in *New Directions*, October 2005, p. 7 (spelling of 'peaces' as original).

> charge: preach the word; be prepared in season and out of season; correct, rebuke and encourage – with great patience and careful instruction.
> (2 Tim. 4:1–2)

The religious leaders in Jerusalem were failing to lead worship thoughtfully or to teach God's Word faithfully. They deserved God's judgment. Time was running out. God's judgment was inescapable. *I will punish* them, says God. If God has called us to leadership in his church, how we need to examine ourselves in the light of his Word! We do well to remember the words of the apostle Paul: 'So, if you think you are standing firm, be careful that you don't fall!' (1 Cor. 10:12). Paul wrote these words in the context of the sins of idolatry, sexual immorality and grumbling. But they equally apply to the sin of intellectual pride and the unwillingness to submit to, and to teach the truth of, God's Word. One day we will have to give account of our teaching as well as our behaviour (1 Cor. 3:10–15). God's judgment is inescapable.

Zephaniah now turns his attention to the next group, the business community. Judgment is coming to them too. He imagines the invading army starting from the Fish Gate (10) and moving through the New Quarter of the city, causing cries of anguish and fear among the wealthy business community. The destruction of their homes, and perhaps the shrines of the pagan gods where some of them worshipped on the hills outside the city (10b), could be seen and heard. It seems that nothing can save them from God's inescapable judgments: *all your merchants will be wiped out, all who trade with silver will be destroyed* (11b). This was worse than the Wall Street crash of the 1920s, Black Wednesday in the city of London, or the credit crunch and recession in 2008. Everything they had worked for in the city would be destroyed. Yet God was still appealing to them to mourn for their sins and to return to him: *Wail, you who live in the market district* (11a). *Seek the LORD . . . Seek righteousness, seek humility . . .* (2:3).

God's judgments are searching and thorough. In a striking phrase, God says: *At that time I will search Jerusalem with lamps and punish those who are complacent, who are like wine left on its dregs, who think, 'The LORD will do nothing, either good or bad'* (12). The idea of God searching Jerusalem with lamps suggests that there were shady deals or dishonest business practices to expose, or that some of the rich were exploiting the poor. Certainly it is a reminder to us that, as the writer to the Hebrews put it, 'Nothing in all creation is hidden from God's sight. Everything is uncovered and laid bare before the eyes of him to whom we must give account' (Heb. 4:13). If that is a humbling truth, it is also a reassuring one. It speaks to us of a God who is just, who hates injustice and knows all about us. He judges the hearts of each of us. He knows our thoughts and motives, and the circumstances of our lives. Just as God searched the many dark corners in Jerusalem 'with lamps', so he searches out the dark corners of our lives with the light of his Word. He does this with perfect justice, perfect knowledge and perfect love.

Interestingly, it is complacency rather than dishonesty that God turns his spotlight on most clearly. Prosperity easily breeds complacency. Those who became rich through business and trade had become so self-sufficient and successful that they no longer felt accountable to God. They believed that they could ignore God with impunity. Their philosophy was *The LORD will do nothing, either good or bad*, even though they had broken God's covenant, compromised their loyalty to Yahweh, and now no longer *seek the LORD nor enquire of him* (6). Here were people who did not deny God's existence, but doubted his relevance. *The LORD will do nothing . . . good* meant that they did not expect God to help them, or see any reason to look for that help. *The LORD will do nothing . . . bad* meant that they did not fear God's judgments or expect him to do anything about their sins. Motyer describes this philosophy as 'practical atheism'. 'It does not say "God is not there", but "God is not here"; not that "God does not exist" but that "He does not matter".'[25]

This 'practical atheism' is widespread in the UK today. A significant proporton of the population still say that they believe in God, but in practice they regard 'God' as irrelevant to their lives. It can be much the same for those of us who are regular churchgoers. We can go through the familiar rituals of a church service, say 'Amen' at the end of the prayers and not mean it; we can sing hymns or songs without ever thinking about the words; we can listen to the sermon while thinking about the lunch ('Did I put the oven on?') or the next game of football or golf. In a word, God has become irrelevant. We are practical atheists. I once heard the late Bishop Festo Kivengere of Uganda preach an unforgettable sermon in which he warned us that it was very easy to come to a church service with some specific problem or 'burden' and to go away again with the burden

[25] For further discussion, see Motyer, in McComiskey (ed.), *The Minor Prophets*, vol. 3, p. 921.

as great as ever and the problem unsolved. This is a kind of practical atheism: often the last thing we expect when we go to church is that we will actually meet the living God, or that he will take away our burden or meet our deepest needs. Zephaniah addressed this problem in his day; we need to let this word from God speak to us too.

Zephaniah uses another vivid phrase (12) to describe these complacent citizens in Jerusalem. They are *like wine left on its dregs* or 'wine thickening upon their lees' (Szeles). A good wine, as it ferments, rids itself of the dregs. These accumulate as the 'lees'. The wine is drawn off from its lees by separating the fermenting liquid from the sludge; but if it is left it becomes bitter to the taste. These citizens had not separated from their sins – like the dregs in the wine – and so their sins contaminated their lives. They had probably neglected that kind of self-examination that would lead to repentance and allow God to take away from their lives the 'dregs' of sinful disobedience.

George Adam Smith points out that to 'settle upon one's lees' became a proverb for sloth, indifference and a muddy mind. Smith believed that Zephaniah was challenging people's complacency arising out of the slowness and limitations of Josiah's reforms:

> Of course disappointments ensued . . . disappointments and listlessness. The new security of life became a temptation; persecution ceased, and religious men lived again at ease. So numbers of eager and sparkling souls, who had been in the front of the movement, fell away into a selfish and idle obscurity.[26]

Whatever the exact causes of their complacency, these 'practical atheists' were under the judgment of God, a judgment that was both near and inescapable. *Their wealth will be plundered, their houses demolished. Though they build houses, they will not live in them; though they plant vineyards, they will not drink the wine* (13). Here was a warning of God's judgment on people who sought to make money, buy property, build houses and extend their real estate simply for their own benefit and well-being, and without reference to God's will and Word. They were like some rich people in the New Testament church who, according to the apostle James, would make their plans without seeking the Lord's will. Like Zephaniah, the apostle confronts them boldly:

[26] G. A. Smith, *The Books of the Twelve Prophets*, vol. 2 (Hodder & Stoughton, 1928), p. 53.

> Now listen, you who say, 'Today or tomorrow we will go to this or that city, spend a year there, carry on business and make money.' Why, you do not even know what will happen tomorrow. What is your life? You are a mist that appears for a little while and then vanishes. Instead, you ought to say, 'If it is the Lord's will, we will live and do this or that.' As it is, you boast in your arrogant schemes. All such boasting is evil.
> (Jas 4:13–16)

How many of us, I wonder, make our life plans without prior reference to God, and boast of those plans? Jesus warned his disciples about doing this and setting their heart on riches in the parable of the rich fool (Luke 12:13–21). God's message to the complacent citizens of Jerusalem in Zephaniah's time was much the same. We too need to hear what the Spirit says to the churches (see Rev. 3:14–22); for spiritual complacency and practical atheism are not unknown in our churches today, nor in our own hearts, if we are honest.

In this section of Zephaniah (10–13) we have learned of God's warning of imminent and inescapable judgment on the business community in Jerusalem and on the wealthy citizens who had turned their back on God. This teaches us that God is concerned with every aspect of our lives – our daily work, as well as personal, family and 'spiritual' matters. God wants us to refer everything to him, including matters of finance, property and fulfilment at work. (His disciplining judgment sometimes frustrates that sense of fulfilment – *though they plant vineyards, they will not drink the wine* – in order to bring us back to dependence on him.) Businesspeople, as well as politicians, are foolish if they say in relation to their work, 'We don't do God.' For there is nothing in our lives that is out of bounds to God. He *will search . . . with lamps* and punish those who are complacent, says Zephaniah. His judgment on our lives is inescapable.

How grateful we should be that God sent his Son to be the saviour of sinners, whether those sinners be found among the civil or religious leadership of a nation, or among other solid citizens, whether rich or poor. Because 'God made him [Jesus] who had no sin to be sin for us, so that in him we might become the righteousness of God' (2 Cor. 5:21), the apostle Paul can assure us that 'there is now no condemnation for those who are in Christ Jesus' (Rom. 8:1). But he also wrote that 'we must all appear before the judgment seat of Christ' (2 Cor. 5:10). Even though true Christian believers are eternally secure 'in Christ Jesus', we will still have to give an account of our lives on that final day of judgment. It is that *great day of the Lord* which Zephaniah now goes on to describe.

4. The end is near (1:14–18)

The words *The great day of the Lord is near* (14a) round off the previous section (7–13) and introduce the next section (14–18).

In the previous passage (7–13) the emphasis was on a day of judgment that was near and inescapable, and which actually came to pass some twenty years after Josiah had died. In this passage (14–18) Zephaniah still has this day in mind. He calls it *a day of wrath, a day of distress and anguish, a day of trouble and ruin* (15). But he also has in mind the *great day of the Lord*, which includes the concept of a final and universal day of judgment, when, *In the fire of his jealousy the whole world will be consumed, for he will make a sudden end of all who live on the earth* (18).

Zephaniah seems to see a pattern emerging which makes certain judgments in history (as in 586 BC) point forward to the final day of judgment at the end of time. The judgment on Jerusalem symbolized for him the judgment of the world.

The reasons for these judgments are identical. The people *have sinned against the Lord* (17) and a just God must punish sin. For Zephaniah and other biblical writers, God's justice and holiness expressed itself in *wrath* (15) and *jealousy* (18). We need to remember, of course, that God's wrath is completely free from sinful human spite, vindictiveness or anger. God doesn't lose his temper. Rather, God's wrath is his holy reaction to sin and evil. As the apostle John wrote centuries later, 'God is light; in him there is no darkness at all' (1 John 1:5). We can understand how light and darkness cannot coexist. If you switch on a light in a dark room, the darkness is expelled. A holy God expelled a disobedient Adam and Eve from the Garden. The prophet Habakkuk rightly says to God, 'Your eyes are too pure to look on evil; you cannot tolerate wrongdoing' (Hab. 1:13). Zephaniah agrees, and foresees that the *great day of the Lord* will be *a day of wrath* – a day when God finally deals with sin and evil (18).

The *fire of his jealousy* (18) is also a term which excludes any idea of sinful jealousy so far as God is concerned. As Kaiser says:

> Jealousy when applied to God denotes that God is intensely concerned for his own character and reputation . . . the metaphor best depicting this

> emotion is that of the jealous husband, which God is said to be when false gods and false allegiances play the part of suitors and potential paramours. He cannot and will not tolerate rivalry of any kind . . . our spiritual lives depend on his tenacious hold of us.[27]

Zephaniah's teaching in this passage (14–18) helps us to prepare for this final great Day of the Lord as he reminds us of some important truths about that day.

a. The Day of the Lord is imminent

I was always glad in my student days that the university where I studied set an examination for my subject at the end of each academic year. Some students with different subjects were only tested at the end of their first and third years. So in the second year, with no exam in the immediate future, it was often difficult for them to keep focused on the work they needed to complete in order to satisfy the examiner at the end of their course. Most of us find that deadlines that are not too far away help to concentrate the mind. They keep us focused.

Zephaniah has warned his hearers about a day of judgment that will come to Jerusalem soon (7, 14). It took place, in fact, in 586 BC. But it is also true that whenever the biblical writers speak about the final day of judgment, the *great day of the LORD*, they also imply that such a day is imminent, and that people need to be ready for that day when it comes. Zephaniah, it seems, saw the impending destruction of Jerusalem in his day as a sign of the final judgment at the end of the age. Such a final examination could come at any time. In that sense, it is always imminent, and we should always be ready for it.

Jesus too saw the impending destruction of Jerusalem (destroyed in AD 70) as a sign of final judgment (Matt. 24; Mark 13; Luke 21). But he did not tell his disciples when that final day would come. When his disciples asked him privately, 'Tell us . . . what will be the sign of your coming and of the end of the age?' (Matt. 24:3), Jesus told them of many 'signs' that would be seen in every generation; but urged them to 'keep watch, because you do not know on what day your Lord will come' (Matt. 24:42). Indeed Jesus was prepared to say, 'About that day or hour no one knows, not even the angels in heaven, nor the Son, but only the Father' (Matt. 24:36;

---

27 W. C. Kaiser, *Hard Sayings of the Old Testament* (Hodder & Stoughton, 1991), p. 232.

Mark 13:32). The point is that both Zephaniah and Jesus are saying that the end of the age is imminent, and that we should always be focused and ready for that day.

It is commonly said that the New Testament writers expected an immediate return of Jesus after his death and resurrection, even in the lifetime of his apostles. So in Mark's Gospel (Mark 13:26–31) when Jesus says that 'people will see the Son of Man coming in clouds with great power and glory', he goes on to say, 'Truly I tell you, this generation will certainly not pass away until all these things have happened.' If 'this generation' refers to the generation of his disciples, then the reference to the Son of Man coming in glory could refer to his immediate return during the lifetime of these disciples. On the other hand, 'coming in glory' could refer to the transfiguration of Jesus; or 'this generation' could refer to the generation that sees the 'signs' of the end times, including the 'sign' that the gospel has been preached to all nations (Matt. 24:14; Mark 13:10). The fact is that an immediate return is not the same as an imminent return. Jesus' return at the end of the age would not be immediate, according to Jesus' own teaching. For one thing, there needed to be time for the gospel to be preached to every nation. Some of the parables of Jesus also imply that the end of the age would not be immediate. In the parable of the ten virgins (or bridesmaids), for example, the bridegroom delays his coming until midnight, the delay causing all of them to become drowsy and to fall asleep (Matt. 25:5–6). It is perhaps significant too that in the parable of the talents, Jesus says that '*After a long time* the master of those servants returned and settled accounts with them' (Matt. 25:19; emphasis mine).

It is true that some in the New Testament church may well have believed that Jesus' return would be immediate.[28] The apostle Peter was also aware of such expectations, as hinted at in one of his letters when he warned Christians in these words: 'in the last days scoffers will come, scoffing and following their own evil desires. They will say, "Where is this 'coming' he promised? Ever since our ancestors died, everything goes on as it has since the beginning of creation"' (2 Pet. 3:3–4).

The consistent teaching of the New Testament, however, is that the final day of judgment, which Zephaniah calls *the great day of the* Lord, is not necessarily immediate, but it is always imminent. As Jesus said,

---

[28] Did some of the Christians become idle and give up work because they believed that Jesus would return in their lifetime? See 1 Thess. 5:13–17; 2 Thess. 3:11–13.

'Therefore keep watch, because you do not know on what day your Lord will come' (Matt. 24:42). Even though the coming again of Jesus is delayed, we should be ready for him at any time.

A friend of mine went home from church on the top of a London bus, with the question from that evening's sermon running through her mind. The preacher had challenged the congregation with the question, 'If Jesus were to come back tonight, would you be ready to meet him?' As my friend wrestled with the question, she knew that she was not ready, for she had never asked the Lord Jesus Christ to come into her life, to forgive her sins and to give her eternal life (1 John 5:11–12). There on the bus she became a committed Christian and began many years of Christian discipleship and service. It was the imminence of the great Day of the Lord which had moved her to respond to the call of Jesus to follow him for the rest of her life.

Zephaniah is aware of this imminence. He may well have wondered whether that day would come with the inevitable judgment that was coming soon to Jerusalem and Judah. In fact that judgment came some twenty years after Zephaniah had completed his ministry and died. But as Zephaniah described the destruction of Jerusalem soon to be completed, he also looked ahead to that final day which was not only imminent and of great importance, but awesome.

b. The Day of the Lord is awesome

Zephaniah now sets before his hearers an awesome scene. It no doubt fitted the judgment on Jerusalem that the Babylonians were soon to bring about (587–586 BC). But it also looked forward to that final *great day of the Lord . . . the day of the LORD's wrath . . .* when, as Zephaniah graphically expressed it, *In the fire of his jealousy the whole world will be consumed, for he will make a sudden end of all who live on the earth* (18b).

There is a pattern[29] about this passage which reveals the focus of Zephaniah's teaching in this oracle. It may be described as follows:

A. The day of God's wrath promised (14b–16a)
B. Human defences useless (16b)
C. Humankind helpless (17a)
D. Human sin is the reason for God's wrath (17b)

[29] Based on the structure set out in Motyer on Zephaniah, in McComiskey (ed.), *The Minor Prophets*, vol. 3, p. 922.

C′. Humankind destroyed (17b)
B′. Human wealth useless (18a)
A′. The day of the Lord's wrath completed (18b, c)

So this passage begins and ends with its focus on the holiness of God, which expresses itself in the overflowing wrath of God against the sin of humankind (15, 17–18). It seems, then, that Zephaniah is challenging his hearers, and us, to recognize at least three truths.

i. We need to acknowledge the greatness of God

The story is told of a young girl who came home from church one day having learned the proposition that 'God is everywhere'. 'Mummy,' she said, 'is God in this house?' 'Yes,' said her mother, 'God is everywhere.' (So far so good!) But the child went on, 'Is God in this kitchen, then?' 'Why, yes', said her mother. 'Is he on this table?' she persisted. 'Well,' said her mother, trying to remember snatches of theology from the sermons she had heard, 'I think so.' 'Is he in this inkpot?' the girl continued remorselessly. 'Well, yes, I suppose so,' replied her mother. The girl slammed her small hand down on top of the inkpot. 'Got him!' she shouted triumphantly.

Many of us have probably treated God like that at times. We have tried to bottle him, to bring him down to our size, to manipulate him. Or we have treated him as some in Jerusalem had done when they thought within themselves, *The Lord will do nothing, either good or bad* (12).

Zephaniah, however, will not let the people get away with thinking about God like that. God is awesome to Zephaniah; he is a great God. He describes him in this passage as the *Lord* or Yahweh (14, 18). He is the covenant God whose steadfast love for his people is constantly affirmed in Scripture (for example, in Hosea). The Lord loves us with an everlasting love. Zephaniah also speaks about the holiness of God. His holiness means that he is distinct, different, 'wholly other', separate from sin, absolutely pure and sinless. So when Zephaniah writes about *the Lord's wrath* (18a), he is not speaking about sinful anger but rather God's holy reaction against sin. When Zephaniah writes about the Lord's *jealousy* (18b), he is acknowledging God's devoted love for his redeemed people that will brook no rival. God is determined to see that sin and evil is finally destroyed and that his righteousness and justice will finally be vindicated. Our God is an awesome God. That day, when *in the fire of his jealousy the whole earth will be consumed*, is an awesome day.

Zephaniah may also be drawing our attention to the greatness and power of God when he calls out to the people in Jerusalem and Judah with these words: *The cry on the day of the LORD is bitter; the Mighty Warrior shouts his battle cry* (14b). It's possible that Zephaniah is referring here to a situation in war where the circumstances are so dire that even brave warriors (the Judean SAS?) are crying out in bitterness and fear. God's judgments are awesome, even to the brave. On the other hand, it is possible that Zephaniah is referring to the Lord as a mighty *warrior.* The cry of bitterness (14b) would then be an expression of the grief and sadness that the Lord feels as he brings just judgment to bear upon his own people. The Gospel writers describe this attitude in Jesus as he wept over the coming judgment upon Jerusalem in his day:

> Jerusalem, Jerusalem, you who kill the prophets and stone those sent to you, how often I have longed to gather your children together, as a hen gathers her chicks under her wings, and you were not willing. Look, your house is left to you desolate.
> (Luke 13:34–35; see also 19:41–44)

So here perhaps is another picture of the greatness of our God. He is a mighty warrior, advancing against his enemies and sure of victory. Certainly the prophet Isaiah saw it like that. He wrote, 'The LORD will march out like a champion, like a warrior he will stir up his zeal; with a shout he will raise the battle cry and will triumph over his enemies' (Isa. 42:13).

The God revealed in these verses through Zephaniah's message is no pushover. He is great; he is awesome. If we are to be ready for the *great day of the LORD*, we need to acknowledge the greatness and glory of God. It is the fear of the Lord that is the beginning of wisdom (Prov. 9:10).

C. S. Lewis captured something of this awesomeness when he depicted Jesus as the lion Aslan in the children's story *The Lion, the Witch and the Wardrobe*. When Mr Beaver describes Aslan to the children, Susan, Lucy and Edmund, he quotes an old rhyme of Narnia:

> Wrong will be right, when Aslan comes in sight,
> At the sound of his roar, sorrows will be no more,
> When he bares his teeth, winter meets its death,
> And when he shakes his mane, we shall have spring again.

Susan is a little fearful of this description of Aslan. So she asks:

> 'Is he – quite safe? I shall feel rather nervous about meeting a lion.'
>
> 'That you will, dearie, and no mistake,' said Mrs. Beaver; 'if there's anyone who can appear before Aslan without their knees knocking, they're either braver than most or just silly.'
>
> 'Then he isn't safe?' said Lucy.
>
> 'Safe?' said Mr. Beaver . . . 'Who said anything about safe? 'Course he isn't safe. But he's good. He's the King, I tell you.'[30]

The writer to the Hebrews teaches us even more clearly about the greatness and awesomeness of God, and the combination of reverent fear and joyful assurance that is appropriate for Christian believers as we come into God's presence. The writer reminded first-century Christian believers:

> You have come to God, the Judge of all . . . to Jesus the mediator of a new covenant, and to the sprinkled blood that speaks a better word than the blood of Abel . . . Therefore, since we are receiving a kingdom that cannot be shaken, let us be thankful, and so worship God acceptably with reverence and awe, for our 'God is a consuming fire.'
> (Heb. 12:23–24, 28)

If we are to be ready for that awesome day, the *great day of the Lord*, we must not fail to acknowledge the greatness of our God.

ii. We need to accept the reality of judgment

If some people in Jerusalem thought, *The Lord will do nothing, either good or bad* (12b), then presumably they were blind to the true glory of God and sceptical about the reality of judgment. There are many people in our Western culture who likewise have no fear of God or judgment. Zephaniah has no doubts about the reality of judgment. *The great day of the Lord is near . . . That day* ***will*** *be a day of wrath . . . the whole earth* ***will*** *be consumed, for he* ***will*** *make a sudden end of all who live on the earth* (14–15, 18; emphasis mine).

Zephaniah emphasizes two complementary truths about judgment. The first is that it is the result of the activity of God; the second is that it is the result of the sinfulness of humankind.

[30] C. S. Lewis, *The Lion, the Witch and the Wardrobe* (Geoffrey Bles, 1950), p. 77.

Judgment is the result of the activity of God

Zephaniah begins this section (1:14–18) by calling on the people of Jerusalem and Judah to listen to God's warnings about the great Day of the Lord. *The cry on the day of the Lord [will be] bitter* (14). Too often God's people turned a deaf ear to God. We often do the same. On one understanding of verse 14, God is depicted as a mighty warrior coming to defeat his enemies. Then Zephaniah describes the consequences of God's activity: *a day of wrath, a day of distress and anguish, a day of trouble and ruin, a day of darkness and gloom, a day of clouds and blackness* (15). We have already noticed that these words describe a kind of reversal of creation. It is an activity of God that is going on all the time. Surely that is what the apostle Paul is teaching us in that famous passage in his letter to the Christians in Rome:

> The wrath of God is being revealed from heaven against all the godlessness and wickedness of people, who suppress the truth by their wickedness . . . Therefore God gave them over in the sinful desires of their hearts to sexual impurity . . . They exchanged the truth of God for a lie, and worshipped and served created things rather than the Creator . . .
> (Rom. 1:18, 24–25)

However, it is God's final action of judgment which is the most awesome. Zephaniah tells us, as we have already noted several times, that on that great Day of the Lord *the whole earth will be consumed, for he will make a sudden end of all who live on the earth* (18). There is no doubt that this truth about final judgment motivates Zephaniah to make an impassioned appeal for God's people to come together and to repent (see note below on 2:1–3, pp. 235–246). The apostle Peter did the same, and may well have been drawing on Zephaniah's description of the end. Peter wrote, 'But the day of the Lord will come like a thief. The heavens will disappear with a roar; the elements will be destroyed by fire, and the earth and everything done in it will be laid bare' (2 Pet. 3:10). Peter then challenges all of us with a question: 'Since everything will be destroyed in this way, what kind of people ought you to be?' (3:11).

We need to face up to this question as we ponder the awesomeness of God's final act of judgment. We also need to consider a further proposition about judgment.

Judgment is the result of the sinfulness of humankind

The sceptic dismisses the concept of a final day of judgment as Zephaniah describes it. 'If God is good and loving, surely he would not destroy the world that he has made and the people in it?' it is sometimes argued. Zephaniah wants us to understand that God is not only good and loving, but also holy and just. As a holy God he must judge sin; and humankind has sinned big time. Right at the heart of this passage (17b), Zephaniah is teaching us that human sin is the reason for God's wrath.

Zephaniah sets out clearly the consequences of people's sin. The turning of the order of creation into the disorder described as *distress and anguish . . . trouble and ruin . . . darkness and gloom . . . clouds and blackness . . . a day of trumpet and battle cry against the fortified cities and against the corner towers* (15–16) is a clear enough picture of the ravages and sufferings of war, which is the result of our inhumanity towards one another. Jesus taught clearly that 'it is from within, out of a person's heart, that evil thoughts come – sexual immorality, theft, murder, adultery, greed, malice, deceit, lewdness, envy, slander, arrogance and folly' (Mark 7:21–22). These things lead to war and violence. As the apostle James put it:

> What causes fights and quarrels among you? Don't they come from your desires that battle within you? You desire but do not have, so you kill. You covet but you cannot get what you want, so you quarrel and fight. You do not have because you do not ask God.
> (Jas 4:1–2)

Zephaniah also uses phrases that remind his readers that judgment comes as a result of disobedience and the deliberate breaking of God's covenant. He warns them that God says, *I will bring such distress on all people that they will grope about like those who are blind, because they have sinned against the Lord* (17). When he does this, some of the people would recall that God had said to Moses, many years earlier, that if the people broke the covenant God had made with them and disobeyed him, then

> these curses will come on you and overtake you . . . At midday you will grope about like a blind person in the dark. You will be unsuccessful in everything you do; day after day you will be oppressed and robbed, with no one to rescue you.
> (Deut. 28:15, 29)

Blind, lost, in darkness, frustrated, making one mistake after another. Isn't this exactly what we experience when we turn our back on God?

The terrible experiences of war, when life seems to be cheap and worthless, may well be captured in this next phrase: *Their blood will be poured out like dust and their entrails like dung* (17b). Sin has terrible consequences. Furthermore, Zephaniah points out, humankind is unable to save itself or escape the just judgment of God. Just as Jerusalem, putting its trust in fortified cities and corner towers, would never be able to defend itself against the Babylonian army with its trumpets and battle cries, so humankind will never save itself when the last trumpet sounds and the last great day of judgment comes (16). Human resources will not be able to save us on that day (18).

It would be wrong, however, to leave Zephaniah's message on a note of total destruction without glimpsing the devoted (jealous) love of God for his people (18b), and the hope and salvation that is implicit in the final, awesome destruction of all sin and evil on the last great Day of the Lord.

iii. We need to rejoice in the certainty of victory

We have already observed that the *day of the Lord* is a day of judgment in Zephaniah's oracle. That *great day of the Lord* is the final day of judgment when God at last triumphs over evil, and when all that deserves his wrath, affronts his holiness and grieves his steadfast covenant love is finally destroyed (18).

Such a *day of the Lord's wrath* is awesome. It should, however, provoke not only the fear of the Lord but also, for believers, joy in God; for it is a day of victory over God's enemies, a day when justice is done and seen to be done. So the psalmist, for example, often calls on God's people to rejoice in his judgments:

> Say among the nations, 'The Lord reigns.'
> The world is firmly established, it cannot be moved;
> he will judge the peoples with equity.
>
> Let the heavens rejoice, let the earth be glad . . .
> he comes to judge the earth.
> He will judge the world in righteousness
> and the peoples in his faithfulness.
> (Ps. 96:10–11, 13)

Or again, 'Zion hears and rejoices and the villages of Judah are glad because of your judgments, LORD' (Ps. 97:8).

Zephaniah has made it perfectly clear that Yahweh is not one who *will do nothing, either good or bad* (12). Rather, he *is righteous; he does no wrong. Morning by morning he dispenses his justice* (3:5). Finally, on the *day of the LORD's wrath*, he completes that work of judgment.[31]

For Zephaniah, however, the great Day of the Lord is not only a day of destruction; it is also a day of deliverance. The day when sin is punished is also the day when righteousness triumphs. In the prophecy of Isaiah God had said, 'See, I will create new heavens and a new earth . . . The wolf and the lamb will feed together, and the lion will eat straw like the ox' (Isa. 65:17, 25). Zephaniah expresses this future hope differently,[32] but he refers to an 'ideal' situation in the future when *all [peoples] may call on the name of the LORD and serve him shoulder to shoulder* (3:9). On that great Day of the Lord, the God who *dispenses his justice* (3:5) will also be *the Mighty Warrior who saves* (3:17).

If Zephaniah does not spell this out as clearly as we would like, Jesus certainly did. When describing the final day of judgment and the signs that preceded 'the Son of Man coming in a cloud with power and great glory', Jesus added: 'When these things begin to take place, stand up and lift up your heads, because your *redemption* is drawing near' (Luke 21:27–28; emphasis mine). The coming great Day of the Lord is not only about the destruction of the world but also about its redemption.

The apostle Peter spells out the certainty of this final victory in his second letter:

> That day will bring about the destruction of the heavens by fire, and the elements will melt in the heat. But in keeping with his promise we are looking forward to a new heaven and a new earth, where righteousness dwells.
> (2 Pet. 3:12–13)

---

[31] NB: One reason for the necessity for a final day of judgment is the imperfect nature of all human attempts at justice. Ralph Martin writes: 'Justice is never perfectly done on earth; the good die young; the righteous suffer; the poor are defrauded. But God's Word speaks over and over of that great day of Yahweh, when God's faithful ones will be rewarded and blessed beyond measure, when God's enemies, and those who have lived unrighteous lives will be definitively punished.' R. Martin, *Is Jesus Coming Soon?*, quoted in R. Chia, *Hope For the World* (IVP, 2006), p. 95.

[32] See exposition of Zeph. 3:9–20, pp. 285–310.

Likewise the apostle Paul teaches us that the whole of creation is waiting on tiptoe with excitement for that day:

> The creation waits in eager expectation for the children of God to be revealed. For the creation was subjected to frustration, not by its own choice, but by the will of the one who subjected it, in hope that the creation itself will be liberated from its bondage to decay and brought into the freedom and glory of the children of God.
> (Rom. 8:19–21).

Some years ago I was walking along the cliffs of north Norfolk when I met a friend I had not seen for a number of years. After exchanging greetings, I asked him how things were going with him and his family. He answered that they had all been through some difficult times healthwise and in other ways. Then he smiled and said, 'But we are on the winning side, aren't we?'

When Zephaniah writes of that great Day of the Lord, he knows that day is imminent and awesome. He knows that God is great, and that judgment is real and serious. But he also knows, as he will spell out in chapter 3, that God's victory over sin and evil is certain. He also knows that God is not only just and holy, but also loving, merciful and a mighty warrior who saves. He knows that believers are on the winning side! God wants us to be sure of these things too. But how can we be sure that we shall be saved on that last great day of judgment? Zephaniah now begins to explain what we must do to be saved.

5. It's time to repent (2:1–3)

My father-in-law, the late Canon Cecil Bewes, was a gentle and faithful minister of the gospel for more than sixty years. His ministry took him to Exeter, Kenya, London, Tonbridge and Cooden. Always he sought to proclaim and teach 'the whole counsel of God' (Acts 20:27, ESV). That included the message of judgment as well as salvation; sin as well as grace. One day a senior church leader rebuked him for his total commitment to the biblical gospel. 'There you go again, Cecil,' he said, 'beating your gospel drum!' Cecil Bewes replied: 'I pray that I may go on beating it until the day I die!' By God's grace, that is exactly what he did.

I like to think that Zephaniah was, by God's grace, a man like that. Certainly, he proclaimed a message of sin and judgment; and as he calls the people of Judah to *gather together*, and *seek the LORD*, he is still warning them of God's *appointed time* of judgment, which will come *like chaff clear gone all at once* (2a).[33] He is still pronouncing boldly *the LORD's fierce anger*, which will come upon them because of their sins. But he also knows that the Lord loves his people (3:14–17). He knows that God is able to save them – *perhaps you will be sheltered on the day of the LORD's anger* (3b). So he calls upon the whole nation to repent and to return to the Lord before it is too late.

'Repentance' has been defined as 'a change of mind leading to a change of direction'. It means far more than 'being sorry for our sins'. In the story that Jesus told about the lost son (Luke 15:11–32), the prodigal had to come 'to his senses' (15:17), acknowledge his sins (15:18) and return to his father with the humble words, 'I am no longer worthy to be called your son' (15:19). Having changed his mind about his rebellious behaviour, he returns to his father (15:20). The parable goes on to teach us that the father (like God our heavenly Father) is always looking out for his lost son to return to him, and welcomes, accepts and reinstates him as his son with the joyful words, 'For this son of mine was dead and is alive again; he was lost and is found' (15:24).

Zephaniah knows that time is running out; but he also knows that it is not too late for the people to return to God and to cast themselves upon his mercy. So, first he addresses the *nation* of Judah (2:1); then he addresses the *humble of the land* (2:3).

a. The nation: there's a place for corporate repentance (1–2)

There is no doubt that Zephaniah is deeply concerned about the state of the nation. When he addresses Judah he uses the Hebrew word *gôy*, which usually refers to a pagan nation. It is almost as if he is implying that Judah has lost her religious identity because of her faithlessness. Certainly he calls Judah a *shameful nation* (1). The Hebrew word literally means 'devoid of feeling', and so comes to mean 'unresponsive to the Lord'. No doubt the complacency of God's people, described earlier (1:12), is a reason for this. The dangerous thing about complacency is that it tends to remove all sense of shame, and the need for repentance. So once again Zephaniah emphasizes the urgency of the situation. God has decreed judgment. It is already scheduled (2a). Furthermore, *that day passes like windblown chaff*,

[33] J. A. Motyer's translation, in McComiskey (ed.), *The Minor Prophets*, vol. 3, p. 915.

which might be better translated as *like chaff clean gone all at once* (2b). For this day, *the day of the* L*ORD's wrath* (2c), may well refer to the final day of judgment when all nations will have to give account of themselves to God (see Matt. 25:31–46). *Gather together*, says Zephaniah, before that final day comes; *perhaps you will be sheltered on the day of the* L*ORD's anger* (3c).

Before we look further at Zephaniah's message to the nation of Judah, we do well to ask ourselves whether we have anywhere near the passion and concern that he had on account of the faithlessness and unresponsiveness of Judah. The people of Judah professed to be God's people. So we need to ask ourselves, first, whether we are concerned enough about the faithlessness of parts of the church to *gather together* to wait for God and to pray for God's mercy upon her. Zephaniah must have shown great courage in pressing his message home. His contemporary, Jeremiah, tells us that there were many false prophets at the time, and God spoke out against them: 'They dress the wound of my people as though it were not serious. "Peace, peace," they say, when there is no peace' (Jer. 6:14). Zephaniah was not like that. But are we? Even some lectionary readings in the Anglican Church have passages about judgment excluded. Do we exclude them from our preaching? Second, how concerned are we in the UK about our once-Christian nation which has largely turned its back on God and his Word? Zephaniah's boldness and clarity should be an inspiration and a challenge to us.

But what point was there in gathering together? In Zephaniah's day, people were used to meeting together regularly for some great festival. Zephaniah now calls upon the nation to *gather together* for the specific purpose of acknowledging sin and seeking the Lord. This is perhaps suggested by the root meaning of the word for 'gather': *qāšaš* literally means 'gather yourselves together like stubble' (cf. Exod. 5:7, 12). This may suggest that the people of Judah should come together in humble acknowledgment of their unworthiness. They are like *stubble*, deserving nothing but God's judgment (Mal. 4:1). So there is an urgent need to gather together in a corporate act of repentance before God's judgment falls (1).

During the Second World War many people in the UK came together in the churches for national days of prayer called for by their sovereign, King George VI. It's hard to imagine such a call having a comparable response today. Since that war, there have been large ecumenical gatherings of Christians in the UK which have met to hear God's Word and to sing his praises. Helpful though these have been, there has often been an element that has largely been missing. That is the element of penitence, and the sense of unworthiness and unreadiness in the light of God's judgment. Perhaps that is a lesson to learn from Zephaniah's message. There's a place for corporate repentance in the life of the church today, and in the life of a nation.

> If my people, who are called by my name, will humble themselves and pray and seek my face and turn from their wicked ways, then will I hear from heaven, and I will forgive their sin and will heal their land.
> (2 Chr. 7:14)

b. The believers: there's a need for personal repentance (3)

Who are the *humble of the land* that Zephaniah now addresses? The phrase may simply refer to the man or woman in the street, the ordinary people, or those 'at the bottom of life's heap' (Motyer), who can easily be pushed around and exploited. But they are also referred to as those *who do what he [God] commands.* So presumably, these people are at least trying to keep God's law and commandments. They want to be on his side; they are in some sense 'believers'. But even 'believers' need to repent. They need to turn from sinful ways and to seek the Lord and his righteousness. So Zephaniah urges them to take three positive steps: to seek *the Lord*; to seek *righteousness*; and to seek *humility* (3).

i. There's a need to seek the Lord

Zephaniah understood that it was not enough to gather the people together at some great festival, unless their attitude to the Lord was right. Religion would not save God's people from judgment then, any more than religion saves us today. Indeed, many would argue today that religion is the cause of many of our problems, not the cure. There is some truth in that. Religion cannot save us. Religious services, rituals and traditions cannot save us. Only God can.

So Zephaniah calls upon believers, not to redouble their religious activities, but to seek the Lord in an attitude of humility and obedience. The word for *seek* (*biqqeš*), when used in the context of human relationships, means 'to long for'. So in the Song of Songs the lover uses that word when he says, 'I will search for the one my heart loves' (Song 3:2). That word conveys much more than casual attendance at temple worship.

Zephaniah is urging believers to seek the Lord because they love him, and long to be in his presence to enjoy his company. When did we last approach God like that in public worship or in private prayer?

Seeking the Lord also involves turning 'to God from idols to serve the living and true God' (1 Thess. 1:9). Those who turned away from following the sinful paths of Jeroboam and his sons in order to follow Rehoboam, the son of Solomon, were described as those who 'set their hearts on seeking [*biqqēš*] the LORD'. Jesus said: 'No one can serve two masters . . . You cannot serve both God and Money' (Matt. 6:24). So to seek the Lord involves putting God first in our lives, while turning away from anything that takes away our first loyalty to him.

In the light of God's imminent judgment, therefore, Zephaniah pleads with God's people not only to *gather together* and to return to the Lord, but also personally and individually to turn from sinful ways and to seek the presence of the Lord.

It is a sad reflection of church life today (at least in the UK) that the weekly prayer meeting has become less and less a priority, even in evangelical churches. Furthermore, the practice of 'the Quiet Time' – when Christians would privately, or as couples, or as a family, read the Scriptures and pray and seek God's blessing on their lives – also seems to have disappeared from the daily life of most Christians. Zephaniah seems clear that there is no hope for God's people unless they repent and truly seek the Lord.

In J. T. Carson's book *God's River in Spate*, which tells the story of the 1859 Revival in the north of Ireland, he describes the way in which Christians met together to pray for revival. The result was dramatic. Whole communities were transformed. Carson wisely commented: 'Things happen when you pray, which do not happen when you do not pray.' The Christians in that revival genuinely sought the presence of the Lord as they prayed. They made time to make prayer a priority. Should we not do the same?

I have no time to read his book,
I have no time to pray.
I have no time to serve Our Lord,
I have no time . . . or so I say.
Before the television set
The minutes pass

The hours flit by.
But when my Lord would meet with us,
I have no time . . . that is my cry.
Thank God he did not say 'I have no time.'
He found the time for you and me,
He found the time for Calvary.
Dear Lord, forgive 'I have no time.'
Before thy cross, I do confess
With tears of shame, my laziness.
You died for me, I did not care.
But now I know 'I have no time'
For it is thine!
And thou must use my life, my time,
As thou dost choose.
(Anon.)

ii. There's a need to seek righteousness

Zephaniah knew that if we truly seek the Lord and meet with him, we will want to reflect his character and do his will in every part of our lives. So he calls upon the *humble of the land* not only to *Seek the Lord* but also to *Seek righteousness* (3b). The tense of the word 'seek' (perfect tense) 'indicates the completion of actions in the future that are also dependent on our present determination and will'.[34] So Zephaniah asks the people to be determined to live a godly and a righteous life, and to reflect God's righteousness in their daily lives. He will take up this theme again a little later (see 3:5) in the context of the failure of both civil and religious leaders to act justly in their dealings with others; and he makes the point that *The Lord . . . is righteous* and that *Morning by morning he dispenses his justice* (3:5).

So here (2:3) Zephaniah calls upon ordinary believers, *the humble of the land*, to *seek righteousness*. Christian believers can understand the significance of this challenge by noting that in Scripture there is a righteousness that God requires, and a righteousness that God offers.

First, we must understand the righteousness that God requires

Zephaniah has already made the point that God is a God of righteousness and justice, a God of judgment (see Zeph. 1). He also reminds the *humble*

---

34 Motyer, in McComiskey (ed.), *The Minor Prophets*, vol. 3, p. 928.

of the land that they are those who do what God commands (2:3a). In the book of Deuteronomy (ch. 5), probably rediscovered in King Josiah's time, we read how Moses brought the Ten Commandments to Israel. These set out the moral standards of righteousness that God required from those he had redeemed. They were prefaced with the words: 'I am the LORD your God, who brought you out of Egypt, out of the land of slavery' (Deut. 5:6). God is not saying, 'If you keep all these commandments you will earn your redemption.' Rather, he is saying, 'I have redeemed you; therefore this is the kind of life I now require of you.' He requires the same from all of us who have been redeemed by the precious blood of Jesus. This is a summary of those commandments:

- You shall have no other gods before me . . .
- You shall not make for yourself an idol . . .
- You shall not misuse the name of the LORD your God . . .
- Observe the sabbath day by keeping it holy . . .
- Honour your father and your mother . . .
- You shall not murder . . .
- You shall not commit adultery . . .
- You shall not steal . . .
- You shall not give false testimony against your neighbour . . .
- You shall not covet . . .

(from Deut. 5:1–21)

It is by keeping these commandments that we demonstrate that we are redeemed by the Lord. We cannot do this in our own strength. But we are to seek to live like this, to seek to live righteously. After the Lord had given to Moses the Ten Commandments, Moses told the people: 'Walk in obedience to all that the LORD your God has commanded you' (Deut. 5:32), and again:

> Hear, O Israel: the LORD our God, the LORD is one. Love the LORD your God with all your heart and with all your soul and with all your strength. These commandments that I give you today are to be on your hearts. Impress them on your children. Talk about them when you sit at home and when you walk along the road, when you lie down and when you get up.
> (Deut. 6:4–7)

So, when Zephaniah says *Seek righteousness*, he means 'Obey God's commandments'! Live like this! God is righteous and he calls us to live righteously.

When Jesus taught his disciples about the Ten Commandments, as in the Sermon on the Mount (Matt. 5), he revealed more fully what it means to keep the moral law of God and to seek a righteousness that 'surpasses that of the Pharisees and the teachers of the law' (Matt. 5:20). Jesus calls us to keep the commandments in thought as well as in deed, positively as well as negatively. So to be 'angry' with someone or to insult them is to break the commandment 'Do not murder' and to be subject to judgment (Matt. 5:21–22). Furthermore, it is not enough to refrain from murder: to keep the sixth commandment positively we need to love our neighbours as ourselves; and that will often mean taking the first step to be reconciled with them and to forgive them (Matt. 5:21–26).

However, in spite of the impossibility of keeping the Ten Commandments perfectly in our own strength, Jesus, like Zephaniah, urges us 'to hunger and thirst for righteousness'. Jesus actually says: 'Blessed are those who hunger and thirst for righteousness, for they will be filled' (Matt. 5:6). In these words lies the clue to the further truth that there is not only a righteousness that God requires, but also a righteousness that God offers.

Second, we must accept the righteousness that God offers

Jesus emphasized the need for intense determination to live the obedient, righteous life that God requires. We are to hunger and thirst after righteousness. This is no casual call to live a decent kind of life. In a country where climate conditions and famine made hunger and thirst a matter of life and death, Jesus' words express strong desire as well as great determination. But his words also remind us that such a righteous life is only possible through the blessing of God and the gift of the Holy Spirit that can fill the life of the believer. Jesus is addressing disciples, just as Moses was addressing the redeemed.

In New Testament terms, then, to seek righteousness is to seek Christ. He lived a perfect life of obedience; he always did those things that pleased the Father (John 8:29). Furthermore, 'Christ also suffered once for sins, the righteous for the unrighteous, to bring you to God' (1 Pet. 3:18). We are all sinners. 'There is no one righteous, not even one' (Rom. 3:10; 3:23). We deserve God's judgment. But God condemned our sin in Jesus (Rom. 8:3); and as we, by faith, lay our sins on our saviour on the cross, he offers us his righteousness to be received by faith (see Eph. 2:8–9). There is a real exchange. As the apostle Paul put it, 'God made him who had no sin to be sin for us, so that in him we might become the righteousness of God' (2 Cor. 5:21).

The story of the conversion of Charles Simeon, who became a famous eighteenth-century vicar of Holy Trinity Church, Cambridge, illustrates the powerfulness of this 'real exchange'. When he was an undergraduate at King's College, Cambridge, he was summoned to attend a Service of Holy Communion in the College Chapel. He felt totally unprepared to do so, and so began to seek God and to read all he could about the meaning of Holy Communion. In one book, he was struck by the comment: 'the Jews knew what they did when they transferred their sin to the head of their offering.'

> Later Simeon wrote: 'The thought rushed to my mind, "What! May I transfer my guilt to another? Has God provided an offering for me that I may lay my sins on his head?" Accordingly, I sought to lay my sins on the sacred head of Jesus' . . . On Easter morning he awoke with these words upon his lips: 'Jesus Christ is risen today, Hallelujah!' He added: 'From that hour peace flowed in rich abundance into my soul; and at the Lord's Table in our Chapel I had the sweetest access to God through our Blessed Saviour.'[35]

However, seeking righteousness is not only about receiving the imputed righteousness of Christ. For God also imparts his righteousness to believers by his Holy Spirit. As Paul argues in Romans 8, God not only condemned our sin in the sinless body of Jesus, but he did this in order that the righteous requirements of the law might be fully met in us (Rom. 8:1–4); and that is possible if we 'do not live according to the flesh but according to the Spirit' (Rom. 8:4). For it is those who are 'led by the Spirit of God' (Rom. 8:14), as sons and daughters of God, who are enabled to live righteous and Christ-like lives.

When Zephaniah calls upon the *humble of the land* to seek *righteousness*, he is pointing towards the kind of obedient, godly life that God requires, which they should seek to live. It is, however, the righteousness that Christ offers to impute and to impart that helps Christian believers

[35] H. E. Hopkins, *Charles Simeon of Cambridge: A Biography* (Hodder & Stoughton, 1977), p. 28.

to understand even more clearly how such a righteous life is possible. Jesus offers us such a possibility; he said, 'Blessed are those who hunger and thirst for righteousness, *for they will be filled*' (Matt. 5:6; emphasis mine).

Zephaniah offers us one further exhortation to consider: *Seek humility* (2:3b).

iii. There's a need to seek humility

Even though Zephaniah is addressing *the humble of the land*, he wants to make sure that these believers are truly humble before the Lord. Micah had found it necessary to remind Israel that God required humility from his people: 'He has shown you, O mortal, what is good. And what does the LORD require of you? To act justly and to love mercy and to walk humbly with your God' (Mic. 6:8). Jesus had taught the same truth in the Sermon on the Mount (Matt. 5:3–5).

In the light of the words that follow (3c), the call to seek humility may include not only the thought of humble dependence on God, but also humble acknowledgment of sin. To seek humility may well be a call to penitence. Yet if true penitence is being called for, why does the prophet say: ***perhaps*** *you will be sheltered on the day of the Lord's anger*? Does that cast doubt on the faithfulness of God to forgive those who truly repent? (See Ps. 51; 1 John 1:9.) There are two main answers to that question.

1. Zephaniah may simply mean that those who seek the Lord and seek humility may *perhaps* be spared death or physical harm on that day, when judgment is delivered to Judah and Jerusalem by the hand of their enemies. There would be no guarantee of that, any more than Christians today can be guaranteed physical safety in this life. What we do know for sure is that nothing 'will be able to separate us from the love of God that is in Christ Jesus our Lord' (Rom. 8:39).

2. If Zephaniah is speaking in spiritual rather than physical terms, then the *perhaps* is more like the phrase 'if by any means' in Paul's letter to the Philippians (see Phil. 3:11, KJV). Neither phrase expresses doubt about the faithfulness of God. Rather, they guard against the presumption of the proud, and the danger of implying what is called 'cheap grace'. We possess salvation through the grace of God; but we are called to work it out 'with fear and trembling' (Phil. 2:12–13). Something of that 'fear and trembling' may be suggested in this passage. Equally, as humble penitent believers, we can be sure that, finally, *on the day of the LORD's anger* we will be

sheltered and safe in Christ. For 'there is now no condemnation for those who are in Christ Jesus' (Rom. 8:1).

There is a further thought from the phrase *perhaps you will be sheltered on the day of the Lord's anger* (3c). The word *sheltered* (*kāpar*) suggests the thought about the way in which the blood of a sacrificial animal makes atonement for the sins of the people, and shelters them from the just judgment of God. Could this have been in the mind of Zephaniah?

So, as we look back over Zephaniah's urgent appeal to the nation and to a remnant of believers, we see that his message includes good news as well as bad. He offers hope to those who are humble enough to seek God and his righteousness, and to return to God in penitence and faith. Time is running out; but now is the time to repent!

The good news is that it is never too late to repent and turn to God. The penitent thief turned to Christ as he was dying, and heard Christ's reassuring words: 'today you will be with me in paradise' (Luke 23:43). The other man crucified with Jesus chose to go his own way, without Christ and without hope.

Bishop Sandy Millar tells the delightful story of an elderly woman who was confirmed by the bishop when she was 101 years old. During the service she was interviewed by the bishop, and blurted out, beaming, 'Don't you think it's wonderful that I've come to Christ at my age?' The bishop thought for a moment, and then said, 'It's wonderful – but risky.'[36]

In one sense it's never too late to turn to God. But we do well to notice the urgency in Zephaniah's appeal. Paul had that same sense of urgency when he wrote to the Christians at Corinth, fearing that some had not received the gift of God's grace and forgiveness. He wrote:

> As God's fellow workers we urge you not to receive God's grace in vain. For he says,
>
> 'In the time of my favour I heard you,
> and in the day of salvation I helped you.'

[36] As a balance to the story about the woman of 101 years, there is an interesting anecdote told by my father-in-law. When he was vicar of Tonbridge Parish Church, he quoted in a sermon a poll that suggested very few people are converted to Christ after the age of fifty. On the night when he preached that sermon he was eating his supper in the vicarage when there was a loud knock at the front door. The vicar went to the door and found a man who had heard his sermon and very much wanted to talk about it. The vicar suggested that it might be better for both of them if they booked a time in the week when they could talk about it. 'No, I can't wait,' said the man. 'I'm fifty tomorrow!' I believe the man was led to Christ that night.

I tell you, now is the time of God's favour, now is the day of salvation. (2 Cor. 6:1–2)

Zephaniah had the same sense of urgency: *Seek the* L*ORD . . . Seek righteousness, seek humility; perhaps you will be sheltered on the day of the* L*ORD's anger.* It was time to repent. It was risky to leave it any longer.

Zephaniah 2:4 – 3:8

7. Judgment and hope for the nations

1. Our God reigns (2:4–15)

Zephaniah now moves on to a new focus in his teaching. This next section has been called the 'Poem of the Nations' and it has been said that it is 'Zephaniah at his literary best'.[1] However, it is even more significant theologically. It focuses on the sovereignty of God, and in particular God's rule over the nations. Starting from Judah, Zephaniah describes God's sovereign rule over the destinies of several neighbouring nations: Philistia to the west of Judah (4–7); Moab and Ammon to the east (8–11); Cush far away to the south (12); and Assyria to the north, for that is the direction from which she always came when attacking Israel (13–15). The fact that Zephaniah has chosen these nations from the north, south, east and west points to the emphasis he wishes to make. They represent nations from every corner of the globe, with different cultures and different political systems; yet the Lord is sovereign over every one of them.

Zephaniah's message in this chapter that 'our God reigns' is an encouraging one for the people of God. It is encouraging because Zephaniah teaches us that God will judge the nations justly; that God cares for his people steadfastly; and that God offers hope to believers universally.

a. God will judge the nations justly (2:4–15)

Zephaniah has already made the point that God will judge his people justly *because they have sinned against the Lord* (1:17). He has also described

[1] J. A. Motyer in T. E. McComiskey (ed.), *The Minor Prophets*, vol. 3: *Zephaniah, Haggai, Zechariah and Malachi* (Baker Book House, 1998), p. 931.

universal judgment, and *the day of the LORD's wrath* when *the whole earth will be consumed* (1:18). Now he applies these general truths to the particular situation that Judah and Jerusalem faced with their enemies. They were surrounded by hostile pagan nations who crossed their borders and attacked their citizens. They were constantly threatened by the possibility of invasion. They must have wondered whether the doctrine of the sovereignty of God meant anything at all. Christians who daily faced bombs, death and kidnapping in Baghdad during the Iraq War in recent years must sometimes have wondered the same thing. Zephaniah encourages us all to look to the sovereign Lord who rules all the nations of the world and will ultimately bring them to account.

Our God reigns. So, inspired by God's Spirit (2 Pet. 1:21), Zephaniah spells out in some detail the judgments which will certainly come to these neighbouring countries, as they will ultimately come to all nations. If we care about justice and God's honour and glory, we shall be encouraged to know that God will act in perfect justice against sin and evil in the world. Therefore let us look more closely at these prophecies against Philistia, Moab and Ammon, Cush and Assyria.

i. Philistia: God will judge those who persistently attack his people (4–7)

We are not told why God's judgments will be so devastating for Philistia. We are told that *the word of the LORD is against* them (5), and we have a description of the results of terrifying warfare that is part of God's judgment upon them, God 'working through the horrific climax of human mismanagement of world affairs' (Motyer). Zephaniah mentions some, though not all, of the main cities in Philistia, as he moves from the north to the south of the country (4). God's judgment would mean that Gaza would be deserted, Ashkelon left in ruins and Ashdod swiftly overcome and emptied. Does *midday* suggest that the battle would be over quickly, that is, literally by midday, or does it suggest a surprise attack at siesta time?

We have no historical record that these promises of judgment were fulfilled. However, we know that God is faithful and keeps his word, and that it is a serious matter if the word of the Lord is against us (5b). We know, therefore, that ultimately justice will be done and will be seen to be done, and that time delays are not a problem with God. For with the Lord 'a day is like a thousand years, and a thousand years are like a day' (2 Pet. 3:8). So, although God's judgments may be delayed, they will certainly come in God's good time, and we can be encouraged by the truth that those who, like the Philistines, continually attack God's people will finally receive God's judgment. The Philistines occupied the fertile coastland west of Judah. It was part of the land that God had promised Israel (Gen. 13:14–15; Deut. 34:1–4). However, Israel failed to subdue the Philistines fully so that they continued to be a threat to God's people and a thorn in their side. It is probably these persistent attacks on the people of God that provide the reason for the severity of God's promised judgments. For God cares deeply for his people (6–7), and believers can easily be discouraged when attacks come upon them constantly (see Ps. 123). When Saul of Tarsus was persecuting Christians, the risen Lord Jesus confronted him with the question, 'Saul, Saul, why do you persecute me?' (Acts 9:4). To persecute Christians is to persecute Christ. To attack God's people is to attack God himself. The *day of the LORD's wrath* (2) ensures, among other things, the just judgment of God upon those who have continually attacked the people of God. Christians in Iraq, Darfur, Pakistan and China, to name but a few of those nations today where there is some persecution of Christians, find hope and comfort in this doctrine of judgment.

We cannot claim, of course, that it is only those outside the church who are hostile to God's people today. There are Philistines among us! Christian leaders, for example, often find themselves continually attacked verbally by other professing Christians. They may be attacked for their style of leadership, their faithful gospel ministry, or simply for their determination to carry through necessary change within the church. We do well to judge ourselves so that we do not come under the judgment of God (1 Cor. 11:31–32). And if we are facing persistent attacks, we need to remember the words of the psalmist as he faced that situation:

> I lift up my eyes to you,
>   to you who sit enthroned in heaven.
> As the eyes of slaves look to the hand of their master,
>   as the eyes of a female slave look to the hand of her mistress,
> so our eyes look to the LORD our God,
>   till he shows us his mercy.
> (Ps. 123:1–2)

Zephaniah wants us to know that a day is coming when we shall all have to give account of our lives to God. God will judge justly those, like the Philistines, who persistently attack his people.

ii. Moab and Ammon: God will judge those who freely insult his people (8–11)

There can be few worse experiences in life than to suffer mocking insults and racist taunts from near neighbours. Even in the relatively tolerant society of multicultural Britain today, Christians are sometimes mocked and insulted.

The Moabites and the Ammonites were close neighbours and kinsfolk to those who lived in Jerusalem and Judah (Gen. 19:37–38). As a result, there was at first much mutual respect and kindness between Judah and her neighbours (Deut. 2:9–11). But after a while there was increasing antagonism. There is, for example, the terrible story of Nahash, the Ammonite, who threatened to gouge out the right eyes of all the citizens in Jabesh Gilead (see 1 Sam. 11:1–2). Furthermore, Nahash's son Hanun, on another occasion, insulted and humiliated some of King David's men by shaving half their beards and baring their buttocks (2 Sam. 10:1–4). This was exactly the kind of insulting, inhumane and insensitive behaviour that stirred up so much hostility in the Middle East during the troubles in Iraq in our present time. Human nature hasn't changed! (See also Judg. 3:12; 10:7–17; 2 Sam. 8:10–12; 2 Kgs 1:1; 3:4; 13:20.)

Zephaniah's message about Judah's near neighbours is an encouraging one for the *remnant* of believers (2:9). He brings them God's promise of a future hope, which we will look at more closely later.[2] But he also assures them that God will judge justly those who mock his people. It will be a just judgment because it is based on God's sure knowledge of the situation. He knows about the insults of Moab and the taunts of the Ammonites. He has not been deaf to what they have been saying about Judah. *I have heard the insults of Moab and the taunts of the Ammonites* (8). They *insulted my people*, complains God (8). He cares deeply for his own people and so will act on their behalf as the living, powerful God who is not only the covenant *God of Israel* (9) but the *Lord Almighty* (9).

The story of Jesus brings home to us still more clearly how much God understands those who suffer taunts and insults because of their faith in God. For God was in Christ as Jesus suffered the mocking and taunts of his enemies in his earthly ministry, and especially in his trial and crucifixion. As the Suffering Servant, Jesus fulfilled Isaiah's great prophecy: 'He was despised and rejected by mankind, a man of suffering, and familiar

2 See pp. 261–266.

with pain' (Isa. 53:3). It was the example of Jesus that inspired the first Christians to face up to the taunts and mocking of others. The apostle Peter reminded those Christians who were being misrepresented and mocked: 'When they hurled their insults at him [Jesus], he did not retaliate; when he suffered, he made no threats. Instead, he entrusted himself to him who judges justly' (1 Pet. 2:23). Our natural instinct is to answer back and retaliate in kind when we are insulted. Maybe we are mocked for being in the 'God squad' or for taking the Bible and its morality seriously, or for being countercultural or politically incorrect. We are tempted to retaliate in our own strength and trusting in our own wisdom. Jesus shows us a better way.

Nevertheless, although Christians should expect the mocking and taunts of others (John 15:20), this does not excuse those who indulge in it. Zephaniah teaches us that this behaviour springs from the pride and arrogance of the Ammonites and the Moabites (10). They believed that Israel was weak and that they could extend their borders into the land promised to Israel by God. They did this in the most cruel way.[3] Ammon and Moab deserved the just judgment of God.

Zephaniah also teaches us that God's judgment is not only just but also appropriate. The Moabites and Ammonites lived close to the Dead Sea. They knew only too well the effects of God's judgment on Sodom and Gomorrah over a thousand years earlier (Gen. 18 – 19). God acted in perfect knowledge of the situation then (Gen. 18:20–21). He would act in perfect knowledge and justice in judging Moab and Ammon.

'Therefore, as surely as I live,'
  [God says]
'surely Moab will become like Sodom,
  the Ammonites like Gomorrah –
a place of weeds and salt pits,
  a wasteland for ever' . . .

This is what they will get in return for their pride,
  for insulting and mocking
  the people of the Lord *Almighty.*

[3] The prophet Amos describes Ammon: 'he ripped open the pregnant women of Gilead in order to extend his borders' (Amos 1:13; see also 2 Kgs 8:12; Isa. 16:6; Jer. 48:29).

The LORD will be awesome to them
when he destroys all the gods of the earth.
(2:9–11)

So Zephaniah reminds us that it is a serious offence to mock or taunt the people of God, for to mock believers is to mock God himself. The extent to which our society in multicultural Britain has become a moral and spiritual *wasteland* (9) in the twenty-first century is illustrated by the fact, for example, that the blasphemous *Jerry Springer: The Opera* did not so much mock the Christian church as mock Jesus Christ himself; and to mock Jesus is to mock God (see also Isa. 1:9; Jer. 49:18; Lam. 4:6; Amos 4:11). However, Zephaniah wants us to see that God will have the last word. In reality, God is not mocked (Ps. 2). God will judge those who freely insult his people. Our God reigns.

iii. Cush: God will judge those who seem far away from his people (12)

You Cushites, too, will be slain by my sword (12). The judgment on Cush is short and to the point. Zephaniah has looked west to Philistia, east to Moab and Ammon, and now briefly south to Cush, which is usually linked to Egypt, Ethiopia (Isa. 20:3) and Sudan.[4]

It is also interesting to note that according to 2 Samuel 18:21 there were Cushites living among God's people in Judah in King David's time. Joab sent a Cushite runner to David to bring to him news of Absalom's death – another sign of God's sovereignty over all nations, and his sovereign choice of Gentiles, as well as Israel, to further his kingdom plans (cf. Luke 4:24–27).

What are we to learn from such a brief oracle of judgment? It seems as though Zephaniah is reminding us that God is sovereign over all the nations and that even faraway Cush cannot escape God's just judgment. For Cush and Ethiopia were regarded as far-off places, rather in the way we might talk about faraway Siberia or outer Mongolia. When Luke wanted to describe the way in which the gospel spread from Jerusalem to 'the ends of the earth', he selected an Ethiopian as an example of someone

---

[4] A land called Cush is mentioned in Genesis (2:13), and Isaiah writes about judgment upon Cushites because of their aggression (Isa. 18). Ethiopia and Egypt are linked to Cush because an Ethiopian dynasty had ruled in Egypt from 664 to 610 BC; and after the fall of Nineveh in 612 BC the Egyptians, with the help of the Ethiopians, went to the aid of Assyria. However, God would have the last word (12) as the Babylonians finally defeated the Assyrians and their allies at the battle of Carchemish in 603 BC.

who had come from afar (Acts 1:8; 8:26–40). He might equally have chosen a Cushite if one had been converted.

We can be encouraged too by the truth that no-one is beyond the knowledge of God. As the writer to the Hebrews put it: 'Nothing in all creation is hidden from God's sight. Everything is uncovered and laid bare before the eyes of him to whom we must give account' (Heb. 4:13). Jesus' teaching brings added encouragement to us when he says:

> Are not two sparrows sold for a penny? Yet not one of them will fall to the ground outside your Father's care. And even the very hairs of your head are all numbered. So don't be afraid; you are worth more than many sparrows.
> (Matt. 10:29–31)

God our Father knows all about us and our circumstances, whether we live in Ethiopia or China. He is the judge of all the earth. So no-one who deserves judgment can escape it. Equally, those who live in remote places are still loved and known by a heavenly Father who will not let a sparrow fall to the ground outside his will. Our God reigns.

iv. Assyria: God will judge those who exalt themselves over God's people (13–15)

Some years ago, in July 1976, an Air France jetliner was hijacked and over 100 passengers were taken hostage and flown to Entebbe airport in Uganda. The Israeli intelligence service reported how President Amin of Uganda was parading in front of the hostages as their protector. Addressed merely as 'Mr President' by a young Israeli mother, Amin rebuked her, thrust out his chest and announced proudly: 'I am His Excellency al-Hajji Field Marshall Dr. Idi Amin Dada, holder of the British Victoria Cross, DSO, MC, and appointed by Almighty God to be your Saviour!'[5]

There was something of this same over-the-top arrogance about Assyria and her leaders in the days of Zephaniah. It's reflected in this passage in the Assyrian claims for her capital city, Nineveh, which boasted, *'I am the one! And there is none besides me'* (15a). However, Zephaniah has a message to shock the Assyrians and encourage God's people. God will judge the proud and arrogant Assyria.

[5] W. Stevenson, *Ninety Minutes at Entebbe* (Bantam, 1976), p. 15.

As we have already noticed, Judah was a small country surrounded by hostile neighbours. Assyria was a declining superpower but still a considerable threat to Jerusalem and Judah. Zephaniah, however, was given a message that put that threat into an entirely different perspective. God's people need not be afraid or discouraged. They could lift up their heads in faith and hope again. For Zephaniah tells them: *He [God] will stretch out his hand against the north and destroy Assyria, leaving Nineveh utterly desolate and dry as the desert* (13). In this context, *stretch out his hand* is clearly a metaphor for judgment, not blessing; and it is a devastating judgment. Nineveh was a well-watered site with rivers on the south-west and the north-west of the city. It also had some famous man-made irrigation canals. Yet Zephaniah describes God's judgment in terms of *leaving Nineveh utterly desolate and dry as the desert* (13). God's judgments are awesome. Mighty Nineveh would be destroyed and Assyria would be depopulated. It would be fit only for animals. *Flocks and herds will lie down there, creatures of every kind* (14). The ruins of the city would become the home of owls and hedgehogs (14, ESV), and the once great buildings would be in ruins with the cedar panels exposed to the elements (14). The scene is one of utter destruction and desolation. *What a ruin she has become, a lair for wild beasts! All who pass by her scoff*[6] *and shake their fists* (15b).

It is hard for us to grasp how astonishing this message must have sounded to those in Judah and Jerusalem who were only too conscious of the might of this superpower, Assyria. Yet Zephaniah was confident that God would overthrow Assyria just as he promised. God would do this in spite of her military power.

In Zephaniah's day, Assyria (part of modern Iraq) was a superpower beginning to decline. But at the height of its power, in the eighth and seventh centuries BC, it had been a constant threat to both Israel and Judah. In 733–732 BC, for example, under Tiglath-Pileser III, Assyria had invaded Judah and received tribute money from Azariah. The Assyrian king had then deposed Pekah in the north and made Hoshea a vassal king over Israel. In 705–681 BC Sargon II founded a new dynasty, captured Samaria and, according to his own records, deported 27,290 people from the northern kingdom. In 701 BC Sennacherib, the son of Sargon, lay siege

[6] The Hebrew word for 'to scoff' is *šāraq*, which means 'to whistle'. Eaton translates it as 'hissing' and points out that hissing is still practised by Palestinian Arabs as an expression of horror or amazement.

to Jerusalem. In the face of much superior military strength it seemed inevitable that Jerusalem would be captured. But God heard the prayer of King Hezekiah and 'the angel of the LORD went out and put to death a hundred and eighty-five thousand in the Assyrian camp' (2 Kgs 19:35). So Jerusalem was saved. But could it happen again? Zephaniah knew that with God all things are possible. He believed that God was a mighty warrior who would certainly defeat all his enemies. *He will stretch out his hand against the north and destroy Assyria, leaving Nineveh utterly desolate and dry as the desert* (13).

Zephaniah teaches us that God is sovereign over all nations, including superpowers with immense military strength. History has shown us the decline and fall of successive superpowers. Those who heard Zephaniah speak of the fall of the mighty Assyrian empire might have dismissed his prophecy as wishful thinking. But, as always, the Word of God never fails, and prayer changes things. Hezekiah's prayer brought deliverance to Jerusalem in his day. Many believe that the collapse of communism in the former Soviet countries in the latter part of the twentieth century, the collapse of the apartheid policy in South Africa, and the changes taking place in mainland China today (including fast-growing house churches) are also due to the prayers of God's people and the sovereign power of God.

So Zephaniah reminds us that God will judge Assyria in spite of her great military strength; but he also makes clear that God's judgment is deserved and just, because of her proud self-sufficiency.

Assyria was especially proud of her capital city, Nineveh. It was described as 'the city of revelry that lived in safety'. *She said to herself, 'I am the one! And there is none besides me'* (15).

There were reasons for this civic pride. Nineveh was probably the world's largest city at this time. It had the reputation for being impregnable. It is said that a wall that was 8 miles in circumference and 100 feet high surrounded the inner city. It was claimed that three chariots could race around the wall side by side. The Assyrian capital had many towers and gates. Around the outer city was built another enormous wall, and inside these fortifications were many magnificent buildings. Lions of bronze and bulls made of marble stood outside the king's palace, and there was a vast area (456 acres) set apart for the king's armoury, chariots, horses and various weapons of destruction. Even allowing for government spin and exaggeration, it must have been a very impressive city. It's not surprising that civic pride was high.

But Nineveh's sin, and the reason for God's judgment on the city, was surely the people's arrogant confidence in their own achievements and security. They really believed they could safety say, *I am the one! And there is none besides me.* As Szeles comments in her commentary on this verse: 'In potential lunacy they had conceived the idea of their own glorious self-divination.' It was surely this arrogance that led to the savage methods of warfare and abuse of human rights that were characteristic of Assyrian military campaigns. The Asssyrians did not have the Scriptures to guide them; but they were human beings made in the image of God, and they had a conscience. As the apostle Paul wrote about the Gentiles who did not have God's written Word to teach them:

> the requirements of the law are written on their hearts, their consciences also bearing witness, and their thoughts sometimes accusing them and at other times even defending them . . . God judges people's secrets through Jesus Christ, as my gospel declares.
> (Rom. 2:15–16)

From the evidence we have, we know that Nineveh grew rich at the expense of the nations that Assyria attacked and conquered. We know too that the Assyrians treated their prisoners inhumanely. For example, some of the kings they captured were made to live in kennels like dogs. Rebel leaders were paraded in chains. Crown princes were taken as hostages, and princesses made to act as slaves and concubines. Many prisoners were beaten, and the more obstinate put to death. Nineveh had become 'the concentrated centre of evil, the capital of crushing tyranny, the epitome of cruellest torture'.[7]

It's not difficult to find modern examples of this kind of arrogance and pride in national achievements, linked with abuse of human rights and callous treatment of enemies. Hitler's Nazi Germany, Stalin's Soviet Union, Idi Amin's Uganda, Pol Pot's Cambodia, Mao's China and Saddam Hussein's Iraq are all examples that come to mind from the twentieth and twenty-first centuries. Nationalism easily becomes a form of idolatry. The state becomes a substitute for God. Each of these nations might well have said with Nineveh and her leaders, '*I am the one! And there is none besides me.*'

---

[7] W. A. Maier, *The Book of Nahum* (Baker, 1980), pp. 89–91, quoted in J. M. Boice, *The Minor Prophets*: vol. 2, *Micah to Malachi* (Zondervan, 1986), p. 59.

It may be harder for those of us who live in a democracy to own up to the same dangers of arrogance and a false sense of security. But a UK government, for example, that 'does not do God', and rides roughshod over biblical standards of morality in relation to such issues as abortion and the plight of immigrants, must be in some danger of the same sinful pride. This is equally true, of course, for the individual. The essence of sin is that human pride and arrogance lead to a life lived without reference to God. To say, as somebody once said to me, 'I do not need God' is not far from the position of those in Nineveh, who said: *I am the one! And there is none besides me.* Zephaniah teaches us that such idolatry and self-sufficiency deserves the just judgment of God.

So in this whole passage (2:4–15) Zephaniah brings home to us the truth that God is sovereign over all the nations. Our God reigns. Christians today should be encouraged by this teaching. God's Word tells us that God will judge justly those who, like Philistia, persistently attack God's people (4–7); those who, like Moab and Ammon, freely insult God's people (8–11); those like Cush who seem too far away from God's people to matter (12); and those like the superpower Assyria who exalt themselves arrogantly over God's people (13–15). Zephaniah is clear that those who attack the people of God will one day experience his judgment. The Sennacheribs and Stalins, the Tiglath-Pilesers and the Pol Pots, the Sargons and Saddam Husseins all perish, with their empires, into the sands of history under the mighty hand of God. No wonder the psalmist writes with great joy:

> Say among the nations, 'The Lord reigns.'
> The world is firmly established, it cannot be moved;
> he will judge the peoples with equity.
>
> Let the heavens rejoice, let the earth be glad;
> let the sea resound, and all that is in it.
> Let the fields be jubilant, and everything in them;
> let all the trees of the forest sing for joy.
> Let all creation rejoice before the Lord, for he comes,
> he comes to judge the earth.
> He will judge the world in righteousness
> and the peoples in his faithfulness.
> (Ps. 96:10–13)

The encouragement of acknowledging that God will judge the nations justly is one important feature of this passage; but Zephaniah has also reminded us of another aspect of the sovereignty of God which should also give us both encouragement and joy: he cares for his people steadfastly.

b. God cares for his people steadfastly (2:4–11)

Zephaniah is keen to point out that Yahweh is not only a righteous God but is also a gracious God. In the midst of his judgment of the nations, Yahweh takes care of his people, the remnant of believers, the company of the redeemed. There are two passages in this section (4–11) which we have not yet looked at in any detail. They both focus on God's providential care for his people.

i. God's message about Philistia – the promise of God's care (6–7)

Zephaniah is clear that God will keep his promise to the remnant of believers. The land promised to them would yet be theirs (Gen. 12:5; 13:12–15; Ps. 105:11). Furthermore, it would be a place characterized by pastoral peace (6b) and complete security (7). Above all, it would be a place where the covenant Lord will care for them and *restore their fortunes* (7c). This last phrase could refer to the restoration of God's people from captivity. However, since Zephaniah was preaching before the Babylonian captivity, there is a case for looking at other possible interpretations. Some commentators suggest that the reference might be to a 'restored ideal' or to 'paradise regained'.[8]

There is no clear historical evidence that the land where the Philistines lived, which had been promised to Israel and is here called *Canaan* (5), ever came fully into the possession of Israel. But Zephaniah probably links Philistia with Canaan in order to draw attention to God's promises which he believed would be fulfilled theologically and spiritually, if not historically. To *restore their fortunes* has been translated 'to restore well-being'. However we interpret the phrase, Zephaniah assures us that God will never let his people down but will always provide for them and protect them in this life and the next.

---

[8] Eaton argues that if the root of the Hebrew verb is *šābâ*, then the likely interpretation is 'restoration from bondage or captivity'. If, however, the root is *šûb* then the meaning is along the lines of 'the restoration of an original ideal'. The future hope of 'paradise regained' might not be far from Zephaniah's thoughts (see Zeph. 3) as he reminded the remnant that God would steadfastly care for them and restore their fortunes.

Charles Haddon Spurgeon, the famous nineteenth-century Baptist preacher, sometimes told the following story to illustrate God's providential care for his servants. A godly minister, running away from his persecutors, found a hayloft and dived into it, covering himself with the hay. The soldiers who were chasing him came with their swords and bayonets, thrusting and testing the hay. The minister felt the cold steel on the soles of his feet but was not discovered; God protected him. God also provided for him. A hen came and laid an egg every day near the place where he was hidden. So that he was sustained as well as protected until the time came for him to leave his hiding place in complete safety![9]

It is unlikely that many of us have found ourselves in as dramatic a situation as Spurgeon describes in his story. But we too can be encouraged by the doctrine of God's providential care for his redeemed people in the midst of our everyday problems and needs. Jesus reassures us too that he will provide for us and protect us, as we put our trust in him and seek first his kingdom:

> And do not set your heart on what you will eat or drink; do not worry about it. For the pagan world runs after all such things, and your Father knows that you need them. But seek his kingdom, and these things will be given to you as well. Do not be afraid, little flock, for your Father has been pleased to give you the kingdom.
> (Luke 12:29–32)

There is a further passage in this section (4–11) which also teaches us about God's providential care for his people. It is part of God's message about Moab and Ammon.

ii. God's message about Moab and Ammon – the promise of God's vindication (8–11)

Amid the awesomeness of the judgments that God would surely inflict upon Moab and Ammon, Zephaniah once more brings home to the remnant the certain hope of God's providential care for them and his vindication of them. The depth of that love and care is expressed in the way that the Lord speaks of *my people* (8), and of himself as *the God of Israel* (9).

[9] This story was recounted in D. R. Davis, *2 Samuel: Looking on the Heart* (Christian Focus, 2004), p. 178. Davis commented: 'Little providences can be grand encouragements.'

As a grandfather I have often noticed with great delight how small grandchildren will talk with great emphasis about 'my' daddy and 'my' mummy, with a marvellous sense of belonging in a very special way. Parents who love their children may not always speak like that about them, but they certainly think of their children in that way. Zephaniah reminds us that God the Creator, the *Lord Almighty* (9), thinks of the remnant of true believers in exactly that way. They are *my people* (8). Furthermore, God looks for trust from his people on the basis of his living reality (*as surely as I live*, 9a) and his mighty power (*the Lord Almighty*, 9a).

Having spoken of God's just judgment of Moab and Ammon (9), Zephaniah records God's words which say: *The remnant of my people will plunder them; the survivors of my nation will inherit their land* (9b). What does this mean? These words seem to mean that God himself will vindicate his people and give them victory over their enemies (11). There is a biblical resonance in the phrase *The remnant of my people will plunder them* (9b). The word for *plunder* (spoil) is used of the spoiling of the Egyptians at the time of the exodus (Exod. 3:22; 12:36). It's also used of Jesus, who on the cross, 'disarmed [spoiled] the rulers and authorities and put them to open shame, by triumphing over them' (Col. 2:15, ESV). It is Jesus who spoiled the enemy in the parable about the divided kingdom in the Gospels (Matt. 12:22–28; Mark 3:22–27; Luke 11:14–22). In each of these examples, the spoiling of the enemy points to the possibility of the remnant enjoying the fruits of God's victory.

So Zephaniah teaches us not only that God judges the nations justly but also that he cares for his people steadfastly. God promises to meet all our needs and to give us victory over our enemies, vindicating our trust in his faithfulness.

There are times when we all find the doctrine of God's providence puzzling. We wonder why he keeps some of his saints wonderfully free of serious illness while others suffer daily. We wonder why some Christians experience amazing deliverance from injury or death when facing persecution, while others are killed and become martyrs. We wonder how we can relate God's providential care for us in the light of the sinful actions of other people, and indeed in the experience of God's judgments. Zephaniah does not raise or seek to answer these questions (see the prophet Habakkuk for another approach). Zephaniah, however, turns our thoughts to the living God who acts both justly and lovingly. He is the faithful Lord who keeps his promises about judgment and salvation. He promises to restore our fortunes in the next life, if not in this. As Christians we can say with the apostle Paul: 'For no matter how many promises God has made, they are "Yes" in Christ. And so through him the "Amen" is spoken by us to the glory of God' (2 Cor. 1:20). So nothing 'else in all creation, will be able to separate us from the love of God that is in Christ Jesus our Lord' (Rom. 8:39). Furthermore, in the light of the cross of Christ, we can also say: 'If God is for us, who can be against us? He who did not spare his own Son, but gave him up for us all – how will he not also, along with him, graciously give us all things?' (Rom. 8:31–32).

There is a further truth that emerges in this passage. God will not only judge the nations justly and care for his people steadfastly; he also offers hope to believers universally.

c. God offers hope to believers universally (2:4–11)

We have already hinted at this aspect of Zephaniah's message. The promise of judgment to come carries with it the hope of salvation. There's a hint of this when Zephaniah tells us that God will *restore [the] fortunes* of the remnant of the house of Judah (7). There's a further message of hope at the end of the message about Moab and Ammon. He underlines the fact that on the day of the Lord's wrath, God *will be awesome* to the Moabites and the Ammonites (11a). They will know that they cannot ignore God or treat him with disrespect. For he is the Lord Almighty and will destroy all other gods (11b). Then Zephaniah adds this phrase: *Distant nations will bow down to him, all of them in their own lands* (11c). These words suggest that the Lord is setting before us a twofold hope.

i. There is the hope that idolaters will come to fear God

Zephaniah tells us that God will destroy the 'gods' or idols which those who lived in Moab or Ammon worshipped and trusted. Idolatry, in both its ancient and modern forms, takes away a proper fear and reverence for the Lord. But Zephaniah's message is one of great encouragement for believers. *The Lord will be awesome to them when he destroys all the gods of the earth* (11a). In other words, God's Word here gives us hope that lives can be changed. Those who have no fear or reverence for the Lord can discover that God is awesome; those who are proud can be humbled to worship the one true God. When the apostle Paul reported on his mission to the Christian converts in Thessalonica, he was able to say that their faith in God had become known everywhere:

> Therefore we do not need to say anything about it, for they . . . tell how you turned to God from idols to serve the living and true God, and to wait for his Son from heaven, whom he raised from the dead – Jesus, who rescues us from the coming wrath.
> (1 Thess. 1:8–10)

Zephaniah believed that the sovereign Lord was able to bring this about. In the midst of judgment there was a message of salvation.

It could be said that 'Jack' (someone I knew personally, but this is not his real name) worshipped 'created things rather than the Creator' (Rom. 1:25). For many years, Jack bowed down to the false gods of money and alcohol. It was while he was on the run from the law that he came into contact with Christians and heard the gospel for the first time. In due course he committed his life to Christ and became a Christian. God changed him. The idolater became a worshipper. His Christian journey had its ups and downs, as it does for most of us. But God's grace kept hold of him all the way. I asked someone who had known him during the last year or two of his life whether Jack had remained faithful to Christ to the end. He told me that he had last seen him a few days before he died 'talking to someone at the local supermarket about Jesus'.

Zephaniah surely believed that people out of every nation would one day turn from idols to worship the living God. It is possible that the phrase *Distant nations will bow down to him* refers to the day when many will involuntarily bow the knee to Jesus (Phil 2:9–11). But it is equally possible to think that Zephaniah believed that, by the grace of God, many idolaters would be changed and come to love and fear God. This leads us to a further message of hope.

ii. There is the hope that people will worship the Lord all over the world

Zephaniah's vision stretches far beyond Jerusalem and Judah. Indeed, it stretches beyond the neighbouring nation states. He reveals a global perspective and clearly expresses the hope that the true worship of the Lord will spread to every shore and every land. *Distant nations will bow down to him, all of them in their own lands* (11).

There are those who have tried to make these words a description of pluralism and multifaith worship. They claim that the prophet is a 'universalist' in the sense that he pictures people all over the world practising different religions but all worshipping the same God. For many people today, 'pluralism' is more than a way of saying that there are many different religions in our multifaith society. Many people use the word, more dangerously and falsely, to say that there are many different religions *and* that they are all equally valid. It is clear from this passage, if we read it in context, that Zephaniah cannot possibly be advocating that kind of pluralism. On the contrary, he is representing exclusivist theology which sees the chosen and redeemed of the Lord as 'the remnant'. However, he clearly believes that the remnant of believers includes Gentiles as well as the remnant of the house of Judah (7); and this passage suggests that in time Gentiles will be found worshipping the Lord all over the world. Zephaniah, of course, was not the only Old Testament prophet who had this global view (see Isa. 40:5; 52:10; 54:1–3; 56:1–8; Obad. 15; Zech. 14:9). The aged Simeon picked up on this prophetic teaching when he saw the Christ-child in the temple and proclaimed that he came to be 'a light for revelation to the Gentiles, and the glory of your people Israel' (Luke 2:32).

Christianity is a global religion. Jesus makes it clear to his disciples after the resurrection that they should make disciples in every nation (Matt. 28:16–20; Acts 1:8) and, according to the vision given to John on the Isle of Patmos, in heaven the remnant, saved by grace, would come from every corner of the earth – a truly international community. This is how John described it:

> After this I looked, and there before me was a great multitude that no one could count, from every nation, tribe, people and language, standing before the throne and before the Lamb. They were wearing white robes and were holding palm branches in their hands. And they cried out in a loud voice: 'Salvation belongs to our God, who sits on the throne, and to the Lamb.'
> (Rev. 7:9–10)

It is easy for Christians, serving Christ in difficult situations, to lose heart or to become discouraged because the work they are engaged in seems to be so small and weak. When we are tempted to see the church as small and struggling, we do well to remember Zephaniah's global vision. He saw that people from every nation would one day be worshipping the Lord. The coming of Christ, his birth, life, death, resurrection and exaltation, and the pouring out of his Spirit on the church, made such a vision a reality. Luke's history of the church in the early days shows how the gospel was spread from Jerusalem to Judea to Samaria and to the uttermost parts of the earth. Jesus once said, 'This gospel of the kingdom will be preached in the whole world as a testimony to all nations, *and then the end will come*' (Matt. 24:14; emphasis mine). Some Christians believe that we may have reached that point already. Whether we have or not, we should certainly lift up our heads and be encouraged by the worldwide growth of the Christian church, which Zephaniah and other prophets foresaw.

The growth of the worldwide church in the twenty-first century is remarkable. One survey I heard about made the following claim, for example:

1. For every African child born, two Africans are becoming Christians (in black Africa).
2. There are 1,600 new Christian congregations formed each week across the world.
3. There are up to 100,000 new Christians every day.[10]

With the strong message of God's judgment, therefore, has come a message of hope and encouragement – hope because God judges the nations justly, cares for his people steadfastly and gives hope to all universally. Zephaniah is to portray this message of future hope in even stronger colours. But before he does so, he returns to his own city of Jerusalem. He is convinced that God reigns. But does he reign in the hearts of his chosen people? Have Jerusalem and Judah learned from God's dealings with the other nations? Will they ever learn?

2. More home truths (3:1–8)

So far in this book, Zephaniah has introduced himself (1:1) and brought home a message of judgment on the world, and on God's people in particular, because they have sinned against the Lord (1:2–18). So he called

---

[10] The broadcaster and agnostic John Humphreys has admitted in his book *In God We Doubt* that the church is indeed growing in many parts of the world. He draws attention to the growth of the evangelical wing of the Anglican Church and the high proportion of believers in the church in the USA. He writes: 'Something similar has been happening in other continents. The chief rabbi, Sir Jonathan Sachs, wrote in 2002 about a revival of evangelical Protestantism sweeping across Latin America, Sub-Sahara Africa, the Philippines, South Korea and even (in spite of persecution) China.' Humphreys quotes *Prospect* magazine's headline 'God Returns to Europe' and the comment of Eric Kaufmann of Birkbeck College that there is a religious revival 'that may be as profound as that which changed the course of the Roman empire in the fourth century' (J. Humphreys, *In God We Doubt* [Hodder, 2008], pp. 125–126).

upon all those in Jerusalem and Judah to repent and return to God (2:1–4). He has also encouraged God's people (the remnant) by reminding them of God's sovereignty in judging the nations justly and in offering his providential care and hope for the remaining believers (2:3–15).

But now Zephaniah is ready to bring some more home truths to the citizens of Jerusalem. They probably felt far more comfortable as Zephaniah described the way in which God would judge their enemies, the neighbouring Philistines, Moabites, Ammonites and Assyrians (2:4–15). But now comes the shock. There are more home truths for Jerusalem and Judah to hear.

Most of us prefer to avoid home truths; yet in retrospect we often recognize their importance. We would be less than pleased if our doctor or consultant offered banal platitudes when our state of health demanded a clear and honest diagnosis of our sickness. Zephaniah was like a wise and courageous physician. He gave the people a diagnosis of their failures. He also offered hope of a cure. Judgment and hope for the nations included the nation of Judah and the citizens and leaders in Jerusalem – at least, we have assumed that, although the name of Jerusalem is not mentioned at this point. Zephaniah simply says: *Woe to the city of oppressors, rebellious and defiled!* (3:1). Can we be sure, then, that Zephaniah is referring to Jerusalem and not Nineveh? I think we can be sure. Zephaniah is addressing a city that *obeys no one* and *accepts no correction* (2). That suggests a city that should be living under the Word of God, a city of God's covenant people where the Lord dwells (5). Zephaniah would not have described Nineveh in that way. It is a city which has *officials* and *rulers* (judges) as well as *prophets* and *priests* (3–4), which is exactly what we would expect in Jerusalem.

So what is Zephaniah saying to Jerusalem? The next section of his prophecy includes two oracles. In the first (3:1–5) we find a message of hope in the midst of corruption; in the second (3:6–8) we hear a message of hope in the midst of judgment.

a. A message of hope in the midst of corruption (3:1–5)

There was a great deal that was wrong with the city of Jerusalem, and Zephaniah was bold enough to bring to God's people a few home truths. He did not spare them. *Woe to the city of oppressors, rebellious and defiled!* (1). Jerusalem was a corrupt city.

There's an important principle here. The three words that Zephaniah uses suggest an important proposition for us to consider.

i. Rebellion against God leads to corrupt behaviour (3:1–4, 5c)

The word for *rebellious* is a word that is almost always used for rebellion against God.[11] The psalmist, for example, speaking of a generation of Israelites who sought to put their trust in God, says of them: 'They would not be like their ancestors – a stubborn and rebellious generation, whose hearts were not loyal to God, whose spirits were not faithful to him' (Ps. 78:8). The psalmist goes on to say that their rebellion revealed itself in the fact that 'they did not keep God's covenant and refused to live by his law' (Ps. 78:10).

Zephaniah makes exactly the same point in this passage. The city that has rebelled against God has shown that rebellion by the fact that *She obeys no one, she accepts no correction. She does not trust in the Lord, she does not draw near to her God* (2).

Let's look more closely, then, at the way in which the citizens of Jerusalem demonstrated their rebellion against God. We may find that it speaks to us as well, as we consider the characteristics of spiritual rebellion.

We refuse to listen to God's Word (3:2a)

The Hebrew word *šāma'* literally means 'to hear', 'to give heed to' or 'to pay attention to'. From that it comes to mean 'obey' (*She obeys no one*). It was the people's failure to pay attention to God's Word and to obey it that led to the corruption in the city. It led to their personal defilement (1) and to the oppressive actions of their leaders (3–4). It led directly to their backsliding and to their apostasy. It is often the beginning of our backsliding too; it is possible to hear sermons, and even to read our Bibles, and not to pay serious attention to what God is saying to us.

Jesus often stressed the importance of proper listening to the Word of God. After telling the parable of the sower (Matt. 13:3–23; Mark 4:1–20; Luke 8:4–15), he makes it clear that it was a parable about listening when he says, 'Whoever has ears to hear, let them hear' (Luke 8:8). The seed that was sown on good soil, yielding a crop that was 'a hundred times more than was sown', stood for those 'with a noble and good heart, who hear the word, retain it, and by persevering produce a crop' (Luke 8:8, 15). In Matthew's Gospel we read: 'someone who hears the word and understands

---

[11] J. A. Motyer says it is used in this way in 36 out of 40 cases, in McComiskey (ed.), *The Minor Prophets*, vol. 3, p. 941.

it . . . produces a crop, yielding a hundred, sixty or thirty times what was sown' (Matt. 13:23). There's more to 'listening' than keeping awake during a sermon, or hurriedly reading a few verses of the Bible before rushing out to work or going to sleep at night!

The apostle James, practical as ever, described 'paying attention to' the Word of God with an apt illustration:

> Do not merely listen to the word, and so deceive yourselves. Do what it says. Anyone who . . . does not do what it says is like someone who looks at his face in a mirror and, after looking at himself, goes away and immediately forgets what he looks like. But whoever looks intently into the perfect law that gives freedom, and continues in it – not forgetting what they have heard but doing it – they will be blessed in what they do.
> (Jas 1:22–25)

If, then, we want to know God's blessing on our lives, and to avoid the corruption and defilement that marked the rebellious citizens of Jerusalem, we shall want to encourage one another to listen to God's Word with attention, understanding and obedience. Reading the Bible one to one, or in a small group, may help us. In church we can encourage one another by having Bibles placed in the pews so that the congregation can follow the passage that is the subject of the sermon. Some churches offer space for sermon notes on the back of their notices sheet. Others give outline sermon notes. Some use PowerPoint for an outline of the sermon. In private study it is largely a matter of finding space and time for unhurried and prayerful reading of the Word of God so that we can reflect upon it, and pray in response to it.

In the early days of the Christian church the apostle Paul warned his young colleague Timothy that in 'the last days' many people would be unwilling to listen to God's Word. 'For the time will come when people will not put up with sound doctrine. Instead, to suit their own desires, they will gather round them a great number of teachers to say what their itching ears want to hear' (2 Tim. 4:3).

Zephaniah warns God's people in Jerusalem of the same dangers. We know from other parts of his prophecy that there were siren voices seeking to draw people away from listening to God's Word. Some were pagan voices – the *remnant of Baal* (1:4); some were complacent voices – *The Lord will do nothing, either good or bad* (1:12); some were the voices of tradition – those who would *avoid stepping on the threshold* (1:9). As a consequence, many failed to pay attention to the Word of God.

The church in the UK today faces similar siren voices. Some Christians seem more ready to listen to the voices of our secular culture than the Word of God. Zephaniah warns us that a refusal to listen to the Word of God is a sign of rebellion against God, which in turn can lead to corrupt behaviour and a corrupt society.

The church today also needs to distinguish between listening to the traditions of people (1:9) and listening to the Word of God. Jesus made that distinction clear when he warned the Pharisees about the way some of their traditions contradicted God's Word: 'Why do you break the command of God for the sake of your tradition?' (Matt. 15:3). Paying too much attention to church tradition may well hinder us from hearing and obeying God's Word. How many church leaders have been brought almost to despair when some church tradition ('We always have the organ to accompany the hymns!') has become more important than listening to what God may have to say to us about the principles of church worship, and about godly and biblical ways of handling disagreements and seeking his guidance.

Somebody has said that God has given us two ears and one mouth so that we are twice as ready to listen as we are to speak! Zephaniah warns us that we can easily become like the rebellious city of Jerusalem by refusing to listen to God's Word and by failing to put it into practice. When we turn a deaf ear to God's Word, we turn a deaf ear to God.

We refuse to submit to God's Word (3:2)

The NIV translates the next phrase, *she accepts no correction* (3:2). When we accept no correction we do things our own way. We act as if we are masters of our own lives. We refuse to submit to God's Word and his will. When Jesus called people to follow him, he stressed the importance of learning from him and submitting to his teaching:

> Come to me, all you who are weary and burdened, and I will give you rest. Take my yoke upon you and learn from me, for I am gentle and humble in heart, and you will find rest for your souls. For my yoke is easy and my burden is light.
> (Matt. 11:28–30)

It is when we submit to God's Word that we find that 'his commands are not burdensome' (1 John 5:3), for his yoke is 'easy'; that is, it fits perfectly. His 'burden is light' because we are yoked together with Jesus. He is with us all the way.

The apostle Paul reminded Timothy that the Scriptures were inspired for the very purpose of 'teaching, rebuking, correcting and training in righteousness, so that the servant of God may be thoroughly equipped for every good work' (2 Tim. 3:16). The implication is that we should submit to its rebuke, correction and instruction. For to reject God's Word is to reject God himself. It is a mark of our rebellion.

God has graciously provided Scripture to be 'a lamp for [our] feet and a light on [our] path' (Ps. 119:105), and to rebuke and to correct and instruct us (2 Tim. 3:16). The tragedy is that many of us, like the citizens of Jerusalem in the days of Zephaniah, will neither listen to God's Word nor submit our lives to its teaching. We too are sometimes *rebellious* and therefore *defiled* (3:1).

There is a further mark of the rebellious citizens of Jerusalem which may also apply to us.

We refuse to trust in the Lord and draw near to God (3:2c)

A refusal to hear and to submit to God's Word inevitably leads to unbelief and a drawing back from God. So we are not surprised to learn that Zephaniah's next comment on Jerusalem is that *She does not trust in the LORD, she does not draw near to her God* (2c).

The Hebrew word for 'draw near' (*qārab*) suggests intimacy and joy in the presence of God. It is used in Leviticus 1:2 when the Lord says to Moses from the Tent of Meeting, 'Speak to the Israelites and say to them: "When anyone among you brings an offering to the LORD, bring as your offering an animal from either the herd or the flock."' A literal translation of the first phrase could be: 'When anyone brings near (*qārab*) a bringing near (*qorbān*)'. An Old Testament believer would seek God's presence on the basis of God's provision of a sacrifice. The shed blood enabled the believer to draw near to a holy God. Perhaps some in Jerusalem no longer trusted in God's provision and were beginning to trust in themselves and their own good works. Or perhaps Zephaniah was making a more general point. Those who were complacent (Zeph. 1:12) may have ceased to be motivated to trust in the Lord and so neglected both private prayer and corporate worship. Or is it more likely that the neglect of private and corporate worship came first and led to unbelief?

A Christian friend once told me that if he were to draw a graph of the highs and lows of his Christian life, they would correspond to the way in which he was finding quality time each day to read the Bible, and to pray, or not. When he was having an unhurried 'Quiet Time' each day, he was conscious of the Lord's presence and help in a way that was not true when he skimped it or missed it altogether. The 'Quiet Time' – a time (anything from ten minutes to an hour or more) set aside each day to meet the Lord as we read the Bible and pray – used to be a priority in the lives of many Christians. In particular, it had a special place in the spiritual discipline of many evangelical Christians. It was said that 'what can be done at any time and any manner, is apt to be done at no time and in no manner'.[12] So we were encouraged to find a regular time and place for a daily Quiet Time. I remember being told a story about the famous concert pianist Paderewski to encourage me to be disciplined about my use of the Quiet Time. On one occasion he is believed to have said: 'If I stop practising the piano for a *day*, I notice the difference; if I stop for *two days* my family notice the difference; if I stop for *three days* my friends notice the difference; and if I stop for *a week*, the public notices the difference.'

In Zephaniah's day the failure to trust in the Lord and to draw near to God led to corruption in the city, which in turn led to God's judgment on Jerusalem. We are in equal danger if the seeking of God's presence is no longer a priority in our lives. Yet Christians know that through Christ and his sacrifice on the cross we 'have access to the Father by one Spirit' (Eph. 2:18). What an amazing privilege that is!

Lord, what a change within us one short hour
Spent in thy presence will prevail to make;
What heavy burdens from our bosoms take,
What parched fields refresh as with a shower! . . .
We kneel, how weak; we rise, how full of power!
Why, therefore, should we do ourselves this wrong,
Or others – that we are not always strong? . . .
Why should we ever weak or heartless be,

[12] I. Abrahams, quoted in E. W. Heaton, *The Book of Daniel: Introduction and Commentary*, Torch Bible Commentary (SCM Press, 1956), p. 164.

Why are we ever overborne with care,
Anxious or troubled, when with us is prayer,
And joy, and strength, and courage are with Thee?
(Richard Chevenix Trench, 1807–86)

So much for some of the characteristics of rebellion against God. Zephaniah teaches us that if we refuse to pay attention to God's Word, refuse to submit to its teaching, and refuse to trust in the Lord and draw near to him, we are showing some of the characteristics of a rebellious people. Now he goes on to teach us some more home truths as he points out some of the consequences of spiritual rebellion.

In the first part of this chapter (3:1–5) Zephaniah draws attention to two distinct consequences that followed the rebellion against God of the citizens of Jerusalem. They could be described as personal defilement and public corruption.

1. The first consequence is personal defilement. Zephaniah describes Jerusalem as defiled, as well as the city of oppressors. The word *defiled* that Zephaniah employs is almost always used of personal defilement – according to Motyer, seven times out of ten. If we disobey God we defile ourselves. Our own personal lives are stained and spoilt. A careful examination of Psalm 51 illustrates this. It is conjectured that this psalm was written by King David after he had committed adultery with Bathsheba, murdered her husband and had been heavily involved in cover-up. We notice that the psalm begins with a sense of personal defilement. The writer feels dirty. So he prays: 'Have mercy on me, O God, according to your unfailing love; according to your great compassion . . . Wash away all my iniquity and cleanse me from my sin' (Ps. 51:1–2). The writer then acknowledges his sin, which he sees as first and foremost against God. 'For I know my transgressions, and my sin is always before me. Against you, you only, have I sinned and done what is evil in your sight' (51:3–4). The psalmist also hints at the consequences of living with unconfessed sin, the taking away of his joy in the Lord (51:8), the physical symptoms he suffered (51:8b), his inability to enjoy God's presence and the power of the Holy Spirit (51:11), and the burden, rather than the freedom and willing eagerness, in serving the Lord (51:12).

We may well experience the same effects if we have unconfessed sin in our lives. Sin stains our lives; it defiles us. Only God, in his grace and mercy, can take away the guilt of our rebellion against God (Ps. 51:14), blot out our sins (51:9), give us a pure heart (51:10), restore our joy (51:12), enable us to lead others to God (51:13), and help us again to worship and serve God worthily (51:18–19).

Zephaniah warns the citizens of Jerusalem that they are rebellious and defiled. Unlike King David, many of them would not trust in the Lord for forgiveness or draw near to him in prayer and worship. Their rebellion against God led to their personal defilement; they deserved God's judgment. They needed God's mercy – as we all do.

Zephaniah now takes us a step further. Personal defilement clearly led, in his view, to public corruption.

2. Public corruption was the second consequence that followed rebellion against God by the citizens of Jerusalem. In Zephaniah's mind there was clearly a link between a city that was rebellious and defiled, and a city that could fairly be called *the city of oppressors* (3:1). For Zephaniah, rebellion against God led to corrupt behaviour. Personal religion affects public morality.

There are many in the UK today who argue that belief in God is a private affair which should have no relevance to public office or to public morality. That is the politically correct and secular view largely accepted by the media. However, there are those, apart from religious leaders, who are willing to challenge that view. For example, William Rees-Mogg, a former editor of the *Times* newspaper, wrote an article[13] in which he said:

> We live in an age when Modernists regard religion with something approaching panic . . . there was a comic example of 'Christianphobia' in the Sunday Times . . . Michael Portillo . . . was hyperventilating at the idea of David Cameron (leader of the Conservative Party) going to church. 'I worry,' he wrote, 'because men of power who take instruction from unseen forces are essentially fanatics.'

Rees-Mogg challenges this privatizing of religion and specifically of the Christian faith. He supports Zephaniah's view that rebellion against God leads to corrupt behaviour, and ultimately to a corrupt society. In this same article in *The Times* he wrote:

> The world needs religion [i.e. true religion] . . . to address the moral issues. In the advanced societies it is these moral issues that now mock us.

---

[13] W. Rees-Mogg, *The Times*, 26 February 2007.

> Europe and North America are largely wealthy regions, but they are morally impoverished. Broken families, drugs, booze, youth gangs, crime, neglect of children and the old, the sheer boredom of shopaholicism, terrorism, the inner city slums, materialism itself are all marks of a global society in decline. Societies can be judged by their care for children. Social education must start in the family, and must have a moral basis. Children need to be taught to distinguish between right and wrong. A recent report by UNICEF showed Britain as 21st out of 21 advanced societies in the welfare of children. Our national failure is a shame and a disgrace.

Why is there so much moral corruption and failure in advanced societies such as the UK today? Rees Mogg concludes his article with these words: 'The 19th century was an age of social reform based on religious revival and the Christian faith. The 20th century was an age of religious decline and an accelerating decline in social cohesion as well as faith.' He then quotes from Oliver Goldsmith's *The Deserted Village*:

> Ill fares the land, to hastening ills a prey
> When wealth accumulates and men decay.

Zephaniah seems to be in no doubt that Jerusalem became *the city of oppressors* because it had rebelled against God. In this same passage (3:1–5) he gives some examples of corruption and oppression in the ranks of civil and religious leaders in Jerusalem.

The first example is the corruption of civil leaders: *Her officials within her are roaring lions; her rulers are evening wolves, who leave nothing for the morning* (3). The term *officials* or 'princes' (Motyer) probably refers to people we would call civil servants – the administrative branch of government. The description of them as *roaring lions* no doubt describes the savage and destructive way they exploited their own position of power and influence for personal gain, and without proper care for the citizens they were called to serve. The *rulers* (or 'judges') were the legislative arm of government. Their task was to apply the Word of God to every situation in life. When Moses first appointed judges he told them:

> Hear the disputes between your people and judge fairly, whether the case is between two Israelites or between an Israelite and a foreigner residing

> among you. Do not show partiality in judging; hear both small and great alike. Do not be afraid of anyone, for judgment belongs to God.
> (Deut. 1:16–17; see Deut. 1:9–18)

However, in Zephaniah's day the judges forgot that judgment belongs to God; they behaved as if he did not exist. They are described as *evening wolves, who leave nothing for the morning* (3). 'Their only desire was to milk the situation of every drop of self-enrichment, leaving not even a bone till morning.'[14] Intensified by hunger, wolves devour everything in sight at great speed. Intensified by greed for their own pockets, these judges must have preyed on their clients and lined their own pockets as quickly as possible.

In a theocracy such as Judah, civil servants and judges were accountable to God and governed by his law. They were also called to care for the welfare of the people (see Exod. 18:13–16). But as they submitted less and less to God's Word and God's standards, so corruption became rife – as it always does in those circumstances. The people of the UK live in a democracy, not a theocracy. Nevertheless, some past governments have acknowledged the Christian basis of that nation more openly than recent governments. To say that politicians 'don't do God' is a chilling indictment of a government. Zephaniah's point is that the failure of the civil leaders to honour God was leading to the lack of care for the people they served, as well as injustice, oppression and corruption. Righteousness exalts a nation. The refusal to seek God and his righteousness leads to corruption and judgment.

Now it is the turn of the religious leaders to face up to some more home truths, as Zephaniah presents the example of their corruption (3:4). When he turns his attention to the religious leaders in Jerusalem, he is equally blunt in what he has to say about the prophets and the priests.

The prophets, whose job it was to bring God's word to the people, are described as *unprincipled* and *treacherous* (4a). The word for *unprincipled* (*paḥaz*) is used elsewhere in the Old Testament. It is used to describe the reckless adventurers hired by Abimelech (Judg. 9:4). The same word is used of Reuben (Gen. 49:4) and translated 'turbulent', and in the context that describes his lack of discipline and self-control. These prophets, then, were unprincipled in the sense that they were reckless and undisciplined

---

[14] J. A. Motyer made this point in a letter sent to me on 5 November 2004.

in their use, and maybe misuse, of Scripture. Perhaps they were like the false prophets mentioned by Jeremiah who, instead of proclaiming God's message of judgment, preached 'Peace, peace . . . when there is no peace' (Jer. 6:13–15).

The prophets are also described as *treacherous.* This word is also used in different contexts elsewhere.[15] It is used in the context of disobeying God's Word (1 Sam. 14:33), being unfaithful in marriage (Jer. 3:20) and even deserting the Lord (Hos. 5:7). Here then were religious leaders who were undisciplined and reckless in behaviour and unfaithful in handling God's Word. Like the Pharisees in Jesus' time, they were blind leaders of the blind.

The New Testament also sets a high standard for those who are called to teach and preach the Word of God. Faithfulness to God's Word is closely linked to godliness of life. The apostle James, indeed, warns those who would be teachers of God's Word to think carefully before they put themselves forward. 'Not many of you should become teachers, my fellow believers, because you know that we who teach will be judged more strictly' (Jas 3:1). More positively, the apostle Paul lays down the need for holiness of life as well as faithfulness to God's Word as essential for Christian teachers and leaders. So Paul writes to his younger colleague in the ministry, Timothy, 'Flee the evil desires of youth and pursue righteousness, faith, love and peace, along with those who call on the Lord out of a pure heart' (2 Tim. 2:22). A little later Paul goes on to say, 'I give you this charge: preach the word; be prepared in season and out of season; correct, rebuke and encourage – with great patience and careful instruction' (2 Tim. 4:1–2).

Zephaniah had the same concerns as the apostle Paul. However, he found that many of the prophets of his day lacked both godliness of life and faithfulness to God's Word.

Zephaniah also had some home truths for the priests in Jerusalem. He wrote: *Her priests profane the sanctuary and do violence to the law* (3:4b). Priests had an important role in the temple at Jerusalem; they were responsible for all that went on in the temple worship. This included the offering of sacrifices, the temple liturgy and the teaching of the law (the Torah). They were called to serve the Lord in a godly way and be known to live a blameless life. They were called to be holy, set apart for God's work. So when Zephaniah accused them of profaning the sanctuary, it was

---

[15] See further Motyer, in McComiskey (ed.), *The Minor Prophets*, vol. 3, p. 943.

clear that they were not fulfilling their calling in a way that was honouring to God. At first sight it seems that Zephaniah was referring to a situation where the priests had become slack and irreverent in the conduct of public worship in the temple. Certainly the conduct of public worship is important, whether in the seventh century BC or in the twenty-first century AD. Modern worship services can certainly bring dishonour to God when they become dead and formal or, in contrast, nothing more than entertainment. But there may be a further significance in these words about the sanctuary. The word for *sanctuary* literally means holiness; it does not necessarily mean a holy place. The word for a holy place is *miqdaš*; the word used here is *qōdeš*. So, Zephaniah's emphasis here may well be on the need for holiness of life more than liturgical correctness. If so, that may well be a message that many of us who lead public worship need to be reminded of. I believe it was that famous nineteenth-century Scottish minister Robert Murray M'Cheyne who was reputed to have said, 'The greatest need of my congregation is my personal holiness.'

There is one further reference to the priests. Zephaniah tells us that they not only profane the sanctuary, but also *they do violence to the law* (4c). The word for *doing violence* (*ḥāmās*) can refer to violent actions against people (e.g. Jer. 13:22) or doing violence by distorting the truth (Exod. 23:1). Motyer neatly sums it up by saying: 'Here it means to do violence to the true meaning and intent of the law (contrast Mal. 2:5–7) and thereby to wrong and hurt people.'[16] The result of this mishandling of God's Word could be seen in the backsliding of the people and widespread corruption in both temple worship and civil life.

One major reason for the moral and spiritual decline of the church and society in Western Europe must surely be the failure of Christian leaders to teach the Bible and to live according to its principles in the grace and power of Christ. Liberal views on the Bible, and the moral scandals in the church which have been widely reported in recent years, have done untold harm to the church in the twenty-first century. We need to take heed to the warnings in Zephaniah. We do well to listen also to the apostle Paul's words about his own ministry:

> Therefore, since through God's mercy we have this ministry, we do not lose heart. Rather, we have renounced secret and shameful ways; we do

[16] Motyer, ibid.

> not use deception, nor do we distort the word of God. On the contrary, by setting forth the truth plainly we commend ourselves to everyone's conscience in the sight of God.
> (2 Cor. 4:1–2)

Zephaniah has demonstrated that rebellion against God leads to corrupt behaviour, and that corruption has extended to both civil and religious leaders in Jerusalem. In turn, their corruption has led to a corrupt society deserving the judgment of God. But that is not the whole story. For although rebellion against God leads to corrupt behaviour, the righteousness of God offers hope to all (5).

ii. The righteousness of God offers hope to all (3:5)

In January 2007 Canon Andrew White, the former vicar of the Anglican church in Baghdad, Iraq, sent one of a number of reports to the *Church of England Newspaper*. He wrote soon after the hanging of Saddam Hussein, and spoke movingly about the murders, the corruption and the dangers of life in the city of Baghdad:

> Murder is committed here every hour, death means nothing, and it is part of daily life . . . everything is difficult, the pain and tragedy cannot be escaped from. The sound of the bombs and the gun fire is unending, and so is our task. Time and time again we say we will not give up; and we will not, but it gets harder every day.

So what hope is there for the remnant of believers in the city? Canon White writes:

> Tomorrow I will be with our church. They will come to me in the International Zone down that road of death where their church stands. Many will be wearing black, mourning the loss of their loved ones. For them this conflict is real, it is their life in the midst of death; but they will worship their God. When we lose everything we realise that Jesus is all we have left. It is he and only he that will keep us going.[17]

There is something of that spirit of Zephaniah in the next verse (5). The prophet has spoken about the corruption and the danger of life in

[17] *Church of England Newspaper*, 19 January 2007.

Jerusalem in his day. But his message is not without hope. God has not abandoned his covenant people; the righteous Lord is present with them. This is how he expressed it: *The* L*ORD* *within her* [Jerusalem] *is righteous; he does no wrong. Morning by morning he dispenses his justice, and every new day he does not fail, yet the unrighteous know no shame* (5).

In stark contrast to the corrupt behaviour of so many in Jerusalem, the righteous Lord is still present among his people, acting justly.[18]

There are two aspects of the righteousness of God to which Zephaniah draws attention.

God is righteous in character

God's righteousness is an aspect of his holiness. God is distinct and separate from sin. His holiness means that he is absolutely pure. As the prophet Habakkuk said to God, 'Your eyes are too pure to look on evil; you cannot tolerate wrongdoing' (Hab. 1:13). Or, as Zephaniah says here: *The* L*ORD* *. . . does no wrong* (5). The apostle John expressed this memorably when he wrote, 'God is light; in him there is no darkness at all' (1 John 1:5). Moses had also proclaimed such a God when he wrote:

> He [God] is the Rock, his works are perfect,
>   and all his ways are just.
> A faithful God who does no wrong,
>   upright and just is he.
> (Deut. 32:4)

In the light of the righteousness of God's character, it is remarkable that Zephaniah can still proclaim that the Lord is present with his corrupt

[18] In his commentary on Zephaniah (in McComiskey [ed.], *The Minor Prophets*, vol. 3, p. 941), Motyer helpfully points out the contrasts in this passage (3:1–5). He writes: 'The thrust of the poem is that the offenses of the city (3:2) and leaders (3:3–4) are inexcusable because of the indwelling God (3:5a–d). Each line of the first two stanzas stands in contrast to the third stanza in an abcdd'c'b'a' relationship.'

The city		*God*	
a.	has not listened (2a)	a'.	was speaking and never heard (5d)
b.	would not accept discipline (2b)	b'.	constantly made his decisions known (5c)
c.	would not trust (2c)	c'.	is totally trustworthy (5b)
d.	did not draw near (2d)	d'.	was always available (5a)
A similar relationship exists between the actions of the leaders and the Lord			
a.	Princes failed their duty (3a)	a'.	was never away from his post (5d)
b.	Judges thought only of themselves (3b)	b'.	was making his judgments known (5c)
c.	Prophets were treacherous (4a)	c'.	was free from deviancy (5b)
d.	Priests defile the holy (4b)	d'.	set the standard (5a)

people. Presumably he was there because there was a remnant of believers in the city. It was much the same when the risen and ascended Lord Jesus sent a message through his servant John to the believers in the seven churches in Asia Minor (see Rev. 2 – 3), reminding them that he 'walks among' them (Rev. 2:1), and knew where they lived – 'where Satan has his throne' (Rev. 2:13).

Christians in troubled situations – such as in Iraq today – hold on to the same truth. The righteous Lord is with us, whatever our particular situation may be, and however much corruption and wickedness may be around us. The God of hope, who is a righteous God, is present with his people.

This ought to have been a challenge to the citizens of Jerusalem, as well as an encouragement to believers. Zephaniah teaches us that they were being reminded of the righteous character of God day by day: perhaps through the teaching of faithful prophets, such as Zephaniah, Huldah and Jeremiah; perhaps through the sacrifices offered in the temple; perhaps through God's common grace revealed in acts of justice and compassion that had not completely disappeared from the city. Zephaniah may well be referring to such actions when he says of the Lord: *Morning by morning he dispenses his justice, and every new day he does not fail* (5b).

This brings us to a second aspect of God's righteousness, namely . . .

God is righteous in his actions

In his *Systematic Theology*, Wayne Grudem gives us a helpful definition of the righteousness of God, emphasizing not only his character of absolute righteousness, but also his actions as a righteous God. He wrote as follows: 'God's righteousness means that God always acts in accordance with what is right and is himself the final standard of what is right.'[19]

Grudem supports this definition with reference to Abraham's question (expecting the answer 'Yes'), 'Shall not the Judge of all the earth do right?' (Gen. 18:25). He also quotes the words of the psalmist, when he says: 'The precepts of the LORD are right, giving joy to the heart' (Ps. 19:8), and God's words to Isaiah: 'I, the LORD, speak the truth; I declare what is right' (Isa. 45:19).[20]

---

19 W. Grudem, *Systematic Theology* (IVP, 1994), p. 203.

20 Grudem, *Systematic Theology*, p. 204.

Zephaniah's message is that God was behaving in a way that was consistent with his character within the corrupt city of Jerusalem. Zephaniah will soon show that a righteous God must judge righteously (6–9) and that a rebellious world deserved judgment. The Lord declares, *The whole world will be consumed by the fire of my jealous anger* (8c). But before Zephaniah speaks further about judgment, he offers a message of hope. The words *he does no wrong* (5) suggest not only that God is absolutely pure and sinless in character, but also that he acts with perfect wisdom and justice. That must be good news and a sign of hope in a corrupt and rebellious world. Zephaniah spells this out still further: *Morning by morning he dispenses his justice* (5). O. P. Robertson suggests that the phrase 'morning by morning' (Heb. *babbōqer babbōqer*) refers to 'the daily regularity of certain sacrifices offered in Israel' (Exod. 30:7; Lev. 6:5; 2 Chr. 13:11; Ezek. 46:13–15); or possibly refers back to the way in which God provided manna for his people morning by morning during their wilderness wanderings (Exod. 16:21). Robertson comments:

> Despite the appearance that corruption prevails on every side, the Lord daily manifests his righteous judgments. Even the faithful remnant, suffering under the oppressive tyrannies of a depraved leadership, must acknowledge the daily realities of the Lord's justice. As faithfully as the Lord provided daily manna for his people during their trial period in the wilderness, so in the chaotic last days of Jerusalem the Lord's righteousness was coming to light.[21]

Motyer has another suggestion for the significance of the phrase 'morning by morning'. He refers to the words spoken to the Servant in Isaiah 50:4: 'The Sovereign LORD has given me a well-instructed tongue, to know the word that sustains the weary. He wakens me morning by morning, wakens my ear to listen.' Such a phrase 'recalls the fellowship into which the Lord daily brought his servant, and within which he made his will known'.[22] Is Zephaniah saying that the righteous and gracious Lord is providing just such opportunities for fellowship day by day for those who would draw near to God, and trust in him (see Isa. 50:10; Zeph. 2:3), even in corrupt Jerusalem?

---

[21] O. P. Robertson, *The Books of Nahum, Habakkuk and Zephaniah*, NICOT (Eerdmans, 1990), p. 322.

[22] Motyer, in McComiskey (ed.), *The Minor Prophets*, vol. 3, p. 944.

The hopefulness of Zephaniah's message continues with the words: *and every new day he does not fail* (5d). Here's a reminder that we can totally rely upon the covenant Lord to keep his promises to us, and to act with perfect wisdom and justice in judging and saving us. The righteous Lord never fails his people, even though they may fail him. He never lets us down, and 'his compassions . . . are new every morning' (Lam. 3:22–23).

It's easy for us to be discouraged by the corruption in the church and in the nation today. Yet Zephaniah's message about the righteousness of God gives us hope. We are not only assured that God will deal with sin and rebellion justly, but we are also reminded that the righteous Lord is still present with his people, acts justly and provides for our spiritual needs day by day. His promises never fail.

It was because of the righteousness of God revealed in the saving work of Jesus Christ on the cross (see Rom. 3:21–26) that the apostle Paul was able to write to Christians in Rome with these reassuring words: 'If God is for us, who can be against us? He who did not spare his own Son, but gave him up for us all – how will he not also, along with him, graciously give us all things?' (Rom. 8:31–32).

Zephaniah speaks similar words of encouragement. The righteousness of God offers hope to all. Sadly, however, Zephaniah has to spell out a further home truth. In spite of God's righteous presence among his people, it is still true that in Jerusalem *the unrighteous know no shame* (5e).

J. H. Eaton points out that the Hebrew could mean, referring to God, 'He knows no shameful iniquity.'[23] If, however, the reference is to 'the unrighteous' (as NIV), then we are reminded that although God's grace and forgiveness are always being offered to us, and God's presence is with us, each of us has a choice to receive or reject God's grace. Zephaniah seems to be saying that there are many who continue to act unjustly and sinfully refuse to return to God, and worse still, *know no shame* (5e). This could be translated as 'they cannot know' or 'they have no way of knowing', with the implication that their conscience is seared and hardened through persistent sin. There is hope in the message of Zephaniah; but there is also a warning about the seriousness of persistent rebellion against God.

In this passage (3:1–5), then, Zephaniah puts two propositions before us. (1) Rebellion against God leads to corrupt behaviour – and that in turn leads to a corrupt society. But (2) the righteousness of God offers hope to

[23] J. H. Eaton, *Obadiah, Nahum, Habakkuk and Zephaniah* (SCM Press, 1961), p. 148.

all – for the righteous Lord did not leave his people. He was present with them, acting justly and providing for them. He offered them hope in the midst of corruption.

The same righteous and loving Lord offers us hope too. He is with us in every circumstance of our lives; he offers to provide for our needs day by day. He has provided a way for our sins to be forgiven – not through animal sacrifices, as in the temple in Jerusalem in Zephaniah's day, but through the once-and-for-all, sufficient sacrifice for sins provided by the death and resurrection of Jesus Christ (see Heb. 10:11–14). There is hope in the midst of corruption, because the righteous Lord is present among us.

Zephaniah now moves on to another oracle.

b. A message of hope in the midst of judgment (3:6–8)

In this next section Zephaniah brings us back again to God's promise of judgment upon the pagan nations (6–7) and his promise of final judgment at the end of the age when *The whole world will be consumed by the fire of my jealous anger* (8b). It's a fierce message, yet in the context of this passage it is also full of grace, love and hope.

The message begins with judgment (6). The devastation of war, both ancient and modern, is terrible. Defeat is so complete that even the *strongholds*, or battlements, the strongest parts of the defence of any city, are demolished. The streets are empty. Great cities are in ruin. The whole area is depopulated. We have seen it all on our television screens in reports from Bosnia, Afghanistan, Iraq and Ukraine, to name but four recent war zones.

But there is still a message of hope. For the remarkable thing is that God seeks to use these terrible events to teach his people. Zephaniah tells us about a God who loves his covenant people, and waits patiently for them to *wait* for him (8a). God seems to be saying to them, 'I wanted you to learn the lessons of history, especially my punishment of wickedness, so that you might submit to my Word, accept correction and be saved. I wanted to spare you; I wanted to give you hope. I hoped you would take the hint!' His actual words, following his description of his judgment of the nations, were: *'Surely you will fear me and accept correction!' Then her place of refuge* [i.e. the dwellings of Jerusalem and Judah] *would not be destroyed, nor all my punishments come upon her* (7a).

The tragedy of Jerusalem in the sixth century BC, as well as in the first century AD, was that her people did not heed God's warnings, or reverence him and his Word, or accept his instruction and correction. The sad truth was that, in spite of God's judgments on other nations, the people and their leaders were *still eager to act corruptly in all they did* (7b). This phrase literally means 'they rose up early' to act corruptly. They did not simply drift into corrupt and evil ways; they gave themselves up to it with purpose and resolve. They got up early to do it! So here, in Zephaniah's prophecy, we are reminded that, in spite of the presence and patience of God, those who claim to belong to God's people may give themselves enthusiastically to a life of sin and corruption. It's a solemn thought.

Is there any hope, then, for God's people and God's world if even those in Jerusalem 'rise up early' to make their deeds corrupt? The answer lies in the words of verse 8a: *'Therefore wait for me,' declares the LORD, 'for the day I will stand up to testify.'* To *wait* for him implies trust and confidence in the covenant Lord and his promises to his people (see Isa. 30:18; 64:4; Hab. 2:3). God reaches out to his people in love, even when they turn away from him. The call to *wait for* God implies the promise of blessing for those who put their trust in him (Isa. 30:18). There is hope here, even in the midst of the promise of judgment. God is pictured as a prosecutor in court in a case against the rebellious nations of the world (8b).[24] It seems clear that God is promising to judge the nations as an expression of his holy reaction against sin and evil. The strength of that reaction is contained in the words translated as *wrath, fierce anger* and *the fire of my jealous anger.* The result, in the final day of judgment, will be that the *whole world will be consumed* (see 2 Pet. 3:11–13).

The description of God as *jealous* is a familiar one in the Old Testament (see Exod. 20:5; 34:14; Deut. 4:24; 6:15; Josh. 24:19; Nah. 1:2; Zech. 1:14; 8:2). However, his jealousy, like his wrath, is wholly without the sin and vindictiveness often associated with human attitudes of this kind. But just as a loving husband is rightly 'jealous' of any attempt by others to take away the love and loyalty of his wife, so God is jealous for the love and loyalty of his covenant people. God wants our complete loyalty (Exod. 20:5; 34:14). He has a burning zeal to fulfil his purposes through his people (see Isa. 59:16–21).

So even this message of final and universal judgment has the seeds of hope in it. God judges the rebellious nations in order to vindicate his name and his people, to demonstrate his righteousness and justice, and to reveal

[24] NIV margin translates 8a as *I will rise up to plunder* in place of *I will stand up to testify*.

his love and wisdom to the remnant of believers. Zephaniah brings us a message of hope in the midst of corruption, and a message of hope in the midst of judgment. He is now ready to describe some even more wonderful things that God has prepared for those who love him.

Zephaniah 3:9–20

8. Hope and restoration for God's people

I bought my wife an engagement ring in the old-fashioned way. I went to the jewellers on my own, asked the man behind the counter to show me a number of rings consistent with my price range, and then fell for his salesmanship when he added one ring outside my price range with the words, 'It's rather special, don't you think, sir?' Then I took Elizabeth to choose one of the rings that were being displayed. This time, however, he put the rings on a beautiful, dark-velvet cloth. They sparkled brilliantly against the dark background – especially the one outside my price range! Elizabeth, who had no idea about the relative cost of the different rings, spotted the expensive one unerringly and chose it without hesitation. The dark background helped to bring out its brilliance and brightness.

The message of hope and restoration for God's people in this last section of Zephaniah (3:9–20) stands out all the more brightly because of the dark background of God's judgment in the previous chapters. It is an essential part of Zephaniah's message. Zephaniah's God is a God of love and mercy as well as a God of wrath and justice.

It has to be said, however, that some Old Testament scholars regard the book of Zephaniah as a composite work, and believe that this last section is written by another hand in post-exilic times. So Rex Mason has written that

> it is not clear how at one and the same time God can judge the nations, avenging the wrongs they have done to his people, and yet promise that foreigners will also join his own people in sharing in the fruits of his reign as a universal King.[1]

---

[1] R. Mason, *Zephaniah, Habakkuk, Joel*, Old Testament Guides (JSOT Press, 1994), pp. 17–18.

There is no compelling reason, however, why we should make this last section of Zephaniah a later addition to the prophecy. On the contrary, as J. H. Eaton has argued, there is a natural development from the first two sections of Zephaniah (1:2 – 2:3 and 2:4 – 3:8) to the third and final passage (3:9–20). Eaton argues:

> The third and final complex presents the positive side of the day of the Lord. If the first complex was as black as the night, and the second brought the early gleams of dawn, the third has emerged at last into the full light of day. In a world unharmed by evil, regenerate mankind now enjoys perfect unity in adoration of the heavenly King.[2]

P. R. House also insists that we look at Zephaniah as a whole. He argues that Zephaniah is best understood as a drama in three acts.[3] House writes that to remove these verses in chapter 3 (9–20) would be 'to destroy the purpose of every part of Zephaniah'.[4]

The clue to resolving the tension between the message of judgment and the message of hope and restoration surely lies with the concept of the remnant (3:13). It is through the remnant that God fulfils his promises. This is not only, in some measure, through the historical restoration of God's people from exile, but also in greater measure through the spiritual regeneration and restoration of believers in Jesus Christ – the remnant of grace. As J. H. Eaton finely expressed it, 'Only in the light of the gospel can it be seen how Zephaniah's "meek of the earth" can pass through doom to the new birth, and, being members of Christ, appear as themselves the transformed Remnant in the perfected Kingdom of God (3:12–13).'[5]

So now let's turn to this final glorious climax to the prophecy of Zephaniah (3:9–20).

There are three oracles or poems to consider. In the first, God promises a glorious future for the remnant of believers (9–13); in the second, God calls for a joyful response from the remnant (14–17a); and in the last section God proclaims final restoration for them (17b–20).

---

[2] J. H. Eaton, *Obadiah, Nahum, Habakkuk and Zephaniah* (SCM Press, 1961), p. 150.

[3] P. R. House, *Zephaniah: A Prophetic Drama* (JSOT Press, 1988).

[4] Quoted by J. A. Motyer in T. E. McComiskey (ed.), *The Minor Prophets*, vol. 3: *Zephaniah, Haggai, Zechariah and Malachi* (Baker Book House, 1998), p. 133.

[5] Eaton, *Obadiah, Nahum, Habakkuk and Zephaniah*, p. 151.

1. God promises a glorious future for believers (3:9–13)

In the Western world in the twenty-first century there is a good deal of pessimism about humankind and planet earth. The brilliant physicist Stephen Hawking, for example, after enjoying an experience of weightlessness, said gloomily, 'Life on earth is at an increasing risk of being wiped out by a disaster such as sudden global warming, nuclear war or viruses or other dangers. I think the human race has no future if it doesn't go into space.' This prompted Mike Hulme to write an article in the *Times* newspaper[6] with the heading 'Go into space . . . well, there's not much future here'. He went on to comment:

> The cry 'the end of the world is nigh!' now comes, not from religious nutters, but from respected scientists with the media to carry their message. Worse, it seems they can support space travel only by depicting other planets as cosmic *Costa del Crime*, where wicked humans can escape punishment for raping and pillaging the earth.[7]

An elderly woman who had just lost her husband gave me a less sophisticated example of pessimism about the future for human beings. Before I could speak about the Christian hope, she stated fiercely: 'When you die, you die, and that's it.' The French philosopher Jean-Paul Sartre said much the same years ago: 'There's no purpose . . . no goal for mankind . . . the world seems ugly, bad and without hope. There, that's the cry of despair of an old man who will die in despair.'[8]

Zephaniah, however, does not share in that despair or sense of hopelessness about the future. He knows that God will judge the world (8), but God's message to him is also a message of hope. God says:

> *Then* [or 'At that time', NRSV; see 3:8] *I will purify the lips of the peoples,*
> *that all of them may call on the name of the LORD*
> *and serve him shoulder to shoulder . . .*
> *They will do no wrong;*
> *they will tell no lies.*

---

[6] 1 May 2007.

[7] Quoted by Andrew Carey in the *Church of England Newspaper*, 4 May 2007.

[8] Quoted by D. Wilkinson in *The Message of Creation* (IVP, 2002), p. 266.

A deceitful tongue
will not be found in their mouths.
They will eat and lie down
and no one will make them afraid.
(9, 13)

Zephaniah teaches us from these verses that we can look forward to a glorious future characterized by united and universal worship (9–10); a holy and humble community (11–13); and a satisfying and secure environment (13d).

a. United and universal worship (9–10)

Zephaniah's vision of the future includes a picture of the remnant of believers worshipping the Lord with pure lips. The priests of the temple may *profane the sanctuary* (4), but the day is coming when the lips of people from every corner of the world will be cleansed and they will *call on the name of the Lord* (9). Isaiah understood the need of such purified worship when he became aware of God's holiness as he worshipped in the temple. He tells us that he cried out, 'Woe to me! . . . I am ruined! For I am a man of unclean lips, and I live among a people of unclean lips, and my eyes have seen the King, the Lord Almighty.' God's response was to touch his lips with a live coal from the place of sacrifice, and to say to Isaiah, 'See, this has touched your lips; your guilt is taken away and your sin atoned for' (Isa. 6:5, 7).

We too need to have our lips (and our hearts) cleansed when we come into the presence of a holy God. For us, the place of sacrifice is the cross, with the promise that 'If we confess our sins, he is faithful and just and will forgive us our sins and purify us from all unrighteousness' (1 John 1:9).

However, there may well be a reference here to another story in Scripture, the story of Babel (see Gen. 11:1–9). In that story we read that 'the whole world had one language and a common speech'. Then at a place called Shinar (Babylonia) the people said, 'Come, let us build ourselves a city, with a tower that reaches to the heavens, so that we may make a name for ourselves; otherwise we will be scattered over the face of the whole earth.' As a result of this project and the proud attitude of those who embarked upon it, God acted in judgment against the people and said:

> If as one people speaking the same language they have begun to do this, then nothing they plan to do will be impossible for them. Come, let us go down and confuse their language so they will not understand each other. So the LORD scattered them from there over all the earth, and they stopped building the city. That is why it was called Babel – because there the LORD confused the language of the whole world. From there the LORD scattered them over the face of the whole earth.

God's message here (3:9–10) may well indicate a reversal of Babel; 'purifying the lips' can be translated as 'clarifying the lips' of the peoples. In Zephaniah, God also refers to the believing remnant as *my worshippers, my scattered people.* Gordon Wenham, in his commentary on the Genesis story, writes on Genesis 11:1–9:

> The Tower of Babel was intended to be a monument to human effort; instead it became a reminder of divine judgment on human pride and folly. Similarly the multiplicity of languages and man's dispersal across the globe points to the futility of man setting himself against the Creator.[9]

But God's message through Zephaniah is that the day is coming when he will put an end to the confusion of Babel. According to Luke's account, that began to happen at Pentecost when the Holy Spirit enabled people from many different nations, and with different languages, to hear the gospel in their own native language (see Acts 2:8–9). The Holy Spirit, who came upon those calling 'upon the name of the Lord' in repentance and faith, also enabled Christian believers from Jewish and Gentile backgrounds to unite in worship, fellowship and service – serving the Lord *shoulder to shoulder* (3:9c; see also Acts 2:42–47). The basis of that worship and service was God's provision of a sacrifice for sin, and the offering of spiritual sacrifices pleasing to God (3:10; Rom. 12:1–2; Eph. 2:14–18; Heb. 9:11–14).

At its best, Christian worship today is both united and universal. Many churches today are truly international. But the church today is also divided and fragmented, and sometimes schismatic. There is a much-quoted piece of doggerel that sums up the situation in many places only too accurately:

---

[9] G. J. Wenham, *Genesis 1–15*, WBC (Word, 1987), pp. 241–242.

> In heaven above, with saints we love,
> That will truly be glory.
> On earth below, with saints we know,
> Well, that's a different story!

God's word to us in Zephaniah lifts up our eyes to a better vision. It's a vision of God's people no longer under the judgment of Babel, but worshipping and serving the Lord together in a truly united and international church. We are challenged to model such a community of the Spirit in today's church. But, on that final day of the Lord, this prophecy of Zephaniah will be fully and finally brought about. The best is yet to be!

> After this I looked, and there before me was a great multitude that no one could count, from every nation, tribe, people and language, standing before the throne and before the Lamb. They were wearing white robes and were holding palm branches in their hands. And they cried out in a loud voice:
>
> 'Salvation belongs to our God,
> who sits on the throne,
> and to the Lamb.'
>
> All the angels were standing round the throne and round the elders and the four living creatures. They fell down on their faces before the throne and worshipped God, saying:
>
> 'Amen!
> Praise and glory
> and wisdom and thanks and honour
> and power and strength
> be to our God for ever and ever.
> Amen!'
> (Rev. 7:9–12)

This vision of the church worshipping God perfectly in the future should challenge any laziness or casual attitude to the worship and service of God today. If God's ultimate purpose for us is united worship of the kind that has been described, then we should be seeking to prepare ourselves for such a day. For example, if we regard Sunday worship in church as an optional extra, if we'll take the trouble to go to church only when it's too wet to play golf, or if our children are not needed for a football match, or if we *feel* like it, then our attitude is far removed from the vision that Zephaniah and the apostle John in the book of Revelation have set before us. The same is true for Christian service. For too many churchgoers it is regarded as a 'hobby' for those who like that sort of thing, rather than one of the purposes for which we have been created and redeemed. To serve the Lord *shoulder to shoulder* (9c) is one of the greatest privileges that a believer can experience. Zephaniah's vision of a glorious future leading to united worship and service 'with all the Lord's holy people' (Eph. 3:18; see Eph. 3:14 – 4:16) should be a powerful incentive for every Christian to take the worship and service of God with the utmost seriousness and commitment.

Zephaniah's prophecy continues with a description of a future transformed city of Jerusalem – a holy and humble community.

b. A holy and humble community (3:11–13c)

The Jerusalem of Zephaniah's time was far from a holy and humble community, as the prophet has already made clear (1:4–13; 3:1–7). In this passage the implication is that the deeds of many are shameful, even though they show no shame (11a); they wrong God (11b) and they are *arrogant boasters* and *haughty* (or rebellious) (11c). Furthermore, they have become known not for their integrity, but for their *lies* and *deceitful tongue* (13).

There's a remarkable similarity between this situation and the moral climate in our own Western culture in the twenty-first century. For example, in the USA and the UK today we too have a problem with integrity and truthfulness. In an article in the *Times* newspaper (3 May 2000) Peter Bee wrote about the way in which dishonesty has invaded our cultures. He explained:

> Research in California revealed that people lie up to twenty times a day; while in a Gallup poll . . . a quarter of respondents admitted being untruthful on a daily basis. Only 8% claimed they had never lied . . . although there is always the chance that even then they weren't being honest! In one study of college students 85% of couples reported that one or both of them had lied about past relationships or recent events. In another it was found that dating partners lied to each other in about a third of their conversations.

It would not be difficult to cite other examples of the endemic nature of lies, deceit and 'cover-up' in our society today. So what hope is there in such a corrupt society? Zephaniah's message emphasizes two encouraging truths about God which can certainly give us hope: God's grace can transform a community, and his promises will be fulfilled ultimately.

i. God's grace can transform a community

Zephaniah's message is about a God who changes things. The people deserved to be *put to shame* (11). But God says: *On that day you, Jerusalem, will not be put to shame for all the wrongs you have done to me.* That day is a day of salvation as well as judgment. We deserve God's judgment. The remnant receive God's grace.

Furthermore, we receive God's transforming grace because God deals with sin and sinners in the community of faith by removing them (11) while sparing the remnant who trust in the name of the Lord (12–13). These no longer trust in themselves but in the name of the Lord – that is, in his revealed character and ability to save sinners. The remnant are marked by humility before God and meekness before others (11–12). By God's grace they are enabled to live blameless lives (13) and 'do not need to feel shame' (Eaton)[10] because God has dealt with it. God promises: the remnant of Israel *will do no wrong; they will tell no lies. A deceitful tongue will not be found in their mouths* (13). God promises to bring about a transformed community.

These promises were partly fulfilled in the New Testament church. The coming of Jesus and the union of believers in him made it possible for truth to become an essential mark of Christian discipleship (Matt. 5:37; Acts 5:1–11; Eph. 4:25; 2 John 4). The Holy Spirit poured out upon the church at Pentecost is the Spirit of truth (John 16:13). Christians are called to be 'walking in the truth' (2 John 4). In other ways, too, all Christians experience the transforming grace of God. The apostle Paul gives us a moving example in his letter to the church in Corinth:

> Do you not know that wrongdoers will not inherit the kingdom of God? Do not be deceived: neither the sexually immoral nor idolaters nor adulterers nor men who have sex with men nor thieves nor the greedy nor

10 Eaton, *Obadiah, Nahum, Habakkuk and Zephaniah*, p. 154.

> drunkards nor slanderers nor swindlers will inherit the kingdom of God. And that is what some of you were. But you were washed, you were sanctified, you were justified in the name of the Lord Jesus Christ and by the Spirit of our God.
> (1 Cor. 6:9–11)

So God's grace can change people's lives and transform a community. Zephaniah knew that; so should every Christian. But Zephaniah is surely looking beyond this life and the New Testament church when he speaks of that day when the remnant of Israel *will do no wrong; they will tell no lies. A deceitful tongue will not be found in their mouths* (13). So here is a second encouraging truth we can learn from Zephaniah about God. We not only learn that God's grace can transform a community; we also learn that God's promises will be fulfilled ultimately.

ii. God's promises will be fulfilled ultimately

Zephaniah's description of the transformed Jerusalem is an ideal one. To do no wrong and to tell no lies describes the remnant of believers living in a perfect community on God's holy hill, with all sinful pride and deceitfulness removed. Zephaniah teaches us that God will bring this about on *that day*, the final day of judgment and salvation. Zephaniah is certain that God will keep his covenant promises to those who *trust in the name of the Lord* (12).

If the promise of united and universal worship in the future inspires us to take the worship and service of the Lord seriously here and now, then the promise of a new Jerusalem as a community where sinful pride is abolished, and where humble, holy living is the norm, should certainly inspire us to model such a community here on earth. There really is no place for pride and haughtiness (that is, spiritual rebellion; see Isa. 1:2) within the Christian church. In the new Jerusalem the *meek and humble* (12) are the only ones who are welcome. Jesus taught us that the same meekness and humility should be the mark of his disciples here on earth. When Jesus modelled such humility by washing the disciples' feet (see John 13:1–17), he said to them:

> Now that I, your Lord and Teacher, have washed your feet, you also should wash one another's feet. I have set you an example that you should do as I have done for you. Very truly I tell you, no servant is greater than

> his master, nor is a messenger greater than the one who sent him. Now that you know these things, you will be blessed if you do them.
> (John 13:14–17)

The Christian community should be a model of practical care, concern and support for others – for those outside the church as well as those within it. We are called to love our neighbour as ourselves.

The apostle Paul repeated this teaching to the Christians in Philippi. He urged them:

> Do nothing out of selfish ambition or vain conceit. Rather, in humility value others above yourselves, not looking to your own interests but each of you to the interests of the others. In your relationships with each other, have the same mindset as Christ Jesus . . .
> (Phil. 2:3–5; see also Phil. 2:1–13; 1 Pet. 5:1–11).

Zephaniah is convinced that God will keep his promises and bring about a new Jerusalem where God's remnant will live in perfect love together, with humility and holiness. The implication is that we should prepare for that day here and now. This is how the apostle John saw it: 'Dear friends, now we are children of God, and what we will be has not yet been made known. But we know that when Christ appears, we shall be like him, for we shall see him as he is' (1 John 3:2). Then, as John glimpses something of what will happen on that day, when Jesus will appear at the end of the age, he challenges Christians now to respond in this way: 'All who have this hope in him purify themselves, just as he is pure' (1 John 3:3). In the light of this future hope, then, there is the challenge to purify ourselves; that is, to repent of our sins and to come to the cross to find in the crucified and risen Saviour cleansing and forgiveness. It is because of Christ's death on the cross for sinners that on that day those who put their *trust in the name of the Lord* (12) will not be put to shame for all the wrongs that they have done (11); for God in Christ has borne that shame and sin in our place (see Isa. 53:4–6; 2 Cor. 5:21; Gal. 3:13; 1 Pet. 2:24; 3:18).

God will keep his promises; Zephaniah is certain about that. God's grace is able to transform us now. God's promise of salvation, as well as of judgment, will be fulfilled then – on that day! God will judge corrupt nations and individuals. But the remnant, who put their trust in the Lord, can look forward with certain hope to a new Jerusalem, a holy and humble community. This is also what the apostle John clearly saw in the book of Revelation:

> I saw the Holy City, the new Jerusalem, coming down out of heaven from God, prepared as a bride beautifully dressed for her husband. And I heard a loud voice from the throne saying, 'Look! God's dwelling-place is now among the people, and he will dwell with them. They will be his people, and God himself will be with them and be their God. "He will wipe away every tear from their eyes. There will be no more death" or mourning or crying or pain, for the old order of things has passed away.'
>
> He who was seated on the throne said, 'I am making everything new!' (Rev. 21:2–5)

Zephaniah's message too is that the best is yet to be! We can look forward to united and universal worship, to a humble and holy community in the new Jerusalem, and, Zephaniah now tells us, a satisfying and secure environment in a restored Eden.

c. A satisfying and secure environment (13d)

They will eat and lie down and no one will make them afraid (13d). Zephaniah now describes the glorious future that God has planned for the remnant of believers in pastoral terms that may also be meant to call to mind the Garden of Eden. The pastoral scene is suggested by the reference to eating and lying down. The people of Israel were often referred to as 'the sheep of Israel' (Gen. 49:24; Pss 23:1; 80:1; Isa. 40:11; Ezek. 34:2–3). God was their shepherd, providing for his people, protecting them, feeding them and leading them in his way. As the prophet Isaiah put it, God 'tends his flock like a shepherd: he gathers the lambs in his arms and carries them close to his heart; he gently leads those that have young' (Isa. 40:11). So here in Zephaniah there is the promise that God will feed his sheep, and give them rest and security so that no-one will make them afraid (Mic. 2:12; 4:4; John 6; John 10:9). Is there a hint here of Eden restored or paradise regained?

It may be said that these words have been partially fulfilled in the lives of Christians since the coming of Jesus, the good shepherd, through his birth, life, death, resurrection and exaltation, and the sending of the Holy Spirit to those who truly repented and believed (Acts 2:38–30).

Jesus promised satisfaction and security for those who followed him (John 6; 10). He also encouraged his disciples to trust him and not to be afraid (see Matt.10:28; Mark 4:40; John 14:1, 27). A friend of mine wrote to me some years ago with the story of her conversion to Jesus Christ. She wrote about the satisfaction she had found in following Jesus, the good shepherd. This is part of her letter, quoted with her permission:

> Having been brought up on the philosophy 'eat, drink and be merry for tomorrow we die' I was determined to get the most out of life. I joined clubs, went to all-night parties and lived in a constant whirl of social activity. To my friends I really seemed to be 'living' but deep down inside I knew it wasn't true. I became more and more dissatisfied and life seemed pointless. Then I heard about the new life that Christ offered. Somehow I knew that this was what I needed and so I asked him into my life to renew it and redirect it. Since then I have known increasing satisfaction and fulfilment more than I had ever known before.

Since she wrote that letter she has continued to serve the Lord at home and overseas, and is still going strong. The Lord has given her satisfaction and security; she has experienced at least partially God's promise through Zephaniah, that the remnant *will eat and lie down and no one will make them afraid* (13d).

But Zephaniah is almost certainly pointing beyond the experience of Christian people on earth. He seems to be looking forward to that day (11) when Eden will be restored, and there will be a 'new heaven and a new earth, where righteousness dwells' (2 Pet. 3:13; Isa. 65:17–25; Rom. 8:18–25; Rev. 21:1–7). Zephaniah is encouraging us to see that 'the best is yet to be' and that God has a purpose beyond this life on that day when the Lord comes both to judge and to save. Then there will be worship and service for the remnant of believers, and holy and humble living for those who will be perfected in a restored Eden or (taking these words of the apostle Peter) in 'a new heaven and a new earth, where righteousness dwells'.

In the light of all this, we need to hear again the same apostle's exhortation: 'So then, dear friends, since you are looking forward to this, make every effort to be found spotless, blameless and at peace with him' (2 Pet. 3:14).

2. Going home (3:14–20)

Over the years I have had the opportunity from time to time to minister overseas, sometimes as far away as Australia and East Africa, sometimes nearer home in other parts of Europe. Although I have always enjoyed the experience and have counted it a great privilege, I have also looked forward to coming home, especially if my wife, Elizabeth, has not been with me. There's no place like home!

In this last section of Zephaniah (3:14–20) the prophet paints a wonderful picture of God gathering his scattered remnant and bringing them home. *At that time I will gather you; at that time I will bring you home . . . when I restore your fortunes before your very eyes* (20). It is possible that Zephaniah is anticipating the return from exile seventy years after the destruction of Jerusalem in 586 BC. Yet the way in which Zephaniah describes this homecoming is far too optimistic in the light of what actually happened historically. The appeal to return to Jerusalem seventy years after the destruction of the city was not a popular one. Those who made the journey faced many hazards and disappointments and a great deal of opposition. If they read Zephaniah's words later, and understood their return as a fulfilment of that prophecy, they would certainly have been disappointed. It wasn't as Zephaniah described it. The fact is that there was a greater fulfilment to come, which we must explore later.

Whatever Zephaniah precisely meant by these words of homecoming, he was certainly bringing a message of hope and joy to those believers who may have been feeling insecure, fearful and despairing (14–16). It's a message we do well to take to heart when we feel similarly discouraged in our Christian discipleship or ministry. For Zephaniah's teaching calls us to do two things in particular: to rejoice in what God has done for us, and to have confidence in what God will do for us.

a. Rejoice in what the Lord has done for you! (14–17a)

There is nothing half-hearted about Zephaniah's call to the citizens of Jerusalem to rejoice in what God has done for them (14).[11] There is a place for exuberant praise in the believer's life as well as for silence and a sense of awe. Singing is a natural way for most people, though not all, to express

[11] 'Daughter Zion', 'Daughter Jerusalem' and 'Israel' (14) in this context are all synonyms for Jerusalem and her inhabitants.

joy in God. To shout aloud is appropriate when we have such good news that we can no longer keep it to ourselves, or when some great victory has been achieved. To *rejoice with all [our] heart* is a reminder that God's actions on our behalf are so great that half-hearted or formal praise can never be enough. The apostle Paul wrote that we should 'rejoice in the Lord', however difficult our circumstances (Phil. 4:4); and he wrote those words while chained to a Roman soldier in prison! We easily get excited about our football team, but we can be strangely silent about our God. Zephaniah teaches us that we have something to shout and sing about, and that we should rejoice in what the Lord has done for us. Charles Wesley captured that excitement a little when he wrote these words:

> O for a thousand tongues to sing
> My great Redeemer's praise,
> The glories of my God and King,
> The triumphs of his grace!

But what has God done for us, according to Zephaniah, that calls forth such joy and celebration? We know from Zephaniah that God is our judge. Now he reminds us again that God is also the saviour of those who put their trust in him (17).

i. God has taken away our punishment (15a)

Zephaniah has faithfully proclaimed the just judgment of God on a rebellious Judah and Jerusalem from the beginning of his prophecy (1:4 ff.). He has called upon God's people to repent and seek the Lord (2:1–3). Now he calls upon those who have put their trust in the Lord, the remnant of believers, to rejoice that God has removed the need for punishment: *The* L*ORD has taken away your punishment* (or, in NRSV and ESV, *The* L*ORD has taken away the judgements against you*) (15a).

It is possible that Zephaniah has in mind the taking away of those instruments of God's judgments – the Assyrian invader, for example. It is possible that he is anticipating the ending of a period of exile, and using the past tense as a way of stating the certainty that what God has promised about salvation he will certainly fulfil. Or he may be reminding the remnant about God's actions in past history; for by a mighty act of redemption God delivered his people from the bondage of slavery in Egypt and the judgment of death, by means of the Passover lamb (Exod. 11 – 14).

Either way, we see a holy and merciful God who must judge sin and rebellion but who has also found a way to take away the punishment and the judgments we deserve. That points the way to God's provision of salvation through sacrifice, which leads us to Christ's death on the cross.

Christians rejoice that 'Christ, our Passover lamb, has been sacrificed' for us (1 Cor. 5:7). He has borne our sins and taken away the punishment we deserve by bearing it in our place (Isa. 53:6; Mark 10:45; John 1:29; 2 Cor. 5:21; Gal. 3:13; 1 Pet. 2:24; 3:18). It is because of what Christ has done for us, once and for all, on the cross, in taking away our punishment, that we should rejoice in the Lord with great joy. For there is now 'no condemnation for those who are in Christ Jesus' (Rom. 8:1; see Rom. 5:1–5).

When Jesus said to his disciples, 'I go and prepare a place for you' (John 14:3), he meant that he was going to the cross to finish the work that God had given him to do, and that by his death, resurrection and exaltation he was going to prepare a home for those who believed in him. He did all this for us so that he could welcome us to his heavenly home. What a glorious gospel! No wonder we are urged to sing and shout aloud and to rejoice in our God with all our hearts. Because of what Christ has done for us we should strengthen our feeble arms and weak knees! (See 3:16 and Heb. 12:1–2.) We should rejoice in the Lord.

There is a further reason to rejoice.

ii. God has turned back our enemies (15b)

The Lord . . . has turned back your enemy. Zephaniah doesn't mention a particular enemy, though he may well have in mind a nation such as Assyria, which God had used as an instrument of disciplining judgment on his people. But here again the words of Zephaniah seem to illustrate a principle. He is surely reminding us that the God who has defeated the enemies of Judah and Jerusalem in the past is *the Mighty Warrior who saves* (17) and can be trusted to defeat all those who oppose God's will and attack his people. We should rejoice in such a God and in his power to deliver his people from their enemy.

Christians should rejoice in the Lord for the same reasons. We can look back to Calvary and see the death of Jesus as a victory over sin, death and the devil. When Jesus cried 'Finished' from the cross, it was a cry of victory, not a sigh of resignation. So the apostle Paul could write to the Christians at Colosse and say, 'God made you alive with Christ. He forgave us all our sins . . . And having disarmed the powers and authorities, he made a public spectacle of them, triumphing over them by the cross' (Col. 2:13, 15).

It is Satan and these spiritual powers that Christians face as their enemy today. As Paul wrote to the church at Ephesus:

> Put on the full armour of God, so that you can take your stand against the devil's schemes. For our struggle is not against flesh and blood, but against the rulers, against the authorities, against the powers of this dark world and against the spiritual forces of evil in the heavenly realms.
> (Eph. 6:11–12)

It is because of Christ's victory on the cross that we can overcome Satan, our enemy. So John, in the book of Revelation, is able to write about Christians who overcame Satan through the victory of Christ on the cross:

> Now have come the salvation and the power
>   and the kingdom of our God,
>   and the authority of his Messiah.
> For the accuser of our brothers and sisters,
>   who accuses them before our God day and night,
>   has been hurled down.
> They triumphed over him
>   by the blood of the Lamb
>   and by the word of their testimony;
> they did not love their lives so much
>   as to shrink from death.
> Therefore rejoice . . .
> (Rev. 12:10–12)

There are some who find it difficult to rejoice in Christ's victory over Satan at Calvary, while evil and suffering seem so rampant and unchecked in today's world. This is difficult to understand. However, in the Second World War, once victory in the battle for Normandy had been achieved, there are historians who would argue that final victory was certain, even though there would still be much fighting and suffering to come. Christ's victory at Calvary, and his death, resurrection and exaltation, guarantees final victory, even though our enemy is still active within the limits of God's sovereign will. So we are right to rejoice in the fact that God has turned back our enemies. Thanks be to God – we're on the winning side!

So Zephaniah has taught us to rejoice because of what God has done for us, as he did for the remnant of believers, in taking away our punishment, turning back our enemies and now coming down among us.

iii. God has come down among us (15–17a)

Unlike Isaiah, Zephaniah does not write about a messianic figure who is revealed as a distinct divine person. It is God, the covenant Lord (Yahweh), who is King of Israel, as well as the Lord of the nations. He is King and he reigns supreme. He is in control of all things. Yet he is also with his people. He dwells in their midst; and because God had come to dwell among his people, he is, as the psalmist put it, 'an ever-present help in trouble' (Ps. 46:1). Because he is with them, they need fear no harm; *he is the Mighty Warrior who saves* (17).

But these words were not completely fulfilled in Israel's past history, or in the days of Zephaniah. Certainly God the King was with them. As a result, *they will say to Jerusalem* [or 'it shall be said', NRSV], *'Do not fear, Zion; do not let your hands hang limp'* (16). The message that God was with them as King and Mighty Warrior, able to save, was intended to move them from fear to faith, from paralysing despair to action. But to say *never again will you fear any harm* (15d) looks to a future that has not yet arrived.

Christians rejoice in the fact that God came down to earth to 'pitch his tent' among us. The apostle John describes Jesus as the Word (*logos*) who was 'with God in the beginning' and 'was God' (John 1:2, 1). He goes on to tell us that the 'Word became flesh and made his dwelling among us. We have seen his glory, the glory of the One and Only, who came from the Father, full of grace and truth' (John 1:14). John also tells us that this same Jesus is a mighty warrior who saves. He is the 'Lamb of God, who takes away the sin of the world' (John 1:29). The whole of the New Testament bears witness to these truths. So, as the apostle Paul said, 'If God is for us, who can be against us? He who did not spare his own Son, but gave him up for us all – how will he not also, along with him, graciously give us all things?' (Rom. 8:31–32).

Christians also rejoice in the fact that God not only sent his Son into the world to redeem the world, but also sends his Spirit into the hearts of those who believe in Christ. The King is with us when the Holy Spirit comes to dwell in our lives to reign there (see John 14:15–27; 16:5–15; Rom. 8:5–17; Gal. 5:13–26).

Yet there is still more to come. In the book of Revelation, John sees a vision of '"a new heaven and a new earth" . . . the Holy City, the new Jerusalem', and hears

> a loud voice from the throne saying, 'Look! God's dwelling-place is now among the people, and he will dwell with them. They will be his people, and God himself will be with them and be their God. "He will wipe every tear from their eyes. There will be no more death" or mourning or crying or pain, for the old order of things has passed away.'
>
> He who was seated on the throne said, 'I am making everything new!' (Rev. 21:1–5)

On that day it will truly be said, *The LORD, the King of Israel, is with you; never again will you fear any harm* (15c–d).

We need to take seriously Zephaniah's exhortation to be *glad and rejoice with all your heart* (14) at what God has done for us. It's easy for us to become discouraged and to give up the fight, letting our hands *hang limp* (16b). It's easy to forget that the King is with us, working out his sovereign will in our lives. *On that day* (16a) suggests that he has a timetable as the sovereign King which may be different from ours. We easily forget that he is a mighty warrior, *who saves* (17a), and that he can do for us 'more than all we ask or imagine' (Eph. 3:20). There's a place for singing, shouting aloud and rejoicing in all that God has done for us. When we are discouraged in our discipleship, or in our ministries, we do well to recall all the good things that our gracious God has done for us. There is much that is spiritually healthy in the old hymn, which said simply:

> Count your blessings,
> Name them one by one,
> And it will be surprise you
> What the Lord has done.

Zephaniah, however, not only teaches us to rejoice in what God *has* done for us; he further encourages us to be confident in what God *will* do for us.

b. Be confident in what God will do for you! (17b–20)

In order to build up the confidence of the remnant of believers in Jerusalem, Zephaniah now describes a number of gracious actions that the Lord will do for his people in the future. Ten times in these last few verses Zephaniah tells us that God will act in a certain way. It's an amazing revelation of God's covenant love and commitment to his people, not only in those times but also today. Here's a summary of what is promised.

i. God will delight in his people (17b, c, d)

He will take great delight in you; in his love he will no longer rebuke you, but will rejoice over you with singing (17). Zephaniah teaches us that the mighty warrior God, who is able to deliver his people from their enemies, is also the God of infinitely tender love who actually delights in us! The words *in his love he will no longer rebuke you* may be understood in a number of different ways. Sometimes the verb (to quieten) is used in a transitive sense. It could then mean 'he will silence you in his love', though in this context it is not altogether clear what that would mean. The NRSV prefers the phrase *he will renew you in his love*, while some Jewish commentators render the phrase, *he will cover up the sins of his people in silence.*

Most commentators, however, believe that the verb is intransitive. Motyer, for example, prefers 'He will be quiet (or silent) in his love'.[12] In other words, the phrase refers to divine feeling rather than divine action. It is perhaps the picture of a mother gazing in silent love and wonder at her baby, or a lover enjoying the presence of a loved one in silence and with deeply felt love. The Hebrew word that is used for 'love' is not *ḥesed* but *'āhăbâ*, which is used for Jacob's love for Rachel (Gen. 29:18); and it is also used for God's love for his covenant people expressed through Hosea's love for his estranged wife (Hos. 3:1).

So God is said to love his people with 'wordless adoration'[13] as well as with joyful song. This is no remote God, distant and cold and untouched by the human situation. Rather, this is the God and Father of our Lord Jesus Christ who demonstrated his love for us in this: 'While we were still sinners Christ died for us'; and the God who has poured out his love 'into our hearts through the Holy Spirit that has been given to us' (Rom. 5:8; 5:5).

---

12 Motyer, in McComiskey (ed.), *The Minor Prophets*, vol. 3, p. 957.

13 Motyer, ibid., p. 958.

Zephaniah reminds us that God will always love us like that. We can be confident that God loves us with a deep personal love and delight that nothing can destroy. When the apostle Paul wrote to Christians at Rome who were suffering persecution and dangers every day, he reminded them of this divine love. He wrote:

> Who shall separate us from the love of Christ? Shall trouble or hardship or persecution or famine or nakedness or danger or sword? . . . No, in all these things we are more than conquerors through him who loved us. For I am convinced that neither death nor life, neither angels nor demons, neither the present nor the future, nor any powers, neither height nor depth, nor anything else in all creation, will be able to separate us from the love of God that is in Christ Jesus our Lord.
> (Rom. 8:35, 37–39)

We may be facing trials in our personal lives, in our family or in the church, which may cause us to wonder where God is and why he doesn't appear to care. Zephaniah reminds us, not only that God (the sovereign King) is with us, but also that he loves us and will always love us; he will take delight in us and rejoice over us as we put our trust in him and, with his help, lift up the hands that *hang limp* (16–17). He is a God to be trusted. He will delight in his believing people.

ii. God will take away our sorrows (18)

It's not completely clear what Zephaniah means in this verse. According to the NIV, the Hebrew means: *I will remove from you all who mourn over the loss of your appointed festivals.* The implication here is that Zephaniah anticipated a time of captivity for God's people when they would feel deep sorrow and reproach for the loss of temple worship and religious feasts (see Ps. 137:1). If so, Zephaniah brings to them God's promise that he will take away their sorrow by restoring them to Jerusalem to enjoy renewed temple worship. Certainly God wants us to enjoy worshipping him with other believers. Yet Jesus made it clear that it was not *where* we worshipped but *how* we worshipped that mattered most (see John 4:21–26).

It's possible to understand the phrase, however, as: 'Those who are grieved because of the appointed feasts I will remove; they will be far from you, the one on whom the imposition was a reproach' (Motyer). On this understanding, Zephaniah seems to be addressing those who find the feasts a burden and may even be using them to exploit the poor (see Amos 8:4–6; 5:11; cf. John 2:12–17).[14] God promises to remove them and the sorrow they caused.

Or was Zephaniah still looking beyond the restoration of the exiles to the dawning of the new covenant when the feasts and sacrifices would be fulfilled in the coming of the Messiah, and religion would no longer be a burden or a wearisome business? (See Jer. 31:31–35; Ezek. 36:24–27; John 4:21–26.) Certainly the apostle Paul made it clear to Christians that one consequence of living life in Christ or walking in the Spirit was freedom from the burden of religion. He wrote: 'It is for freedom that Christ has set us free. Stand firm, then, and do not let yourselves be burdened again by a yoke of slavery' (Gal. 5:1).

Some years ago I was travelling by train from Edinburgh to London and found myself sitting next to an Orthodox Jew. While we travelled, I had been reading Ezekiel 36 and its teaching on the new covenant, and when we both stopped to enjoy a cup of coffee we entered into conversation. I asked my friend how he understood the words in Ezekiel when God says:

> I will give you a new heart and put a new spirit in you; I will remove from you your heart of stone and give you a heart of flesh. And I will put my Spirit in you and move you to follow my decrees and be careful to keep my laws.
> (Ezek. 36:26–27)

My Jewish friend paused for a moment. Then he said something like this: 'Ah! At the moment it is very difficult to keep God's laws. It's a struggle and we often fail. But the rabbis tell us that when the Messiah comes we will have the inner power to keep God's law.'

Was Zephaniah pointing to such a time when the keeping of God's law would no longer be a burden and a reproach? Jesus called people to come to him and urged them to submit to his teaching. 'Come to me, all you who are weary and burdened, and I will give you rest. Take my yoke upon you and learn from me . . . ' But Jesus then goes on to say, 'I am gentle and humble in heart, and you will find rest for your souls. For my yoke is easy and my burden is light' (Matt. 11:28–30). To follow Jesus and to submit to

14 See Motyer, ibid., p. 960.

his teaching is not a burden. As the apostle Paul said to the Christians in Philippi, 'I can do all this through him who gives me strength' (Phil. 4:13).

Zephaniah's vision of a God who will remove false religion, or the sorrows and the burden of religion in our own strength, points yet again to the Lord Jesus Christ and the new Jerusalem where there will be no more sorrow (Rev. 21:4).

iii. God will rescue and honour the weak (19)

Once again these words might apply to those in Judah and Jerusalem who would later be taken into exile as part of God's disciplining judgment. Exile would mean oppression, lack of freedom to worship, and various other forms of suffering. Probably the weak and vulnerable (for example, *the lame*, 19b) would suffer most. But God is now speaking directly to his people: *At that time I will deal with all who oppressed you; I will rescue the lame* (19a). Furthermore, God promises to honour the remnant in the very countries where they had scattered and been put to shame. A little later he says: *I will give you honour and praise among all the peoples of the earth* (20b).

It's important for us to recognize, with Zephaniah, that God cares deeply about the powerless and the oppressed. In the New Testament, Jesus reveals God's care for the weak and vulnerable in his messianic ministry. He fulfilled Isaiah's prophecy 'to proclaim good news to the poor . . . to proclaim freedom for the captives and release from darkness for the prisoners, to proclaim the year of the LORD's favour' (Isa. 61:1–2; Luke 4:18–19).

Sometimes as we watch our television screens, or read our newspapers, and see the hopelessness and despair on the faces of millions of starving and oppressed people, we lose sight of God's love and compassion for them. Of course we have a responsibility, here and now, to do all we can for those in such desperate need; and Christians are often involved deeply and sacrificially in bringing aid and offering practical and professional help. From time to time also, those who perpetrate oppression are brought to justice. But in Zephaniah's day, as in our own, justice and deliverance can only be partial and temporary. Once more we find that Zephaniah is pointing towards a future hope beyond this life when 'The kingdom of the world has become the kingdom of our Lord and of his Messiah, and he will reign for ever and ever' (Rev. 11:15). At that time God will deal in perfect justice with those who oppress the poor, and God will deliver his people.

But what is the meaning of God's promise to give praise and honour to those who have been scattered, oppressed and shamed? In our culture, wealthy celebrities are honoured far more than ordinary, unknown caring people. In God's kingdom the opposite is true. God promises to honour those who put their trust in him, however weak, powerless and vulnerable they might be. In Zephaniah's prophecy God says: *I will give them* [i.e. *the lame*, representing the weak and vulnerable] *praise and honour in every land where they have suffered shame . . . I will gather you* [the remnant?] . . . *I will give you honour and praise among all the peoples of the earth when I restore your fortunes* [or 'when I bring back your captivity', suggests Motyer[15]] *before your very eyes* (19–20).

Although Daniel, Nehemiah and Esther were honoured to an extent by some of their pagan contemporaries, it's hard to see their 'honour' as a fulfilment of these promises. In New Testament times, after the Holy Spirit had been poured out upon the church at Pentecost, we read that believers enjoyed 'the favour of all the people. And the Lord added to their number daily those who were being saved' (Acts 2:46). But we know that persecution, imprisonment and martyrdom soon came to many of them; we know that God honoured the weak and powerless. When Paul wrote to the church at Corinth, he said:

> Brothers and sisters, think of what you were when you were called. Not many of you were wise by human standards; not many were influential; not many were of noble birth. But God chose the foolish things of the world to shame the wise; God chose the weak things of the world to shame the strong. God chose the lowly things of this world and the despised things – and the things that are not – to nullify the things that are, so that no one may boast before him.
> (1 Cor. 1:26–29)

There is no doubt that God honours those who put their trust in him, however weak and powerless they might be. He rescues and honours the weak – and that is an immense encouragement for all of us. But it is not necessarily true that the 'world' honours Christians. Indeed, the Christian church worldwide is currently facing unprecedented persecution. So once more we must look forward to that day, or that time (in God's good time) at the end of the age, for these promises to be completely fulfilled. On that day, the God who will

[15] Motyer, ibid., p. 959.

continue to love us, take away our sorrows and burdens, rescue us and honour us, will also *restore [our] fortunes* and bring us home (20).

iv. God will bring us home (20)

It's hard to believe, as some do, that Zephaniah is simply describing a situation where, after a time of exile, God would gather his people together, restore their fortunes, give them honour and praise, and bring them home to Jerusalem. If it does mean no more than that, then many of the promises that God gave to the people here (9–20) were unfulfilled at that time. It is much more likely that Zephaniah is pointing forward to *that time* or *that day* when God will come with judgment and salvation, and bring home the remnant of believers to his heavenly home. In his commentary on Zephaniah, J. H. Eaton concurs with this interpretation. He writes on verse 20: 'It is not necessary to connect these lines directly with the historical exile of Judah and the subsequent dispersion.' He then goes on to comment on the phrase 'when I restore your fortunes' or 'when I turn back your captivity'. He says it summarizes tersely

> the consummation of God's work with his creatures . . . [T]hrough all the hazards of history and through the fires of the final catastrophe, he [God] has at last achieved the perfect result which was in his mind at the beginning; he has secured his people in that glorious state for which they were originally destined. New creatures they are indeed, but their new creation is achieved through the old.
>
> It is prophesied that the work shall be accomplished 'before your very eyes' so the new people are still the same people, though changed from glory unto glory. Thus the old order is not emptied of significance and God's first creative word does not return to him void. Through devastation and death, by means of the remnant, the new man is accomplished from the old, transfigured as the perfect man of God in accordance with his eternal destiny.[16]

Certainly Jesus taught his disciples to look for a heavenly home:

> Do not let your hearts be troubled. You believe in God; believe also in me. My Father's house has many rooms; if that were not so, would I have told you that I am going there to prepare a place for you? And if I go and

[16] Eaton, *Obadiah, Nahum, Habakkuk and Zephaniah*, pp. 158–159.

> prepare a place for you, I will come back and take you to be with me that you also may be where I am.
> (John 14:1–3)

The writer to the Hebrews also claims that the Old Testament saints, such as Abel, Noah and Abraham, lived their lives in the light of the future hope of heaven:

> All these people were still living by faith when they died. They did not receive the things promised; they only saw them and welcomed them from a distance, admitting that they were foreigners and strangers on earth. People who say such things show that they are looking for a country of their own. If they had been thinking of the country they had left, they would have had opportunity to return. Instead they were longing for a better country – a heavenly one. Therefore God is not ashamed to be called their God, for he has prepared a city for them.
> (Heb. 11:13–16)

The apostle Paul likewise wrote to Christians in Philippi and claimed, 'But our citizenship is in heaven. And we eagerly await a Saviour from there, the Lord Jesus Christ' (Phil 3:20; cf. Rev. 21 – 22).

Zephaniah wants his readers to be confident in what God will do for them in the future, including the promise that God will bring the remnant of believers into the new Jerusalem, God's heavenly home. In the New Testament this hope of heaven motivated Christians to live holy and godly lives (1 John 3:2–3); to commit themselves to continue God's work steadfastly (1 Cor. 15:58); to endure suffering (Rom. 8:18); and to preach and teach with urgency, accuracy and great patience (2 Tim. 4:1–8). And these are but a few examples of the motivating power of the Christian hope. There have always been critics who have sneered at the Christian hope of heaven as 'pie in the sky when you die' leading us to be 'so heavenly minded that we are no earthly use'! The fact is that those who have done most for people on earth (such as the social reformers of the nineteenth century, including Wilberforce, Shaftesbury, Barnardo and Hannah More) were often those who were motivated by the hope of heaven. C. S. Lewis put it in this way: 'Aim at Heaven and you will get earth "thrown in"; aim at earth and you will get neither.'[17]

---

[17] C. S. Lewis, *Mere Christianity* (HarperCollins, rev. edn, 2002), p. 134.

So the book of Zephaniah begins with judgment but ends with salvation, restoration and hope. The prophet encourages us to rejoice in what God has done for us and to be confident in what he will do for us. God promises to give to those who trust him enduring love, freedom from captivity and sorrow, deliverance and honour, and a welcome to his heavenly home. The forces of evil and wickedness will not have the last word – God will, on that day of judgment and salvation.

The challenge of that day confronts each of us. Maybe our response will be to pray 'Your kingdom come!' or 'Come, Lord Jesus!' If so, then perhaps we need to ponder the words of C. S. Lewis:

> I wonder whether people who ask God to interfere openly and directly in our world quite realise what it will be like when He does. When that happens, it is the end of this world. When the author walks on to the stage the play is over. God is going to invade, all right: but what is the good of saying you are on His side then, when you see the whole natural universe melting away like a dream and something else – something it never entered your head to conceive – comes crashing in; something so beautiful to some of us and so terrible to others that none of us will have any choice left? For this time it will be God without disguise; something so overwhelming that it will strike either irresistible love or irresistible horror into every creature. It will be too late then to choose your side. There is no use saying that you choose to lie down when it has become impossible to stand up. That will not be the time for choosing: it will be the time when we discover which side we really have chosen, whether we realised it before or not. Now, today, this moment, is the chance to choose the right side. God is holding back to give us that chance. It will not last for ever. We must take it or leave it.[18]

The prophecy of Zephaniah began with the statement *The word of the Lord that came to Zephaniah* . . . It ends with the words *says the Lord*. It is God's word that confronts us in this book. It is God to whom we have to give account – a God of justice *and* love.

[18] Lewis, *Mere Christianity*, p. 65.

The Bible Speaks Today: Old Testament series

The Message of Genesis 1 – 11
The dawn of creation
David Atkinson

The Message of Genesis 12 – 50
From Abraham to Joseph
Joyce G. Baldwin

The Message of Exodus
The days of our pilgrimage
Alec Motyer

The Message of Leviticus
Free to be holy
Derek Tidball

The Message of Numbers
Journey to the Promised Land
Raymond Brown

The Message of Deuteronomy
Not by bread alone
Raymond Brown

The Message of Joshua
Promise and people
David G. Firth

The Message of Judges
Grace abounding
Michael Wilcock

The Message of Ruth
The wings of refuge
David Atkinson

The Message of 1 and 2 Samuel
Personalities, potential, politics and power
Mary J. Evans

The Message of 1 and 2 Kings
God is present
John W. Olley

The Message of 1 and 2 Chronicles
One church, one faith, one Lord
Michael Wilcock

The Message of Ezra and Haggai
Building for God
Robert Fyall

The Message of Nehemiah
God's servant in a time of change
Raymond Brown

The Message of Esther
God present but unseen
David G. Firth

The Message of Job
Suffering and grace
David Atkinson

The Message of Psalms 1 – 72
Songs for the people of God
Michael Wilcock

The Message of Psalms 73 – 150
Songs for the people of God
Michael Wilcock

The Message of Proverbs
Wisdom for life
David Atkinson

The Message of Ecclesiastes
A time to mourn, and a time to dance
Derek Kidner

The Message of the Song of Songs
The lyrics of love
Tom Gledhill

The Message of Isaiah
On eagles' wings
Barry Webb

The Message of Jeremiah
Grace in the end
Christopher J. H. Wright

The Message of Lamentations
Honest to God
Christopher J. H. Wright

The Message of Ezekiel
A new heart and a new spirit
Christopher J. H. Wright

The Message of Daniel
His kingdom cannot fail
Dale Ralph Davis

The Message of Hosea
Love to the loveless
Derek Kidner

The Message of Joel, Micah and Habakkuk
Listening to the voice of God
David Prior

The Message of Amos
The day of the lion
Alec Motyer

The Message of Obadiah, Nahum and Zephaniah
The kindness and severity of God
Gordon Bridger

The Message of Jonah
Presence in the storm
Rosemary Nixon

The Message of Zechariah
Your kingdom come
Barry Webb

The Message of Malachi
'I have loved you,' says the Lord
Peter Adam

The Bible Speaks Today: New Testament series

The Message of Matthew
The kingdom of heaven
Michael Green

The Message of Mark
The mystery of faith
Donald English

The Message of Luke
The Saviour of the world
Michael Wilcock

The Message of John
Here is your King!
Bruce Milne

The Message of the Sermon on the Mount (Matthew 5 – 7)
Christian counter-culture
John Stott

The Message of Acts
To the ends of the earth
John Stott

The Message of Romans
God's good news for the world
John Stott

The Message of 1 Corinthians
Life in the local church
David Prior

The Message of 2 Corinthians
Power in weakness
Paul Barnett

The Message of Galatians
Only one way
John Stott

The Message of Ephesians
God's new society
John Stott

The Message of Philippians
Jesus our joy
Alec Motyer

The Message of Colossians and Philemon
Fullness and freedom
Dick Lucas

The Message of 1 and 2 Thessalonians
Preparing for the coming King
John Stott

The Message of 1 Timothy and Titus
The life of the local church
John Stott

The Message of 2 Timothy
Guard the gospel
John Stott

The Message of Hebrews
Christ above all
Raymond Brown

The Message of James
The tests of faith
Alec Motyer

The Message of 1 Peter
The way of the cross
Edmund Clowney

The Message of 2 Peter and Jude
The promise of his coming
Dick Lucas and Chris Green

The Message of John's Letters
Living in the love of God
David Jackman

The Message of Revelation
I saw heaven opened
Michael Wilcock

The Bible Speaks Today: Bible Themes series

The Message of the Living God
His glory, his people, his world
Peter Lewis

The Message of the Resurrection
Christ is risen!
Paul Beasley-Murray

The Message of the Cross
Wisdom unsearchable, love indestructible
Derek Tidball

The Message of Salvation
By God's grace, for God's glory
Philip Graham Ryken

The Message of Creation
Encountering the Lord of the universe
David Wilkinson

The Message of Heaven and Hell
Grace and destiny
Bruce Milne

The Message of Mission
The glory of Christ in all time and space
Howard Peskett and Vinoth Ramachandra

The Message of Prayer
Approaching the throne of grace
Tim Chester

The Message of the Trinity
Life in God
Brian Edgar

The Message of Evil and Suffering
Light into darkness
Peter Hicks

The Message of the Holy Spirit
The Spirit of encounter
Keith Warrington

The Message of Holiness
Restoring God's masterpiece
Derek Tidball

The Message of Sonship
At home in God's household
Trevor Burke

The Message of the Word of God
The glory of God made known
Tim Meadowcroft

The Message of Women
Creation, grace and gender
Derek and Dianne Tidball

The Message of the Church
Assemble the people before me
Chris Green

The Message of the Person of Christ
The Word made flesh
Robert Letham

The Message of Worship
Celebrating the glory of God in the whole of life
John Risbridger

The Message of Spiritual Warfare
The Lord is a warrior; the Lord is his name
Keith Ferdinando

The Message of Discipleship
Authentic followers of Jesus in today's world
Peter Morden

The Message of Love
The only thing that counts
Patrick Mitchel

The Message of Wisdom
Learning and living the way of the Lord
Daniel J. Estes

The Message of the Second Coming
Ending all things well
Steve Motyer

The Message of the Kingdom of God
T. Desmond Alexander